Second World War Infantry Tactics

Second World War Infantry Tactics

The European Theatre

Stephen Bull

Pen & Sword
MILITARY

First published in Great Britain in 2012 by
Pen & Sword Military
an imprint of
Pen & Sword Books Ltd
47 Church Street
Barnsley
South Yorkshire
S70 2AS

ISBN 978 1 84884 070 6

A CIP catalogue record for this book is available from the British Library

Typeset in Ehrhardt by Phoenix Typesetting, Auldgirth, Dumfriesshire

Printed and bound in England by CPI UK

Pen & Sword Books Ltd incorporates the Imprints of Pen & Sword Aviation, Pen & Sword Maritime, Pen & Sword Military, Wharncliffe Local History, Pen and Sword Select, Pen and Sword Military Classics, Leo Cooper, Remember When, Seaforth Publishing and Frontline Publishing.

For a complete list of Pen & Sword titles please contact
PEN & SWORD BOOKS LIMITED
47 Church Street, Barnsley, South Yorkshire, S70 2AS, England
E-mail: enquiries@pen-and-sword.co.uk
Website: www.pen-and-sword.co.uk

Contents

Preface

Only once have I felt, rather than heard, a bullet pass near to my head – close enough, quite literally, for the shock wave to make hair stand up. Objectively, a shot from close range is a bit like being at the centre of a storm. Everything is simultaneous: report, bullet, sensation – no luxury of identifying one from another. That was on a shooting range, in Wales, when somebody, who should have known better, let fly from behind the firing point. It was thirty-two years ago. Yet simply conjuring the incident to mind recalls the immediate and visceral reaction: one of pure rage, of wanting to shoot back, of 'why me?'. Only hours later did such feelings subside into involuntary shudders at realisation that only by grace of inches was there was still sentience and breath. A trivial incident, yet still a measure of distance between life and eternity. Just one shot, in ignorance, rather than in anger, and on a pleasant afternoon just minutes away from a hot meal, comfortable bed, and every convenience of a Western civilian life. Similarly, perhaps, you too have stood unwisely close to, and vaguely north of, a tank or field gun when it fires: if so you will know that one becomes part of the blast rather than experiencing it as an independent phenomenon. It makes no matter whether this is a Royal salute or innocent target practice: ripples pass through the body shaking internal organs. A second shell is usually strangely silent as the first has already induced temporary deafness: and these are merely the 'outgoing'.

So how then did an infantryman function in combat, when not just an odd round, but whole belts of ammunition and train loads of shells were indeed meant not merely to kill him, but blow him to pieces over a period of weeks, months, and even years? Besides, wars of all eras feature rain, snow, brutality, hunger, accidents, dirt, shattered buildings, and broken people. As Radford Carrol, an infantryman with US 99th Division, put it,

> The infantry walks, except when it runs, and lives in the open as best it can. Battles and wars are not won unless the infantry is standing on the land that once belonged to the enemy. The infantry fighting is not remote from the foe; the enemy is visible and the bodies of enemy and friend alike show the results of the fighting. The infantry lives under the hardest conditions and suffers the most danger of any branch of the military. It is the pits, a place to stay out of . . .

Nevertheless, only seventy years ago, and in Western Europe of all places, vast numbers, many of them conscripts, were taught to fight in very specific ways; not just to pull the trigger or control the desire to run. For more or less effectively, and on every battlefield of the Second World War, orders were given and tactics followed.

Chaotic as combat is, the models for infantry actions are a complex choreography. Not for nothing did the Duke of Wellington once describe battles as being like balls, in which the movements might be well known, but the exact sequences of events are extremely difficult to describe.The mid-twentieth century 'dance of death', conducted in khaki, green, and grey, was not of course as obvious as that of earlier wars with their close lines and dense columns of red, white, and blue: but if more deliberately hidden, and intentionally irregular, the design was even more complicated. Interestingly, it is also true that techniques did change between 1939 and 1945, and that, perhaps even more than in 1914 to 1918, armies learned from one another, becoming more similar in their tactical outlook as the war progressed. Moreover, whilst we tend to think of the Second World War as a war of technological leaps, of radar, atom bombs, and submarines, troops still had to advance, taking ground and cities, still had to kill and be killed. As the British *Operations* manual of 1939 observed, it was infantry that confirmed success in war, infantry that 'compels the withdrawal or surrender of the enemy', and infantry that holds objectives. In short, 'it is the most adaptable and most generally useful of all arms, since it is capable of operating over any ground by day or night and can find or make cover for itself more readily than other arms'.

This was nothing to be taken lightly. For, whilst the fighting foot soldiers made up a smaller segment of armies than they had done hitherto, they continued to absorb most of the punishment. In Normandy British infantry represented about 70 per cent of the army's losses, though only one in four men was in the infantry arm. In the autumn of 1944 over 89 per cent of 15th (Scottish) Division's casualties came from its infantry. Over the longer campaign in Italy the New Zealand infantry eventually suffered twice as many casualties as the number of troops it had started out with. Many US infantry divisions that fought in North West Europe had final casualty lists as long as their original orders of battle. The 90th, landing a few days after D-Day, and gaining huge if painful experience in the *bocage*, had an eventual turnover of 196 per cent. The 'Big Red One' 1st Division, actually landed on 6 June, needed just over twice its original strength in replacements in 292 days of combat. The US record holder however was the 4th, which in 299 days of action had a total turnover of a staggering 252 per cent. In the Hurtgen Forest US 28th Division suffered 6,184 combat casualties, 738 cases of trench foot, and 620 instances of battle fatigue. Over a few weeks the majority, rather than a minority, had suffered some injury of war. As in the First World War, infantry officers suffered disproportionately. In 4th Division some companies ran through three or four commanders in a couple of weeks: 'Staff sergeants and sergeants commanded most of the rifle platoons. The few officers still running platoons were either replacements or heavy weapons platoon leaders displaced forward. Most squad leaders were inexperienced privates or privates first class. One company had only 25 men including replacements . . .'. British figures suggest that proportionately speaking more officers were put *hors de combat* relative to the number of other rank casualties than in the First World War.

There have been vast numbers of books on battles, weapons, and generals: pitifully few on tactics. This is all the more odd when one considers that it is very often tactics that win or lose the many little fights that make up the battle and dictate the way weapons are used and men are organised for war. All too often it is assumed that weapons and tactics are a form mathematical chess game, and that if ranges and effects are calculated, and 'force multipliers' applied, outcomes of combat can be predicted. Yet in reality men are not numbers, nor do they always act in accordance with what theorists might recognise as logical courses of action. This is not necessarily because they are fanatics, or because of national, political, or cultural differences – though all of these things may apply – but very often because individuals cannot see, or perhaps do not understand, bigger pictures. Some do not know that they are in range – or that a rifle bullet can go right through the man, or even the wall, in front of them. Some are already in despair – others can clearly see the gates of heaven, or a quick way home. Others are too tired or hungry to care. Even so, as SLA Marshall, First World War veteran and Second World War combat commentator, said in 1947, 'it is the soldier who fights and wins battles, that fighting means using a weapon, and that it is the heart of man which controls this use'.

Soldiers and commanders usually act in context – according to what they know, feel, or believe, have been told – by the next man up the command tree, or their scouts – or are trained to do. Sometimes they act from a deep-seated conviction or loyalty, sometimes because they fear their own more than they fear the enemy. Frequently, it is only because they do not wish to let down either their comrades or themselves. In histories and novels bravery is often 'suicidal' – in reality it is rarely so. Those that truly act as machines, or take theoretically perfect and consistent decisions, are rare indeed. Response to training, decisions – intelligent or otherwise – battle 'fever', and traumas, are all far more powerful factors. For every circumstance is different and actions in stress of combat may be products of anything ranging from extreme altruism and comradeship to total ignorance or selfishness. Sometimes there is little conscious thought at all and Pavlovian reactions to instruction and situation intervene. Moreover, not a few disasters are written up creatively to put best gloss on a tragic situation for the benefit of the printed citation. Through printed word or moving picture many things become accepted, or even parts of national myth. The role of 'willpower' may be out of fashion, but the annals of war are littered with instances in which commanders believed themselves to be at a disadvantage, or beaten, and acted accordingly. Conversely, as Clausewitz observed, sensible leaders and commanders only go to war or commit themselves to battles they think already won.

What put soldiers out of action, and what they feared, clearly impacted on what they might do, or were prepared to venture. British figures, probably not untypically, suggest that roughly three-quarters of all wounds during the war were caused by shells, bombs, mortar rounds, and grenades. Bullets and anti-tank rounds added a rather modest 10 per cent; the same as mines and booby traps. The remaining and unlucky one in twenty were injured by a miscellaneous mix of blasts, crushings, chemical burns, and 'other'. It has to be admitted that this is not quite the whole story, since this list omits those killed outright – but it is probably fair to guess that a majority of these were caused by similar means, and particularly shells and bullets. Nevertheless, the idea that infantry more often had things done to them, rather than inflicting harm themselves, would appear valid. With remarkable if unimaginatively insensitive seriousness the US Army handed out questionnaires to its men regarding their fear. Nobody should have been at all surprised when the symptoms reported included almost everybody with pounding heart and sinking feelings, with a fair incidence of cold sweats, faintness, and vomiting. Perhaps more remarkable was that only a relatively small minority admitted to losing control of their bowels. Another survey of US veterans of Italy discovered that at one time or another roughly three-quarters felt as if it was just a matter of time before they were hit. Understandably, shelling and bombing were very high on the hate list of the US infantry, with the '88' top of the tree of terror. At the end of such a catalogue lay not only death or physical injury but 'battle fatigue', the point at which a man could no longer carry on.

SLA Marshall later claimed that a significant failing of the infantry, and the US infantry in particular, was reluctance, failure even, of a majority to actually fire at their enemies. Doubtless some did 'freeze' involuntarily, and many others, very understandably, ducked their heads below parapets and crests when shot at. This, after all, was what suppressive or 'neutralising' fire, and sensible use of cover, were all about. Careful observation of shooters, even on a range, also shows that a percentage blink, or even shut their eyes for a moment, on squeezing a trigger. Yet many Germans died, and truck loads of ammunition costing millions of dollars went somewhere. There are also many first-hand accounts of soldiers shooting – sometimes over enthusiastically – at nothing. It is said that Marshall deliberately deceived his readers: a more charitable interpretation is that like the manual, and like General Patton, what he sought to do was make them shoot even more than they already did, this being more likely to keep them alive.

Another major pitfall to be avoided is the idea that there are tactical absolutes, some perfect movements and dispositions – that if only they could be discovered and applied would always prove successful. In the Renaissance this Chimera was often assumed to be the tactics of the ancients, that, somehow being forgotten, could now be rediscovered and applied in an age of gunpowder. Thereafter the exemplars were successively the motions of the Spanish, Dutch, Gustavus of Sweden, Frederick the Great, Napoleon, and from the later nineteenth century the German armies, commencing with the wars of unification. Whilst every period holds useful or interesting examples, the only genuine certainty appears to be that every age is different. Mighty nations and empires in one historical period may well not be so mighty in the next. Technology and economics change very obviously: but so do people, and often more subtly. This notion of change on the grand scale also holds true for changes in the minutiae, as what works very well one day may not apply at all a few days later. For not only does the enemy often learn the painful lessons that new ruses teach him surprisingly fast, but new weapons and training can appear very quickly in time of war. Similarly, lack of spare parts or ammunition for weapons of a particular type, a change of light conditions or weather, or temporary interruption to orders, can have the consequence that an otherwise successful tactic fails. For the 'want of a nail' indeed.

All too often anachronism appears in writing about tactics that would not be tolerated in any other form of history. For rather than attempt to construct, as best we can, how it was, and, if possible, why a commander or unit acted as it did, simplistic fingers are pointed at 'poor tactics'. Smug assumptions are made that what is done now is 'better' and that our ancestors were simply stupid in their supposed inability to identify obvious truths. Accounts, even those from eyewitnesses, disagreeing with anything established after the event are pushed to one side. This, however, gets us nowhere other than the cul-de-sac of complacency that we have arrived at a better place. It suggests that further research is pointless, as we already have the answers. Such lazy thinking will at least serve to amuse future generations.

Though infantry are but part of the story of tactics, and the Second World War is one war amongst many, the subject is so vast that it has been necessary to tighten the focus of this study very sharply. To this end we deal here only with the European theatre, and three major players, the USA, Britain, and Germany. Important as the Soviet Union, France, and Italy might be, they have been relegated to odd remarks where these impinge upon the conduct of our chosen three. Commonwealth and Empire forces are likewise mentioned only very briefly in the context of European combat. It has to be admitted that to take some countries and ignore others is arbitrary, but there is method in selection. The three chosen nations were the drivers in Western Europe after D-Day; Germany was arguably the trendsetter early in the war; the USA was destined for great things inside and outside Europe after 1945; and elements of commonality between the USA, Canada, and Britain on the one part, and the US study of German and British methods on the other, forms a cohesive narrative from which conclusions may be drawn. To include for example Japan, Yugoslavia, and Poland would make for an interesting volume – but a work easily twice the length, and less amenable to useful analysis. Moreover, the primary sources required – and the command of multiple languages needed – to look at the tactics of such countries on more than a very superficial level would expand the narrative, and the time it would take to construct, to unmanageable proportions. To further clarify the subject we look only at the methods of the majority. Special forces, other services, and the defenders of fortresses – to name but a few – also saw action as ground troops, and all had a least some tactics that were not identical to those of the 'line infantry', or the 'rifle' and 'motorised' battalions, but the specialists are ignored here in the search for clarity and an intelligible storyline.

Tactics themselves could change surprisingly quickly, and the often theoretical problems of formulating new methods were compounded by the practical issue of just how often updated training could be introduced or manuals revised and actually published. During the period under consideration here the main US Army key infantry tactical manuals were revised in 1940, 1942, and 1944. Many gaps on specific subjects and situations were filled in during intervening periods, with substantial documents on for example fighting against fortifications and in built-up areas, armour and infantry co-operation, and warfare in different climates. Arguably US effort in this direction was the most thorough and exhaustive. The key British document, *Infantry Training* of 1937, was replaced only once, but revised very thoroughly, in 1944. Nevertheless, substantial documents containing improved methods were created in 1942, and many more slender instructions were produced all the time. German methods were advanced in 1939, and official revised infantry manuals were produced at intervals, notably in 1940 and 1941, and like the British endeavours were supported by a stream of other documents, both official and unofficial. In the last two years of war it appears that at times the German Army had problems keeping up with new weapons and tactical training. In an ideal world all nations would probably have revised their instructions and completely retrained their infantry every eighteen months, though this was never achieved.

Apart from painting a picture and attempting to draw lessons from the interactions of human beings, tactical developments, and weapons, it is hoped that something can

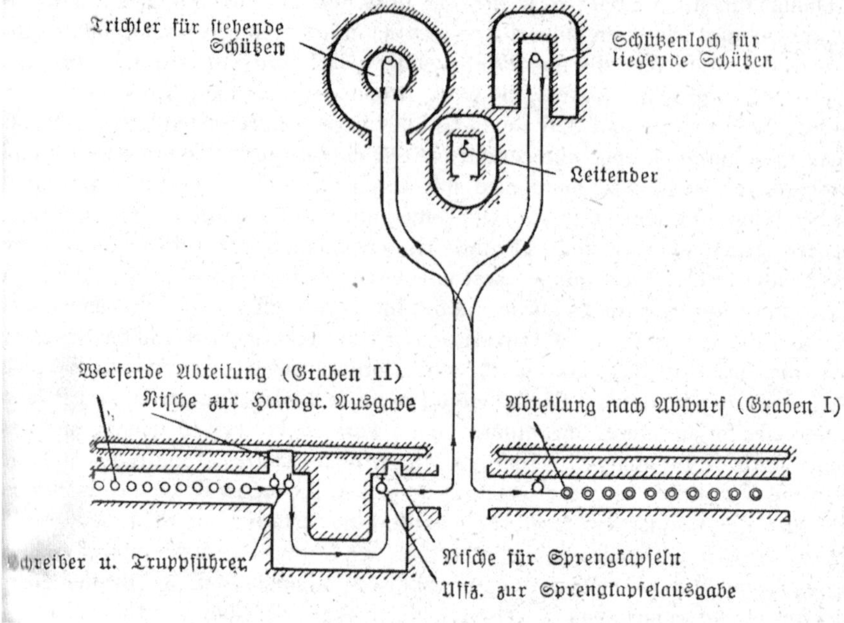

German hand-grenade practice range from Captain Weber's *Unterrichtsbuch für Soldaten*, 1938. The waiting trainees are kept well back from the thrower who can lob his grenade from special standing or prone positions under the eye of an instructor.

also be said about trends. Terrain, objectives, training, quality of manpower, politics, and circumstance all complicated the scene so that it is very difficult to make sweeping conclusions about what is 'better' or the importance of that abstract idea 'national characteristics'. What should become very apparent is that not only did tactics change with time, but armies changed as well. The tiny, and in may ways antiquated, US Army of 1940 bore little or no relation to the ground forces of the superpower of 1945. The victorious German *Heer* of 1940 was totally different to the technically very advanced – but totally enervated and very diverse – army that fought amongst the ruins of Budapest and Berlin. The British Army was clearly jerked from a somewhat insular professionalism into a practical proletarian modernity; but also realised that it had to be European facing, taking into account the new superpower realities of the USA and USSR.

For those who wish to probe deeper there is a bibliography at the end of this volume. A glance here will show the diverse sources, covering mainly manuals, reports, memoirs, and secondary works. It is to be hoped that this range will provide a measure of corroboration of salient facts. One has to beware, however, that not only do manuals – taken alone, in vast quantities, and possibly out of context – lead almost inevitably to ennui and eventually severe mental indigestion, but lack of connection with real actions. Eyewitnesses to combat often provide us with some inkling of how successful a particular tactic might have been, or how well it was learned and remembered in a particular army. They also lend a notion that however well planned actions in the real world frequently broke down into a flurry of existential confusion that could on occasion make nonsense of 'drills' or theory. General works set campaigns, units, and outcomes into context. Only a fool completely ignores secondary sources: for even if disagreed with, they still provide significant food for thought. Some of the most closely studied and influential here have included Paddy Griffith, *Forward Into Battle*; Michael D Doubler, *Closing with the Enemy*; David French, *Raising Churchill's Army*; and Joseph Balkowski, *Beyond the Beachhead*. The manuals, once relatively difficult to obtain, have become much more accessible in the digital age, and many of the most important have now been reprinted. Quite a few can also be found in public collections. In Britain most regimental museums have at least a sample, and larger collections are to be found within the Liddell Hart Archive at King's College, London, and the National Army Museum, Chelsea. The Imperial War Museum collections include a broader selection with some US and German material represented.

Second World War Infantry Tactics

Chapter One

The Human Resource

'War is launched, waged and won by will power' - Hans von Seeckt

It has frequently been asserted that key factors underlying combat, and in particular the performance of the infantry, are 'national characteristics'. In such an explanation – of the often apparently inexplicable – simple stereotypes stand in for the complex detail of research. So it is that Germans are illustrated as naturally obedient to orders, good soldiers, and tactical experts – or automatons – depending on whether they have just been victorious or otherwise. British troops are frequently dismissed as slow moving and relatively unimaginative – though stoic in defence, and willing to continue against overwhelming odds. Americans are pictured as gung-ho and trigger happy. Such trite characterisations can be traced back through the First World War and into the nineteenth century: but they also have remarkably ancient echoes, as for example when words like 'Barbarian' and 'Spartan' eventually became adjectives through their understood use in describing the attributes of entire peoples. Similarly, the idea of the 'other side' being vilified as primitive, idiots, heretics, or infidels, remains with us still.

The notion of national characteristic as the defining attribute of the fighting soldier was widely accepted during the Second World War. As Major EM Llewellyn, editor of *Stars and Stripes*, put it, 'The British believe that, regardless of mistakes made today and tomorrow they will fight on courageously and win final victory. The Yankee feels that no power on earth will stand his might . . .'. On the other side, German propagandists portrayed their fighting soldiers as 'Europe's shield', bred from the outset as the guarantors of the homeland, like the Spartans 'endowed with soldierly virtues by destiny'. As Major Dr Wilhelm Ehmer explained in one editorial, 'Peoples which have to fight for and secure their existence on a poor soil under hard conditions regard soldierly virtues as the expression of an attitude forced upon them by necessity'. This was their 'historical fate'. In the post-war decades some analysts, and notably Colonel Trevor Dupuy, went so far as to suggest that the 'superiority' of the German fighting soldier could be quantified numerically. This pseudo-scientific approach mirrors mathematical calculations that US Army trainers used in computing likely outcomes of pitching different weapons against each other. Yet the idea of reducing people to numbers was at best gross oversimplification – at worst a complacent assumption upon which disasters were built. Perhaps the most obvious instance of this error was a widespread readiness in the West to dismiss the Japanese soldier as somehow inferior, this being promptly followed by the shock of repeated defeats and the huge expansion of the Japanese 'co-prosperity' zone in 1941–1942. If the notion of 'national characteristic' has any validity at all it cannot be merely one simple idea, but as a portmanteau of very disparate factors, education, indoctrination, training and 'morale' being just some of the most obvious.

Of all the agents of victory some abstract genetic propensity to fight is surely the least important – if indeed such a thing ever actually existed at all. Some may have believed in this mystic quality at the time as a 'magic ingredient', much as the Nazis did, but as an explanation of fighting prowess or tactical virtuosity it quickly falls apart under historical examination. 'Tommy' was first defeated by, then learned to respect, and eventually beat for example the Pathan and Zulu; the Greeks – once masters of the known world – underwent years of Ottoman domination to emerge only as very junior partners in modern alliances. The Italians moved through just as dramatic a trajectory. Moreover, the gene pools of Britain, Germany, and the USA had distinct areas of overlap with Britons, Germans, and Irish being major contributors to the makeup of the USA, with many of them having arrived there less than a century before 1941. Hence part of the very real fear of Axis sympathy in America. At the time the US Army conducted a survey on the attitudes of its men to the enemy, making the interesting discovery that whilst more than a third 'really wanted' to kill a Japanese soldier, less than 10 per cent felt the same about their German adversary.

The simple fact of nationality must therefore be put to one side as at most a very minor contributor to the differing qualities of fighting soldiers of the 1940s, and something that is well nigh impossible to assess. Or to put it another way simply being 'American' or 'German' for example did not explain very much – though jingoism was definitely given full play as means of motivation. If nationality by itself was but an uncertain factor, this nevertheless leaves us with a plethora of other environmental influences. Of these, education; training; politics and ideologies; history; social organisation; conflicts of demands; and willingness to fight in given circumstances, are perhaps the most obvious. Nevertheless, it may be contended that the interactions between weapons and tactics, and the suitability of tactics to situation, can be even more important. Significantly, it also has to be recognised that the character of specific armies changed radically between 1939 and 1945, with the progress of the war itself limiting or enhancing performance. From the outset there was dramatic divergence, with Germany prepared for a short aggressive war; the USA prepared for no war at all; and Britain partially prepared for the wrong war.

In the German instance 'militarism' played a highly significant part, but this was of a very specific historic type – with its own internal logic. In the Prussian state martial service and civil service had been inextricably bound by military servants of the King moving on to other departments of state and bureaucracy. With a weak navy, the geopolitical position, conscription, and limited finances, the army, together with the patronage it entailed, became a more significant pillar of society than in the democracies. It provided the 'blood and iron' with which Bismarck had forged the German state, and it was also the army that guaranteed its continued existence precariously sandwiched between the old Leviathans of France, Russia, and Austria. Its training became the 'school of the nation'. German Army officer training material was apt to stress duty, honour, 'military thinking', and the fact that the forces were the 'weapon carriers' of 'the people' – to be armed in the service of the state being the historic obligation of the free man. As Gesting's primer *Zwanzig Offizierthemen*, reprinted in 1935, explained, the soldier had to be 'an idealist, not a materialist'. 'Dishonour' came not just from the big things, but the details, as for example poor posture and dress, boastfulness, loutish behaviour – each soldier being responsible not only for his own honour, but for that of all soldiers. In the military sense genuine 'freedom' was not an abstract external, but the ability of the individual soldier to master his heart and spirit to overcome 'internal demons' – such as fear.

Crucial for the subsequent development of German strategy and tactics was the situation between the wars, and the character of the *Reichsheer*. A glance at the map of Europe showed that a German Army limited to 100,000 men could not hope to be an offensive force against France or Poland, and was probably no overwhelming menace for Belgium or Austria either. This indeed was the intention of the Allied powers when framing the Treaty of Versailles. For whilst some of the articles of that document – such as the trial of the former Kaiser – were not carried into effect, and the US Senate did not finally ratify the agreement, the substantial military and territorial clauses were implemented. Alsace and Lorraine, parts of Prussia and Schleswig, and Memel were all ceded to other powers, and the German Army reduced to 10 divisions – 3 cavalry and 7 infantry. Almost equally significantly there would be no conscription: men would serve for twelve years, and there would be no easy way to build up the large reserve forces on which immediate expansion of the army had depended in 1914.

What was more when Colonel General von Seeckt, Chief of the *Heeresleitung*, looked at his resources in 1920 it was apparent that the new and diminutive German Army was insufficient even for a traditional static defence of national boundaries. The only possible solution was that it should become highly trained, mobile, and able to fight a complex running battle of surprise counter attacks, retreats, and buying time. It should also be a *Führer Armee*, in the sense of being 'an army of leaders'. With no ready trained reserve the most important problem in the event of war would not be a lack of men, but rather lack of good officers and NCOs capable of leading the mass levies that the government would doubtless attempt to call to the colours. To this end all German soldiers were to be trained in peacetime to act above their notional grades. Initially, officers were chosen from those with experience both in, and before, the First World War. Thereafter, new officer candidates were first taken on as private soldiers, serving fifteen months before being considered for examination and posting to the NCOs course at the Dresden infantry school. Next candidates studied for and sat an officer's exam, and those who were successful were taken by a regiment on a trial basis. Not until four or more years had elapsed from the student's first enlistment was he promoted to substantive commissioned rank, and even then this step had to be confirmed by the officers of his unit. From 1921 staff exams were made compulsory for lieutenants of middle seniority, even if they had no wish for a staff career. Other ranks in general were recruited twice a year from medically fit, unmarried, German nationals in the age range 17 to 21 with no criminal record. Even those who did not actively seek promotion to NCO were trained over time in basic tactics and leadership of small units.

Commentators have observed that von Seeckt was a difficult individual, no fan of technology, traditional in outlook, ambitious and controversial. Perhaps surprisingly he also regarded the British professional army of 1914 as something of a role model, and doubted the efficacy of the tank. Be that as it may, he nevertheless laid the foundation of an army in which action, willingness to seek initiative, and intelligent professionalism were all highly valued, and this lead was also followed by his successors, Generals Wilhelm Heye and Kurt von Hammerstein-Equord from 1926 to 1934. Training was focused primarily on combat in the European theatre, from a starting point that took for granted that the army might be outnumbered and would require good tactics and great energy to be successful. New manuals were written based on the vital importance of 'Combined Arms' and mission-led tactics: these included not only the *Führung und Gefecht der Verbundenen Waffen*, or 'Combined Arms Leadership and Battle', of 1921, but infantry training regulations in 1922 and 1925, and volumes on the rifle squad and umpiring exercises, all of which influenced later documents. There was already a presumption that orders could be simplified, usually delivered verbally, and that subordinates would be capable of filling in whatever blanks existed in the spirit of the mission and in accordance with techniques they had already assimilated. Von Seeckt's 'observations' based on his inspections of 1925 explicitly approved the notion of the *Kampfgruppen*, or 'battlegroups', for independent action that were already being used in exercises provided they did not become 'stereotyped'. Basic 'battalion drills' for reactions to specific combat circumstances were promoted as early as 1924 by Colonel Stollberger in his volume *Kampfschule für die Infanterie*, or 'Battle School for the Infantry', a title that would have huge, and probably not totally coincidental, resonance almost twenty years on. The German Army of the mid-1920s was not yet capable of 'lightning' aggressive war, but it was already being trained in the *Bewegerungskrieg*, or war of movement. US military attaché and observer Colonel AL Conger declared that it was a 'first-class fighting machine' comprised of the best soldiers on the Continent.

The Weimar Republic with its brave attempt at democratic government and tiny army was an untypical interlude. Conscription was reintroduced under the new Nazi regime, and in 1933 under the direction of General Ludwig Beck the new service regulations, or *Truppenführung*, were published. Though much updated, this owed a considerable debt to the doctrine of the 1920s. The General Staff, hitherto disguised as the *Truppenampt*, was recreated in 1935. Interestingly, whilst German manuals, tactical or otherwise, were generally attributed to the chief who signed them off, most were in fact framed by relatively junior officers. In the interwar period these individuals included some of the most promising talents of the day. Notable amongst them were writer, philosopher, and all-round polymath Ernst Jünger and the as yet relatively unknown former Württemberg mountain troop officer Erwin Rommel. Serving with the 73rd Hanoverian Fusiliers, Jünger had won the Pour Le Mérite ('Blue Max'), during the First World War when aged only 23. Though a conservative who regarded Jews as a threat to German unity, he later fell out of favour with the Nazis. Posted to Paris during the Second World War, he was out of the public eye and developed an interest in art and artists. Rommel, also a Pour Le Mérite winner, was an instructor at the Dresden infantry school from 1929 until 1934, the year he authored the manual *Gefechts Aufgaben für Zug und Kompanie*, or 'combat tasks for platoon and company'. This was followed by commands at the Potsdam war academy and in 1937 the publication of his well-known *Infanterie Grieft an*, or 'infantry attacks', a series of observations on battle and tactics based on his experiences in 1914–1918. This volume brought him to the notice of the *Führer*, who promptly put him in charge of War Ministry Liaison with the Hitler Youth, and the attention of Goebbels who would later promote him as the model of the quintessential German officer. So it was that he came to serve as escort to the *Führer* headquarters early in the war, and was set on the path to later stardom.

By 1939 the Nazi state was only six years old, but in some of its particulars it revived old causes such as the return of German nationals to the Fatherland, and embraced genuinely popular ideas like high employment and revision, or renunciation, of the Treaty of Versailles. Many Germans believed in the justice of the occupations and re-occupations of 1936 to 1938, and the war aims of 1939 to 1940. Such feelings were reinforced by nationalisation of the film industry, state domination of publishing, and the production of pamphlets such as *Warum und wofür kämpfen wir?*, 'Why and for what do we fight?'. The changes to the map of Europe and the relatively few concessions to wartime economy made prior to the end of 1940 appeared to justify either active support for, or at least acquiescence in, military conflict. The German population would be far less enthusiastic after years of war with Russia, and a fight with the USA that lacked clear aims or benefits.

German Army basic training was a notional sixteen weeks, but shrank to eight, or sometimes even less with the progress of the war and the difficulty of the situation. It was remarkable in that everybody had to learn common skills – and tactics – before going on to the specialisms of an arm of service. As artillerist Siegfried Knappe explained, following a brief induction:

> Our training began in earnest the next day with six weeks of infantry training. This included handling our rifles, shooting them on the firing range, moving on the ground under fire, and digging in. Of course that was in addition to marching, drilling and learning to parade. We kept cadence while marching by singing. We also had training with hand grenades and machine guns . . . During this infantry training period, we would get up at five o'clock, perform stable duty, have breakfast, fall out, and begin a very full day that ended only when we went to bed, exhausted, at ten o'clock. The training was interesting, well planned, and well organised. Lunch was our main meal of the day. The food was good and it was well prepared. After lunch we would get fifteen minutes or so of rest, then we would typically change uniforms (the clothing was prescribed for different activities) and get a lecture on espionage or German national history.

Amongst other things all recruits were taught infantry tactics – 'because tactics usually determined the outcome of a battle'.

The infantry training schedule often began with learning about weapons, but soon graduated to practical exercises that stressed both 'combat shooting' and battlefield movement. Such is certainly the picture given by Kühlwein's handy digest *Fielddienst ABC*, or the 'field service ABC' of 1934, and *Der Feuerkampf der Schützenkompanie* in 1940. Tactics similarly bulked large in the training schedules of officers, and whilst other ranks and NCOs tended to focus their efforts on matters relating to squads, platoons, and companies, the officer was encouraged to think much bigger. Those on divisional courses commonly included 6 hours a week on either the tactics of the infantry regiment – or the division.

Captain Clifford Shore acknowledged that a major strength of German training was the way in which the theoretical and the practical were quickly brought into one.

> Their policy certainly seems to have been to merge weapons training and field-craft into its tactical application on the ground at the earliest possible moment and to allow the two to run, hand in hand, instead of separate entities as was the British policy. There are many British officers who once having caught the idea of this type of training are most enthusiastic about it, and wish to incorporate much of the Teuton idea into present and future training. That it has excellent points cannot be denied . . .

US observer Frederick Sondern saw in German training methods a significant strand of 'standard operating procedures' – what the British would later think of as 'battle drill'.

> Not a moment of a German soldier's day is wasted. Clerical labour, kitchen police, manual work around the post are all done by a civilian military corps of men unfit for combat duty. Every day the German soldier goes through 'standard practice'. A hand grenade is thrown at him, which he must pick up and throw back as quickly as possible. He must advance through a wood and fire at the hip at a target which is suddenly raised in his path. He must be able to throw himself into a shell hole without breaking a leg. He must practice getting through an entanglement without letting his helmet clank against the barbed wire. 'The casualties in the last war, through ignorance', a German Staff Officer once told me, 'were much too high. We shall cut them down by 75 percent this time.'

Significantly, the German interwar generation would become widely militarised, even if only a portion actually served in the army. German education, traditionally of a high standard, was gradually 'coordinated' with party precepts with almost all teachers becoming members of the National Socialist Teacher's Alliance. More than half of German youngsters were in the Hitler Youth by 1935, in which hiking and military style activities played significant parts. Youth was particularly susceptible to the joys of cinema with leaders able to remark by 1937 that the young were now 'directed towards the heroic' by educational film and were therefore 'psychologically prepared' to withstand 'all pressures'. Six months with the state labour service was compulsory in the age group 19 to 25, and this duty had a distinctly military flavour with smart uniforms and drilling with spades. Fitness became something of a cult, whilst the instruction of paramilitary organisations such as the *Sturm Abteilung* (SA) was largely military. In qualifying for the *Wehrabzeichen*, or defence badge, for example, the SA candidate had to complete three groups of tests. The first was 'physical training' and included running up to 3,000m, long jumping, putting the shot, and long-distance hand-grenade throwing. The second were the 'military sports': route marches; small-bore rifle shooting; grenade throwing from prone, kneeling, and standing positions;

first aid; and running in a gas mask. Swimming was not obligatory, but offered as an option, the alternative activity being cycling. The final series of tests was a programme of field activities. During qualification scores were marked by the tester in a booklet, the second and third groups of tests carrying by far the majority of the possible points.

The prewar *SS* began as 'protection' unit for the Nazi party, and it is commonly acknowledged that even in the 'armed', or *Waffen SS*, units raised later political motivations and loyalties remained strong. What is less clear, and remains very much a matter of live debate, is the degree to which the army was also politicised or 'Nazified'. Traditionally, many commentators maintained that the army remained broadly conservative, pointing to the Hitler bomb plot of 1944 and continuing army–*SS* rivalry as evidence, but more recently some academics have claimed that all of the German fighting forces were 'barbarised' in fighting for a Nazi state. Very probably both perspectives are oversimplifications as the picture undoubtedly changed with time. For in the early 1930s the army was resistant to both socialist and extreme right-wing influences. Later with mass conscription, political control of the media, the weeding out of critical voices from positions of military influence, and finally a growing danger that the *Heimat* would be invaded by Russian 'hordes', matters would be very different.

That there were sustained attempts to raise political awareness within the German Army is undoubtedly true. Often this was done in a broad way by emphasis on external threats to the nation, or by means of exhortation to duty to comrades and leaders. Up-to-the-minute popular features in periodicals also played their part. The colourful twice-monthly *Signal* magazine produced by the *Wehrmacht* under the authority of the Propaganda Ministry was European market leader, and ultimately published in 20 languages with peak circulation of 2,500,000 million copies. It reached occupied populations, in their own tongues, as well as German soldiers. The periodical *Soldatenblätter für Feier und Freizeit*, 'Soldier's Paper for Holidays and Free Time', was aimed specifically at the serviceman, and whilst often schmaltzy and frivolous also carried pictures of the *Führer*, odd snippets from speeches, and reminders of the bravery of comrades or the solidity of the home front.

Yet some messages were much more detailed and specific. In the High Command sponsored booklets *Tornisterschrift* (literally 'pack pamphlets') for example the ordinary fighting man was presented with a series of arguments on different aspects of the German world view by academics and other personalities. The tendency of all was to stiffen resolve, inform the individual of the justice of the cause, and boost morale by either positive or negative means. Issue 18, of 1941, gave the soldier the official line on Alsace and Lorraine: that they were historically German, and should remain so. In issue 19 *SS Hauptsturmführer* Dr Lück presented the argument for German ethnic minorities in the east as part of the fatherland within the 'new order'. Later that year came a helpful map of south-east Europe and the Balkans, covering campaign areas. Issue 61 of 1942 gave a picture of German historical achievements and interests within the 'old' Austrian Empire. *Tornisterschrift* was not so unusual, and in its more benign aspects mirrored Allied publications of like purpose. In the British periodical *War* for example the Army Bureau of Current Affairs offered observations on the international scene, flattering pictures of Britain's allies and how to co-operate with them, as well as helpful tips on enemy forces. Yet *Tornisterschrift* was much more overtly political – and often far darker. Issue 29 of 1941 for example was devoted to Dr M von Stämmler's monograph *Deutsche Rassenflege*, the case for 'German racial cultivation'. The people being in an emergency, and the nation being in 'biological danger', it was the duty of all – doctors, politicians, and population alike to act. That Nazi ideology had roots in the trenches of 1914–1918, and a fundamental basis in notions of willpower triumphing over the material, and national and personal 'superiority' it could doubtless serve as spur to action. The counterpoint, that a totalitarian state, locked in a life or death struggle, could easily imprison or execute its citizens for the least sign of hesitancy in the face of the enemy, could be an equally powerful, if essentially negative motivator.

By such standards the morale and propaganda fare of Western Allied armies was tame indeed, though officially sponsored films for example made it abundantly clear what servicemen and their families might stand to lose by enemy victory. Later, especially in the case of Britain, soldiers were encouraged to look forward to an improved, more equitable homeland with better health, education, and housing. British Army morale-raising material, though by no means socialist in general outlook, made frequent appeals to 'Britishness', 'fair play', sense of personal – and to a lesser extent, patriotic – duty. Heavy stress was placed upon the duty of officers to their men, already a strong point when compared to some parts of Europe. As *The Officer and Fighting Efficiency*, 1940, issued to every officer and officer cadet, explained,

> The immediate responsibility for the care and preparation of men for battle rests on the shoulders of the junior commander – a responsibility that he must seize eagerly and tackle firmly in the knowledge that the British officer who measures up to the job has no more loyal supporters than his own men . . . The future of the Army lies with its officers, and, in particular, with its junior officers. It is their contribution that will determine morale and fighting spirit of the troops in battle.

This may be seen as paternalistic, and rooted in class concepts of *noblesse oblige*, but the value of 'fairness' as an idea to engender loyalty was arguably crucial in the army of a democracy. Whilst soldiers were not to be 'pampered', the 'care of men' was to be regarded as the necessary foundation of successful training, not least because the discontented and unwilling were obviously far more difficult to teach. The officer had to remember that his recruit was a man, not merely 'an automaton in battle dress'. Key to this was what *Fighting Efficiency* called the 'man's mental background'. The officer must find out what the men are thinking and what they are worried about:

> The officer who visits the men at mealtimes and calls out 'any complaints?' is merely asking for the most inevitable response – a response as meaningless and automatic as the question itself. An officer who is really doing his job will look for himself and check up. The intelligent officer will ask, 'are the dinners good today?', 'are the potatoes better than they were yesterday?' – and ring the obvious variations. If he puts parrot questions he must expect parrot answers.

As far as complaints were concerned officers were encouraged to take them seriously, since even if the complaint itself was found to be baseless it might be indicative of some other problem or discontent. Ideal ways to get to know the troops was to be involved in sports and games, and continually ask oneself if there was anything else that could be done to make their lives more bearable. In bad times it was to be understood that the good officer 'sticks it out with his men'. Fighting efficiency was further linked to welfare by the instructions of *The Soldier's Welfare: Notes for Officers*, 1941. The prime objects of military welfare work were two fold:

1) To make men as happy and contented as is possible, in the varying circumstances of war, so that they may be at all times fighting fit and fit to fight.

2) To link officers and men together in a bond of mutual friendship and respect, which will not only stand the hardest tests of war, but will be strengthened by them.

In training officers were to make every attempt to ensure not only that the men were not bored, but that their brains were engaged, 'the first yawn' being regarded as 'devastating criticism' of the officer's powers of exposition. Illusive as the notions of 'care of men' and 'mental background' might appear, officers who managed these things well were indeed followed willingly, even loved by their men, whilst those who failed often failed spectacularly – and were frequently despised. A vital part of being a good officer was not wasting the lives of the men.

> Thus it may be said that it is an officer's responsibility during training not merely to fit his men for their work on the battlefield, but to ensure that they will stand a chance of survival, and live to fight another day. In the average battle with imperfectly trained troops only a small proportion of the casualties can be directly credited to the enemy.

It should be recognised that this sort of attitude was both a reaction to the public and political response to the casualties of the First World War, and an increasing realisation that attitudes to casualties in general were changing. In a situation where a small professional army had to be expanded into a large conscript or citizen army this was probably inevitable. Yet practically where British infantry officers and tacticians came from such a starting point there was likely to be an almost in-built tactical caution, and an aversion to risk that was completely alien to the German way of thinking. For whilst British officers were taught that unacceptable risks had to be programmed out, German officers were taught that inactivity was the worst sin and that in the event of choices having to be made the high-risk option was more likely to be correct.

Interestingly, Dunkirk was in many respects a motivational turning point for the British Army. In many quarters there was a feeling that hitherto not only had existing methods of drill and training been old fashioned, but that the war itself was not being taken seriously enough. The enemy was not seen to be playing fair, and by the same token both attitudes and resolve in the military had to be stiffened with a willingness to do whatever it would take to prevent successful invasion of Britain, and ultimately to win. Some of the manifestations of the Dunkirk and Blitz 'spirit' were general – whatever individuals thought of them – Churchillian speeches and efforts at community identification in the face of adversity being only the most obvious. In retrospect the change in attitude to the *Führer* was also remarkable, for between 1938 and 1940 'Herr Hitler' the statesman was transformed into criminal buffoon in the mind of the masses in an interesting parallel to the cartoons of Napoleon as 'Boney' almost a century and a half earlier.

Yet the works of Western Allied propagandists were usually more abstract than those of the enemy, and frequently too gentle or cerebral to raise any sense of immediacy in the breast of the fighting man. Indeed, titles of popular publications such as *Hell! I'm British* were assumed by both reader and author to be humourous rather than patriotic works. This would change markedly after June 1940, with the rise of a veritable cult of unarmed combat, and later even of officially sponsored 'hate training' in the British Army. There was a rash of unarmed and close-combat manuals, many of them private or unofficial, ranging from more conventional Gale and Polen publications on bayonet drill to catalogues of knife and otherwise 'dirty' fighting, the best known of which was undoubtedly Fairbairn and Sykes, *All in Fighting*. Though this actually appeared in 1942, it was based on courses that had been taught since 1940. In *Rough Stuff*, by Sydney Duffield and Andrew Elliot, the reader was given the low down on 'close quarter weapon technique', the 'psychological factor', 'treatment for fifth columnists', 'kicks, stones and helmets', and 'unusual facts about hand grenades'. In many such works, and especially those of Fairbairn, trainees were advised to abandon 'Britishness' and 'rules', adopting instead what was assumed to be a stereotypically 'oriental' school of combat in which no quarter was given and no move too underhand for use in fighting an unfair enemy.

'Hate training' reached its zenith in late 1941, and in some instances included trainees being shown photographs of German atrocities, trips to abattoirs, and encouragement to chant 'Kill! Kill!' or 'Hate! Hate!' during exercises. Lionel Wigram's lectures to infantry recruits after mid-1941 included hair-raising descriptions of German treatment of Russian prisoners, grim warnings of enemy 'efficiency'. This was just too much for traditional generals who thought that such material would unnerve the men, and for many other ranks who found the whole proceedings ridiculous. Hate training was therefore officially abandoned in mid-1942. Yet the need for 'aggression' in the broader sense remained, and ultimately to win meant to attack. As the mantra of the NCOs manual *Surprise the First Principle of Attack* explained: 'Defence must be aggressive and mobile if it is to succeed. Therefore, even when preparing defensive positions, think always how to attack. Your men must survive for a counter attack. Surprise is the first principle of attack. By concealment you will achieve surprise.'

Whilst political indoctrination, or lack of it, remains a controversial area in terms of military motivation, recent studies have come to stress the notion that in the actual heat of combat such abstracts become largely irrelevant. The soldier fights not for an ideal, but for his own survival, and not to let his friends down. As Eastern Front veteran and novelist Willi Heinrich put it, the common soldier's fundamental decency 'doesn't permit him to leave his comrades in the lurch'. In US accounts front-line soldiers are often referred to as 'fox-hole buddies', being the smallest 'team' on the battlefield – or variously as a 'band of brothers' or even, more recently, a 'deadly brotherhood'. Looking back, Harry Arnold of the 99th Infantry Division went so far as to describe the infantrymen as a 'breed apart', thinking that very possibly they had more in common with the enemy than they did with their own rear echelon. Though some have since attempted to deny it, the British manual *Infantry Training* 1944 was fully aware of the reality, even at the time. The infantry section was 'the team' and those in it were to be altered as little as possible: everything was to be done that could be done to foster this 'group morale'. There were also 'soft' skills acknowledged in other instructions. These were that good leadership required good welfare; good officers make good troops; welfare embraced mind body and spirit; and 'care of men' was the first concern of an officer and properly done this fostered 'self reliance'. On the other hand, officers were to note that boredom, unfair treatment, and discontent all undermined morale.

Perhaps more obviously the Nazis drew a good deal of inspiration from the experience of 'comrades' in the First World War, and made capital of the notion of *Frontgemeinschaft* or the comradeship of the 'front-line soldier'. Whatever the relevance of this, the memoirs of individual German soldiers certainly speak of *Kameradschaft*, 'comradeship', the willingness to bear hardships and make sacrifices for one's peers or a particularly valued leader.

With commencement of US conscription in 1940 suddenly over 16 million Americans realised that at some point they might be liable for service. Just one of those swept up by Uncle Sam that year was Carl Cox of Freeman, West Virginia, who actually volunteered before the draft could catch up with him, and whose progress into the army was observed by the lens of a *Look* magazine photo journalist. Like many others, his first stop was Fort Slocum, New York, the 'receiving barracks', where he was given not only a medical examination, hair cut, and uniform, but basic drill, along with 90 to 150 other men per day on the induction production line for preliminary training. The mess hall at Fort Slocum was designed for 600, so the 2,400 troops already there in December 1940 had to eat in 4 shifts of 20 minutes each – their beef hash and vegetables being scooped up and gobbled from the distinctive institutional metal trays with divisions for the contents. Clothing issue was reasonably lavish by wartime European standards comprising the woollen uniform, 2 tropical kits, 2 blue-denim suits for fatigue duty, 4 sets of underwear, and 2 pairs of boots and headgear. 'Civvies' were to be sent home and army clothing was numbered to attempt to prevent what was euphemistically called 'laundering mix-ups and borrowing'. Bunk beds were made up and squared off military style.

Cox was allotted to a training 'section' of about fifty, in essence an overgrown platoon under a sergeant and corporal. Punishment for rule breaking included extra duties, being 'restricted to post grounds', loss of leave or other privileges, and for slightly more serious issues confinement to the guard house. The recruit's daily timetable was highly structured with reveille at 6.15, breakfast at 6.30, and work details or drill from 7 to 12. Lunch totalled a 45-minute break followed by more fatigues or drill until 4pm and a ridiculously early 'supper' at 5pm. Lights out came at 9, with the final 'taps' at 11. As in hospitals and prisons, there were stated 'visiting hours' and lucky men might obtain 'weekend passes'. *Look* magazine remarked with no apparent irony that Cox was able to 'wear his uniform correctly', and march to the mess using the new 'simplified drill' by the end of his first day. Real business came later.

The key US Army training document at the time of entry into the war was FM 21-5, *Military Training*, of July 1941. This saw 'assurance of victory' as the ultimate purpose of all training, and asserted that though there were regulars, reserves, and National Guard, in fact there was only 'one army'. Training was not only to develop ability, but the wish to take offensive action in combat. For, 'To develop an offensive spirit a major objective of training must be the development of aggressive, resolute, thoroughly capable individuals and units whose skill, initiative and confidence have instilled in them the desire to close with the enemy and destroy him'. Interestingly, the ambitious list of qualities that military training needed to instil were morale; discipline; health, strength and endurance; technical proficiency; initiative; adaptability; leadership; teamwork; and, lastly, tactical proficiency.

Basic training was twelve weeks, but under pressure to produce new divisions swiftly this fell to eight, before rising again to as much as fourteen weeks later in the war. At the end of 1942 it was calculated that the entirety of US basic training – once eating, sleeping, housekeeping, and rest periods were deducted – amounted to just 472 hours. Of this 20 hours went on the 'close-order drill' of 'square bashing'.

Ideally, training was to be 'decentralised' and proceeded in a balanced and progressive manner, with 'applicatory tactical exercises'. However, the task was a big one, and even the manual admitted that when time, means, and suitable instructors were lacking, elements of training could be 'centralised' to speed basic and technical training. This turned out to be a nice way of saying that in many subjects large numbers of men had to be herded together quickly, often to attend mass lectures given by instructors who were not very experienced themselves, and to learn to parrot sections from different manuals. Veterans returning from the front were sometimes amused or annoyed by such high-volume, 'by the book' techniques. On the positive side, any prospect of the invasion of the USA was still a very distant one, and mass bombings of American production facilities would never occur. However, it is a little known fact that US planners did consider the possibility that Britain would succumb to invasion, and that Canada might one day become hostile territory. This was used as part of the rationale for development of US mountain and ski-troop capabilities.

Interestingly, whilst the US Army never seems to have explicitly recognised 'hate training' in the same manner as did the British, there were signs of concerted attempts to get the soldier 'mad enough' to fight with determination an enemy that he had never met – and might even have been distantly related to. So it was that bayonet drill and unarmed combat either remained important parts of the syllabus, or were soon re-introduced. FM 21-150 *Unarmed Defense for the American Soldier* was issued in June 1942, and was intended not merely to help the soldier protect himself, but to give 'confidence in his own ability unarmed' which, like having confidence in his weapons, 'makes a man a better soldier'. Like Fairbairn and Sykes in Britian, and like some of the sniper trainers of the First World War, *Unarmed Defense* makes reference to the schools of oriental unarmed combat, but claims that Americans – having discovered these frustrating or ineffective – went on to found their own style of judo. Removing the 'oriental terminology', they then produced 'as good a system as the Japanese and far outstripped it in the effectiveness of the method'.

Having thus calmed the rookie GI that he was not about to be taken apart by some fiendishly effective Kung Fu, the manual went on to reassure him that he himself should have 'no stigma' regarding any and every tactic that he could imagine for, 'In hand to hand combat there are no referees, no judges, and no timekeeper. You are on your own. No measure of defense is too extreme when your life is in danger'. By means of photographs the principles of balance and a succession of blows, disarmings, throws, chops and strangulations were then explained. The opponents were not only unarmed themselves but equipped with rifle and bayonet, knife, club, pistol, and – somewhat improbably – a sabre. Interestingly, though the 'enemy' depicted was larger than the man who invariably came out on top, he was also shown with a darker coloured shirt or jacket. In this way the reader was given a ready Hollywood style reference as to which party represented the forces of evil. Perhaps surprisingly a new manual, *Bayonet*, was produced as late as September 1943. Again there was an emphasis on confidence, and perhaps sensibly, upon a disarmed man becoming armed again as rapidly as possible.

That US trainers had a mammoth task is an understatement. From the tiny pre-war army grew a leviathan of 8 million at peak strength. In 1943 alone 2.6 million men were processed through its reception centres. Yet there was growing realisation that front-line combat infantry did not get the best. Recruits were graded as they came in, and efforts were made to direct those with civilian skills and qualifications towards like jobs in the army. Men who volunteered rather than being drafted were given choice as to branch of service. The net result was that those who chose tended to select Air Services, Marines, and Navy, whilst those with skills that did go to Army ground forces went disproportionately to rear area Corps. As General LJ McNair, Commanding General Ground Forces, observed, troops had preference for the 'more genteel forms of warfare'. No special skills therefore often meant entry into the infantry or field artillery. Statistically, the USAAF and the army accountancy branch mopped up many of the very best men, whilst the infantry got 44 per cent of those graded most poorly. The official history did not mince its words: the ground combat arms obtained, 'less than their share of high intelligence men'. In a surprisingly early and advanced piece of internal market research conducted in 1943 the US Army asked its own men whether they preferred their own branch of service, and whether they were satisfied with their present assignment. Three-quarters of the Air Corps preferred their own branch, and just over half professed themselves 'satisfied'. Only a tenth of the infantry preferred their own branch and less than a fifth declared themselves 'satisfied'.

The replacement system, in which new men were fed to combat units piecemeal, and often found themselves isolated, if not shunned, as inexperienced and likely to take the next bullet, came in for much criticism. Finding the right officers was also problematic. At first there were far too few. West Point could not hope to satisfy any significant proportion of demand and there was much reliance on the National Guard, and the new officer schools that in the event provided much of the junior front-line officer corps. Eventually, late in the war, the schools actually produced too many officers, and the production line had to be slowed. Even Major General HR Bull, head of the Replacement and Schools Command, admitted that, 'emphasis on filling officer candidate quotas had influenced commanders in many instances to sacrifice quality for quantity'. Little wonder that there is often an impression that the US infantry regarded itself as forgotten or unappreciated.

By 1944 with a large army in, or on its way to, Europe, and increasing casualties, infantry manpower reached a crisis, and a series of measures were introduced both to increase the flow of men, and, perhaps less successfully, to raise quality. About 200,000 mainly well-graded personnel were found by combing out the rear areas of the Air Corps and supply branches, whilst at the same time the net was widened for those judged adequate to proceed overseas. This meant specifically that those with poor teeth, but who had held jobs in civilian life, were made avaliable – as well as, more controversially, those with 'mild psycho-neuro' problems of a 'transient' character. Perhaps even more remarkable for the time was a proposal from a member of G-3 branch at the War Department that not only should African Americans be raised for combat units in 'proportionate number', but that black troops should be integrated with their white comrades to fight alongside each other in mixed units. Whilst attempts were made to increase African American enlistment, the latter proposal did not come to full fruition until much later.

In other initiatives the age of the draft, and the age at which men were permitted to go overseas, were adjusted a number of times, but with mixed results. Originally, men had been drafted at 20, but this was lowered to 18 in 1942, but rules in place from June 1944 precluded the sending of any going abroad as replacements until 19. Also in June 1944 came a concerted attempt to tackle the systemic problem by dint of which the best men avoided, or were directed away from, the infantry. The new process involved 'physical profiling'. Under this recruits were graded primarily by physical attributes rather than previous work experience, and the infantry was given entitlement to a larger proportion of the grade 'A' men. Though this began to have an impact a few months later, it came too late to change the general character of the infantry before the end of the war. Moreover, there was further competition from the Navy, which had, in the meantime, added its own entrance tests that also tended to screen out some of the least able.

If the recruitment process never did succeed in getting the very cream of the USA nose to nose with the Nazi in the foxholes, the Army did at least manage to do a number of things that made the infantryman's lot somewhat more palatable. There was a clear awareness, even if only patchily achieved in practice, that the army of a democracy had to make significant concessions to its fighting men to keep them motivated. As Lieutenant General McNair put it, 'My whole experience fixes my belief that the first essential of an efficient command is a happy one – the happiness, or contentment if you will, being based upon confidence in the leadership and a realisation that the leader's demands are just, reasonable and necessary for victory in war'.

Pay was certainly a department where the GI scored significantly over his European counterparts. The basic infantry average was about $700 at the start, but rose to approximately $743 by 1944 with the introduction of special pay status comparable to certain other specialisms. At the same time efforts were made with image. The idea of redefining the qualified infantryman as a 'fighter' turned out to be a non-starter, but special 'Combat Infantryman' badges were actually issued. Supplies of food and equipment were also usually maintained at levels and quality that were clearly ahead of the British, and far outclassed those of the Germans in the latter stages of the war.

Though recalcitrant US troops could be punished in various ways, threat of the 'ultimate sanction' was largely held in abeyance – if not entirely absent. The military legal code demanded that a Court Martial had to be able to prove that a man who left his unit intended to do so permanently in order to prove desertion. Such intent was difficult to demonstrate and so many apprehended were charged with 'absence without leave'. Desertion cases ultimately reached into the low thousands, and there were many more absences without leave, but only 130 deserters were given a death sentence, and just one of these was actually carried out. Private Eddie Slovik, a replacement of 109th Division, was 'shot to death by musketry' by order of a Court Martial in January 1945. Not the brightest of soldiers in the first place, he had not only suffered badly through shelling, but, apparently unsolicited, gave a full signed confession of repeated and intentional desertion. This probably still would not have resulted in execution, but he added that he intended to run away again, and to keep doing so.

The development of US infantry tactics was aided not only by growing experience, but by the translation of enemy manuals and the sending of representatives to Britain to take part in British training courses – most notably those of the new Commandos. This began even before the USA entered the war as in places *Rifle Battalion*, 1940 reads like a direct translation of German manuals. Later chunks of lectures to British troops by battle-experienced officers were repeated almost verbatim in the pages of Military Intelligence documents such as *Technical and Tactical Trends*. Whilst lack of originality could be viewed as criticism, for the most part this was a sensible and valuable way to proceed and emulation and learning by the mistakes and successes of others probably worked rather better in 1940–1941 than it had done in 1917–1918. Accusations of plagiarism meant nothing in war, but wasting lives undoubtedly did.

Film made a growing contribution to instruction: the nationalised German film industry made training films from an early stage, including pieces on the handling of infantry weapons. By May 1942 there were 154 British Army training films, with a further 107 under production. British films were divided into 'basic', 'instructional' – covering specific pieces of equipment, and 'background' features. Prints were held in area 'Kinema Section Libraries' and lent out to units as required. US endeavours, backed by the colossus of Hollywood, were even more remarkable. FM 21-6 *List of Publications for Training* of early 1942 went so far as to claim that training films and 'film strips' (comprising sequences of still frames), supplemented by illustrations in printed manuals, were already 'the primary visual aids for training the army'. Training 'movies', being minor 'sound motion pictures', had the huge benefit that by teaching through the eye and the ear they compelled interest and left lasting pictures of the lesson.

US training motion pictures were provided on 16mm and 35mm film, the larger versions being shown on regular theatre-sized projectors. Film 'strips' were less impressive, and could not show movement, but had the value that individual images could be held on the screen and discussed or explained. Films were not a substitute for practical application, but 'instructional aids' taking their inspiration from the latest methods of teaching in other spheres. Whilst film could never do everything, it had huge advantages. Being shot and edited in advance, films produced polished presentations focusing on salient points, and might well include examples of equipment not yet available to troops. Potentially, film also saved time and resources as one film could be used many times in many places and locations and actions that would otherwise require movement of large numbers of men to distant venues. One projector might well suffice to show not only training films but news and information from the Army Motion Picture Service and entertainment features in off-duty hours. The standard projection equipment was described as 'rugged' and 'durable' as well as simple to operate. Each Corps HQ maintained a large central stock of training material in a film library, lending out in batches to sub-units and reception centres which in turn kept smaller 'sub libraries'.

US Army training films were divided into four major categories: basic; mechanical; technical; and tactical. The 'basic' films were applicable to all branches of service giving enlisted men general factual information. These films were thought especially useful as many men already regarded cinema as a source of both education and entertainment in their civilian lives. Basic films included titles such as *Military Courtesy and Customs of Service* and *Sex Hygiene*. The 'mechanical' films dealt with the function and operation of equipment such as weapons and vehicles, and their organisation. Typical examples included a 28-minute piece on the sighting of 60mm and 81mm mortars, and *The Anti Tank Mine*. 'Technical' films illustrated the actual use of weapons and equipment, 'and the actions of an individual or group in performing an operation or series of operations'. Examples in this category included films on techniques of fire, manning crew-served weapons, and the use of various types of pioneer equipment. Several were of special reference to infantry including the 19-minute *Small Arms Ammunition – Loading*, covering all the squad weapons, and *Infantry Hasty Field Fortifications*. 'Tactical' films proper naturally covered 'the application of basic combat tactics of the different arms and services', just one example being *Platoon Scouts*. In reality, both the mechanical and technical films contributed to tactics in the broader sense. Interestingly, the substantial list of issue films also contained a few oddities such as *Interrogation of Prisoners*, 1941 – actually a British War Office production, 'partially re-edited by the United States Signal Corps'. As of February 1942 seven of the basic titles were obligatory viewing for all recruits. Some silent films were still in circulation at this time but the majority were 'talkies' and silent pictures were being withdrawn as more up-to-date productions replaced them. Though 35mm films were shown to very large audiences, it was recommended that 16mm features were used to groups of no more than a company in size. Troops were marched to the film halls and commanders and trainers were encouraged to give a brief introduction to the piece and its content and usefulness.

Whatever the nationality the practical business end of the infantryman's training had common targets, and these were driven by the tactical realities of the modern battlefield. The soldier had to be taught to use his weapons, to move unobtrusively, use surprise, and defeat the enemy in combat. In short, he had to remain alive long enough, and in such a manner, that he was able to shoot effectively at his enemy. The ideal, as Basil Liddell Hart put it, was a contemporary infantry soldier who was 'stalker, althlete and marksman'. Movements taught in the British publication *Battle School*, 1941 included crawling, with 'chest and crutch flat on the ground, all motive power provided by a thrust forward from the thighs. Body keeping flat, hugging the ground but rolling slightly from side to side like the crawl stroke in swimming'; and walking by day, observing. At night the options included walking by lifting the foot well off the ground and freezing when needed; a 'squatting' or Cossack walk; and crawling. Crawling with the rifle involved holding the weapon across the body, clear of the ground. Bren guns were not to be dragged in low stealthy movement, but held low by two men at butt strap and bipod. Alternatively, one man could crawl with the Bren transverse in front of him, or more slowly on his side, with the weapon resting on the lower leg.

In *Fieldcraft and Elementary Training* the recruit was taught the 'Section Stalk' in which a team crept up on the 'enemy' over a distance of 200 or 300yd, with the section commander choosing the final position, line of advance, and best formations. A second section, representing 'defenders', lay in position and practised observing the attackers. The field movements for the rifleman taught in *Infantry Training*, 1944 were the walk; 'leopard' or stomach crawl; a hands and knees crawl with the rifle round the neck or in one hand; and the roll. Bren gunners were also coached in methods of running; with the gun held between two, or over the shoulder, or with it hung from a sling. This last was described as most comfortable, having the advantage that the weapon could still be fired. Some of the German equivalents were very similar with recruits taught to throw themselves to the ground, and *kreichen* or *gleiten*, that is to crawl with an elbow and knee movement or glide by pushing with the feet.

Camouflage and cover tips also formed part of fieldcraft. The 1941 US *Soldier's Handbook*, or its 1942 update, was issued to all recruits and gave advice on observing around cover, and not silhouetting against an obvious background or skyline. Furthermore,

> You are provided with an olive drab uniform because that color blends in with the color of nature and is difficult to see even at a short distance. If there is not sufficient natural concealment at hand, you can still further increase the concealment which your uniform affords you by using leaves, grass, nets, sacking or other material which may be at hand. No piece of your equipment should glisten in the sun. When the ground is covered in snow concealment may be provided by wearing a cape or jacket of white sheeting.

In *Protective Measures*, 1942 the GI was also taught not to look up at flares at night as this would illuminate his face, to use the correct 'dispersion' to make groups of men less obvious, and to avoid straight lines.

Many pieces of advice stressed breaking up outlines and use of shadow as well as simply obscuring or colouring. As the British manual *Section Leading and Fieldcraft for Cadets* put it, 'shadow is the best protection, keep in it'. Interestingly, some of the Home Guard and privately produced literature went further than the official *Camouflage* manual. In *How to Teach Battlecraft* Captains Humphrey and Ardizzone, of the King's Royal Rifle Corps and Buffs respectively, gave a number of useful hints. These included cocoa powder or flour and soot as face camouflage; dulling of boots; and helmet camouflage intended to disguise and increase breadth, rather than accentuate height. Insulating or darkened adhesive tape around the rim of the helmet was recommended to kill 'shine'. In the *Home Guard Fieldcraft Manual*, students were encouraged to think of 'tone' as much as colour and the natural patterns and devices of snakes, fish, and other animals. Simple but effective were 'wire concealment screens', suitably camouflaged to block the enemy point of view, net hung from the helmet, and green poster paint – so long as arsenical types were avoided.

The bedrock of Second World War infanty tactics would be 'fire and movement'. Though a recognisably modern form of this existed as early as the first decade of the twentieth century, and alternate rushes by platoons or sections were accepted at an early date, the idea took time to develop. In 1914 no real integration of machine guns and platoons had been possible, since there were few machine guns and these were almost all too heavy to be moved at the same speed as an attacking squad. Platoons, or even entire companies, were therefore the individual currency of the 'fire unit'. Light machine guns and automatic rifles were gradually introduced during the First World War, with the result that by late 1916 or early 1917 most front-line platoons included one or more such light support weapons. Occasionally, before the end of the war mixed light machine-gun and rifle sections were also used, as for example in the 1918 *Einheitsgruppen* of the Bavarian guards. Nevertheless, even in the German Army such integration at the very lowest tactical level was not the norm, or was an ad hoc arrangement for a specific purpose, and in the early interwar period the leading military nations settled on infantry organisations in which light machine weapons formed one or more 'sections', or *Truppen*, within the platoon.

British instructions, as expressed in *Section Leading*, 1928, represented one milestone in the 'fire and movement' process, as by now it was well nigh universally accepted that: 'success in the attack depends on firepower which makes possible movement in the face of opposition'. However, the platoon was still regarded as the smallest unit that could be divided into 'interdependent bodies' each capable of fire and movement, an entire section being earmarked as the body to move or fire as required. Within the platoon the Lewis guns formed their own powerful fire sections, and the rifle-section elements were more capable of the actual close assault – if weaker in firepower. Both rifle and Lewis sections were six-men strong, under a section leader. The 2 rifle sections had 7 rifles each; the 2 Lewis sections comprised 1 Lewis and 5 rifles. How ideal platoon fire and movement should be taught was still in some flux, however, as *Section Leading* remarked,

> Care must be taken that exercises to teach the combination of fire and movement are not carried out as a drill. When a platoon is attacking advances must not be made by alternate section rushes, without consideration of the ground and the enemy's fire. Every advance should, if possible, be from fire position to fire position. Training on these lines in peace can only result in heavy and unnecessary casualties in war.

Whilst this was light years ahead of what had pertained on 1 July 1916, it also contained the nub of future arguments about the viability of 'battle drill'. Many more important steps would be taken from 1937 to 1942.

The final stage of infantry training, tactical or otherwise, was exercises. Some were purely theoretical, designed to test commanders rather than units. These might take the form of indoor conferences with maps and plans in the manner of the old German General Staff *Kriegspiel*, or 'wargame'. In the British version there were 'TEWTs', 'Tactical Exercises Without Troops' – one step closer to realism that included movement around the countryside with officers studying features and problems on actual terrain. These had their roots in the old 'staff ride' idea. The full-blown 'field exercise' saw bodies of troops manoeuvre against each other in what were effectively pre-planned marches and mock battles. Again, the general notion was a venerable one, having a history that spanned not only the nineteenth century and Napoleonic periods, but had some echoes as far back as at least the seventeenth century.

In the Second World War some exercises lasted hours, the biggest a number of days. Some involved complete divisions, and even, as in Britain in early 1944, fully combined land, sea, and air components. The most successful were those that aped most accurately the conditions and results of actual combat, were mounted for specific objectives, and attempted to take into account interaction between various arms of service and with air power. Realism could be enhanced by explosions, smoke, and ammunition, blank or otherwise. Yet sometimes troops took exercises less than seriously with encounters degenerating into fisticuffs, or guffaws of raucous laugher at less than realistic aspects of counterfeit casualties and barrages. Many contained a competitive element with 'red' and 'blue' teams for example being judged on general performance or mission success. In the German Army, immediately prior to the outbreak of war, teams were often 'red' and 'yellow' with 'manoeuvre bands' of these colours being widely issued for use on the steel helmet. Some exercises were asymmetrical in that it was really the efforts of one side being assessed, the 'defender' being a token force or even non-existent. So it was that the British for example somctimes pitted one regular unit against another – but on occasion used Home Guards, Commandos, or even boy scouts to represent the opposition. Interestingly, the Home Guard itself joined in with the notion of field exercises with great alacrity, though not always the greatest realism. One of the first units to mount their own in the summer of 1940 was the Great Rollright Platoon of the Oxfordshire Local Defence Volunteers (LDV). In the exercise the LDV defended their own village, being attacked by local regulars and a dive-bombing raid by the RAF. Red Cross volunteers dealt with 'casualties'. Despite lack of verisimilitude, the day was a considerable boost to morale and a curtain raiser to the many more serious efforts that followed later.

In full competitive field exercises assessment was crucial, and the arbiters who reported to the commanders and staffs that organised exercises were the individual 'umpires' who observed and judged the outcome of events such as the effect of enemy fire, interference of extraneous factors, limitations of intelligence, and the ultimate results of combat. Often an umpire was attached to a specific unit, but nevertheless would have to move swiftly over the terrain, listening in to officer groups, checking what the 'enemy' were doing, or telling sentries what they had observed in 'picture painting' sessions designed to stimulate forces into action. These word pictures were often drawn from or embellished upon a 'narrative' devised to give structure to the exercise. To be a good umpire required not just a decisive, and sometimes commanding, demeanour but an intimate knowledge of tactics, weapons effectiveness, diplomacy, and skill in understanding the purpose of the exercise. Umpires were cautioned not to tell the troops what to do, and to remain impartial.

Finding enough suitable umpires in time of war was problematic. British divisions in Britain had an umpire ranking as colonel or lieutenant colonel permanently attached, but many more were required at unit level, and it was sometimes necessary for formations to provide their own. During exercise Cuckoo in 1943, in just one example of many, 5th Battalion the Wiltshire Regiment was forced to use its own company commanders who issued orders then rapidly changed roles to judge the results of their own instructions. By this time US regulations specified a very generous allowance of independent umpires: for a single infantry battalion on exercise it was recommended that there should be 5 umpires ranking as officers, 5 as NCOs, and 7 men to act as 'flag orderlies'. These umpires were to have the use of a truck, complete with 'chauffeur'. Very sensibly it was recommended that the umpire staff should be supplied by the director, 'preferably from sources other than participating troop units', and in any event should never sit in judgement on their own parent unit. Whether this high standard was always possible in practice is unclear.

Another problem was the difficulty of umpiring the detail of 'mopping up' and hand-to-hand fighting: indeed British instructions of 1944 suggested that it was best not even attempted. US regulations suggested that it was the complete impossibility of replicating hand-to-hand combat that was one of the main reasons for needing umpires in the first place. On other occasions issues also arose when one side suddenly achieved an unforeseen advantage and thereby risked seriously upsetting the 'back story' or bringing the exercise to a sudden and premature conclusion. Though exercises with umpires had obvious and serious drawbacks in tactical terms, it would be difficult to argue that even the most amateurish did not have value in testing the ability of formations to absorb orders, move from place to place, react to events, and co-operate with each other as they did so. In retrospect, umpiring also has much to offer the student of tactics, as umpires came to judge exercises by a system of assumptions about combat within which armies were expected to operate in the real world.

In the US example a mimeographed 'Umpire Manual' of February 1941 was the best that was available on the outbreak of war, but a new and much more professional volume, *Field Manual 105-5*, was published in April 1942 giving umpires a uniform set of parameters by which they were to judge the outcomes of combat. According to these instructions the best manoeuvres were, free; continuous; and brief. That is the participants were to have maximum freedom to choose their own courses of action, the flow of events was not to be artificially stultified by unnatural pauses, and exercises involving units of divisional size or smaller were best kept within 48 hours duration. Since hand-to-hand combat could not be 'real', troops were to be stopped short of physical engagement. Fire would be simulated, ideally with blank ammunition and the effect determined by the umpires who were to be organised under the 'Director' who was tasked with overall planning and conduct. Umpires working with infantry were to be of three general types: 'unit' umpires attached to units; 'fire' umpires to mark out artillery fire; and 'bridge' umpires who were to deal with crossing points, especially where these had been subject to notional air attacks. Separate species of umpire were to be attached to tanks, signals, artillery, and other arms. For the purposes of exercises it was to be assumed that,

> An infantry element or any element acting as infantry should be permitted only to advance when it has decisive superiority of fire as compared with the elements immediately opposing it. This superiority never should be less than 2 to 1, and generally should be 3 or 4 to one. If the defender has good cover and a good field of fire, or the attacker has little cover, there should be no hesitation in requiring a superiority of 5 to 1, or even more . . . The tendency is to favour the attacker, permitting him to advance with only a small fire superiority, whereas war experience has shown conclusively that a determined defender, well placed, can delay or even stop a greatly superior force.

US umpires were not to attempt to calculate the effect of each individual infantry weapon, but were given a table by means of which they could determine the likely effect of a number of weapons by multiplication. Naturally, it was impossible to 'evaluate precisely'. Nevertheless, umpires could produce a numerical yardstick for the strength of units and then factor in such things as aircraft, tanks, and artillery to a given situation. A 1940 US rifle squad was thus allotted a notional firepower of 12, whilst an automatic rifle or BAR added a further 3. A typical company, with machine guns and mortars firing at various ranges, might therefore total about 150 firepower points in a confrontation. Interestingly, it was assumed that infantry were neutralised by any tank within a hundred yards, whilst artillery fire halved the effectiveness of infantry. Aircraft were to signal the umpires that they had sighted a ground target and where there was a single aircraft a battery or company was assumed to be temporarily neutralised by low-level attack, three being sufficient for a battalion and nine for a regiment. Aircraft could demonstrate the perceived threat to ground troops by dropping flares, small bags of flour, and other devices. Infantry could likewise simulate anti-tank grenade attacks on vehicles and tanks using flour. As time progressed the calculations necessarily became more complex as losses, assessed as a percentage of the troops engaged, had to be deducted from the firepower totals.

Whilst the idea of calculating firepower was a useful one, and shows what the US Army believed were the relative merits of various weapons systems, flour-throwing battles were not without surreal and slapstick overtones. Moreover, some of the assumptions of the 1942 *Umpire Manual* were highly questionable, and soon proved to be totally out of date. For example, in its remarks on 'horse cavalry' it suggested that when attacking deployed infantry losses to the mounted troops would be a notional 5 per cent. In the event there were exceedingly few cavalry charges anywhere after 1939, and it is difficult to think of even one that took place against deployed US infantry. It was also true that reliance on mechanistic calculation of firepower and range did not test the nuances of the smallest unit tactics, nor take very much account of any of the human elements – such factors as morale, fatigue, and previous levels of experience.

Perhaps the most interesting aspect is that in US theory it was taken as read that getting to the vital spot with the greatest firepower was already accepted as the ultimate determinant of combat.

Whilst exercises with umpires presented obvious difficulties it has to be remembered that these remained a prime method of 'realistic' training on both sides as long as opportunity allowed. In the German official manuals of 1940 it was assumed that the final stage of infantry training would be umpired exercises, and that it might be necessary for units to umpire themselves. In the most extreme example it was sometimes suggested that in small-scale tactical problems that the umpire functions could be assumed even by squad leaders. In the USA the final goal of infantry training was the large-scale exercise. Nevertheless, due to pressures of time thirteen of the eighty-seven divisions trained in the USA never managed to get this far before deployment overseas.

Chapter Two

The Germans

'An unbounded spirit of self sacrifice' - Erwin Rommel

As might be expected the early part of the war saw rapid production of several new German manuals – both commercial editions based on existing official publications to satisfy burgeoning demand, and, more importantly, new versions taking into account both experience of early campaigns and new weapons. The main official manual covering small-unit infantry tactics was the *Ausbildungsvorschrift für die Infanterie*, volume two (130/2a), updated editions of which appeared in both 1940 and 1941. These covered small-unit organisation, squad, and platoon tactics and training, weapons, hand signals, and some basics of fieldcraft and orienteering. However, as we shall see in certain respects, the official army publication lagged somewhat behind existing practice, and doubtless many forward-thinking infantry commanders and NCOs were already using some of the wide variety of commercial material.

Such unofficial contributions included Weber's *Unterrichtsbuch für Soldaten*, of 1938, which for many was probably the first technical introduction to the new MG 34, and the important January 1940 edition of Dr Reibert's much-respected *Der Dienst Unterricht Im Heere*. Reibert worked at the infantry school, Döberitz, and his compendium, first appearing as early as 1929, covered a mass of material at much greater length than any single official booklet. This included not only tactics but history and traditions, details of organisation, ranks, uniform and insignia, orders and correspondence, gas drill, weapons, ammunition, horses, and indeed virtually everything an infantry junior leader might be expected to know. Its popularity therefore appears to have been in part due to the fact that it covered much of the likely curriculum under a single cover. Given Reibert's background, position, and depth of his work – as well as the fact that it is mentioned in the memoirs of veterans, it is fair to infer that it was influential. Though much shorter, another work of some significance was *Die (neue) Gruppe*, a semi-official manual of 1940 by Major Bodo Zimmerman, the content of which corresponds essentially with the second part of the official manual of the same year. Zimmerman's work appears to have been prompted both by the outbreak of war, and by realisation that much existing literature was out of date – being based upon earlier organisations. Zimmerman was thus, as he himself observed, also updating his own 1930s *Soldatenfibel*. Major, later Colonel, Zimmerman was clearly a character of some note being later promoted to the position of first staff officer of the commander in chief of the German Army in the West. He survived until 1963, and so was able to offer well-informed if retrospective comment on the events of the D-Day campaign.

Conveniently, the official manual *Ausbildungsvorschrift* (130/2a) was later translated,

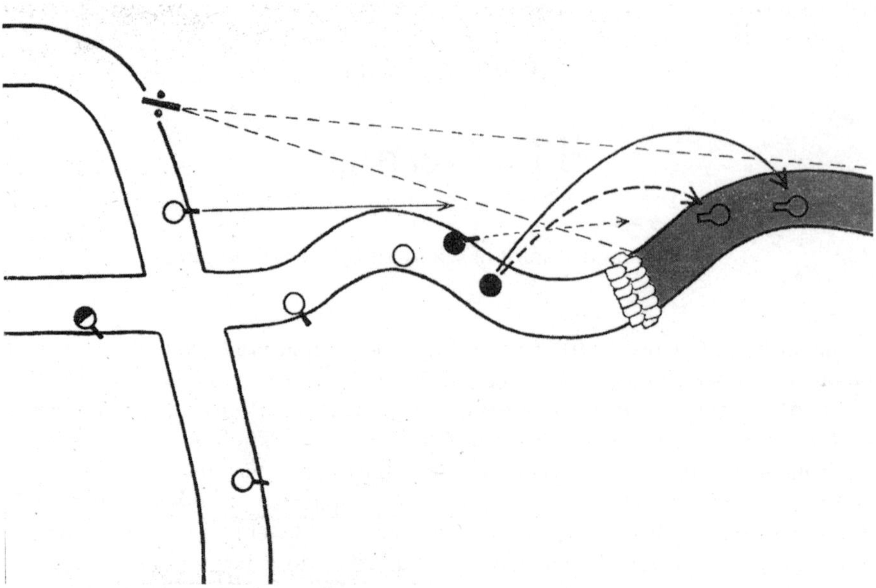

Recommended method for attack along a trench. The squad light machine gun gives covering fire as the team advances, with a grenadier and rifleman in the lead. The remainder follow up guarding against possible threat from other directions. When close grenades are thrown over the block in the trench. With the bursting of the bombs the team are ready for close assault. From *Der Feuerkampf der Schützenkompanie*, 1940.

albeit somewhat inexactly, by US Military Intelligence, with updated drawings, as, *The German Squad in Combat*. An example of the oddities encountered in the US version is the rendering of *Taschenlampe* – meaning literally 'pocket lamp', but usually translated as 'flashlight' or 'torch' – as 'search light'. Yet however, and by whomsoever, it was absorbed the official German infantry manual does seem to have had considerable impact over time, and indeed also appears to have permeated a number of British synthesises. These included the handy and fairly widely available crib *German Infantry in Action (Minor Tactics)*, which had indeed been printed as far afield as India by February 1941, and Wilhelm Necker's commercial booklet *The German Army of Today*, 1943. Necker was already the author of three morale-raising titles including the upliftingly simple *Nazi Germany Can't Win*.

Die Neue Gruppe makes the important point that, '*Die Gruppe ist die kleinste, im neuzeitlichen kampf wichtigste kampfenheit der Infanterie*' – 'the squad is the smallest infantry unit of significance in modern combat'. It was indeed the building block of the German platoon, which consisted of four squads, each of a leader and nine men. A platoon headquarters of a leader and three men, and a light mortar squad of a leader and two men completed the platoon. The squad as outlined in the *Ausbildungsvorschrift* of May 1940 was still shown as thirteen-strong, being the *Gruppenführer*, or squad leader, with a *Truppenführer*, or troop leader, as second in command. In action the latter would usually find his place leading the riflemen, but also acted as deputy for the leader. The main body of the *Gruppe* was still shown as two sub-elements; a four-man machine-gun team and a seven-man rifle team – respectively the *LMG Trupp* and the *Schützentrupp*. The *Richtschütze*, or LMG 'No. 1', fired the support weapon, and acted as leader for the *LMG Trupp* in the absence of both the squad leader and his deputy. The three other men of the *LMG Trupp* serviced the gun-carrying equipment and acted as ammunition numbers. The troops of the *Gruppe* were equipped according to task and the type of machine weapon that supported it.

Squad Leader: rifle; binoculars; dispatch pouch; wire cutters; and compass.

Assistant Squad Leader: rifle; binoculars; dispatch pouch; hatchet; and tape measure.

Richtschütze, or LMG 'No. 1': LMG; pistol; and folding mattock. Where the weapon was an MG 08/15 he also carried a drum magazine attached, and the long-range sight and spare lock in pouches. In case of an MG 13, an ammunition belt with four magazines; pistol; tool pouch; and folding mattock.

***Schütze* 2**: pistol; and folding mattock. For the MG 08/15, ammunition box with belt; tool pouch; water container and condenser pipe; spare barrel; and carry strap. For the MG 13, two ammunition-carrying belts with magazines; carry strap; spare barrel; and mitten for barrel changes.

***Schütze* 3**: with the MG 08/15, two cartridge boxes; rifle; short spade; and carry strap. With the MG 13, two ammunition belts with magazine pouches; rifle; carry strap; and short spade.

***Schütze* 4**: with the MG 08/15, tripod; pistol; cartridge box; and short spade. With the MG 13, tripod; pistol; ammunition belt with magazine pouches; and short spade. Tripods were only needed on 'special service', where these were not required an extra ammunition box or pouch was carried.

Seven riflemen of the *Schützen Trupp* were equipped with rifles and standard equipment and distribution of grenades and digging tools as per the instructions of the company commander.

Interestingly, this summary of equipment was already incomplete, and the precise composition of the German squad was in flux. For the general purpose MG 34 machine gun was now in widespread use with front-line troops, and many squad leaders were carrying the MP 38 sub-machine gun as early as the invasion of Poland. Indeed, the official company manual '130/2a' lagged a very considerable way behind actual practice since the MG 34 machine gun, inspired by a Swiss design, had been officially introduced in 1936 and had seen service in the Spanish Civil War. This new weapon featured prominently in Weber's *Unterrichtsbuch für Soldaten*, and in the 1940 edition of Reibert, where the MG 13 was already relegated to an appendix. Many of the MG 13s were sold off, and even early in the war were seen mainly in second-line and training units, and in rear areas with formations such as the army postal service.

The MG 34 has been justifiably described as revolutionary, being the first mass-issue weapon that could realistically fulfil virtually any task expected of a machine gun. In design terms points of interest included a relatively light weight of just over 12kg; an ability to use either ammunition belts or drums; the options of firing from a tripod, pintle, anti-aircraft mount, or lightweight bipod; and a brisk rate of fire averaging a maximum cyclic rate of well over 800 rounds per minute. On the bipod reasonable accuracy could be attained up to about 800m, whilst on the *Lafette 34*, with its optical sight and shock-absorbing spring-loaded cradle, the gun worked exceptionally efficiently in a 'heavy' machine-gun role. It could equally well be fitted to vehicles, including half-tracks, motorcycles, and tanks making for simplicity in training, and commonality of many component parts as well as ammunition. It was also a competent anti-aircraft weapon as its rate of fire was adequate against the propeller-driven craft of the day, and it could be put in twin mountings. Put together this spelled a remarkable versatility, and, perhaps most critically from the point of view of tactical application in the context of infantry, a gun with the capability to deliver high volumes of fire without sacrificing speed of movement.

The drawbacks were remarkably few. One of these was certainly the relatively fine tolerances of manufacture, which made for an accurate and elegant weapon, but entailed high production costs and might lead to fouling of the mechanism. Another more controversial issue was that the high rate of fire and belt feed, advantageous in many circumstances, also led to high ammunition consumption. The British had believed that such a characteristic was unacceptable in a squad weapon: the squad had to move fast, carry everything with it, and could not afford to 'waste' ammunition that weighed a great deal and might be difficult to replenish. A light and accurate machine gun with box magazines with a maximum capacity of thirty-two rounds was therefore ideal. The Germans accepted the potential burdens that ammunition belts might entail.

The *Maschinenpistole* 38 was also a contributor to increased firepower, but one of a very different sort. The German Army had been the first to adopt a true sub-machine gun, in the shape of the old Bergman MP 18, in 1918, when the weapon had been seen as the answer to a specific need in trench warfare. Trenches were confined spaces, and traditional rifles were powerful and accurate at longer ranges, but hampered by small magazines and long length in a rapidly developing environment of close action. Much consideration was therefore given to finding something that fired rapidly, but was short and handy in a confined space. One option was to add a stock to a semi-automatic pistol, another was to shorten and lighten traditional carbines firing full-size rifle cartridges even further. Neither solution was satisfactory. A carbine was still a carbine, slow to load, and with a massive muzzle blast if lightened or shortened too much. Pistols were more handy and rapid, but required larger magazines and additional parts to transform them into small carbines – and were really too delicate for prolonged use as impromptu assault weapons. The Bergman was a nicely calculated half-way house, managing to incorporate full automatic fire without being too bulky or heavy. It achieved this by means of 'blow back' operation and 'advanced primer ignition'. The secret of these principles was to take full advantage of the moving bolt, the forward impetus of which chambered the cartridge, but also helped retain explosive force before being blown back again to eject the cartridge and repeat the cycle. The weapon therefore required only a relatively light bolt, and no overcomplicated locking mechanism. By luck or judgement the 9mm parabellum round, already a standard for German semi-automatic pistols, proved ideal for the sub-machine gun. It was powerful enough at the sort of ranges that were needed, whilst not so large as to be unmanageable even when firing fully automatic. The Bergman's magazine was the 'snail' drum already produced for use with some Luger pistols.

Whilst most interwar sub-machine guns followed the lead of the Bergman with its traditional woodwork – and 'short carbine with shoulder stock' outline, the MP 38 represented another leap forward. Designed under the auspices of Berthold Giepel, director of Erma armaments, it took advantage of recent work by Heinrich Vollmer, but also incorporated a number of novel features to produce a highly innovative weapon. Perhaps most obvious of these was the furniture. Gone was any wood at all, and in its place came a folding metal skeleton buttstock and phenolic resin grips. There was no barrel jacket and sheet-metal stampings and aluminium castings were used alongside high-quality steel tubing. Its box magazine and pistol-style grip were tested features that may have been inspired by the Thompson, though its feed was less sturdy than that of the American gun. Sighted at up to 200m, but more accurate and effective at about half that range, the MP 38 weighed about 4kg and carried a thirty-two-round magazine. It was best used in short bursts and proved extremely useful both in close-assault and close-defence situations.

The decision that machine weapons and firepower in the forms of the MG 34 and MP 38 should take priority had the natural corollary that squads could be smaller, but also that there would be just a single element rather than two small '*Trupps*' making up the Gruppe. So it was that the new edition of the *Ausbildungsvorschrift* of March 1941 showed a drastically revised format for both men and equipment, economising on manpower whilst maximising firepower – a trend that would be further extended later in the war. The latest squad consisted of the squad leader and nine men.

Gruppenführer: equipped with machine pistol; six magazines in pouches; magazine filler; binoculars; wire cutters; and whistle.

Schütze 1, or *Richtschütze*: carrying and firing the MG 34; with a drum magazine; pistol; tool pouch; and pocket lamp.

Schütze 2: acting as gunner's assistant, carrying spare barrel and case; carry strap; an ammunition box and four belts, one of which held armour-piercing ammunition; pistol; short spade; and sun glasses.

Schütze 3: acting as ammunition carrier, with spare barrel and case; carry strap; two ammunition boxes; rifle; and short spade.

Schützen 4–9: were the riflemen and *Nahkämpfer*, or literally 'close-combat' element, the most senior of which was the assistant squad leader. All equipped with rifle; two ammunition pouches; short spade; hand grenades, plus smoke grenades; machine-gun ammunition belts; concentrated charges; and tripod as ordered.

This arrangement produced a selection of squad weapons of polar opposites – being two of the most modern machine weapons, one of which generated extremely heavy fire to long ranges, and a small group of riflemen whose main weapon was essentially a carbine version of a bolt-action rifle from the end of the previous century. These Mauser K98 k rifles, whilst by no means the worst of their class, had only five-round magazines, were not particularly swift to load and fire, and required some skill to achieve the full accuracy that was arguably their best design feature. British sniper officer Captain Clifford Shore found the standard German Mauser accurate with convenient sights, especially up to 300yd, but declared the bolt action and finish vastly inferior to the Enfields that he was used to,

> To anyone familar with the crisp, clean and easy bolt action of the SMLE and No. 4 the Mauser bolt was nothing but a headache, and absolutely hopeless for anything in the nature of rapid fire. If one filled the magazine and fired the five rounds fairly quickly it took quite an effort to open the bolt for the last round. The furniture of these rifles – of 1940 to 1942 vintage – was very poor and on more than one occasion I saw definitely warped butts. Another feature of the normal German service rifle, to many, was the vicious kick which every rifle of this type possessed . . . in assessing its capabilities as impartially as possible I place it a long way behind the No. 4 and the Springfield. The safety catch on the Mauser was a clumsy contrivance, and very awkward of manipulation. But I do grant that it was a 'mobile' weapon.

Hinlegen und Aufstehen

Kommando „Hinlegen!" (siehe Bild)

Der Mann setzt zunächst den linken Fuß etwa einen Schritt vor und läßt sich auf das rechte Knie nieder. Er ergreift gleichzeitig das Gewehr mit der linken Hand im Schwerpunkt, Mündung etwas angehoben, beugt den Oberkörper nach vorn und

legt sich nach vorwärts flach auf den Boden. Hierbei dient zunächst das linke Knie, dann die rechte Hand und zuletzt der linke Ellbogen als Stützpunkt des Körpers. Alle Bewegungen fließen ineinander über.

Merkspruch: Rechtes Knie, linkes Knie, rechte Hand, linker Ellbogen.

Das Gewehr wird zwischen Ober- und Unterring und mit links aufwärts gedrehtem Lauf auf den linken Unterarm ge-

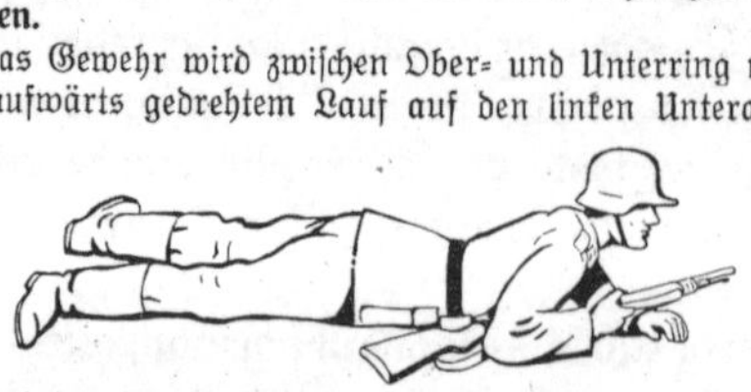

legt, wobei weder die Mündung noch die Schloßteile die Erde berühren dürfen. Der Kopf ist etwas angehoben, der Blick nach vorn gerichtet, der Mann rührt sich.

Fehler:

a) Karabiner wird nicht in die linke Hand gegeben.
b) Hacken werden hinten hoch geworfen.
c) Der Mann sieht nicht nach vorn, sondern auf den Boden.
d) Falsche Karabinerlage, Lauf zeigt nach rechts. Karabiner liegt zu weit vom Körper entfernt. Karabiner nicht im Schwerpunkt erfaßt.

The most basic fieldcraft: going prone quickly. From Dembrowski's privately published *Exerzieren und Kommandieren*, Berlin, 1940, in a copy sold by the Karafiat book dealers in Herman Göring Strasse, Brünn.

The result of having an old and rather slow and basic, but short, light and handy rifle was German units revolving around the light machine gun, a high volume of total firepower, but a great imbalance between the support weapon and the riflemen who were very often supports and beasts of burden for the gun. Conversely, German infantry maintained an ability to lay down very heavy fire, even when units were badly depleted – an extraordinarily useful characteristic particularly in the defensive battle.

In Reibert's summary detailed tactics boiled down to the specific capabilities of each weapon. The rifle was to be regarded as 'the chief weapon of the infantryman working mainly at middle ranges'. The light machine guns, by contrast, were the 'main strength' of the rifle company working up to 1200m. The light mortar of the platoon was deemed useful between 50m and 450m. Machine pistols and pistols were quick-fire 'close-combat weapons' (*Nahkampfwaffe*). The hand grenade was the 'stick fire weapon' of the infantry for combat up to 40m range, with a blast effectiveness of 3–6m and fragments doing damage in a radius of 10–15m. The edged weapons, such as the bayonet, were obviously close combat, and worked only by *Stich, Stoß oder Schlag*, that is by stab, shock, or blows.

The formations of the squad divided essentially into those of close order and those of extended order – mainly the latter being used in combat. In close order, lines, single-file column, and marching order by threes covered the basics of drill. For combat and manoeuvre there were three key deployments. The first of these was the *Schützenrudel*, a simple scattering of the riflemen across a space about 15m sq, thus reducing the potential impact of enemy fire. The term translates somewhat misleadingly as rifle 'flock' or 'pack', since the main consideration was not to bunch too closely, but to maintain dispersion amongst the riflemen whilst maintaining contact with each other and the leader. The *Schützenrudel* as such appears to have received less emphasis with time as squads were no longer considered to be composed of separate 'rifle' and 'MG' groups. Nevertheless, the 'open-order' squad remained a valid and important concept. The other two combat formations were the extended squad column, or *Schützenreihe*, and the *Schützenkette*, which translated as skirmish 'line' or 'chain'. Strictly speaking, chain was the more exact, since this formation was not strictly linear, but a roughly linked frontage upon which individuals took 'positions according to the terrain', usually building up the skirmish line on both sides of the light machine gun. Commonly, the squad was expected to move seamlessly from squad column to line when required to enter the firefight, the light machine gun remaining 'centrally located in the squad skirmish line' with the riflemen spreading out to either side as they advanced. Nevertheless, they could also be deployed to the left or right of the gun team where required by terrain or circumstance, though 'bunching around the gun must be avoided under all situations'. The distance between individuals was about five paces unless otherwise specified. In open-order cross-country movement it was expected that all members of the team would ensure that their weapons were loaded with safety catches on, and magazines and boxes secured. The basic command to move on was '*Marsch*!' with '*Kehrt Marsch*!' for falling back. Leaders were expected to remain on the enemy side of the unit whether advancing or retiring. From forward movement it was probable that the squad leader would give one of three orders: '*halt*!', to stop; '*hinlegen*!', or 'lie down'; or '*Volle Deckung*!', meaning 'full cover' to avoid enemy fire and observation. In going into full cover individual members of the squad were to attempt to preserve contact with the leader, unit cohesion, and ability to observe ground around them.

> The use of other formations, or the omission of parts of the squad, is permissible only when the situation makes it necessary. In this case special orders should be given. Cohesion within the squad must be maintained at all costs. The formation of the squad may be changed from column to skirmish line (or vice versa) to reduce casualties from hostile fire or to negotiate difficult terrain. Formation changes in rough terrain are often necessary in surmounting or avoiding obstacles of all kinds, or in closing up on rear squads. It is less important that the distances and intervals be maintained exactly than it is that the squad avoid losses – in other words, that it reach the enemy position in full strength. The attention of the riflemen should be directed more in the direction of the enemy and less on the formation. The squad leader is not restricted to any given position or place. As a rule he moves before his squad. On occasion it may be necessary for him to leave his squad temporarily in order to observe the enemy, reconnoitre the terrain, and maintain connection with adjacent units. His place is then taken by the second in command.

The squad was no longer regarded as two differently armed sub-units, but as a single flexible entity that might be divided in various ways as required for tactical purposes such as fire and movement. In the firefight it was often controlled as one, where generally attacking troops would open fire whenever possible at relatively short ranges – with the squad leader personally directing the fire of the light machine gun. Sometimes, indeed, as against a small target at close range, the fire of a single marksman could suffice. For the attack some or all of the riflemen might remain under cover until called upon. Nevertheless, once under fire, and with the squad scattered, it might prove difficult for the leader to control everyone simultaneously and in such circumstances the riflemen 'assist in the firefight of the squad by conducting their fire independently, unless the squad leader concentrates the fire of his riflemen upon one target'. Where the squad had been told to 'fire at will' the individual soldier was to aim at the target that 'interferes most with the accomplishment of the squad's mission'. If no such order had been given the squad held fire unless targets suddenly appeared at close range. Sometimes the squad leader would designate areas of the target on which individuals were to fire, or against a 'very broad target' the rifleman simply shot against that portion 'directly opposite him'. In any engagement it was vital that the squad leader consider ammunition expenditure. Given only what they carried it was not feasible for the squad to continue intensive combat for prolonged periods, and it was recommended that the light machine gun retain a final reserve of 200 to 250 rounds for as long as possible. In order to conserve ammunition effectively the squad leader was to keep track of how much was available, and have an idea of when it could be replenished. Individuals were to keep track of their own ammunition during pauses in firing, and when asked could inform their leader what was left.

The *Ausbildungsvorschrift* offered several possible tactical scenarios for the firefight. One very likely possibility was that the squad would be in position and concealed when

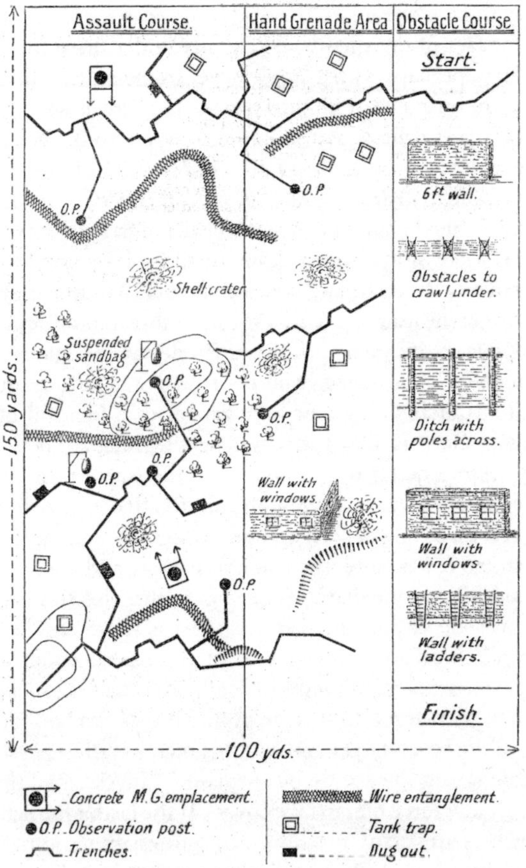

A 'training area for fighting at close quarters' from a 'semi-official' German publication, as rendered in the British publication *Periodical Notes on the German Army*, No. 35, February 1941. The whole space is only about 150 by 100yd but contains a wide variety of possible scenarios and terrain encountered on the battlefield. Parts of the area are devoted to assault and obstacle courses and realistic hand-grenade training.

the enemy was noticed. It was the duty of the squad leader to identify the best way for targets to be engaged, maximising surprise, and perhaps using only the light machine gun initially. Having spotted what was to be fired upon, he would give an order specifying an estimation of range, type of target, and location – as for example: 'Direction: farm houses, pile of bright stones. One finger to the right, an enemy machine gun'. The gunner signified he understood by answering perhaps that he could see smoke from the enemy weapon, or by other confirmation such as, ' gun appears to be about 100 yards behind a bright green bush'. Following the actual fire order the gun team would then make ready the LMG under cover, before bringing it into position and opening up, the assistant gunner remaining as well concealed as possible, perhaps a few paces to the left and rear, but ready to help or replace the *Richtschütze* as required. In instances where the squad was in the face of the enemy and already under fire it might be necessary to abbreviate everything, perhaps with a single order to the entire squad such as: 'squad, posts. Machine gun in bushes, left oblique, range 450, fire at will'. As a rule any such engagement would involve the squad falling into cover to deliver fire, or be swiftly followed by the squad being ordered into *Volle Deckung*, or 'full cover'. In extreme cases it might only be possible to order 'fire at will' or 'full cover'.

In training for firefights the squad was positioned and flags raised from different locations to simulate presence of the enemy. The squad leader reacted by ordering fire on the different spots in a swift, clear, and concise manner. Multiple flags shown simultaneously were used to get the team to identify the most threatening targets, and encourage the squad leader to engage his men with them. Productive reactions to different situations were also taught. For instance, where a squad was already dug in and enemy riflemen appeared advancing singly at long range, or a handful of men were seen crawling cautiously as close as 500yd, fire was best withheld. These were not 'paying targets' – it was therefore better not to give away the squad position but to keep the enemy under observation until close enough for effective engagement. Conversely, a machine gun being set up at 400yd, perhaps immediately behind the individual riflemen, was a worthwhile target. It was larger than a single person, and was a definite threat. The squad leader should issue immediate orders for a 'surprise fire attack' and thereby remove the threat as soon as possible – and as soon as the enemy were neutralised or disappeared order his own LMG to locate to an alternate position so as to avoid any quick retaliation. Likewise, large numbers of enemy riflemen advancing, even at 600yd, were considered an urgent target. In such an eventuality it was best for the squad leader to indicate sectors of the broad target and allot his men to different parts of it, ordering rapid fire, if possible taking the enemy by surprise – 'the essential thing is to stop the advance of the enemy and force him to take cover'. If the leader himself identified a critical new target, such as an enemy machine gun, not easily indicated to his own light machine gunner he was to have no hesitation but take charge of the weapon directly, and by firing bursts in the right direction show the team where they should be aiming.

The key problem was to 'develop in the squad leader the ability to adapt himself readily to various and unexpected situations, and, on the basis of a sound decision made quickly, to issue a brief and clear order'. In organising his men in the firefight the leader was to remember a few main points. First, he was to make sure that the target was clearly and briefly designated. Secondly, to check that the men had their sights adjusted to the correct setting, and that their fire positions were suitable. Thirdly, he was to ensure that the LMG had an alternative fire position to which it could be moved when it came under accurate return fire. In relocating he was to make sure that it did so by disappearing back under cover before occupying the new post – rather than moving in view of the enemy.

The attack was seen as the *métier* of the infantry since the offensive was understood to bestow a 'feeling of superiority', with the attacker determining where and when battle would be fought. In attacking it was the infantry that would bring about 'the final decision in combat', and it was the arm that all other arms had to support. Further,

Ausbildungsvorschrift encouraged its readers to believe that superiority in numbers was not always the decisive factor, the big battalions being potentially balanced out by leadership, training, and a willingness to exploit favourable circumstances. Interestingly, this was a clear echo of *Der Angriff im Stellungskrieg*, the 1918 manual of 'Attack in Position Warfare' that had spoken of 'fighting power' based on such factors as training, equipment, preparation, and determined action being able to overcome numbers.

In developing the attack an infantry company was likely to march to within a certain distance of the enemy, redeploy taking advantage of any cover, and break down into its platoons, and then shake out into the separate squads. Though no longer compressed into a single unit, the squads were still expected to remain fairly compact, in squad columns, probably receiving their final orders at this stage. Such instructions might well be phrased simply as a couple of sentences to the platoon, ordering for example an objective, and a formation or distribution. In going forward common platoon formations included the 'wedge' and 'broad wedge' – the one having three squads in a rough arrow shape to the fore, and one to the rear, the latter having two in the lead followed by two more to the centre rear. The wedge, with its single squad thrown forward, was seen as particularly valuable in terrain where observation was difficult, or enemy positions were only vaguely located. The remaining squads could take appropriate action as soon as the leader made contact. As long as the situation allowed, as for example where they were under cover and not receiving fire, the troops advanced at a walk. By staying in small rough columns the squads allowed supporting machine-gun fire to continue as long as possible.

At the command 'spread out' the squads finally moved into skirmish line, usually with the LMG group at their spearhead. Under fire they now moved by rushes, either as a unit or as individuals. Whether this was by bounds, or by crawling, depended on the amount of support, enemy fire action, and the terrain:

> If under effective hostile fire, the advance of the squad must be supported by its own fire. Here the fire can serve its purpose only if it is used quickly and decisively to gain fire superiority, thus permitting the men to work forward. Fire and movement must always be closely co-ordinated. The terrain must be used in a skilful manner. In terrain with little cover the infantryman must dig quickly. Here the machine guns must protect the entrenchment until a makeshift cover has been provided. If possible, areas covered by enemy artillery fire are avoided or circumvented insofar as the terrain and mission permit; otherwise, quick rushes are made during a pause in the firing.

The squad assault was usually part of a bigger plan involving platoons or companies: as the British precis *German Infantry in Action* explained, 'The rifle companies are the deciding factors in the infantry battle. Close co-operation with the infantry support weapons, the artillery and on occasions tanks and aircraft, and a quick and determined exploitation of their action ensures the success of the rifle companies'. To co-ordinate with neighbouring units the squad leader needed to bring his men to the jumping off point at the specified time. Where this needed to be accomplished swiftly the best method was a combination of moving at the double and walking – so travelling reasonably swiftly without becoming prematurely exhausted. Normally, this required no specific order, men simply followed the pace set by the leader. In picking his route the leader was not required to stick slavishly to the sector assigned if this might lead to casualties, but was free to deviate to avoid observation or fire.

Under ideal circumstances, where it was possible for the entire squad to go from cover to cover, movement bounds for the complete unit could be prepared systematically, with the LMG being loaded and signalled as ready before a rush. The *Gruppe* could then make a surprise move, with the leader specifying the destination before the orders, 'Entire squad; prepare to rush; up!'. Often, however, it might only be practical for the men to go forward singly, working their way 'independently at irregular intervals of time and space to the objective'. Where covering fire was required from the LMG during the advance this was achieved by having one of the gun team go forward with some ammunition, and select a good fire position. Once he was secure the next member of the team would quickly bring up the gun and drop into cover, allowing the man who had already been in position for a moment or two to take over the gun and start firing. As a general rule if the squad was under enemy observation covering fire would be needed to aid movement, whether this came from heavy weapons, fire from the rear, or from the squad's own assets.

Conversely, where the squad was moving through particularly close cover riflemen could be thrown forward to reduce the chance of the LMG being taken by surprise. The squad leader chose the method of approach according to the tactical problem at hand. In crossing a bridge covered by enemy artillery, for example, the best solution might be long bounds during pauses in fire. In seizing high ground overlooked by the enemy it might well be possible to advance stealthily, before rushing the entire squad forward on a final bound. If shells began to fall near the advancing squad during an assault the best choice was often to 'rush obliquely forward' out of the area of fire, rather than to go to cover in a bombardment zone, or retire through it. Where supporting artillery kept the enemy under cover this was to be taken full advantage of by advances in long bounds. If, however, the squad was fired upon by an enemy located in a strong defensive position at close range the only practical option might be a mixture of short bounds and crawling.

> In the attack the fire fight is conducted initially by the heavy weapons. The destruction or neutralisation of enemy strongpoints is the most important mission of the artillery, the infantry cannon, and the heavy machine gun. At effective ranges the light machine gun is also employed. The riflemen participate in the fire fight in the early phases when good results may be expected, or when they have insufficient cover. But it is not the task of the riflemen to engage in fire fights of long duration in order to gain fire superiority. In the attack, in the final analysis, it is the vigorous shock power of the riflemen with bayonet which overcomes the enemy. Fine leadership on the part of the squad leader consists in bringing his riflemen into contact with the enemy in as strong a condition as possible. The outcome of the attack will depend upon the will of each individual soldier to attack, and particularly upon the will of the leader.

Under ideal conditions squads worked their way forwards 'as far as possible without firing'. When there was no longer sufficient cover, or when the fire of other arms proved insufficient, the LMG was to be employed against enemy positions offering resistance to the advance. One obvious instance might be when a machine gun held up the squad: the textbook response would be to leave the majority of the men under cover – as for example in a depression – and indicate the target to the LMG. Only exceptionally would rifles be brought into play at 'mid ranges', such occasions might include loss of the LMG, or the appearance of particularly favourable targets. However, at closer ranges, when the support of heavy weapons was no longer fully effective the riflemen opened aimed fire – nevertheless, 'their fire should be in heavy bursts of short duration'. The objective of such fire action was not merely to hit the enemy but as Hauptmann Weber had observed in his *Unterrichtsbuch*, '*Niederkampfen*', or beating down the opposition so as to neutralise return fire.

Reibert's detailed advice on the rifle firefight was that it should begin with the squad prone and shooting from cover, commencing on the command '*Stellung! Feuer frei*', 'Fire at will', from the commander. More than one rough line of troops might engage the enemy under propitious circumstances, with rifles and machine guns firing through comrades ahead of them, if gaps of ten or twenty paces were observed and the rearmost firers were closed up sufficiently to those in front. Local tactical movement or assault preparation might be continued by crawling under cover, on all fours, or by worming on the stomach pushing with the feet. In doing so individual soldiers might hang their arms around their necks, cradle them low and slightly to one side, or hold them transversely to the front.

Further detail of the micro tactics of the firefight were given in *Der Feuerkampf der Schützenkompanie*, 1940, which, though technically an unofficial document, quoted freely from official sources. It included advice on judging distances, tips gleaned from the First World War and Polish campaign, and a summary of key information on squad formations, application of fire, and basic signalling. Drawings showed how machine gunners could crawl with their weapons through dead ground, or pop down into 'full cover' positions if observed or countered by heavy fire. Individual 'accurate and quick' shooting was the ideal, and sketches showed how single shots in combat were best aimed at the centre of mass of the visible target. For standing or kneeling adversaries this was usually the lower part of the chest or abdomen. When confronted by a prone enemy the best shot was often the upper chest, or for a head popping up and down the centre of the face. Interestingly, fire against cavalry was directed at the centre of mass of the rider, not the mount, as had sometimes been recommended in previous centuries. In certain circumstances the actual human target might not be visible at all, but betrayed by the presence of equipment such as binoculars or range finder. Nevertheless, intelligent engagement was still possible, either by prediction of the position of the user, or by firing at the equipment itself to deny observation. For moving targets a quick method of 'aiming off' to the front was offered in which widths of the target formed a unit of measurement. So it was, for example, a walking figure crossing at 600m might be hit by aiming off three 'target widths', whilst running figures at half that distance were given four. A mounted horseman walking at 300m required just half a target width in 'aim off' as the target was both large and not moving at great speed.

Where any degree of preparation was possible distances to landmarks were determined in advance and ammunition supply calculated. Machine gunners received priority in positioning, ideal posts being concealed but with a broad field of fire and covered line of retreat. In forward field positions guns were placed so as to just clear an apparent crest with the users head well down, though gunners had to be wary of the fact that the sight was higher than the bore of the weapon and avoid shooting into their own cover. Local lumps and bumps that interfered with bipod positions could quickly be sorted out with digging implements, usually by levelling the ground slightly, or creating a small depression that enabled the gunner to get his head lower. Tree positions were less flexible, but where a simple platform could be created might give a considerable element of surprise firing over intervening cover from unexpected angles. Riflemen were easier to get aloft, and good for observation purposes. For clearance of stoppages or minor repairs, MG teams were to duck back into cover, not remain helpless targets to an enemy they had just alerted with their own fire. Where to put the gunner's assistants required some judgement since adequate feeding of the gun was vital, but team members were not to betray the position, nor distract the gunner from his main task. In ideal circumstances the number two man was within a metre or so, but well concealed, as for example in a depression, or on the reverse of the slope. As a yardstick for winter fighting banks of snow less than 2m wide were to be regarded as insecure against fire.

Baumschütße – sharpshooting from a tree position. A good surprise manner to open a firefight, as described in *Der Feuerkampf der Schützenkompanie*, 1940.

Assaults might be the work of entire companies or platoons, as well as very local affairs, and could be planned in a number of ways. The 1940 edition of Reibert outlines outright frontal attacks, *Frontalerangriff*, flank attacks, or *Flankenangriff*, and rear attacks. Also possible were 'wing attacks', or *Flügelangriff*, in which assault was angled onto a corner of the enemy position, so to strike diagonally across. Finally, attacks might be executed as enveloping attacks or *Umfassenderangriff*, that sought to pin the front as part of the unit moved around the enemy flank. Interestingly, these definitions, based on essentially linear assumptions about enemy battle formations, were dropped by the time of the appearance of the 1942 edition. Though usually part of a bigger plan, the actual initiative to close with the enemy often came from the squad leader, each leader taking advantage of 'every opportunity' even in the absence of orders. 'In penetration [*Einbruch*, literally 'break in'], the whole group rushes or fires as a unit. If possible the platoon leader employs several squads advancing from various directions against the objective. In this way the defensive fire will be scattered.' Such a close assault might be prefaced by throwing hand grenades, but the squad leader was to ensure co-ordination between the throwers, machine gun, and riflemen.

The 1939 edition of the *Ausbildungsvorschrift* contained interesting detail of the *Nahkampf*, or 'close combat' – stated to depend on the not inconsiderable determination required to take on the enemy 'man to man' and 'destroy him'. In the final advance the troops were to go on, bayonets fixed, but with rifles loaded and safety catches on, perhaps through woods, or hedged in country, so as to give themselves the best possible preparation and chance of surprise. When moving at speed over the last few metres riflemen were instructed to indulge in assault fire, canting the rifle over onto its left side at the hip, letting fly at no more than 5–10m range, and thus being ready on arrival to use the weapon with both bayonet and butt. Light machine gunners also took part in the final charge, their ideal assault posture being at the forefront of the squad with the weapon held couched under the right arm close to the body and the muzzle controlled by holding the bipod with the left hand. In this way the gunner was ready either to fire on the move, whilst preventing the muzzle rising, or immediately to throw himself down and set up the weapon on its bipod to fire. This might be needed if the squad came under heavy fire as it came in, or on the position once taken. 'Assault fire' from the hip by German troops was indeed observed by the French during the Second World War as early as November 1939. This was thought to be a new technique at that time, the object being supposed to be to, 'frighten the enemy by making him think that he has to deal with overwhelming numbers, and thus cause him to surrender'.

Though grenades were best thrown from cover, or at the start of close action, they could also be used on the move. In such cases the advancing rifleman held his gun in the left hand, a grenade in his right. At an opportune moment he could then use the fingers of the hand holding the rifle to pull the fuse cord and throw with the right. Where the squad leader saw a need for showers of grenades he would simply shout '*Handgranaten*!'. 'With hand grenades, submachine gun, rifles, pistols and spades, and shouting "hurrah", the men charge the last enemy position. The whole squad takes part in the hand to hand fighting.' As Reibert put it, the attack 'should destroy the enemy, bringing the decision'. Having arrived on the enemy position the squad was to reorganise to continue the advance, but not to bunch together, ideally with the men on a frontage of about 30–40m with the LMG near to the centre and the leader so positioned as to be able to maintain control. To resume a breakthrough a common method was for the platoon commander to designate one squad to support fire, and for it to concentrate its efforts 'upon the place of penetration' or on any enemy in flanking or rear positions. Even if it succeeded on only a narrow front the attack was not to halt at the first enemy position but to be pushed deep, especially where it proved possible to pursue at points of weakening resistance.

Interestingly, some of the key elements of German raiding tactics, and willingness to mix together different sub-units and weapons, were observed by the French on the Saar front before the main 1940 campaign. This information was put into English by direction of the British War Office in May 1940 as part of *Periodical Notes on the German Army*. Usually German preliminary planning was carried out by 2 officers and 3 or 4 NCOs, and the post to be attacked reconnoitred the day before the assault by a patrol of 8 to 10 men. The attack proper was carried out by a *Stosstrupp*, rendered in the English translation as a 'raiding party', but more literally a 'shock troop'. This select group was not a 'circus of specialists', but in most cases was 'organized with a view to the particular operation planned', the bulk of the personnel being drawn from an infantry battalion or regiment under a lieutenant:

> Numbers may vary between 25 men and 60; engineers are often included, and it is they who lay the Bangalore torpedoes, the use of which has many times been reported. Once selected, the party is specially trained for the raid and rehearsals are often staged. Specially trained dogs are frequently made use of. . . . As regards weapons, officers carry their revolvers [probably 'pistols'], NCOs sub machine-guns, and the rest of the party rifles and hand grenades (four per man). According to a prisoner's statement, raiding parties are also armed with light, and even heavy, machine guns. Large scale raids are preceded and supported usually by the fire of infantry weapons; frequently by artillery fire also. The preparation may continue for several hours, but more commonly it lasts not longer than about 20 minutes. An artillery box barrage, reinforced and continued by MG fire is common . . . In the raid proper, the officer, accompanied by one or two NCOs, leads the advance on the objective, in order to reconnoitre the ground and co-ordinate the action of the rest of the party, each portion of which has a special task to perform. Then, after telephone lines have been cut, gaps made in the wire, and the covering parties posted, and when the objective has been surrounded or outflanked, a surprise assault is delivered.

Night offered special opportunities, for both raids and full-scale assaults, as attackers stood a better chance of getting much closer to the enemy before being detected. Indeed, German theory stressed the value of deployment and development under cover of darkness, even if an actual assault was to be delivered in half light or daylight. As the US digest *German Tactical Doctrine*, 1942, observed,

> Although night marches initially tax the strength of troops, this disadvantage is minimised after troops become adjusted to resting in day bivouacs and eating

> regularly on a changed schedule. Night marches have decided advantages: they deny altogether or restrict materially hostile ground and air reconnaissance, and by keeping the enemy ignorant, they contribute to surprise; also, night marches bring troops into position for battle with fewer losses and consequently higher morale.

The speed of such movement varied according to moonlight and other factors, but on poor roads on dark nights could drop to well under 3km per hour. To minimise the inconvenience of darkness bodies of troops made liberal use of 'connecting files' to maintain contact with units ahead and behind, and 'security units' to flanks were drawn in closer. Distances between moving units might profitably be increased so as to provide more 'buffer' in the event of minor delays that could otherwise cause a concertina effect and dangerous bunching.

Specific small-unit night-combat tactics were reviewed in light of experience in Russia where the Soviet Army showed considerable skill in such matters – focusing on small operations on narrow fronts, dawn surprises, digging under darkness, and the use of flares for the sudden illumination of short-range targets. Accordingly, German instructions of 1943 were that if possible troops should approach in twos, against the wind, taking note that 'men who have not bathed for a long time can be smelled down-wind at some distance' and that sound carried better at night. In the event of encountering a single enemy the drill was to take cover, let him pass, then 'spring at him from behind'. In negotiating wire obstacles cuts were to be made against dark back-ground, or amongst craters, hollows, or bushes where crawling or movement was less obvious. Diversions, such as sacks hung up or small-arms fire, at other points might provide sufficient distraction for troops to move undetected. Bird calls or other simple signals could also be used to maintain contact if sufficiently unobtrusive. When working as an 'assault troop' by night the best order of march was almost a reversal of daylight tactics with riflemen being followed by the leader, then long-distance grenade throwers, short-distance grenade throwers, and men carrying grenades. The light-machine-gun team brought up the rear. Flank protection with machine guns and additional riflemen was also advisable.

The German theory of defensive combat was based upon old principles: making attack difficult for the enemy; forcing the enemy to attack against unfavourable odds; or economising on troops by using weaker but well-positioned forces at some points in order to free up manpower for other tasks. By skilful dispositions, as for example organ-isation in depth and security of flanks, and making use of factors such as camouflage, natural or artificial obstacles, and automatic weapons, a smaller force could halt a larger one temporarily, or even indefinitely. Machine guns and good observation were assumed to be critical factors 'in determining the framework of the position, because heavy weapons constitute the backbone of every defensive position'. To this ends guns were to be located so that together they would sweep the entire front of the position with effective frontal and flanking fire.

In defence the duties of the squad leader began with his being assigned a sector by his platoon commander. Following personal reconnaissance he would allot places to the riflemen, then supervise organisation and camouflage. Commonly, the frontage of the squad defence was 30–40yd, and that of the platoon less than 300yd, with gaps covered by fire – much more and it was difficult to control the squads in combat. How much digging in was possible was governed by time available, but ideally best-prepared positions included not only foxholes but linking trenches and obstacles to impede the enemy. The placing of the light machine gun was crucial, being best disposed when it not only had a good field of fire but was also supported by adjacent units with flanking fire. Several positions were chosen immediately, fifty or more yards apart, so placed that the gun could be moved without being overseen by the enemy. These enabled the machine-gun crew to evade fire and recommence shooting in different directions. With time these ad hoc positions could be further organised or improved.

Riflemen were often also given more than one battle position, being placed either as a reserve, or forward in the front line. In the forward positions the squad was able to sweep the whole terrain to the front with fire, though commonly at close or very close range.

> As a rule, two riflemen are grouped together, usually in a small trench or ditch sufficiently close so that they can easily understand each other even in combat. In order to decrease the effectiveness of enemy fire, these separate nests should not be on the same level but should be echeloned. If sufficient time is available after the squad groups have been established, the squad leader may order the squad members to dig foxholes or trenches somewhat to the rear of their positions. The foxholes should be concealed from ground observation and, if possible, from air observation. The men may remain under such cover until the squad is employed in the fire fight.

Der Feuerkampf der Schützenkompanie was prepared to accept that squads might be employed on fairly narrow fronts if two-man pits or shell holes were available, positions being arranged to avoid deployment in a straight line, and with the squad leader toward the centre.

The squad leader selected his own battle position so as to best direct the fire of his unit, especially the light machine gun, also determining the range to conspicuous points and other factors likely to affect fire. Methods of employing fire were then discussed with the men. Whilst the digging of trenches or other preparations were underway, a member of each squad was detailed as lookout, so that the team was not taken by surprise from ground or air. In occupying an area the group would avoid very obvious or isolated points of reference such as lone trees, the edge of a wood, or a local high point, as these would easily attract fire. Where time was available particularly conspicuous trees or bushes could be removed, so denying aiming points for heavy weapons and artillery. For night defence it was advisable that fixed lines be set up before darkness, with pegs set so that the soldier could automatically position his rifle pointing in the most likely direction of the enemy. In the event of an alarm or incursion he was then able to fire in approximately the right direction to break up attacks or intimidate individual enemies with unexpectedly accurate fire.

In preparing trenches and rifle pits, *Schützenloch*, disposal and concealment of freshly dug earth was vital, and in all field defences sharp corners, straight lines and obvious shadows were expressly avoided. In many instances it was possible for the squad leader to draw off some distance and check for himself the effectiveness of camouflage methods. Where meadows or other areas of uniform vegetation were dug into troops were cautioned to avoid laying out the sods that were being retained for covering works later in a regular manner. Instead, they were to be hidden along hedges, between fields, or under bushes where they would not attract attention particularly

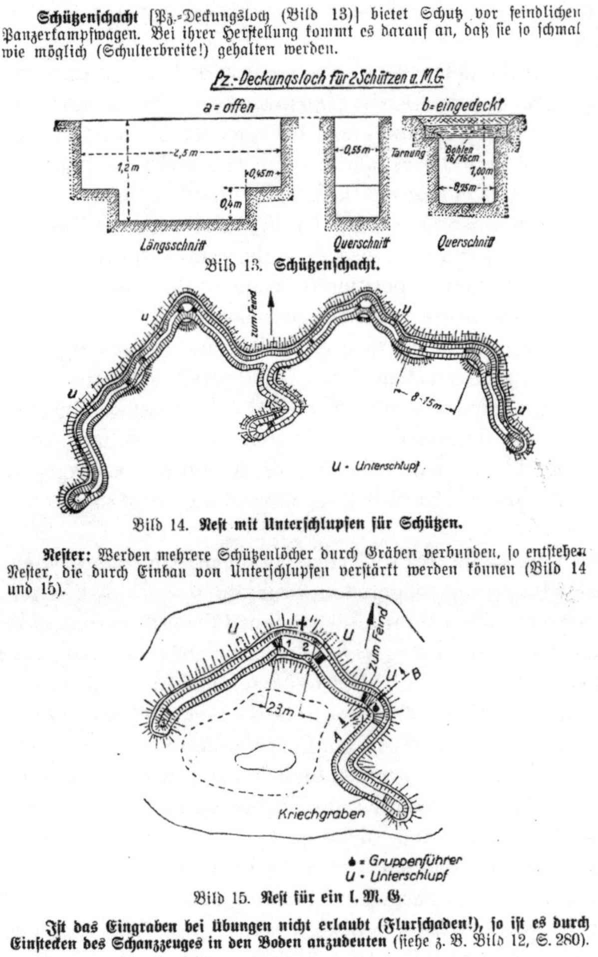

Schützenschacht [Pz.-Deckungsloch (Bild 13)] bietet Schutz vor feindlichen Panzerkampfwagen. Bei ihrer Herstellung kommt es darauf an, daß sie so schmal wie möglich (Schulterbreite!) gehalten werden.

Bild 13. **Schützenschacht.**

Bild 14. **Nest mit Unterschlupfen für Schützen.**

Nester: Werden mehrere Schützenlöcher durch Gräben verbunden, so entstehen Nester, die durch Einbau von Unterschlupfen verstärkt werden können (Bild 14 und 15).

Bild 15. **Nest für ein l. M. G.**

Ist das Eingraben bei Übungen nicht erlaubt (Flurschaden!), so ist es durch Einstecken des Schanzzeuges in den Boden anzudeuten (siehe z. B. Bild 12, S. 280).

Battlefield squad defensive positions according to the 1940 edition of Reibert's *Der Dienst Unterricht Im Heere*. The pit, illustrated at the top, is for a two-man MG team to take cover against armour. The trench, middle, is designed essentially for riflemen and includes small shelter dugouts under its forward lip. The bottom illustration is a light machine-gun 'nest' incorporating crawl trenches to allow the team and leader to move around under cover.

from the air. Even before work started it was wise to lay in a handy stock of camouflage material for throwing across the excavations quickly if the enemy was spotted at a distance. Similarly, premature firing or unnecessary movement were both to be avoided as surprise and much concealment value would thereby be lost. Longer range targets were best reserved to the artillery and heavy machine guns. The squad light machine guns would come into play at effective range, aimed primarily against targets that could not be engaged by the heavy weapons. In the event of close attack every member of the squad was to fire without regard for concealment. Very likely the enemy would throw grenades: the defenders avoided these by springing into cover, or, *in extremis*, throwing the missile back.

Further detail on the defensive position was added by Zimmermann in *Die Neue Gruppe*. This suggested options such as burrowing protective holes into the near side of banks into which defenders could crawl for considerable security; taking advantage of sunken roads and boundaries; and a small and easily constructed machine-gun bunker with overhead cover that was designed primarily against observation or premature discovery. Zimmermann observed that in occupying the *Schützenloch* there were two basic positions, alert and with the rifle at the ready just over the lip of the pit, and the *Volle Deckung* or full cover position in which the troops disappeared like rabbits into their holes, helmets firmly on their heads to avoid the worst of bombardment. The helmet could be removed during 'pauses in fire', and the soft cap worn in its place. The rifle pits could vary from about 1.5–1.7m in depth depending on local conditions and outlook. In Zimmermann's fully developed squad position the fox holes could be linked by a basic but well-concealed trench to the rear, creating what was effectively a very unobtrusive field fortified chain. A short length of dog-legged communication trench leading back towards friendly lines allowed the squad to get out of the position unseen.

Similar descriptions appeared in Weber's popular 1938 *Unterrichtsbuch*. In Weber's version the field MG pit was roughly four times the size of a foxhole for an individual, and whilst working to enlarge it the team concealed themselves under a camouflage net. Holes cut under the forward lip provided a place for the crew to squeeze themselves or munitions, and an *MG - Unterschlupf* or 'machine-gun refuge'. This lined cavity protected the gun during bombardment or heavy rain. Both the MG position and the rifle pits could have the benefit of a sump at the bottom to drain away the worst of the rain, perhaps with suitably trimmed branches and twigs on top to keep men out of any gathering ground water. Where individual foxholes were dug the occupant could keep his shelter half pegged and folded back to the rear of the top of the pit. This allowed him to pull it over for complete concealment or basic rain protection.

In Reibert's 1940 summary are shown not only details of a similar *Schützenloch* but methods for the development of a shallow scrape providing basic cover to a prone soldier into kneeling and standing cover. In these examples the hole has a rudimentary parados and parapet behind and in front of the hole. The front has a rise of about 30cm of earth, though 60cm are heaped up behind. In such an arrangement the occupants of the hole could not be skylined as their heads were in front of the rear spoil heap. Camouflage could be rigged in such a way as to connect parapet and parados, so concealing the position entirely. Reibert also illustrates a petrifying looking

Panzerdeckungsloch, or 'tank cover hole', into which a two-man machine-gun team could be crammed in the event of close-armour assault. This tiny pit, 'as narrow as possible', was normally just 55cm or 'shoulder wide' and 1.2m deep. The addition of a thick planked cover and camouflage reduced the height to just a metre, but at least in theory made the gun team entirely undetectable to armour which could run over the position without discovering them. Another point shown by Reibert is fire positions taking advantage of 'natural masking' as in the case of using sunken lanes and tracks as improvised fire positions. In such scenarios existing trees and vegetation or banks might be left along the side of the feature whilst the troops improved the ground behind, ideally excavating a trench-type profile with elbow rest and trench or pit at least a metre deep. Reibert's advice would remain virtually unchanged in the 1942 edition.

Against tank attack the basic drill was to go to ground, in field works or any nearby depression. Running away was strictly prohibited as inviting 'certain death'. Tanks were to be engaged specifically by anti-tank weapons and artillery, though small-arms fire could be directed into slits or other openings where hot lead spray or bullet fragments might endanger crews. Nevertheless, the primary target of rifles and machine guns was the infantry who usually accompanied an armoured attack, 'being immediately subjected to concentrated fire'. If the enemy employed smoke this would be fired into as it might neutralise or slow up the opposition even if they were not hit. In the event of adjacent positions being penetrated the squad was instructed to hold its position, allowing rear units to counter attack the incursion. Squads to the rear of the main line of resistance were to dig in and could contribute to the firefight by firing through gaps or flanks, or employing surprise fire against closer targets. Rear squads were ready to make counter attacks, convenient routes for such blows being identified by their squad leaders. If not otherwise needed, light machine guns of rear squads could be held in reserve as 'silent guns' waiting for close-range targets, or groups of the enemy who broke through the main line. Such ruses were 'highly destructive' especially if organised for flanking fire.

Squads could also be deployed as 'combat outposts'. These were generally positioned close enough to the main line of resistance that they could be seen by artillery observers and supported by artillery fire. Such squads might defend themselves, or, if needs be, fall back under pressure. In either instance the team was to be ordered in advance as to the appropriate action under given circumstances, and in case of retirement informed of safe routes back to the main position. The usual method for setting up combat outposts was for the squad leader to reconnoitre the ground first, protected by two men who provided security to his front whilst he studied the ground. The leader then selected the best positions for the light machine gun, bearing in mind factors such as field of fire, camouflage, and routes in and out. Multiple positions allowed for relocation, and, by fire from different spots, simulation of a much larger defending force. Having decided on machine-gun locations the leader then picked out some rifle posts where the men could be set in twos and threes so as to be mutually supporting each other and any adjacent units. With the outline of the defence decided the remainder of the squad was brought up by the second in command. The entire area occupied would not usually extend over more than 200yd in any direction, and took into consideration ease of evacuation unseen by the enemy.

The tactical purposes of outposts were to: make the enemy's approach difficult; disguise the location and nature of the main line of resistance; act to stall an enemy advance whilst forces to the rear were prepared for combat; and provide close-in reconnaissance of, and maintain contact with, the opposition. Squads deployed in this manner could act as outposts for platoon or company sectors, and were likely to be reinforced by machine guns and anti-tank weapons.

> The outposts are grouped in individual nests, which are echeloned in depth so that the rear nests can later give fire protection for some time in case the forward elements must withdraw. The battle outposts must energetically prevent the enemy scout patrols from getting through their line. By means of patrols, and at times by small advances, they themselves reconnoitre the enemy.

Combat outposts could also confuse the enemy by means of different ruses, for example, by setting up dummy positions, or by creating genuine duplicate positions, and relocating to them unseen, perhaps by night. During offensive action combat posts might similarly be established by an aggressor as security for his own main position.

The demands of the combat outpost placed particular stress on troops, not least the squad leaders:

> The squad is more difficult to control because of its broader and deeper formations. The squad leader must frequently make independent decisions during the course of the battle as to when and how he will break off the fight, and when and how he will lead his squad back to the main line of resistance. The difficulty in this situation results from the nature of his mission, which is to hold off the enemy as long as possible and yet be able to disengage his squad and return to the main defensive position before he is cut off.

Such withdrawals, like advances, might be executed as 'fire and movement' by alternate elements of the squad, or perhaps taking advantage of fire of heavy weapons from behind the main line of resistance. The precise moment to retire was necessarily a judgement call, but as a rule of thumb open terrain spelt a need to go back before the enemy reached within about 600yd – this being regarded as the practical range of light-infantry weapons, otherwise, 'in view of the effectiveness of modern weapons' the squad would suffer 'heavy losses'. Rolling ground, woods, or the availability of other cover or smoke might allow the outpost to remain in place somewhat longer.

'Outguards' could fulfil some similar duties to 'combat outposts' but were intended primarily as security against the surprise of larger bodies of troops at rest, or as cover for defensive features. Outguards might be posted to overlook roads, bridges, or anti-tank defences, or protect observation posts on hills. Such outguards would usually be posted less than a mile from their main body, and strength depended on perceived need. Nevertheless, outguards were expected to provide for their own safety by means of sentries, reconnaissance patrols, and positioned machine guns. Sentries might possibly be posted as much as a few hundred yards from the main position, and were best used as a chain able to see each others posts. Such chains of sentry posts were to be visited by patrols, more frequently when visibility was poor, or terrain made observation difficult. Like the men of combat outposts, outguards were given sufficient briefing to perform their tasks well, as for example specific things to look out for, and what signals to give in different eventualities. Perhaps most importantly troops were given an outline plan for use in the event of being attacked, when to open fire, and what routes to fall back on if overrun. A supplement to 'outguards' proper was the positioning of observation and listening posts, usually located out in front of the sentinels of larger units. Particularly useful points might include exits from villages and bridges.

Zimmerman's *Die Neue Gruppe* also offered some interesting minor tactical ruses that could be used by combat outposts and outguards as well as in 'delaying actions'. In one of the most useful of these squads were hidden away behind, or a short distance to the side of, the most obvious cover, such as a farmhouse or copse. Only the leader or assistant leader positioned himself forwards – well camouflaged, perhaps with binoculars, within a garden or similar. In such an observation post he was unlikely to be detected, or indeed hit by speculative fire aimed at the house. On sighting enemy troops advancing on the tactical point in question the leader could signal the squad up into alternative forward positions in cover, overlooking the approach. Properly timed this allowed his men to catch the enemy at their most vulnerable, advancing through open terrain, whilst at the same time preventing enemy observers from spotting them. Retaliation from artillery or otherwise could be avoided by moving the squad smartly back again.

Effectively, the opposite duty of a squad was its role when called upon to act as part of an 'advanced guard', or as 'point', to formations on the move. Nevertheless, neither was regarded as substitute for genuine reconnaissance, nor could they do the jobs more properly assigned to aircraft, armoured cars, or cycle patrols. Commonly, it was recommended that advanced guards were strong, being anything from a sixth to a third of the entire force, and that the infantry 'point' should be about 500yd ahead with cyclists or cavalry still further forward. Swift communication between the elements could be maintained by cars, motorcyclists, or 'connecting files' of men. The density of deployment of the various parts depended on a number of factors, but was reduced to half normal where air attack was considered likely. At night, or in low visibility, the parts of the force could close up for better connectivity.

The 'infantry point' – usually consisting of between one and four squads – was there to protect the front of the advanced guard, and drive off weaker forces by 'swift attacks'. Some of its number were to observe to the front, others to the sides and rear. Its own early warning was provided by a couple of scouts equipped with binoculars and a signal pistol, the latter being mainly used to raise the alarm if enemy armour was encountered. If they came across defiles the scouts were to advance cautiously around both sides in order to outflank any ambush force. The leader of the point was to take advantage of any hill or rise for observation that could be made without undue delays. The point was not to go to ground in the event of enemy aircraft appearing, but take advantage of size and scattered deployment to continue on its way by using trees, roadside ditches, or any other means of continuing its mission unobtrusively. When halted the point was to move off the road into cover, posting an observer and quickly setting up a light machine gun to give maximum security. When the enemy was thought to be close, or danger of contact high, the point changed formation accordingly, going into skirmish line, and searching any buildings thought to present a particular hazard.

In the event of contact with the enemy the point had a number of default actions. Where the enemy was small this was immediate attack, bringing the light machine gun into a suitable position and commencing fire, whilst the point leader led his men forward taking advantage of cover, then perhaps working a way around a flank. Scouts and reconnaissance parties were to be engaged immediately, not being allowed 'even a glance' at a main body. Where the point bumped into an obviously superior enemy it took cover straight away and fought defensively, though the leader was encouraged to determine the extent of the enemy and his machine-gun positions. If possible a reconnaissance patrol was organised. In the event of being attacked the leader was to order his entire body to open fire 'in order to bring the attack to a standstill'.

As well as armoured cars and other swift-moving elements infantry could also form reconnaissance patrols, moving independently of larger formations. How strong a patrol should be, and the nature of its arming, was dependent upon 'situation and mission'.

> The reconnoitring patrol must move cautiously and quietly. It should halt frequently in order to observe and listen. Cunning and cleverness, a quick eye and resolution, a love of adventure and boldness are the prerequisites for the successful execution of every recognisance mission. The reconnoitring patrol should get as close to the enemy as possible without being seen in order that the patrol may obtain information on his position. The men of the patrol must become acquainted with the terrain so that on their return they may give information about it and, if necessary, serve later as guides.

Often reconnaissance patrols were mounted to cover areas not occupied or observed from static posts, and most useful at night or in areas of broken terrain. Patrols sent by 'outguards' could be as few as a pair of men.

Though the basis of German infantry tactics was laid even before 1939, and the fundamentals of squad and platoon action were in place early in the war, there were significant changes over time. These changes appear to have been made mainly in reaction to alterations in technology, and to the situations in which armies found themselves. Fundamental to much of what transpired were losses, and loss of initiative in the face of enemy attack, placing a premium on methods that enabled German forces to do more with less. Key to this was a proliferation of automatic weapons. On the Eastern Front in particular it was quickly apparent that more machine weapons were vital, both to combat superior numbers and, initially at least, relatively unsophisticated tactics involving 'human waves'. In retrospect this is unsurprising since in the First World War, after the halting of German advances in 1914 and 1915, similar emphasis had been put on the mass production and development of machine guns for the defence in response to strategic and tactical pressures.

As just one part of the drive for 'total war' and the more effective mobilisation of industry, great efforts were put into the revamping the infantry arsenal. The intro-

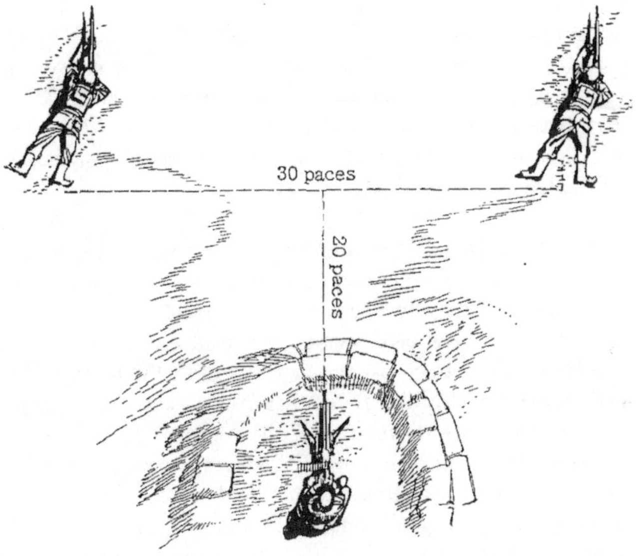

A deployment to allow machine guns to fire through a line of prone infantry, from the US summary *The German Squad in Combat*, 1944.

duction of the simplified MP 40 in 1940 addressed the issues of relatively slow and expensive production that had been experienced with the MP 38. In 1941 a new and simpler general-purpose machine gun developed by the *Heereswaffenampt* and Dr Gruner at the Grossfuss works was battlefield trialled. This not only decreased the resources required for production but actually increased the cyclic rate of fire to a then remarkable 1,200 rounds per minute. The significance of this was not that any one gun could actually fire that many shots in a minute, given the need to change belts and supply ammunition, but that this very rapid delivery was more likely to catch moving targets with effective fire, even if they were only briefly exposed. Formally accepted early in 1942, the new gun was now known as the *Maschinengewehr 42*, or MG 42. That Allied infantry found the new weapon unnerving is something of an understatement, describing its distinctive sound as being akin to loud ripping cloth or a 'buzz saw'. US infantrymen of any experience could tell the MG 42 from their own .30 calibre Brownings in a second, the latter giving a much more leisurely 'tat, tat, tat', or a 'chatter'. As a begrudging Captain Shore put it, German machine guns were 'morally' devastating. With the 5th Seaforths Alistair Borthwick actually believed that British infantry would rather have been shelled than shot at by an MG 42 – it was 'much too personal'. Wherever they were actually made, many troops continued the First World War habit of calling them 'Spandaus'.

Like the MG 34, the MG 42 was an excellent 'general-purpose' machine gun: it could be deployed in a 'heavy' machine-gun role using a tripod and optical sights, but also was light enough as a squad weapon firing from an integral bipod. In the bipod role the MG 42 was certainly accurate enough, but the lack of a steady cradle made longer range fire less productive, and the difficulty of providing enough ammunition in a mobile role demanded more effective husbandry of rounds. It was also true that unless firmly clamped the rapid spray of bullets and attendant recoil was likely to make the MG 42 wander off target more quickly than the slower firing MG 34 and the older Maxim designs. Fire control and tactics for the MG 42 were examined in the December 1943 edition of the US *Army Intelligence Bulletin*:

> They take the high commanding ground and try for long grazing fire. In defense they can pick their own ground of course. In siting machine guns they often use the military crest of the hill as well as its base . . . [rate of fire] is 25 rounds per second. Most of the disadvantages as well as the advantages of the gun can be attributed to this single characteristic. As a result of the high rate of fire the gun has a marked tendency to 'throw off', so that the fire stays on target for a much briefer time than does the slower fire of the MG 34 . . . The Germans are instructed to fire bursts from 5 to 7 rounds when they employ the MG 42 as a light machine gun, since the operator cannot hold his gun on target for a longer period. The gun must be re-aimed after each burst. Under battle conditions the MG 42 can fire about 22 bursts per minute – that is, about 154 rounds. Although the Germans believe that when the weapon is properly employed the compactness and density of its fire pattern justify the high ammunition expenditure, recent German Army orders have increasingly stressed the need of withholding machine gun fire until the best possible effect is assured.

The effectiveness of the MG 42, combined with decreasing general manpower, had the result that, particularly in defensive actions, it was interlocking zones of automatic fire that became ever more important to German tactics. As Lieutenant Sydney Jary of 4th Somerset Light Infantry discovered in Normandy: as soon as the forward platoon crossed a stream, 'concentrated Spandau fire came from both flanks. There must have been about 12 machine guns firing at one time. This devastating firepower stopped the battalion dead in its tracks. There was no way forward or around it and no way to retire'. With the Canadians at Bienen in March 1945 Lieutenant Pearce got even more closely acquainted,

> My platoon assaulted in a single extended wave. Ten tumbled down nailed on the instant by fire from two, or maybe three, machine guns . . . The rest of us rolled or dropped into a shallow ditch, hardly more than a trough six inches deep at the bottom of a dyke. The Bren gunners put their weapons to their shoulders but never got a shot away. (I saw them after the battle, both dead, one still holding the aiming position) . . . A rifleman on my left took aim at a German weapon pit, and with a spasm collapsed on my arm. His face turned instantly a faint green, and bore a simple smile.

Increasing mechanisation did not ignore rifles either. For though it was realised that to replace the millions of bolt-action Mausers and similar foreign-manufactured and

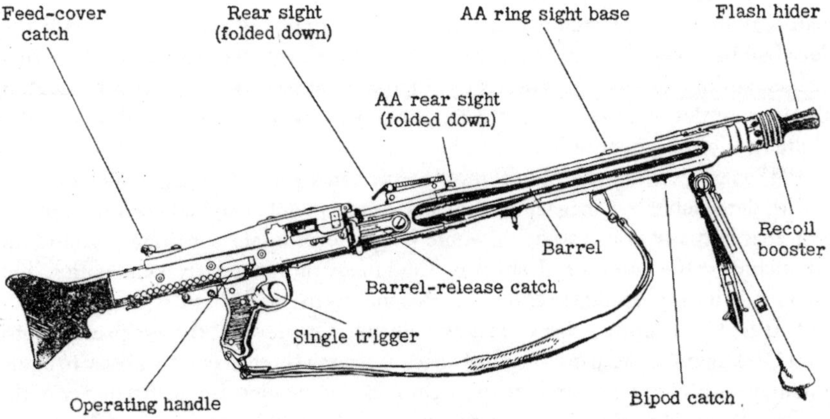

The MG 42 in its light bipod-mounted squad role; as seen in the US *Company Officer's Handbook of the German Army*, March 1944.

captured weapons in service, and to retrain forces, was a Herculean task that might never be achieved, significant efforts were put into both semi-automatic and fully automatic rifles. As early as 1937, following the appearance of the US Garand, the army had considered the possibilities of a self-loading arm, and by 1940 Walther had begun an experimental programme to produce a new rifle. The following year the firm began manufacturing the G 41, a semi-automatic in the ordinary rifle 7.92 calibre with a ten-round box magazine. Though not well balanced, and only produced in small numbers, this laid the way for the G 43, first used in the East in 1943. This solved many of the problems seen in the earlier semi-automatic, and featured a fixing point for a telescopic sight. So it was that this useful weapon was widely deployed as a specialist arm, and often with snipers. Captain Shore declared the G 41 a 'fair weapon of sound basic design' though not as handy as a US Garand, and the G 43, though an improved design, not as well finished.

The real breakthrough, however, came from the idea that the ideal infantry weapon was neither rifle, nor sub-machine gun, but something combining the best characteristics of both: a sort of arm that could be fired on the move, had a decent range, but was also capable of full automatic operation. Various weapons had attempted this trick, but none were entirely satisfactory. Anything that fired the 9mm round was still a relatively short-range sub-machine gun or pistol; whilst fully automatic weapons using full-size rifle cartridges were effectively abbreviated machine guns, with the attendant handling problems thereof. In this respect the parachutists' FG 42 was a case in point – it bestowed heavy firepower, had a twenty-round magazine, but was hard to control. What eventually made a new hybrid piece possible was not really mechanical innovation, but a new cartridge. Experiments with 'short'-rifle-calibre cartridges of less power than the full-blown military round had taken place as early as the 1920s, but financial concerns, combined with worry that less power meant less effective, had ensured that none was adopted in the short term. Vollmer machine carbines using one form of 'intermediate' cartridge were tested in the period 1935 to 1938, but rejected. Nevertheless, the idea had been kept alive by the army weapons office which commissioned the firm of Haenel, and its famous chief designer Hugo Schmeisser, to continue investigating similar lines of development. A new *Kurz*, or short cartridge, was now developed by the Polte firm of Magdeburg.

By 1941 a new gun, capable of full automatic fire, made mainly of sheet-metal stampings, with detachable box magazine, and back-swept pistol grip, had been designed: a weapon that in many of its essentials would later inform infantry weapons around the world, including the famous Kalashnikov – and many more modern assault rifles. The original made its appearance in three-dimensional form in 1942 under the titles MKb 42, or 'MPS' 42, denoting a 'heavy machine pistol'. The new hybrid was presented by Colonel Drekmann of the army weapons office as having three major purposes: to equip the infantry with a lighter weapon with a lighter cartridge; increase the firepower of the squad; and to simplify the arming of the infantry. It would be used as a self-loading rifle, one aimed shot at a time, for precise targets, but like the machine pistol when required. Ideally, it would replace all rifles in service, all machine pistols, and all pistols. The new weapon was not universally welcomed. Early demands had included something with a bayonet, the primary object of single-shot accurate fire, and the ability to fit a telescopic sight. There were now also doubts as to whether something automatic ought also to be able to use belt feed, and that whether using more rounds, albeit lighter ones, did actually promise to reduce the soldier's burden. Eventually, however, such internal misgivings were overcome by the office of the General of Infantry, convinced that the new concept represented the beginnings of a fundamental change to infantry armament. Only one significant obstacle still stood in the way of the new weapon: Hitler himself. The new weapon was rejected, at least temporarily, on grounds that its effective range of 500m was too short, and mass manufacture of gun and new ammunition would place too big a burden on industry. In December 1942 an elaborate live-firing demonstration was put on at Rastenburg in which a nine-man squad of the *Führerbegleitbataillon* assaulted a dummy enemy battle position with the new gun and grenades. The dictator failed to turn up to see the very impressive results of this exercise, and so it was that army trials and development were carried on, without official approval, and in low-key fashion.

Only in 1943, after further work, and by the subterfuge of a new name, *Maschinen Pistole 43*, or 'MP 43', did the latest version manage to creep onto production schedules. Even then Hitler only agreed on the basis that the MP 43 replace the MP 40. Nevertheless, that autumn it was decided to arm squads of trial regiments, excepting machine-gun numbers, snipers, and rifle grenade men, with the MP 43. How it was to be used tactically was explained in a secret 'information sheet' to accompany the trials,

> The MP 43/1 is a weapon which first of all shall be employed for individual fire (like the self loader), and secondarily as a machine weapon. With the development of this weapon the long expressed demand of the troops for a fully automatic weapon for the individual fighter shall be answered. The value of the weapon is in its high rate of fire and accuracy of individual fire, as well as in the possibility

> of increasing the rate by firing bursts. The rate of fire of the MP 43/1 is 22–28 rounds per minute single fire (rifle 8–10), while in burst fire 40–50 rounds per minute can be fired . . . Performance of the ammunition of the MP 43/1 (short cartridge) is sufficient to engage living targets with success up to 1,000m. The steel helmet will be pierced up to a distance of 600m . . . Considering the high rate of fire of the MP 43/1 a strict fire discipline for each MP gunner is mandatory. Fire discipline means especially the proper use of individual fire and burst fire. With the MP 43/1, on principle individual fire is to apply to individual targets. However, if a decision is necessary for example in the case of break-through or in defending against enemy attack at close range, the highest rate of fire in the form of burst fire is necessary. Bursts are to be restricted to 3–4 rounds. Continuous fire is not allowed under any circumstances.

In action it was recommended that the complete squad engage 'within the decisive fighting distance of 500 m', the advance to combat still be conducted in squad column.

The trials gave the new weapon glowing reports, *Grenadier* Regiment 43 noted for example that the MP 43 was superior even to machine guns in close combat because of its great agility. It could be brought to bear on sudden attacks, and even when the enemy entered the German trench it could quickly be turned upon him. On patrol it was resistant to dirt, more 'combat ready' than a machine gun, and much more powerful than the bolt-action rifle. In the assault it was better still due to its combination of accuracy and 'immense increase of firepower'. Interestingly, the MP 43 was also seen to add to tactical fluidity, since formerly when the squad machine gun was up and moving the firepower of the riflemen had been modest. Now any element of the squad or platoon could move with a confidence that there was plenty of firepower to cover it. Men who had confidence in their old weapons were quickly won over when they saw its work in practice. At the end of 1943 orders were issued for the re-equipment of the army on the Eastern Front, and part of the forces in Italy with the MP 43.

In February 1944 a new short provisional manual *Der MP Zug Der Granadier Kompanie*, 'MP Platoon Grenadier Company', appeared. This reiterated the main points of the troop trial instructions, noting that basic provision of ammunition for the new gun would be 720 rounds, 180 of which were held in 6 30-round magazines on the soldier. Within the MP platoons 9-man squads would be arranged as follows:

Squad Leader: MP 43; binoculars; wire cutters; and whistle.
***Schütze* 1**: Bolt-action rifle; grenade launcher; and grenades.
***Schütze* 2**: Rifle with telescopic sight; and entrenching tool.
***Schützen* 3–8**: MP 43; and entrenching tool.

As before, the leader was responsible for the mission and his men, and directing the use of the sniper and rifle grenadier. The rifle grenadier fought as an ordinary rifleman unless there were targets to be engaged not accessible to other arms. The second *Schütze* fought as a sniper hitting difficult 'individual targets'. The MP 43 gunners were the 'close-combat fighters' and one of them acted as the assistant squad leader. In combat the MP 43 platoon was instructed to hold its fire, relying as long as possible on support weapons. Generally, they were not to open fire until within 600m, and even then the emphasis would be on short firefights, engaging the 'entire squad', with good fire discipline. Ideally, the whole action was conducted from cover, with the squad leader in full control, but gunners could fight and fire as required by necessity or mission. MP-equipped platoons were especially suitable for combat patrols and reconnaissance missions, as a flexible reserve in defence or assault, or in the pursuit and riding on tanks and in vehicles.

Despite stepping up manufacture and a monthly average ammunition production of 48 million rounds in 1944, getting enough weapons to the troops was proving extremely difficult. Confusingly, the gun's name was now changed again, with few actual tweaks to the hardware, first to MP 44, then finally to *Sturmgewehr 44*, literally 'assault rifle 44'. However, by May 1944 more than thirty divisions and other units had received some MP 44, and questionnaires directed to them returned a resounding endorsement. Virtually all wanted a complete replacement of bolt-action rifles, semi-automatic rifles, and sub-machine guns with assault rifles: even the precision rifle enthusiasts of 5th *Jäger* Division conceded that they would be better off if 80 per cent of their weapons were automatic assault rifles. Not many formations were worried about bayonets, and some were happy that a proportion of machine guns could also be dispensed with if a general issue of assault rifles was made. Despite the fact that far from all infantry (now *VolksGrenadier*, 'people's grenadier') companies yet possessed 'MP Platoons', in September 1944 it was decided that the assault rifle would become the general-purpose infantry arm. It was projected that 70 per cent of all infantry divisions would achieve two 'assault platoons' with assault rifles – in the summer of 1945.

If individual tactics actually changed relatively little over time, how infantry co-operated with other arms – and groups were assembled to achieve objectives – continued to increase in significance. Central was the idea of the *Kampfgruppe*, or 'battle group', a team put together according to task – being a concrete expression of form following function in *Aufträge*, or 'mission-led' tactics. The basic concept was not new, however, having featured in the manuals of the *Reichswehr* in the 1920s. As the 1944 US *Company Officer's Handbook of the German Army* would explain,

> A high degree of flexibility is a characteristic of German organisation, and it is best exemplified in the fluid composition of combat teams, or 'battle groups' (*Kampfgruppen*). Consequently, German tables of organisation, though useful for a basic understanding of unit strength, are of little practical value for operational purposes. A German division, whether it is on the offensive or defensive is organised into one or more combat teams . . . In the German conception, an infantry combat team may vary in size from a reinforced rifle company to a reinforced regiment.

Such groupings often brought together troops from different arms of service and were normally known by the name of the commanding officer. Furthermore, the composition of the team might change over time. It was by no means unusual to create *Kampfgruppen* mixing together *Panzergrenadiere* with tanks, or infantry with artillery, engineers, or other combinations.

Combat teams were intended to create strong balanced formations, but sometimes, as when they were scraped together at times of emergency, might lack self sufficiency or cohesion. In Sicily, for example, the Hermann Göring Panzer Division created a number of different teams, Öhring; Hahm; Rebholz; Fährmann and others that mixed Panzer troops, tanks, assault guns, Flak guns, and even Italian infantry for specific purposes. Also included were so-called *Märschbataillons* of the infantry, these being units that were officially temporary, and formed to transfer replacements to the combat zone, but by force of circumstance were committed to the fighting complete. In the case of *Kampfgruppe* Paulus, formed at the end of July 1943 for protection against landings, the team was named after the commander of a Panzer reconnaissance company, but included two batteries of heavy guns, a company of armoured infantry, and a 'special company' allotted by divisional HQ. In Italy *Kampfgruppe Heilmann* brought together parachute troops, with a selection of anti-tank and other artillery and three self-propelled guns, into a much-reinforced battalion to fight a protracted delaying action in northern Apulia. With little apparent logic, the formation was topped off with thirty-two Italian parachutists, of whom a quarter were officers. Much more modest was *Kampfgruppe* Rau, an emergency measure for the defence of Termoli. This comprised just 383 all ranks of 8 different units, including artillery and one self-propelled gun. Despite its small size and ad hoc creation, 'Rau' fielded no less than ten tubes of ordnance and twenty-four machine guns.

In early 1945, towards the end of the war, US observers attempted to distil the ideas behind the *Kampfgruppen* into coherent theory. Essentially, it appeared that the enemy regarded the 'headquarters pool' of combat units as something that could be dipped into in order to create a tailored formation for the task. In doing so they normally started from one large unit, and added to it according to suitability and availability. Remarkably, *Kampfgruppen* were not limited to one service, such as the *Heer*, or army, but might include elements drawn from the air force, navy, and *SS*. Where assets from disparate origins were mixed the commander was chosen from the service that predominated or the interests of which were paramount. Once formed the task force was ideally tactically and administratively independent, and not reliant on other units to carry out the mission: 'the belief of former years that the German Army was inflexible and lacking in initiative has been completely destroyed in this war, in which aggressive and daring leadership has been responsible for many bold decisions'.

The detail of the German infantry attack of the late war period combined the old notions of the approach march, and the *Entwicklung*, in which units then deployed in detail. For infantry companies this meant deploying in depth, and usually into column of files, as they came within artillery fire. If they then had to negotiate terrain or encountered stiffer enemy fire, the companies broke down into sections, these being less vulnerable and easier to handle. Once deployed, rifle companies exploited all possible cover as they advanced, but did not extend into skirmish lines until required in the fire-fight. For the actual assault the key phases were penetration, exploitation, and breakthrough. First to go in were the 'assault detachments' (*Stosstrupp*) in a series of local attacks designed to overcome key points in the enemy defences so that wedges into the enemy's forward positions could be established and from which the attack could be driven forward into the depth of the position, or the flanks of the wedge rolled up.

Chapter Three

The British

'What is wanted in the infantry is a return to faith and confidence in their own weapons based on practice' – Lionel Wigram

After the First World War the British Army shrank rapidly. It then got back to what many professionals recognised as 'proper soldiering'. This consisted mainly of policing a world empire – in the process ensuring that recruits, however badly schooled, were clean, reasonably sober, shot straight, marched well, and responded to discipline. Infantry tactics were relatively low on the priority list, not least because little garrisons scattered from Bermuda to the Hindu Kush rarely had opportunity to practise them in groups of any significant size, and working with artillery and machine-gun barrages had no place in quelling colonial riot. As a weary General Sir Ivor Maxse put it, 'we are hardly doing any tactics at all'. As early as 1919, Christopher Stone referred to a 'reactionary boredom' – caused, at least in part, by demobilisation of 'all the best men'. Nevertheless, it would be wrong to assume that tactical theory was ignored entirely.

One of the key figures in the interwar development of British tactics – not least in his own estimation – was Captain Basil Liddell Hart. Born in Paris in 1895, he went up to Cambridge in 1913 where his academic performance was initially mediocre; though it was here he had his first military experience with the university Officer Training Corps. Prior to the First World War he had described his views as those of a 'socialist, a pacifist, an anti-conscriptionist' and 'an anti-disciplinist'. If this was ever true they would soon change to almost the diametric opposite. Joining the King's Own Yorkshire Light Infantry, he was at the front near Albert by the end of September 1915. On 1 July 1916 he was held in the 'immediate reserve' of officers when his battalion attacked on the Somme, a fact that may have saved his life since many of his comrades were killed or wounded that day. As it was it fell to Liddell Hart to help rally the remnants after the assault, and later he participated in the defence of Mametz Wood. Gassed and withdrawn from action, he was now deemed fit only for light duties. His experiences, and his views on the generals of 1914 to 1918, would inform all his work thereafter. He was inclined to dismiss the commanders of that war as 'recklessly cautious' and Field Marshal Haig as honourable but 'dim'.

After the end of the First World War Liddell Hart emerged as protégé of General Maxse, lately the Inspector General of Training with the expeditionary force, and as collaborator of tank guru JFC Fuller. Soon he was part of the team producing the new *Infantry Training* manual, and in 1921 he published a little book entitled *The Framework of the Science of Infantry Tactics*. Perhaps most importantly, Liddell Hart was soon elaborating his own theory of the 'expanding torrent'. This was an outline for a method to 'sweep through and overwhelm' successive layers of defence. Under this system forward sub-units would find or make a breach in the enemy's position and continue forward so long as they were backed up by the 'manoeuvre body' of the force. Formations on the wings that were held up would also push towards the breach, attacking the enemy on the flanks of the opening, so widening the gap. Rear units would 'press through the gap and deploy to take over the frontage and lead the advance in place of the temporarily held up units'. Finally, those elements that had been held up would follow on in support of those that had been more successful. In so far as this was a direction to reinforce success, rather than failure, it was good common sense and fitted neatly with Maxse's own predilection for the simplification of military problems. Liddell Hart claimed that his key inspiration was nature – streams cutting their way through earthen banks or dams – but some of what he said was already very much along the lines of *Der Angriff im Stellungskrieg*, the German manual of 'attack in position warfare' of early 1918.

Who had thought of what, and when, remained significant concerns to Liddell Hart, who always wrote with an eye to history. So it was when he penned a letter to Fuller in 1928:

> In the eyes of the Army and the public we are the two chief advocates of mechanisation. When this comes about, origins may be obscured. So I will put on record this fact, lest others forget, that you were the pioneer and that my conversion did not begin till 1918 and was not complete until 1921. Up to that time I was essentially a pioneer in the field of infantry tactics and had hardly studied mechanical warfare. Which of us had greater influence in recent years in paving the way for the military and public acceptance of mechanisation is a matter for later and public opinion to decide. Again, on the 'phases' of the campaign, I think that it is right to say that you were the pioneer in the conception of armoured forces, of the results of cross country movement, of the attack on the enemy's military command and control etc. and that I was pioneer in assailing the 'armed forces' objective (devastation v. demoralisation), in making the defensive power of the machine gun the staple argument for mechanisation, and in using the ancient horse archer as an historical argument for it.

Whatever the exact truth, Liddell Hart would go on to either identify, or at least popularise, many of the major issues addressed during the Second World War. In 1937 he began to draw up a long list of army reforms. Some of these later appeared in his 1939 work *The Defence of Britain*. Many of these notions were strategic in scope, or otherwise not relevant to our themes, but some were crucial to the development and practical application of infantry tactics. These included the following ideas:

1) The complete motorisation of all infantry battalions.
2) The incorporation of armoured carriers in every battalion and the abandonment of separate machine-gun battalions.
3) A reduction in size of both infantry battalions and divisions but an increased ratio of firepower to manpower.

4) Provision of 'Battle Dress' suitable to modern conditions.
5) Creation of motorcycle units for use as 'skirmishers'.
6) The adoption of a 'modernised and simplified, system of infantry drill for all purposes including ceremonial'.
7) Increase in the responsibility of NCOs.
8) Soldiers not on duty to be allowed to sleep out of barracks.
9) Creation of a 'tactical school' for junior commanders.

Though this list neatly summarises some of the main axes of direction, many of these reforms were in fact already in train. Reduction in the number of battalions in divisions was recommended by the Kirke Committee as early as 1932. 'Battle Dress' was trialled in 1937 and was actually on issue to front-line units at the outbreak of war. Soldiers 'sleeping out' became the norm of the Commandos in 1940. Motorcyclists, on the other hand, were already proved good for reconnaissance tasks and for message carrying, but not regularly used in a skirmishing capacity. Drills in the sense of 'standard operating procedures', 'battle drill', and the increasing importance of teaching NCOs tactics would be taken up by others much more seriously after Dunkirk.

The key documents for British infantry tactics on the outbreak of war were *Infantry Training*, 1937 and *Infantry Section Leading*, 1938. The whole philosophy behind *Infantry Training* was that in combat the work of infantry, artillery, and armour should be fully integrated so as to take full advantage of the attributes of each branch, and that as far as possible casualties should be minimised. Apart from the value this placed on human life, this approach was calculated to husband resources, and maintain morale for as long as possible in the face of sustained action. It was particularly sensible in contexts where a relatively small professional British Army faced either a larger conscript Continental force – or a colonial enemy with less technological or skilful battle tactics. As David French has noted, this methodology was prompted primarily by the heavy losses of the First World War, particularly 1914–1916, when it was gradually deduced that 'success depended upon the intelligent co-operation of all arms to overwhelm the defenders by weight of fire', enabling the infantry to manoeuvre without incurring unacceptably high losses.

The first security of infantry formations was seen to rest in air reconnaissance, outlying mobile troops, detachments, and especially patrols. These last might watch a flank, gather intelligence, keep contact with the enemy after an attack or retreat, or merely harass him. Individual patrols were framed for specific tasks: 'reconnoitring patrols' might be as few as two or three scouts. 'Fighting patrols', on the other hand, generally required a strength of two or more sections commanded by an officer; they were thus strong enough to manoeuvre supported by fire, hold prisoners, or carry back their own wounded. The equipment of the patrol similarly depended on the task,

> The clothing, equipment, including anti gas equipment, and arms carried by a patrol will depend on the task in hand, the nature of the country and the length of time they are expected to be out. Mobility will often be of the greatest importance and equipment should therefore be as light as possible and may on

> occasion consist only of a rifle with a few rounds carried in the pocket. It will often be advisable to dispense with light machine guns, particularly if the patrol is operating in woods or very close country. Nothing bright should be worn or carried and equipment should be tested to see that it does not rattle. Particularly when operating at night, silence is vital.

Patrol formations would vary – with more compact bodies at night, more widely spread with observation in all directions during the day. Objectives might be approached from flanks, but preferably not from an obvious direction or via an isolated piece of cover or prominent hill. Patrols would be withdrawn by 'bounds' with one element at a time covering each other as they moved. The places in which elements stopped should have good fields of fire, and a covered line of withdrawal. When a large body of infantry was moving towards the enemy patrols would be seconded by one or more 'advanced guards', which were usually composed of all arms. The front element of the advanced guard was the 'vanguard', which might well be a whole company, moving ahead of a 'main guard' of a battalion strength.

When attack was contemplated it was likely that the force would initially be strung out along roads or other avenues of advance, with patrols and advanced guards actually in contact with an enemy. When the mobile troops were held up the commander could then decide to deploy onto a wider front, time now being of the 'utmost importance' as swift decisions allowed weaknesses to be identified and exploited before the enemy could attack or withdraw. 'Penetration' was attempted where there were weaknesses, and where 'infantry tanks' were employed these could be used either with a section or two probing ahead of the infantry, or with a party following behind the lead infantry where they could advance by 'short bounds', coming to the fore to deal with any resistance the infantry could not overcome. Whilst brisk decisions were encouraged, fire support was seen as critical,

> As in all attacks, it is essential to allot sufficient fire resources to make success reasonably certain. Battalions will advance with support of such artillery, machine guns and mortars as are immediately available . . . As the leading troops fight their way forward, they will eventually encounter stiffening resistance and localities of such strength that it may be necessary to organize a fire plan of artillery, machine guns and mortars to deal with successive localities to limited depth by means of a short programme.

Within the attack forward rifle companies were 'directed against definite objectives'. As they came under 'effective fire' they would be forced to fight their way forward with their own weapons and 'such assistance as may be obtained from machine guns, mortars, artillery and possibly tanks'. The action was to be one of 'fire and manoeuvre'. The battalion commander was encouraged to keep well forward, maintaining 'momentum', and looking out for any weakness through which his force could pass to 'turn the flanks of the defences'. View points and tactical features were to be identified, seized, and held – in order that further attack 'may be planned and prepared successfully'. Whilst the defender might select his ground and prepare, attackers were to take steps to minimise the effect of his fire, as for example by manoeuvre and use of ground; smoke; darkness; or return fire.

The exact nature of attack varied according to whether enemy resistance was 'organised' or 'uncoordinated'. Organised resistance might include not only dug positions, but defence in depth, barbed wire, and other preparations: this was expected to form a series of 'defended localities' offering mutual support. If any sort of daylight attack was to be mounted against this without 'excessive' casualties it required 'deliberate and methodical preparation' with much effort devoted to keeping enemy fire 'in subjection'. A typical plan of assault included an initial attack, 'supported by smoke, artillery, machine guns and possibly tanks', on a timed programme, to gain clearly defined objectives. Individual battalions were tasked by superior commanders and often given a 'starting line' and frontage. The infantry would advance to the 'full distance that pre arranged supporting fire and tanks can take it'. Individual rifle companies operated their own fire plans for mortars and machine guns, and held their own local reserves. 'The guiding principle is to employ the smallest number of forward platoons consistent with the execution of the task'. If platoons were checked they were to take up firing positions to 'pin the enemy to his ground with fire and endeavour to create weak points in his defence by working round the flanks' of centres of resistance. Individual sections of the platoon would move in turn, covered by the fire from others. Attacks were to be made at 'a steady pace' – the idea being that troops would not tire themselves when they did not need to do so, but conserve enough energy to rush across dangerous ground, and remain fresh enough when called upon to make the final assault. This last push might well have to be made with the bayonet, led by platoon and section commanders.

In the second phase important captured features were used as 'jumping off places' to keep up the momentum of the attack. Success depended largely on the ability of the infantry 'to move forward close under cover of supporting fire' – and at the outset 'close' was defined as about 200yd. They were supposed go on steadily and without opening fire themselves unless forced to do so. Artillery support might take the form of 'a barrage moving ahead of the assaulting troops', preparatory fire, concentrations on successive localities, smoke, counter battery, or 'harassing fire'. In the initial stages artillery support was likely to be controlled centrally. During attacks commanders might keep reserves consisting of complete units with which they might outflank stubborn defence. Tanks were expected to operate essentially as localised surprise tin-openers with the infantry advancing rapidly 'immediately the tanks make such forward movement possible'. In this way armour and infantry co-operated, but it was hardly seamless or in the manner of a single unit. Where enemy resistance was 'uncoordinated' there was greater emphasis on speed in the attack, striking before the enemy could improve his situation. Individual thrusts aimed at weakness rather than strength, and commanders had to accept that there would be less chance for elaborate fire plans. Quick schemes more reliant upon 'infantry fire and manoeuvre' were likely to be the order of the day. In such a situation the leading infantry 'move forward with boldness', seeking opportunity for infiltration and with a willingness to take risks. Nevertheless, all attacks called for 'reconnaissance and preparation'.

In defensive battle the systematic approach of *Infantry Training*, 1937 was even more apparent. Ideally, battalion commanders were allotted sectors, covered by artillery, and infantry and artillery commanders were put in touch as soon as possible. Considering the defence from the enemy perspective battalion commanders would detail companies to positions taking into account the need for concealment and protection by means of slopes and woods, and for forward posts to protect observers. The battalion was divided into 'forward' and 'reserve' companies, with individual defended localities so positioned as to cover the ground between them with small arms. Machine guns could be set up on 'fixed lines' so remaining useful after dark and in fog, but were to be provided with alternative positions. Where used intelligently in enfilading positions the machine guns would help economise on the number of riflemen required in forward areas. The reserves could be used to create defence in depth, or as a local counter attack or reinforcement.

To natural cover troops would soon add field defences, camouflage, and wire. First priority was likely to be small-weapons pits and machine-gun emplacements, but if the position was occupied for more than 48 hours it was usually 'expedient to confront the enemy with an extensive trench system' and covered communications between front and rear. 'Isolated entities' could soon be made to disappear by the simple expedient of 'rapid and extensive digging between platoon and company localities'. In creating the network best procedure was to dig one set of weapons pits and erect the first wire, then dig 'intermediate' pits between units. The pits would then be linked up by means of shallow 'crawl trenches' which were themselves progressively deepened to 3ft. After

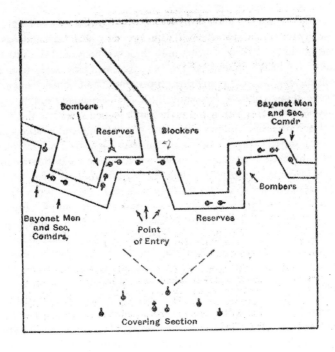

Method of trench clearance as given in *Training in Fieldcraft and Elementary Tactics*, March 1940.

just six days an ideal defence plan would see the whole frontage locked by 'extensive digging' with two or three trench lines, belts of wire, anti-tank mines, and zigzag communication trenches. The overall effect was very much like that created on the Western Front in the middle of the First World War. Indeed, the general ethos of *Infantry Tactics*, 1937 was methodical and systematic, with gains to be properly consolidated, advances thoroughly reconnoitred. To many, particularly in the early part of the Second World War, this could be interpreted as slow and over reliant on material – rather than full of initiative and dash.

For the smallest unit the tactical bible was *Infantry Section Leading*, issued on the last day of 1938, and seeing its widest production and distribution in 1939 with 135 copies going to every infantry battalion. Perhaps wisely, but unusually, it began with remarks on man management – a subject hitherto little covered at the level of the humble corporal. Key points to consider were leadership, loyalty, discipline, and the time element. To get loyalty from his section the junior infantry NCO needed the confidence of his men: good ways to ensure this were calmness, decisiveness, and discipline tempered with common sense and fairness. Some space was also devoted to the apparently obvious: encouraging the men to keep clean, ensure that their equipment was properly fitted, look after their feet, and similar matters. In his own appreciation of tactics the junior leader was to consider the importance of surprise, the value of looking ahead, and have knowledge not only of his own immediate duties but some appreciation of what other arms were expected to do.

At this date the British section numbered just eight armed with one light machine gun – now usually the Bren – and seven rifles. In a properly trained unit it was expected that everyone would be capable of firing both these weapons, and the anti-tank rifle. On the march individuals were expected to carry the small haversacks from their web equipment on their backs, containing mess tin, rations, water bottle, and waterproof sheet or gas cape, though photographs show the bottle suspended from the equipment. A total of fifty rounds were carried in pouches, more when there was threat of immediate action. Larger packs containing clothing, greatcoats, some weapons, and other bulky items were stowed in the recently issued platoon 15cwt trucks. Though not capacious enough to lift the entire platoon, these vehicles made a significant contribution to lightening loads, or *in extremis*, could be used to shift groups of men.

The smallness of the British section has been criticised on grounds that even without losses it was really of insufficient strength to split into two elements for fire and movement purposes. Moreover, there was no sub-machine gun in army hands, and the Bren, though highly accurate and popular, weighing just 22lb, was not much of a sustained fire weapon. The Short Magazine Lee–Enfield or SMLE was likewise reliable, generally accurate, and well thought of, fairly swift, and not over cumbersome in its length and weight: but it was of a design almost forty years old, and could be out shot in volume fire by the newest semi-automatic arms. All of this was essentially true, but these problems arose mainly from factors beyond the control of both tacticians and individual officers. The biggest single issue was arguably paucity of resources, for the army equipment procurement budget of the middle 1930s was barely £1 million per annum, and units were rarely kept up to strength. As a by-product of this situation there was pressure to retain existing stocks of weapons, including massive numbers of SMLE rifles dating back to the First World War. Another restricting factor, somewhat paradoxically, was the attempt to gain mechanised mobility – not only battlefield mobility, but mobility of stores and troop mobility within theatre. Large stocks of ammunition were difficult to shift and so seen as a potential limit to the use of automatic weapons.

Whilst the supposedly modernist reformers pushed the mechanisation agenda, and eventually got the trucks and some of the carriers demanded, the Bren was really the only genuinely new infantry weapon of any great significance introduced between 1918 and 1939. The emergency of 1940 would see a serious shortage of arms of all descriptions. Old Lewis guns were then dug out, and over the next couple of years many weapons were imported from the USA, including the Browning Automatic Rifle, P17 rifle, Browning machine gun, Thompson, and a venerable selection of handguns. The majority of these, with the exception of the precious Thompsons, went to the Home Guard – almost 2 million strong at its zenith, and to other second-line formations and reserves.

Nevertheless, *Infantry Section Leading* saw weaponry and firepower as defining characteristics of the section. Most important was the 'Light Machine Gun' (Bren), 'the principal weapon of the infantry and, except where extreme mobility outweighs the need for firepower, it should always be carried by sections in action'. Training focused on two modes of fire, single rounds, conserving ammunition and keeping the enemy unsure whether they faced rifles or automatic arms until a significant opportunity target presented itself, and busts. The ideal burst fire was four or five rounds at a time from the bipod mounting, repeated as necessary: this made best use of ammunition, and increased the time taken to cause overheating. As a general yardstick 'normal' single-round fire was a leisurely 5 shots a minute, and rapid 30. 'Normal' automatic fire was about 5 bursts of 5 rounds per minute from the light bipod, with longer 10- and 15-round bursts from the sustained fire tripod.

The rifle, by contrast, was seen as 'the personal protective weapon of the individual'. For this 'normal' fire was five rounds per minute, but the rate could be increased in 'rapid' to 'as fast as a man can fire with accuracy'. Practically, this equated to a maximum of about fifteen to twenty rounds per minute. The 1937 manual *Application of Fire* added the point that individual riflemen could be detailed as snipers or for protection of the Bren. In applying fire, sections were encouraged to make maximum use of short-range surprise and enfilade fire, both of which were far more effective than commencing at long range or against speculative targets. Good views, covered approaches, and adequate space for deployment were all important, but a field of fire of 100 or 200yd was sufficient for forward posts if covering fire from other units was available. Section leaders were to consider carefully what form fire should take: whether to use all weapons or just the Bren gun, and if shots should be concentrated on a narrow target or perhaps distributed over a broader one. Advantage was to be taken of lulls in actions to top up magazines, and collect spare ammunition from riflemen and any casualties and pass it to the Bren gunner. Platoon commanders were to be informed when ammunition began to run low, and arrangements made to bring up more from the platoon truck. Mills grenades, which could be thrown from 25 to 35yd, were a powerful adjunct to the infantryman's arsenal. Indeed, though the usual 'lethal radius' was much less some fragments were expected to fly upwards of 100yd particularly when used on stony ground.

For this reason they were best used from cover, or when the thrower threw himself flat. Their primary uses were in street fighting, trench-to-trench action, or in 'uncivilised theatres of war, against an enemy who takes cover in caves or behind rocks'. Mortars and anti-tank rifles were deployed at company and battalion level, later with platoons.

The little tracked carriers were battalion assets, organised in their own platoon, and in the first instance these had been designed as means of transport for a light machine gun and crew to positions of advantage – where ideally the weapon would be dismounted before use. Tactics envisaged by *Infantry Training*, 1937 included close support to tanks; assistance to the advance of infantry by 'infiltration method'; flank protection; 'counter attack by fire'; maintaining contact with the enemy or covering withdrawals. In the event this proved a rather vague, incomplete, and sometimes over ambitious summary of what the carrier platoons achieved in the first years of war. According to the *Army Training Memorandum* of June 1940 the campaign in France and Belgium saw carriers used to rush forward 'bombers', and at night confused the enemy who mistook them for tanks. More negatively it became painfully apparent that they were vulnerable to small arms from above, as well as to heavy weapons. Their cross-country agility was good, but they could be stopped by anti-tank and other obstacles. It was pointed out that the normal modus operandi should be to advance, debus weapons teams, and then withdraw the vehicles under cover. As the manual *Carrier Platoon* put it, 'if in doubt, dismount'.

Infantry Section Leading also assumed that the section leaders would have cognisance of other arms on the basis that infantry would usually fight in conjunction with artillery, machine-gun battalions armed with Vickers medium machine guns, and possibly tanks, anti-tank guns, aircraft, and even horsed cavalry. Of the various supporting arms it was anticipated that artillery and tanks would play particularly important roles, and of the artillery the new and handy 25pdr guns of the Royal Artillery Field Regiments would take the most directly co-operative part. These would 'shell or smoke' the enemy during an infantry advance, and perhaps cut wire entanglements: in support of a defence they would shell the enemy by hitting targets inaccessible to small arms. Tanks were stated to be, 'the most valuable support for infantry, especially in an attack against a prepared position. Owing to their armour being proof against small arms fire, they can precede the infantry, make gaps in the enemy wire and neutralize or destroy his automatic weapons.'

That the *Blitzkrieg* of 1939 and 1940 came as a considerable shock to the Western Allies scarcely requires elaboration: but it is also true that defeat and evacuation from Dunkirk were salutary lessons against lingering complacency. Whilst tanks and dive bombing received much attention, infantry tactics also came under the spotlight, and, in some aspects at least, underwent considerable revision. With further expansion of the armed forces and recruitment of the 'Local Defence Volunteers' from May 1940, it could be argued that to some extent infantry training and tactics were both increasingly 'deprofessionalised'. Yet, on the other hand, in the depths of national emergency, training also received both a sudden influx of realism, and healthy exposure to new ideas from quarters hitherto regarded in establishment circles as beyond the pale. In the forefront of the new were many Home Guard trainers who, by dint of necessity as much as choice, introduced training methods shorn of all subtlety and ceremony – but all too often blighted by total lack of equipment. Though sometimes well-meaning efforts descended into the ridiculous with broom sticks, carving knives, and garrottes, the crisis of 1940 also betokened an unearthing of hidden talent as veterans of not only 1918, but the war in Spain, took up duty. Of these last officialdom never quite overcame its suspicions, since the men of the International Brigade had fought for political ideals, as well as against Fascism.

In truth, the key figures of the Home Guard movement were a mixed bag indeed – coming almost indiscriminately from all walks of life and all shades of opinion, only entirely united in their determination to thwart invasion. Major John Langdon-Davies, author of the widely used volumes *Home Guard Fieldcraft Manual* and *Home Guard Training Manual*, was both Spanish veteran and Commandant of the South Eastern Command Fieldcraft School. The left-wing writer John Brophy, who produced *Home Guard: a Handbook for the LDV*, was a teacher and author, but encouraged in his efforts by Major General Percy Hobart. Captain Simon Fine was a Royal Fusilier turned Home Guard training officer and pundit. Yank Levy was an international adventurer and soldier of fortune turned close-combat instructor. Another veteran of Spain was painter, journalist, and staff officer Hugh Slater, author of *Home Guard for Victory*. SJ Cuthbert, who penned *We Shall Fight them in the Streets*, was a captain in the Scots Guards. At the same time many Home Guard platoons were led by pillars of the establishment, and more senior positions were often occupied by retired colonels and generals. The exploits of such characters are worth volumes in their own right, but if only one had to be singled out for his significance to the story of tactical development it would arguably be Tom Wintringham.

Maverick is an overused term, but for Tom Wintringham entirely fitting. A former senior British Communist who had served a prison sentence for his revolutionary activities, Wintringham had fallen out with the party – first over his choice of girlfriends, and then the Soviet tyranny unleashed by Stalin – and was expelled from the Communist Party of Great Britain in 1938. Thereafter, he had quickly become a convinced democrat, albeit one of the extreme left wing. An Oxford graduate of very middle-class Lincolnshire roots, he was described by friends as a 'sincere radical' with a genius to inspire, and remarkable capacity to invent weapons. His military career had begun as early as June 1916, when, as a young man of 18, he had joined the Royal Flying Corps, soon becoming a mechanic and dispatch rider attached to a balloon unit. He caught influenza in 1918, and in a farcical incident whilst attempting to break out of hospital for a recreational visit to Etaples, was arrested and accused of mutiny, a charge soon reduced to one of being absent without leave.

He arrived in Spain in 1936, whence he had been sent by Harry Pollitt, chairman of the CPGB, to act as representative of the party in Barcelona. Soon, however, Wintringham had become directly involved in the Republican war effort against the Nationalists, and a moving force in the formation of the International Brigades. By a strange quirk of fate, when one officer accidentally shot another with a pistol, Wintringham then found himself commanding the British Battalion. This command had lasted just two days when he was wounded at Jarama. A jealous 'comrade' put about that this was a self-inflicted wound, but more reliable witnesses confirmed that he had stood up to lead a charge, only to be immediately shot through the thigh. Partially recovered from the wound, he was later appointed instructor to the officer training school at Pozorrubio near Albacete. Sent back to the front as a staff officer, he soon demonstrated his impetuosity again, when, during a personal reconnaissance at Qunito, he took a bullet through the shoulder resulting in a nasty wound requiring repeated operations to the splintered bone. Ambitions to go to the aid of the Chinese Communists in their struggle were cut short by both personal circumstance and the stirrings of a more general conflict in Europe.

Interestingly, though Wintringam obviously gained very useful and up-to-date knowledge in the organisation of irregular warfare, and specific skills such as training, anti-tank work, and street fighting, his view of events always retained a marked political dimension – being shot through with the theory that how wars were fought was inextricably linked to political developments, and by extension to history in general. As he explained in *On the Coming World War*, roughly quoting earlier work by Engels, 'Gunpowder and firearms completely revolutionised methods of warfare. They required industry and money and both of these were in the hands of the burghers of the towns. The feudal lords' supremacy of the castles was broken. With the development of the bourgeoisie, infantry and guns became more and more decisive types of weapons'.

Of much more direct relevance to development of modern infantry tactics was Wintringham's reading of the First World War, and specifically of Ludendorff's war memoirs. A reduction in the size of the smallest tactical units had made possible breakthroughs in the trench stalemate, and made necessary both responsibility and a certain freedom of thought amongst junior leaders. In the transfer of such a notion to the Spanish militias he saw a 'mosquito cloud' of tiny 'almost independent units' working not by wrote, but speedily by initiative, understanding, and consultation. Such devolution of command might or might not be 'revolutionary' in either sense, but certainly required the introduction of a degree of democracy and problem solving hitherto alien to the traditional British Army. He had faced tanks personally and Wintringham's grasp of how infantry might sooner or later strike back was remarkably percipient:

> The verdict of Spain is not that the tank is an utter failure but that it has restricted use as a weapon of opportunity. Tanks cannot replace infantry as the basis of an army because they cannot hide, go to ground, become dangerous vermin hard to brush out of the seams of the soil. Tanks are short sighted, noisy, and bad gun platforms; they can be knocked out by handy little weapons.

In 1940 Wintringham immediately set about organising and training. The force of his efforts was materially aided not only by his break with the Communist Party, but happy accident of his employment by *Picture Post*, the proprietors of which were keen to do their bit for the war effort – and at the same time obtain thrilling patriotic stories for the magazine. So it was that Wintringham first published articles on experience in Spain and proposals for new auxiliary forces, then, with the encouragement and co-operation of Sir Edward Hulton and Lord Jersey, went on to help establish the 'Guerilla Warfare Training School' at Osterley Park, of which he became director on 10 July. So it was that revolutionary former Communist, press baron, and titled aristocrat worked together against the common foe. Wintringham's fellow instructors were Hugh Slater; Captain Wyatt-Foulger; Stanley White; Wilfred Vernon; and Roland Penrose. Wyatt-Foulger was a First World War veteran of broad experience who specialised in 'anti-aircraft musketry'; Stanley White a chief instructor of the Boy Scouts Association; Penrose was a surrealist painter specialising in camouflage; whilst the batty looking Vernon was described as a 'mixer of Molotov Cocktails and dispenser of improvised explosives'. Even some of his more extreme colleagues regarded him as 'rather mad'.

By the end of September 1940 about 6,000 men had passed through Osterley Park. The syllabus they followed was strictly practical. As Wintringham explained in *Picture Post*,

> We left out of our teachings things necessary to the Home Guard that we believed could better be taught to them elsewhere: drill, signalling, much of musketry. Our lectures and demonstrations included: modern tactics in general, and German tactics present and future. The use and improvisation of hand grenades, land mines and antitank grenades. The use of various types of rifles, shot guns, pistols etc. Camouflage, fieldcraft, scouting, stalking and patrolling. Guerilla warfare in territory occupied by the enemy. Street tactics and defence of cities; the use of smoke screens. Troop carrying aircraft, parachutists, and defence measures against them. Field works, road blocks, and antitank methods. Observation and reporting. The aim of the school was to teach members of the Home Guard to become first class irregulars.

Soon Osterley and its methods were being copied not only in other parts of the country, but in other parts of the Empire.

This was a magnificent effort of both practical and publicity value, but authorities were much alarmed that this friend of George Orwell, and critic of 'Colonel Blimps', might want to achieve much more. Already at the forefront of what was effectively a popular militia, Wintringham also recommended that the Home Guard should have its own 'Army Council' separate from the existing official body. Despite many political reservations, the school had well-placed and appreciative friends, and later in the summer of 1940 parties from the regular army also attended courses. These even included soldiers from the Brigade of Guards, the commander of which, General Augustus Thorne, had been an early supporter of Wintringham's ideas on army reform. Moreover, Wintringham was perceived as useful enough in his place, and was thus co-opted into the writing of official Home Guard training literature. As danger of invasion passed, establishment forces gradually and quietly absorbed the revolutionary wing of counter Fascist training. Osterley Park was closed, but reopened under a regular army officer at Denbeis, still with scout leader Stanley White on the staff. If more or less gently elbowed aside, Wintringham and his ilk left an indelible mark – ideological and practical. For though Home Guard schools were commonly dubbed mere 'training schools', it cannot really be doubted that they were close cousins of the battle schools and often their precursors. In overcoming the idealism of Home Guard lobbyists the army had been infected with their enthusiasm.

It has been suggested that since the universal manual *Infantry Training*, 1937 was not replaced until 1944 British infantry tactics and regular instruction must have remained out of date. This point of view fails to take into account the fact that though the whole was not revised, the parts certainly were. Indeed, many detailed aspects of infantry combat were examined and reviewed, and if anything output of new manuals and instructions was rather too great for training programmes to keep up with. Whilst new or revised pamphlets in the *Small Arms Training* series dealt with weapons, the *Military Training Pamphlet* publications looked at tactics and general principles. *Army Training Memoranda* offered smaller titbits and latest advice, often before it had been fully digested into manual form. *Periodical Notes* contained material on the German Army. Other subjects sometimes merited special volumes outside the normal series. Though it is unlikely that anybody in official positions would have been willing to admit it, as early as September 1939 aspects of enemy doctrine were already beginning to creep into British theory. This was certainly the case with the 1939 *Operations* manual in which remarks on the characteristics of infantry for example appear to be an approximate summary of enemy statements.

Part two of the 1939 *Operations* manual 'Defence' also updated earlier advice, remarking that, 'the fire power of infantry is the real backbone of the defence; its effectiveness depends on fieldworks combined with concealment, surprise, and the use of ground and obstacles'. Webs created by arcs of fire of multiple Bren guns were made all the more effective by concealment of weapons adding considerable surprise to the defence. Though trenches and wire were still seen as useful, greater emphasis was put on the idea of 'defended localities', weapons pits, and improvement of existing cover: 'Defended localities will be held by platoons or companies with their section posts so disposed as to afford each other and neighbouring localities mutual support. They will protect by their dispositions the sites chosen for medium machine guns and anti tank guns.' As might be expected, revised *Operations* manuals of 1941 also considered the actions of British formations in relation to the dispositions of a German defender, rather than against a notional anonymous foe, informing the reader what to expect and the steps needed to overcome it. These documents gradually departed from the existing *Field Service Regulations*, though the idea was maintained that they were essentially new versions of, or supplements to, the regulations of 1935.

Army training memoranda certainly looked at a wide variety of subjects pertinent to infantry tactics, albeit in brief and piecemeal fashion. The September 1939 edition addressed infantry training, fieldcraft, and patrols. Importantly, it also stated that training manuals were to be regarded in two categories: the tactical, dealing with training and employment of formations and units in war; and the technical with their instructions 'on the handling and equipment, with as much technical knowledge as the regimental officer and man need know'. Under the 'tactical' were lumped together all versions and revisions of the *Field Service Regulations* and training regulations, whilst the weapons manuals, drill, engineering, signals, and others were somewhat arbitrarily labelled 'technical'. The November 1939 'ATM' contained sections on the Bren gun; 'infantry war craft' in static warfare; and equipment.

One particularly remarkable Military Training Pamphlet was *Notes on the Training of Snipers* of 1940, reprinted in July 1941. This was significant as the first official attempt to update British sniping in any serious manner since the First World War, mixing the methods of 1914–1918 with more recent ideas. Official policy was that eight dedicated snipers be grouped within the intelligence section of 'all infantry units'. In infantry battalions normal practice was to draw two snipers from each company, which was also responsible for providing replacements in the event of casualties. Within the companies reserves were therefore earmarked and maintained. One of the eight dedicated snipers was an NCO, qualified wherever possible in a course at an army school. He acted as an assistant to the battalion intelligence officer. Nevertheless, it was not intended that sniping be limited to 'specially trained men with special weapons', as it was the duty of every man to be skilled in the use of his rifle and fieldcraft.

Sniping was defined as 'the art of the hunter coupled with the wiles of the poacher and the skill of the target expert, armed with the best aids that science can produce'. The primary duty of the sniper was 'to kill'. Sniper activity included both static warfare, and war of movement, when they might act on the flanks of attacking troops or single out crews of heavy weapons. Tactics in defensive open warfare situations might see snipers used as adjuncts to the defence of pillboxes, roadblocks, or field works where they could shoot from concealed posts to pick off any enemy who attempted to attack the more obvious position. A good ruse was to place the sniper on the blind side of the main defence, or in a position to fire into a covered approach. Conversely, in a counter sniping role snipers had special care to check trees, points overlooking friendly positions, fallen trees, sunken roads, and long grass, all of which were possible lairs for enemy snipers.

The key skill was to 'pick out targets exposed only for short periods and kill them with a single shot from a concealed position' – day or night. In order to achieve his mission the sniper needed to be trained in the use of equipment such as telescopes and telescopic sights; observation and fieldcraft; reports and map reading; the construction of hides and loopholes; camouflage; stealthy movement and identification by sound. Snipers could work alone, as was usually the case in open warfare, or in a pair with an observer, and shots were usually taken within 400yd, beyond which range 'sniping is rarely effective'. Part of the reason for this was that any moving target would take considerable 'aiming off' to hit at long range, and there was rarely time for the adjustment of sights. Moreover, even if a man was skilled enough to shoot consistent 3in groups at 100yd his spread of rounds would be a foot at 400yd, making hits to vital organs, or shots through vision slits very difficult to achieve.

Yet the value of the sniper well used was out of all proportion to the number of rounds fired, as the ability to hit the enemy any time he showed himself, preventing freedom of movement and observation was well calculated to help gain 'moral ascendancy'. It is interesting to note the similarities of the official instructions with the work of former Canadian reconnaissance officer Major Nevill Armstrong, who also published his unofficial but rather fuller manual *Fieldcraft Sniping and Intelligence*, as endorsed by Lord Cottesloe, in 1940. In this the links with methods of the First World War were even more obvious, right down to repeating images of the sniper suits and hides of 1918, and the use of posts in no-man's-land. Armstrong also reiterated the strong traditional connection between 'scouts' and 'snipers', updating some earlier patrol techniques and formations. One significant concession to modernity recommended for model fighting patrols was the use of 'gangster guns', to be issued four or five per battalion. These weapons, usually Thompson types, were to be placed at the points of the diamond-shaped formation and in the hands of the patrol leader, or carried, 'by someone right next door to him, more or less his loader'.

Practical experience and greater availability of equipment quickly moved tactics on. By 1942 snipers were considered company rather than battalion assets, with two to each company headquarters. Moreover, each section was now supposed to have a nominated sniper, though these might be limited to rifles without scopes. Sniper robes, already in limited use, were now commonplace, with a type of home-made smock cut from Hessian and painted to match the local environment recommended to both Home Guard and regulars. Different patterns recommended included an early disruptive type for 'agricultural, hedge, field and parkland'; a scheme of large patches suited to 'rocks, stone, earth, and sandbags'; and modernist-looking stripes and rectangles of dark brown and brick or stone shades for built-up areas. Dedicated sniper schools were established in the Mediterranean as the war spread southwards. By 1944 and the time of Normandy snipers proliferated, partly in response to increased enemy efforts. By this time camouflage Airborne-type Denison smocks, veils, and binoculars were general issues to infantry snipers.

As important as that of Wintringham, but in rather a different and perhaps ultimately more successful way, was the work of Lionel Wigram, a London-based solicitor and property developer and Royal Fusiliers territorial officer at the outbreak of war. Wigram was not only talented, but in the right place at the right time. If something of an outsider, by luck or judgement he managed to work for a while within the established system. Despite resistance to innovation, and suspicion, he was politically untainted and crucially had well-placed support. Wigram's brother-in-law was an instructor at 1st Corps school, and this formation, under the influence of Major General Alexander, had begun using simple general drills for the quick learning of basic tactics by the latter part of 1940, if not earlier. Alexander, experienced in similar training ideas at the end of the First World War, was more than receptive to their more general adoption, going so far as to encourage the circulation of 1 Corps tactical notes in October 1940. These helped form the syllabus at the Platoon Commander's School at Lincoln, and those of divisional section commander's schools. These developments certainly influenced the 1941 supplement to *Infantry Training*, entitled *Tactical Notes for Platoon Commanders*. However, the new official document for mass consumption attempted to avoid the term 'battle drill', and notice was taken of voices who complained that the very notion of combining 'battle' and 'drill' would straightjacket talented leaders and brave men. It would, therefore, be some time before the concept became mainstream.

In July 1941, however, Major General Utterson-Kelso's 47th Division formed the first divisional battle school at Chelwood Gate with Wigram as commandant. A two-week course imparted lectures, observation, and fieldcraft, with a strong emphasis on practical exercises. Both Utterson-Kelso and Wigram spoke to attendees, and Wigram attempted to include ideas on best practice culled from pre-existing training establishments. Interestingly, Wigram's later published work included a description of this phase, thinly disguised by omission of names. The ten instructors included a couple of ex-lawyers, as well as 'business men', regular soldiers, expert 'fieldcraft men' and a tank-hunting expert. These all pooled their experience together with the material recently gathered and held a no-holds barred 'Soviet' arguing the case from many different perspectives 'late into the night'. The rows were described as 'frequent and inevitable', but as a result a viable programme was hammered out. The school instructed not only its own division's regimental officers and junior leaders, but admitted personnel from other units and the Canadian Army. The work was not unnoticed, nor unappreciated, and that December Lieutenant General Paget, new Commander in Chief of home forces, ordered that similar schools be established in every division. To train the trainers a Central Battle School was set up at Barnard Castle in County Durham, and Wigram was posted there as chief instructor. In the summer of 1942 the new School of Infantry was also opened at Barnard Castle, and soon visited by Winston Churchill – lending the project his gravitas and approval.

Divisional battle schools also went on with the work locally, often using, as had been planned, officers honed at Barnard Castle. One of these was Captain Denis Forman of the Argylls who became Chief Instructor at perhaps the farthest flung of the British battle schools at Voxter in the Shetlands. Later, after being wounded at Monte Cassino, Forman returned to training, now working on the development of new instructors. Another prominent battle-school instructor to mix a career of front-line action with behind the lines teaching was Major Derek Lang of the Queen's Own Cameron Highlanders. Following active service in Belgium and Eritrea, he was posted to the Middle East Battle School in 1941, and from here went on to succeed as Chief Instructor at Barnard Castle. Interestingly, like the Achnacary Commando Basic Training Centre, some of the infantry battle schools were also used by American troops in Britain. The story promoted by the Ministry of Information was that at the British battle-school troops learned 'through ordeal' and in the nearest possible approximation to war conditions, 'nerve and brain are steeled' with a new soldier becoming a 'hardened veteran before he takes to the field'. In opening their use to US troops 'battle schools are another item Britain gives to the US in return for lend lease'.

Wigram's ideal battle-school syllabus commenced on arrival with his own address, that of the Divisional commander being given the next morning. The rest of that day and the next were devoted to fieldcraft in all its guises, with individual sessions, practical or lecture, of about 40 minutes to an hour. By the third day squads were learning and practising specific small-unit tactics, infiltration, and pincer movements. Day four had the units 'following a retreating enemy', followed by lectures on night patrols. After dark theories were put into practice. Day five saw trainees divided into two platoon-sized groups, one of which tackled village fighting and 'action across country' against an 'unlocated enemy', whilst the other worked on exercises 'without troops' as well as 'village fighting'. The first Saturday saw the platoons reversed, dealing with subjects they had so far missed. Sunday was a well-deserved day of rest, but from Monday to Wednesday of the second week the platoons were again divided to study tank traps, roadblocks, fighting in woods, crossing rivers, and guarding VIPs and bridges. Some of this was conducted under live-firing conditions. There was also another night exercise, this time against 'tanks in harbour'. The next day was devoted to 'the killing power of the platoon' – weapons and live firing, more river crossing and another night patrol. The final Friday was a hunt for enemy parachutists 'up hill and down dale'. On the last morning of what was effectively a thirteen-day course, with a rest day in the middle, the troops looked at anti-aircraft fire before lunch, followed in the afternoon by closing addresses, one of which was a summary of 'the tactical picture on which battle drill is based'.

As they were in operation for some years, and courses were presented at widespread locations by different staff, changes over time were not unexpected. Arguably, those not under the personal direction of Wigram were more conservative in approach. Nevertheless, many of the elements formulated in 1941 were retained. At the Voxter Battle School a 'demonstration platoon' showed the recruits how it should be done, the 'first essential' being a 'formidable' assault course, 'starting with an ascent up a naked cliff, passing through all manner of obstacles, including a pool of liquid mud, and ending with a three hundred yard walk through the freezing water of the voe or fjord, chest high, weapons carried above the head and live .303 bullets whipping up the sea all around'.

The battle school at Ullswater in the Lake District was attended by young signals officer and former Home Guard MG Jefferies in November 1943. One of the first parts of his two-week course was also a very special type of assault course. In this instance the most important obstacle was a multi-stranded Dannert Wire (barbed wire) entanglement, with three-, two-, and single-coil layers. This a squad was taught to cross, with no little pain, by thrusting one of their number up to the top and releasing him. On the way down the human wire crusher covered his face: the rest of the squad then ran over the human bridge. The last two across then paused to lift him vertically from the barbs before going on to the next obstruction. Other instruction included swimming in the ice-cold lake, with and without battle dress and boots; rafting; jumping from heights and landing; mile run in full kit; and weapons training. Revolvers and mortars were treated with particular imagination. For the revolver the trainee was given the weapon and a supply of ammunition. He then had to walk through a dense wood engaging plywood enemy figures marked with target areas. As the targets were shot the student counted off his rounds, and having used the sixth, dived flat behind a tree to reload. On the mortar men worked in pairs, learning to avoid overhanging objects that might explode the bomb prematurely, to keep the head back on firing, and to estimate range from angle. Rounds were fired to bracket and then hit chosen targets.

How his course ended Jefferies was unsure, as a particularly vigorous exercise resulted in a suspected broken back. Others did finish: two of these were Ron Goldstein and Frank Alison, tank men who were put through an infantry course at Barnard Castle for good measure. Goldstein remembered 'denims and mud' and a good deal of live ammunition, plus the stream-crossing element. The climax of his course was the tactical night exercise enlivened by tracer bullets and thunder flashes. Alison was on the grenade-throwing lesson when he dropped a live bomb in a slit trench. His fellow trainees immediately learned to exit a field work in record time, and the most realistic manner possible. Some of the Canadian officer students, earmarked as instructors of the future, came away with more professional and overtly tactical observations, as for example the catchy mantra 'down, crawl, observe, fire', and the crucial importance of 'dispersal' in squad movements when 5yd gaps between men was regarded as ideal for avoiding being caught together as an easy target. Experienced section leaders and platoon sergeants from many different units were impressed with the need to operate squads as two or three 'teams' in action, one of which was the Bren team specialising in covering and flanking fire.

Wigram complied his training notes from 1941 in book form as *Battle School*, a volume apparently completed before the end of the year, but not actually published, privately, until April 1942. Only 1,000 copies were produced, and *Battle School* was eclectic if not eccentric in its style, beginning with a lengthy quotation from a US newspaperman regarding the German Army of the 1930s and sideways criticism of flagging British morale. Moreover, *Battle School* would not have endeared itself to authority in any case since it castigates the infantry for 'wholesale ignorance of the realities of modern battle' and acknowledges German tactical inspiration, referring very specifically to Operation Michael as a lesson that has yet to be learned,

> One of the most remarkable things about the last war was the failure to note and study a very significant change in Infantry fighting technique adopted by the Germans in their final offensive in March 1918. Call this technique by any tactical catch phrase you fancy; but in effect it amounted to a return to faith in infantry weapons, properly used as a major factor in winning battles.

Battle School then goes on to point out the crucial nature of fire and movement, quoting precisely the same passages from German manuals that US theoreticians were simultaneously translating and integrating into their own new instructions on the other side of the Atlantic. It also includes a section from the interwar US publication *Infantry in Battle*.

Battle School focuses specifically on drills for fieldcraft; small-unit movements and what weapons and equipment platoons should carry; drills for the assault; games to develop interest and 'team spirit'; street fighting and defence. Many of the instructions were boiled down to simple movements that could be demonstrated on a parade ground, and it was clear that the intended recipients of the lessons should be platoon and company commanders and sergeants. Wigram was particularly keen that platoon sergeants should be included whenever possible, these being 'one fairly stable institution' in an 'evanescent army'. The offensive tactics included infiltrating around the enemy, a pincer movement and a basic drill for a section assault. In this the Bren and rifle groups began spaced apart, preferably angled at 90 degrees to maintain 'fire superiority' as long as possible. A sniper and 'grenadier' then crept stealthily forward under covering fire, with the former detailed to 'kill anyone trying to interfere with the grenadier'. Once close enough the grenadier threw a grenade or smoke bomb, and then, 'On burst of grenade, or thickening up of smoke, rifle group assault. All firing from the hip as soon as they have come level with the sniper and grenadier who join the assault'. In the attack the section leader went in about the middle of the assault maintaining control. All the enemy were to be killed, with the section carrying on about 50yd beyond the enemy post – with 'resting and smoking' on the enemy position being regarded as a specific sin to be avoided.

Important as *Battle School* might be it was essentially a book of lectures and notes, and delivered as such was very good – by turns pithy, entertaining, and inspirational. Yet as a durable and accessible reference book of tactics it fell short of its full potential.

The real landmark in British tactical development was *The Instructor's Handbook on Fieldcraft and Battle Drill*, published in October 1942 as a 'provisional' document pending the long-awaited rewriting of *Infantry Training*. This was essentially Wigram's work, but polished, better integrated, and with much of the anecdotal and incidental material removed. These asides and illustrations had doubtless much enlivened lectures, but were of dubious relevance in a printed manual for general distribution from which instructors were themselves supposed to learn. It was then thought that the revision of the 1937 *Infantry Training* would finally be accomplished in 'some months', but in the event *Instructor's Handbook* remained a mainstay of tactical training from late 1942 through to early 1944, and even then some of its contents were merely repeated

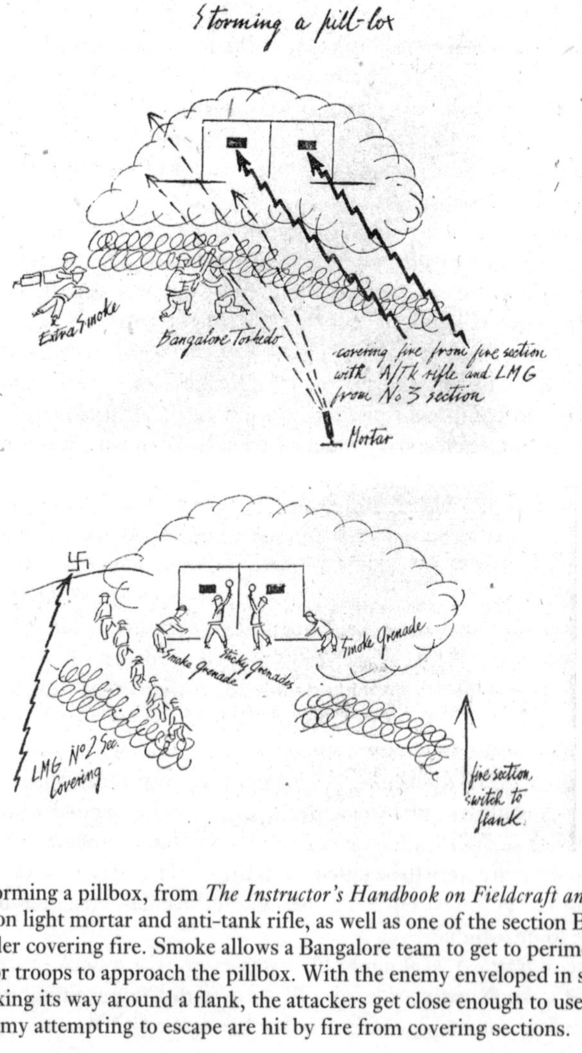

Technique for storming a pillbox, from *The Instructor's Handbook on Fieldcraft and Battledrill*, 1942. The platoon light mortar and anti-tank rifle, as well as one of the section Brens, bring the target under covering fire. Smoke allows a Bangalore team to get to perimeter wire breaking a gap for troops to approach the pillbox. With the enemy enveloped in smoke and a Bren team working its way around a flank, the attackers get close enough to use grenades. Enemy attempting to escape are hit by fire from covering sections.

in the new treatment. What made the *Instructor's Handbook* important was not just its durability through vital stages of the war, but the methodology that lay behind it. For now the notion of 'battle drill' was embraced systematically, becoming accepted as the orthodox way to teach tactics to the entire infantry arm.

Though far less well known than either edition of *Infantry Training*, the handbook was widely used, with 175,000 copies of the 190-page soft back in circulation by the end of 1942. Its roots in Wigram's original *Battle School* publication are obvious, not only in subject matter and treatment, but in its style and spidery diagrams. It did not claim to teach 'new or revolutionary tactics', nor, properly imparted, would it cramp innovation or lead to 'stereotyped action'. Rather it was intended as a firm base from which junior commanders could develop 'individual initiative' in the same way as 'young cricketers' taught basic principles then went on to develop their own styles. If the instructor's book replaced much that went before, its emphasis was clearly different to that of *Infantry Training*, 1937 in that its focus was on small-unit tactics and behaviour of squads and platoons and far less on macro decisions. Broadly, the old *Infantry Training* addressed itself primarily to majors and lieutenant colonels speaking the language of regulations, 'paragraphs', and issuance of orders, whilst *Instructor's Handbook* aimed at the platoon commander and senior NCO instructor and was couched in the speech of practicality, with quickly grasped simple diagrams and cartoons.

The principles of battle drill were to take movements and operations, breaking them down to the bare essentials, then work out an ideal plan for ideal conditions. This outline became the drill relayed to all, and as it was mastered variations were introduced and students impressed that the blueprint was really a 'means to an end'. With the basics thoroughly implanted individuals were now free to adapt them to suit the individual circumstances of a situation. Down to the private soldier it was expected that everybody would know 'what is being aimed at, what the battle is all about, what everyone is trying to do – things he seldom knows now'. Even if a man had 'no imagination' and carried out drills 'woodenly' he would still perform better than before. As battle drill,

> ensures that every individual in the platoon team knows what action he has to take and why he has to do it under any circumstances in battle. It ensures that each member of the team knows at all times what his comrades are doing, and what action is required on his part to help on the team's task of destroying the enemy. It ensures that all action is carried out at high speed and that the minimum of orders is necessary to put this into effect. At the same time, battle drill, by insisting on the discipline of the barrack square on the battlefield ensures the strictest attention by all ranks to the smaller details on which success is based. It has a psychological effect which arouses the aggressive spirit, brings out latent qualities of leadership, and, in its more advanced stages, eliminates nervousness of battle sounds and battle experiences.

Many of the tactics of *Battle School*, such as basic schemes for assault and pincer movements, appear again in the *Instructor's Handbook*, and the general arrangement of subjects actually follows the syllabus suggested by Wigram for the battle schools' courses a year earlier. Nonetheless, the *Instructor's Handbook* is longer, often more specific and undeniably more comprehensive. Though the precise phrases are not used, what it teaches are even closer to 'close-quarter battle' and 'standard operating procedures' than what was being used just a year earlier. Trainees are taught the importance of attack as soon as supporting fire stopped, pushing forward Bren guns 'to very short range' to cover the final attack, and of having 'one foot on the ground' at all times – this being the art of having one group stopped and firing whilst another advanced. Tactical handling of weapons received detailed treatment. The 2in mortar for example is regarded as, 'probably the most important of the platoon weapons'. However, it,

> emits a puff of smoke with every bomb that is fired, and it is therefore the most difficult of the platoon weapons to conceal. Except in the case of a 'quick bomb on the ground', previously referred to, and when firing low angle, this weapon must always be fired from a carefully concealed position which is behind bullet proof cover, the cover being of sufficient depth to give concealment both to the firer and to the smoke emitted from the barrel.

The *Instructor's Handbook* recommends that going into action the mortar No. 1 should carry the mortar, plus four bombs in his pouches, whilst the No. 2 is armed with rifle and bayonet but holds a bomb carrier of six bombs. This arrangement means that both of these numbers have a hand free. The No. 3, 'usually the platoon commander's batman', can carry a further six bombs. If ordered to fire immediately, the No. 1 uses one of the rounds from his pouches without assistance. If there is more time, he seeks a suitable observation point to see both the target and platoon line of advance. Nos 2 and 3 use team work and 'intelligent anticipation', keeping not far away. The No. 1 'should never have to yell for the rest of his team'. As soon as they are together No. 1 repeats the fire orders, as for example range and number of rounds, and whether smoke or high explosive, and puts out 'aiming posts' for direction – commonly two bayonets stuck in the ground – and goes to his observation point. He is now positioned so as to see the target, without being obvious, and with the team entirely under cover but knowing the direction of fire and what range and munitions to use.

Advanced instructions for Bren guns state that the section commander should straight away determine the position of the enemy as soon as fired upon. Then the default action is to work the Bren around into a concealed fire position. Such locations were best well round to the flank, or even rear, of the enemy, so as to create flanking fire, or 'cut offs', gauntlets of lead that the enemy would have to brave to move. Such tactics might deter reinforcement or 'ensure extermination' of a trapped enemy. Submachine guns and rifles are taught the importance of 'snap firing'; perhaps using lanes within woods as ranges for the rifles in which targets are rigged to pop up suddenly from the ground or from behind trees. Similar SMG training is within enclosed spaces, at no more than 25yd, with figures popping up from dark corners or out of cupboards in houses. During the advance all were instructed on the benefits of concealment and good cover, both of which had to be balanced with the advantages of gaining good fire positions. Those commanding during the advance were to remember four maxims: 'sweat saves blood'; 'brains save both sweat and blood'; 'dead ground – live men'; and 'take essential risks as far away from the enemy as possible'.

For advance against the enemy platoon commanders were encouraged to get the men to take everything they needed with them – but nothing else. For 'if our enemies lighten the loads they have to carry, we cannot afford to deny ourselves similar advantages'. The really necessary items could be reduced to a 'light battle order' of basic equipment with weapon, ammunition, water bottle, bayonet, entrenching tool, and respirator, though on occasion even the latter was dispensed with. The bayonet could be 'slung by the frog from the left brace at the point of the shoulder, the tip of the scabbard being fastened to the belt with cord', and the water bottle slung on the right side. Presumably, this arrangement, seldom seen in photographs, was recommended as more convenient when prone or seated. With the troops in light battle order extraneous kit went on the platoon truck, preferably packed into haversacks marked with names and neatly stacked on improvised 'stretchers'. At the order of the Company Commander trucks went forward and redistributed haversacks to the men, correct platoons getting the right kit being aided by different shaped 'platoon tallies'. Where the troops were not readily accessible to vehicles the stretchers could be used to bring up the equipment whilst the majority stayed in position. Ammunition and food would go up in similar manner, or by carrying parties in case of necessity.

Naturally, the point of lightening burdens was to make men faster, more agile, and less prone to tire. Quite how fast *Instructor's Handbook* would have infantry move in action is open to question, this being in essence 'the maximum speed of which they are physically capable, allowing for the fact that they must be fit to fight when they reach their destination', but this was something that 'only a commander who knows his men and their physical capabilities intimately can gauge'. Training and fitness being achieved, 2½ miles an hour was regarded 'as the minimum', but for short distances and when having to take risks much more rapid movement was demanded. The British Army in particular had been criticised as moving at plodding rates during the attack during the First World War, but if men exhausted themselves running half a mile or a mile from the enemy they could easily become tired, slow, easy targets when clearly within enemy sights at 200yd. *Instructor's Handbook* was well aware of the dilemma, but the solution was left to company and platoon leaders bearing in mind that speed, well used, gained surprise and presented difficult moving targets as briefly as possible, and cut down the amount of covering fire needed. Yet poorly used speed was a handicap – 'it is speed you want, not haste'.

Battalion and higher infantry commanders were encouraged to consider making their attacks by means of a 'main effort' in which, although the enemy was engaged along a wider front, the main force was concentrated in one area – as for example with two companies and much of the supporting artillery focused on a fairly narrow frontage within a battalion area. Though fought with new weapons, this was a very old idea, and indeed a micro version of the Napoleonic 'central position' where the bulk of a force was brought against a smaller portion of that of the opponent. It also followed current German notions of the battlefield *Schwerpunckt*, or 'main point of force' or focus of attack. If ordered to make a frontal assault, a 'main-effort' company could itself put two of its three platoons forward. In such an example two British platoons could achieve preponderance over one German, first by artillery support, then by outnumbering it in infantry weapons and men. Best of all a British company should attempt to locate and then deliberately attack an enemy platoon position. In such a scenario the first British platoon to arrive would take up a 'first-class fire position', perhaps supported by 3in mortars 'to thicken up fire'. Whilst the enemy was engaged the other two platoons manoeuvred to a flank from which to attack. Critically, numerous Bren guns employed from different angles kept the enemy down in his trenches until the last possible moment. Such a calculated approach was seen as ideal to overcome the natural advantages of defence, nevertheless, 'it must be remembered that the balance in casualties is always likely to be against the attackers'. Things would only go well if fire superiority was maintained, and 'intimate' close support provided to the attackers both before and 'actually during the assault'.

Three key assault methods for small units were suggested. The first was a basic attack, as already described, in extended order, pushed forward by automatic weapons, smoke, and grenades. The second was the so-called 'pepper pot' in which each section split into three fire groups. At any given moment any one of the groups was up and running, covering about 20yd before throwing itself flat again. During this brief sudden movement one or both of the other two parts of the section gave covering fire. Of particular value in fields of standing crops and hayfields, from the enemy's point of view a 'pepper pot' attack presented only fleeting targets difficult to engage quickly enough, especially when more than half the attackers were firing. The third attack was the 'lane method'. In this the attacking platoons stayed in lose single files as long as possible, taking advantage of field boundaries, hedges, or ditches during their advance. As they went on the open lanes between them could be used by Bren guns to give unimpeded supporting fire. Where a company made an attack supported by the fire of 3in mortars and the fire of Brens the whole could adopt 'snake' formations in dead ground, and the Bren teams leapfrog forwards by turns covered by smoke from 2in mortars. Once the Brens were close enough they gave concentrated crossfires allowing at least one attacking snake to make a penetration – going in from an unexpected angle.

Like a number of his fellow battle-school instructors, Wigram might have gone on to greater things, but after the appearance of the *Instructor's Handbook* he went overseas to gain practical experience, and to see how new ideas were being put into practice. What he found in Sicily fell well short of his now very well-informed, but arguably inflated, expectations. Acting first as observer, and later as commander of small units, he became increasingly frustrated. For a while he ran a small battle school for NCOs, and finally, ranking as temporary lieutenant colonel, had power to order modification of methods in his own battalion – but little to alter the procedures of higher formations. In a mix of exasperation and well-meaning desire to do the job as well as possible, and save lives, he began to annoy his superiors. In a report of 16 August 1943 he criticised organisations as 'out of date', poor reinforcement procedures, sections as too small, patrols as inadequate, and the very battle drills he had helped devise as poorly applied. Specifically platoons relied less on fire and movement and proven responses to emergencies, than half a dozen 'gutful men'. This was not 'fire and movement' but 'guts and movement'. In most platoons the key six were usually accompanied by '12 sheep who will follow a short distance behind if they are well led', and '4–6 who will run away'. What was needed was a simpler form of battle drill thoroughly drummed into all, more battle inoculation, more smoke, and supporting fire from 25pdrs using a form of napalm. Perhaps the most controversial idea was that some soldiers had to be categorised as unfit for the infantry battle before they reached the front. This would avoid the 'panic and hysteria' that sometimes ensued with heavy shelling. Whilst some accepted this as 'provocative', but useful, Montgomery reacted extremely badly to such presumption and called Wigram to him for a severe dressing down, blocking his future promotion.

In Italy Wigram was soon effectively sidelined by appointment to collaborate with Partisan forces – this he, nevertheless, carried off in some style, clad, according to witnesses, in black cape and purple Homburg. Several successes were scored. Italian irregulars were, however, even less receptive to the idea of battle drill than senior British generals, as was noted by an incredulous Denis Forman in a dispatch to Brigade HQ:

> In the assault, they adopt a hedgehog formation, as a conglomerate mass moving forward at a snail's pace, all facing outwards and discharging their weapons in the air and sometimes in the ground to the detriment of troops nearby. As soon as their objective is reached there is an immediate uncontrolled rush for booty. Boots are the main prize. The guerillas do not speak of killing a German but of winning a pair of boots. They are not above looting our dead if it places them in no danger.

Under such circumstances Wigram found himself doing less co-ordinating and more fighting. On 3 February 1944 he led the little Anglo-Italian 'Wigforce' in a dawn assault against the rocky fastness of Pizzoferato. The enemy was well prepared: Wigram was shot, his men defeated. Aged barely 37, he was buried on the spot, but was later re-interred at the Moro River Canadian War Cemetery.

With Wigram permanently out of the way, none of the original officers of the team still working at Barnard Castle, and specific 'battle-drill' training discontinued there later in 1944, it is assumed by many that the movement was effectively over and forces of conservatism had won out. This, however, is a gross oversimplification; for whilst there was no longer a militant or outspoken lobby in favour of battle-drill style of teaching, this was at least in part for the very reason that battle drills had now been accepted as part and parcel of ordinary infantry training. True it was that instruction was shorn of overt criticism of hierarchy, and of any perceived taint of copying German methods, but 'battle drill' in its least confrontational form, addressed directly to junior officers and NCOs, was now the norm. That this was so was confirmed by the most important tactical manual to be issued by the British Army during the Second World War.

Infantry Training of March 1944 was ambitious, comprehensive, and practical – but also realistic in the sense that it was appreciated that with the progress of time and experience parts of it would necessarily need updating or replacement. Perhaps for this reason it was produced as a series of parts, and of these Part VIII, 'Fieldcraft, Battle Drill, Section and Platoon Tactics', was the most significant. It should be noted that not only did the words 'Battle Drill' appear in the title, but that all the attacking moves were taught as drills, and that assault courses, battle discipline, and battle inoculation were all important parts of the whole. Part VIII was intended specifically, 'to help junior commanders in handling and training their sub-units for war', it was not to be followed 'slavishly', nor was it a complete syllabus that would in any way 'cramp initiative'. It would help every section commander to know his duties and lead intelligently making teaching of tactics interesting. The platoon should then work 'like a pack of hounds' not 'a pack of sheep'. Training was to be realistic and commanders would, as a matter of course, learn to look at problems from the perspective of the enemy.

> On the modern battlefield the close formations of past wars cannot survive; dispersion is therefore essential. Dispersion means that small units and even individuals will have to decide on the action they must take to carry out the general intention of their commander. This situation calls for initiative, intelligence, and military knowledge on the part of every private soldier.

Wherever possible section leaders were trained first, being brought together as a platoon and put through a separate course to instil both knowledge and confidence. Battle drills were to be wisely used to enable deployments to be speeded up, and help units develop 'maximum battle power quickly', but never allowed to become the master of the decision-making process. Drills did not 'give the answer to every problem', nor absolve the leader from thinking, but taught him to think on the right lines, and rapidly. If possible, situational examples were organised using 'demonstration platoons'. All this was pure Wigram, better organised – but minus invective.

The instruction course recommended by *Infantry Training*, 1944 commenced with fieldcraft, movement, and cover, replicating in many particulars advice given by *Instructor's Handbook* and other earlier manuals. To this were added sections on night movement and listening. It was further explained that in the First World War troops had often been 'seasoned' by periods in quiet sectors, but in this total war men often had to move from peace to '100 percent war' over night. Under these circumstances men could only be inured to 'terror of war' by three methods: battle discipline; battle inoculation; and measures to support morale. 'Battle discipline' may have begun in the time-honoured way with a short period of traditional drill, but quickly moved on to battle drill – the modern equivalent in more interesting form, giving the NCO more scope, variety, and test of intelligence. This was to be followed by assault courses and more realistic periods of section battle drills in which basic orders were learned. Assault courses could be 'miniature', packing typical field obstacles such as barbed wire, anti-tank ditches, gates, and hedges into a small area, or 'full scale', allowing sections to be manoeuvred over terrain. Students would be forced to take cover along the route, preferably with the addition of some live firing to make them dodge about to avoid, or attack, an enemy. When menaced from a flank they were trained to use smoke and deploy the Bren accordingly, when checked from the front they were to assault – aided by a grenade represented by a thunder flash.

Battle inoculation now involved live firing by night and day. It might begin with a version of the old Commando-pioneered 'crack and thump' exercise with students

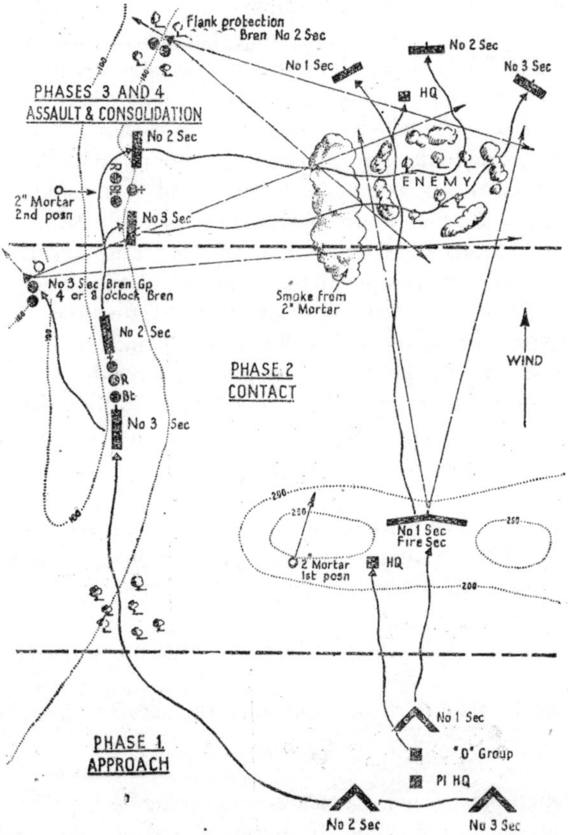

Platoon flanking movement from *Infantry Training*, 1944. The move is in three phases. One section advances to a good position to bring the enemy under covering fire whilst the other two move through cover onto the enemy flank. Smoke from the mortar and fire from the Brens allows the attackers to get close before the actual close assault.

spotting enemies and identifying their weapons by sound, but quickly moved on to scenarios that included rounds directed nearby by trusted marksmen. In one exercise trainees were given a solid, but very low, bank to crawl behind, into which LMG fire was directed. Thunder flashes were to be used as liberally as possible, and buried charges represented artillery fire. Yet 'rigid discipline' and good training were not enough: the soldier had to be given reason to feel enthusiasm and pride, factors encouraging him to act intelligently and bravely without waiting to be told what to do in an unusual situation. Accordingly, the cause for which he fought needed thorough explanation, and his skill and prowess due recognition. He had to feel the energy and enthusiasm of his officers, and leaders had to understand the difference between morale and discipline and 'aim at both'.

Sections went into battle with every man knowing his job, usual organisation being two 'groups', the Bren group and the rifle group. The alternative of two rifle groups and one Bren group would only be used if the section was up to strength, and enough men present with experience to lead sub-groups in action. Three key men including junior NCOs would lead the sub-sections, and whilst the section commander concerned himself only with giving leadership to them, he did not try to lead a group at the same time. Groups were formed as far as possible from friends that would 'keep together and fight together', any sub-group leaders who were not already NCOs being chosen for their 'natural gifts of leadership and because the rest of the group look to him as leader'.

Section formations were chosen with regard to control, the ground, fire production, and enemy fire. Wherever needed during an advance, formations were to be changed to meet circumstance. In all formations except 'blobs', and on very dark nights, men were expected to maintain distances between individuals of about 5yd. Given that this would mean a single section being deployed over about 50yd, commanders had to give instructions by simple signals, or very brief orders. The five key formations, and their advantages and disadvantages, were now:

The 'blob', of two to four men. Good for concealment and control.

Single file. Useful for cover such as hedgerows but poor for fire production.

Loose, or 'broken' file. Good for control and rapid movement or change of direction, but poor for fire production.

Irregular arrowhead. Facilitating rapid deployment to flanks, but difficult to control.

Extended line. Ideal for the final assault but difficult to control and vulnerable from the flank.

The three main principles of the attack were 'covering fire', without which 'forward movement would often be impossible'; assaulting from flanks, allowing covering fire to continue for as long as possible; and timing, as,

> There must be no interval between the cessation of covering fire and the beginning of the assault. If there should be such an interval, the enemy will be able to begin shooting again. Remember that if the enemy is dug in, covering fire seldom kills him; it merely makes him keep his head down so that he is unable to shoot back.

As soon as advancing sections came under 'effective' enemy fire they would carry out whatever 'anticipatory' orders they had been given. In the event of none being in place they dropped to the ground 'instantly as if shot' and crawled forward or sideways into a fire position and returned fire independently until ordered to stop. The slogan to be remembered being, 'down, crawl, observe, sights, fire': or much what it had been at the original battle schools, with only the injunction to take aim being added to the basic mantra.

With this taking place the section commander summed up the situation and issued his own orders, as perhaps directing the team to better cover, or follow him on a particular line of advance. In the event that fire and movement was necessary the Bren team

100

155. Diagrams.—The following figures illustrate the above drills :—

CLEARING SMALL WOODS OR ISOLATED COVER

(Diagrammatic only)

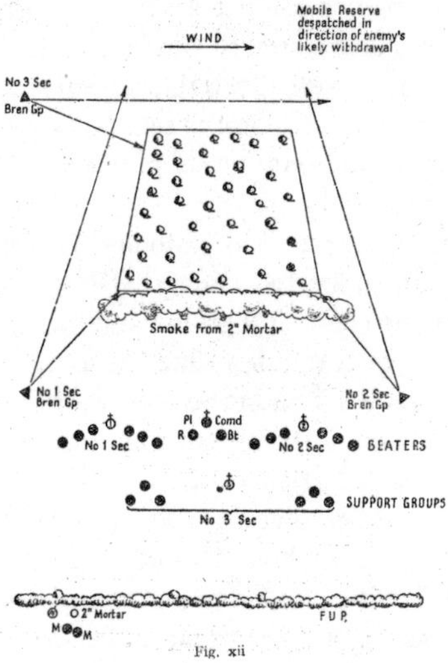

Fig. xii

101

CLEARING ISOLATED COVER OR WOODS

(Diagrammatic only)

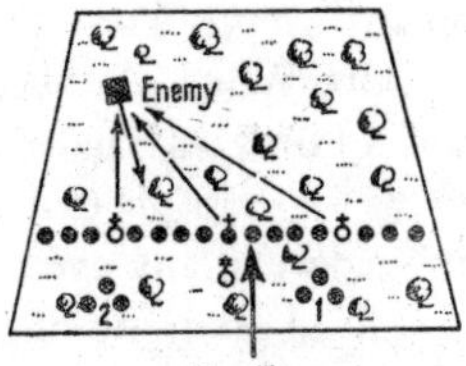

Fig. xiii

Beater locates the enemy ; he fires, calls " 2 Sp Gp " and " beaters down." All beaters take cover and FIRE, if they are able to locate the approximate direction of the enemy.

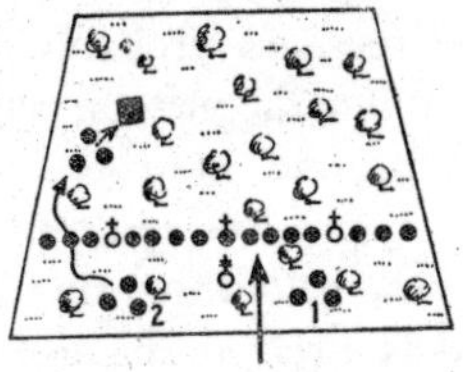

Fig. xiv

Beater indicates approximate location of the enemy to the sp gp. They go in with the bayonet, ready to fire from the hip. They either kill the enemy or report the ground clear.

102

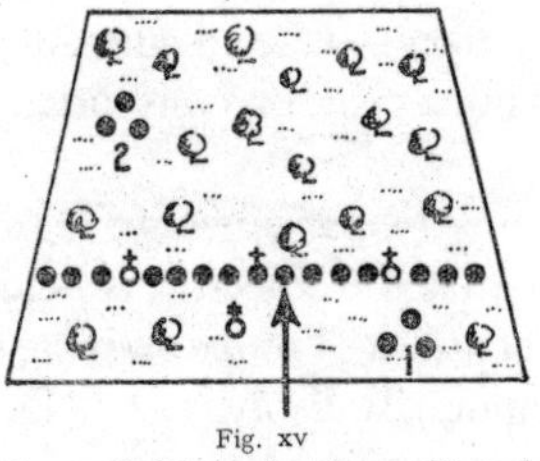

Fig. xv

The sp. gp. has reported clear and got down. Pl. comd. now orders " Forward." All now move forward except No. 2 Gp. who wait until the line of beaters has passed them.

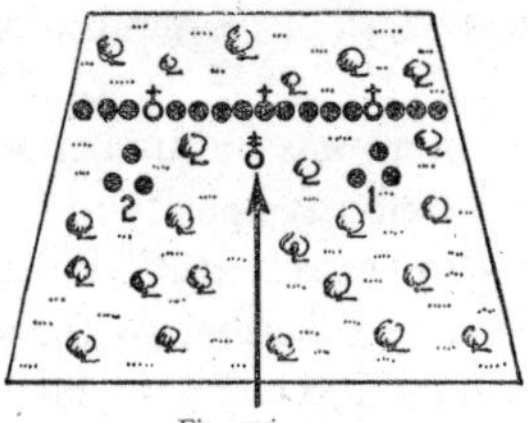

Fig. xvi

All have resumed original positions and the advance is continued.

SECTION 39.—**RIVER CROSSINGS**

See also Military Training Pamphlet No. 74, Part III (to be issued shortly).

156. Forward troops will cross the rivers by any means that are available, including :—

(*a*) Existing sources, *e.g.* fords, locks, intact or partly demolished bridges, boats, hauling across on ropes, improvised rafts.

Clearing woods or isolated cover from *Infantry Training*, 1944. The attacking platoon is divided into 'beaters' and support groups. The beaters force the enemy to reveal their position, then bring him under fire from cover. This allows the support groups to advance from another direction and attack the enemy whilst occupied and pinned.

was given a fire position and the rifle group moved on its firm base of fire – as for example on the order, 'left' or 'right flanking'. The two groups would then advance alternately by 'bounds', one covering the other. Eventually, the rifle group would reach a position sufficiently close to the enemy to make their assault, with the Bren group able to support. Whenever possible, the attack would be covered by smoke or grenades. The benefit of drill was that if anticipatory instructions were given the section reacted instantly – as for example to double to a covered position – or if not to react very swiftly to a 'snap' order. In any event, the train of events would only be set in motion if the section was fired upon, not if other units were shot at.

Sections that mastered the basics were ready to be exercised as platoons. The order of advance for platoons across country against 'an unlocated enemy' was with one section to the fore as a 'scout section', followed by the command group, and finally the two other sections, probably deployed in skirmish or 'extended' lines in more open country. When the platoon came under fire the default action of the scout section was to return fire, and try to 'get on alone'. If the platoon commander saw that this was not immediately possible, or deemed it necessary, he ordered a platoon attack. The leading section, now halted in firing positions, became the 'fire section' and the other two advanced as directed, making best use of flanking and any less-obvious covered lines of movement. In the event that it was not possible for the platoon to make progress the action moved up a tier with the company commander reading the situation and deciding whether to put in a company attack. It was not a worry that every platoon should succeed since action in one spot might allow others to advance elsewhere. Merely by engaging the enemy a section or platoon would force the enemy to reveal his positions, allowing others to take advantage.

On taking a position consolidation was often difficult, but vital:

> Once a particular objective is captured, then it is the duty of attacking troops to ensure that the objective is held and not allowed to be recaptured by an enemy counter attack. Troops arriving on an objective may be exhausted, and will often be temporarily disorganised. They have probably had some hand to hand fighting with the enemy, and some may have been wounded or killed. Therefore, great dash and energy are required by the platoon commander, who must at once set about the task of reorganisation and consolidation.

Where there was no further advance the platoon dug in immediately preparing an 'all-round' defensive position. Enemy mortar and artillery fire was soon likely to force defenders underground and it was better that they should prepare straight away rather than wait for retaliation. At the same time communications were re-established with other platoons and company HQ, wounded tended, and any prisoners evacuated. Part of the process would be to inform higher commanders of the location of units, presence and intentions of the enemy, losses, and situations to the flanks. Where wireless sets were not available platoons would need to send a runner.

Infantry Training, 1944 put significant emphasis on patrols, these being vital day and night when a unit was forced to remain on the defensive, keeping in touch with the enemy in order to discover his strength and positions. Though all patrols sought infor-

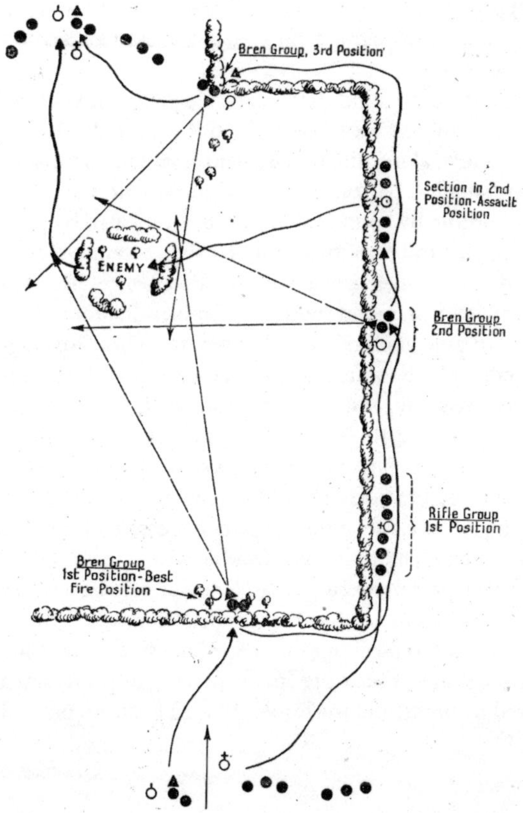

Section flank attack as depicted in *Section Leading and Fieldcraft for Cadets*, 1945. The Bren group gives covering fire as the rifle group works its way around the enemy under cover. The Bren then relocates as the rifle group fires on the enemy. This allows the Bren group to relocate, and as the Bren fires again the rifle group obtain their jumping off point for the assault. Finally, the Bren group is able to work its way around to the rear, catching the enemy if they attempt to escape.

mation, they might be primarily 'reconnaissance' or 'fighting' dependent on situation. Reconnaissance patrols specifically avoided combat, moving around enemy positions or taking cover at a distance for prolonged observation. In either event the patrol was given clear instructions and definite questions and objectives to satisfy. Every patrol ended with the submission of a report by the leader, ideally on a pre-prepared 'pro forma'. Long-range patrols might last days rather than hours, having specified routes to follow, and even locations to lie up by day and then act by night. Every member of the patrol was informed of the vital facts, as it could not be guaranteed that the leader would not become a casualty. For fighting patrols it was often advisable that the commanders should first mount a smaller patrol to scout the ground, and lay plans for movement and surprises by the main body. Patrol formations and actions were to be tested beforehand, and in daylight, with obstacle crossings, signals, and encounters with the enemy practised.

Reconnaissance and observation patrols were usually only an officer or NCO and two men, though they might be a whole section if required. Movement of the reconnaissance patrol was slow, along ditches and banks, seeking points from which to make observations. In the smallest patrols single-file movement was often most convenient, with the lead man working by bounds along a route indicated by the leader. The leader moved in the centre and the rear man, dubbed the 'getaway man', was to watch the flanks and rear, and in case of emergency his duty was to get back to the main body. In patrols larger than three, a diamond was the recommended formation, with six men for example being able to give good all-round observation and coverage. On dark nights the system of movement by bounds was replaced by a steady, silent pace with frequent halts to listen, check the route, and allow the team to close up. In single file it was wise to put two riflemen and the patrol leader just to the fore of the main body, so positioned that they could be seen by the men behind. Road movement was along the sides, and individuals were cautioned to keep low and in shadows. In the event of surprise collision with the enemy it was recommended that the patrol 'go straight in with the bayonet' before the enemy had time to collect his wits.

Full-blown fighting patrols were prepared to act offensively, and designed to be strong enough to deal with enemy patrols, take prisoners, and bring back wounded. Of about twenty men, strong, typical fighting patrol missions might include delaying the enemy during a withdrawal, combating enemy patrols, or protecting units. Usually the fighting patrol acted by night, and the leader divided his team into sub-groups of about four under an NCO.

British bayonet training the old fashioned way – from 'Small Arms Training', Vol. 1, No. 12, *Bayonet*, 1942.

> The patrol will advance slowly and silently, halting frequently for listening, checking direction, and maintaining touch. Wherever the patrol halts, each man will automatically lie down and face outwards, i.e. away from the centre of the patrol, so that all round observation is maintained throughout. The control of the patrol is carried out by signals for example bird calls, mouth whistles, clicking of fingers. Whispering should be cut down to an absolute minimum, being only used by the patrol leader himself. 'Getaway men' should be detailed and should be part of the patrol HQ group, with instructions what they are to do in the event of the patrol meeting unexpected opposition.

In defence *Infantry Training* saw the role of the section and platoon as building blocks of the 'company defended locality'. To do their jobs properly platoon commanders had to be informed of crucial features to be denied to the enemy, locations and fields of fire of adjoining units and support weapons, and details of local anti-tank and counter-attack plans. The platoon commander, given his orders and aware that he was responsible 'for holding his post to the last man and the last round', then looked to his detailed dispositions. In making his decisions he was to reconnoitre personally, getting 'down on the ground' and viewing in all directions thus imagining himself in the enemy's position, and bearing in mind areas covered or not covered by fire, as well as tank-proof obstacles and concealment. Time also required consideration since if there was no attack expected some unpromising positions could be much improved by field works; conversely, if action was imminent the platoon would have to fight using only natural features and concealment. Generally, long fields of fire were not required, 100 to 150yd being regarded as adequate for both rifles and LMGs. Having come to conclusions, the platoon commander called his 'O' group together and issued orders.

Section commanders now acted upon instructions, expecting to be informed of such matters as locations of friendly units, the platoon HQ and 2in mortar, the platoon task, whether any friendly patrols were out, and important terrain features. Usually, sections would be given their own 'arc of fire', and told what digging was required. It was the specific responsibility of the section commander to see that his men were properly dug in, well concealed from ground and air, had the ranges of likely targets, and that, 'the section weapons are so placed that they can actually fire on the ground allotted to them. The platoon commander, in selecting the section position, will have taken this point into consideration, but the section commander must select the site for each weapon; this selection must be made with the eye close to the ground'. In using natural cover full advantage was taken of such things as banks, ditches, and hedges, especially where these afforded cover to the front for elements tasked with oblique or enfilade tasks. Walls and rocks were also good, but apt to splinter and easy to range upon. Shell holes were viewed as instant weapons pits, but care had to be taken that they were not overcrowded, and that section commanders were aware that control was difficult with his team in several different holes.

In any event, troops had to be clear that concealment was vital, as 'an outstanding lesson of the present war' was that positions that could be accurately located by the enemy could be 'neutralised' by overwhelming firepower. The standard type of field work now recommended was the two- or three-man 'weapon pit'. These were to be vertical sided and narrow, and not to have parapet or parados all the spoil being 'removed and hidden'. Silhouetting of occupants' heads was to be avoided by positioning against a suitable background, and elbow rests provided within the pit as required. Camouflage was very important, any branches and foliage being renewed from time to time. Section pits were to be located close enough to the commander that he be able to direct them in battle. Though the basic pit accommodated two men, side by side, variations included a V-shaped three-man pit and a cross-shaped pit. Ideally, pits were revetted and well drained, reverse slopes being generally a good idea, and dug in stages so that men were assured of shallow basic protection very quickly, improving upon it as time allowed. According to *Infantry Training*, weapons pits were not normally given overhead cover so allowing freedom for anti-aircraft fire, but in practice where troops stayed anywhere for significant periods of time efforts were made at weather and splinter protection. Depending on location, rain capes, corrugated iron, layers of soil, doors, shutters, and earth-filled wardrobes were all brought into play by inventive infantrymen. Seaforth officer Alistair Borthwick saw holes lined with parachute silk, others protected by mosquito nets, and even some illuminated with electric light.

Chapter Four

The Americans

'Move Forward Under Fire' - George S Patton

Many of the issues that bedevilled development of the British Army and its tactics between the wars also affected the USA. Arguably the position was even worse, and by the end of 1919 the US Army was again entirely volunteer and reduced to about a quarter of a million men. As in Britain, the prospect of a major war was now regarded as extremely unlikely – but in the case of the USA the notional location of any theoretical conflict was also viewed as distant. The most immediate concerns were internal disturbances and the Mexican border: small expeditionary forces and overseas garrisons were furnished essentially by the Marine Corps. The Wall Street Crash and restatement of the isolationist 'Monroe Doctrine' by President Herbert Hoover pushed the profile of the army even further into the background. Given the world situation, the US Navy was given preference and the regular army shrank again to below 150,000, and only the maintenance of a larger National Guard lent any credibility to the force. As Chief of Staff Douglas MacArthur pointed out, the US Army was now just seventeenth in the world in numerical terms – and many units existed only as 'skeleton' in peacetime. Under the catch phrase 'Fortress America' it was assumed that the navy and tiny army would be adequate to keep foes at bay until there could be huge expansion. Indeed, it was only in the late 1930s that the seriousness of the world position was really apprehended, and with the outbreak of war in Europe a sum of $8 billion was found for the army – together with an aspiration for expansion to over a million men by October 1941. Major corps and army training manoeuvres were mounted in April 1940.

There were, however, a few potential advantages held by the USA, even though some of these might have appeared as negatives at the time. The first was that in having a small army, few colonial possessions, and relatively little equipment, there was not much to stand in the way of the development of new hardware and doctrine. The numbers of men tied to obsolete equipment were few, and the USA had massive potential both in terms of industrial and human material. It was also the case that 'Fortress America' was indeed a long way from potential major enemies and this geographic fact alone would help buy time. A genuine bright spot was a realisation of the importance of military education and staff training, and in addition to the US Military Academy, the Army War College at Washington, and the Command and General Staff School at Fort Leavenworth, there were thirty-one special service schools for branch training. Particular awareness of infantry tactics was cultivated by the infantry school at Fort Benning, Georgia. This produced the semi-annual publication *Infantry School Mailing List*, a journal intended to contain 'the latest thought on infantry'.

Another highly relevant offering of the interwar period was a volume entitled *Infantry in Battle*, a digest of First World War infantry tactics and lore drawn from the examples of 1914–1918. This first saw light of day in May 1934 under the sponsorship of George C Marshall, and was revised and reprinted in 1938 and 1939. Amongst the maxims it offered was the following – something that already sounded as though it might have been loosely translated from the German *Truppenfuhrung*,

> the leader who would become a competent tactician must first close his mind to the alluring formulae that well meaning people offer in the name of victory. To master his difficult art he must learn to cut to the heart of the situation, recognise its decisive elements and base his course of action on these. The ability to do this is not God given, nor can it be acquired overnight; it is a process of years. He must realise that training in solving problems of all types, long practice in making clear, unequivocal decisions, the habit of concentrating on the question at hand, and an elasticity of mind, are indispensable requisites for the successful practice of the art of war. The leader who frantically strives to remember what someone else did in some slightly similar situation has already set his feet on the well travelled road to ruin.

Highly pertinent also was the comment of *Infantry in Battle* on 'fire and movement'. 'Fire without movement is indecisive. Exposed movement without fire is disastrous. There must be effective fire combined with skilled movement.' The format of *Infantry in Battle* gave concrete examples followed by 'discussion' and 'conclusion'. Hence, for example, Chapter 18 focusing on the 'Infantry-Artillery Team' using examples drawn from French experience in 1914 and US experience in 1918. Sage and replete with good examples as *Infantry in Battle* might have been, it was hardly up to date by the Second World War, and the majority of the sources quoted were in fact written prior to 1930. The *Infantry School Mailing List* attempted to remain more up to date with periodic articles – and some of these did in fact turn out to be crucial to the direction of US infantry tactics after 1941. In July 1936, for example, the *Mailing List* carried a particularly important piece entitled 'The Tactics of the New Infantry Rifle Platoon'. This represented the 'tentative infantry school teachings on the new unit', which, for the first time, included riflemen with the new Garand semi-automatic M1 rifle. Significantly, it was recognised that organisations were not fixed, being 'merely the best machine we can devise for putting certain tactical principles into effect'.

The purpose of the recent changes was to increase firepower, without at the same time, decreasing mobility. As was explained, adopting the semi-automatic rifle was thought to increase firepower by a factor of about 2.5 : 1, whilst a Browning Automatic Rifle had just under half the firepower of the old heavy machine gun. Later training literature specified that the actual rates of fire for the M1 were '20 to 30 aimed shots' per minute and 10 to 15 for the bolt-action Model 1903 rifle. Nevertheless, if semi-automatics replaced bolt-action rifles, and larger numbers of light machine guns (and 'automatic rifles') replaced the heavies, the firepower of the battalion increased, whilst its mobility – without cumbersome heavy machine guns – actually went up.

What may have been less apparent at the time was that formations made up of BARs and Garand semi-automatics actually led to units with high firepower quite evenly distributed amongst the team – as the Garands fired faster than bolt-action rifles, whilst the BAR with its twenty-round box magazines fired much more slowly than true belt-fed machine guns. It was also apparent that general issue of the new rifle, and information on how to use it most effectively, took time. In July 1936, for example, it appears that just 3,000 copies of *Mailing List* were produced, and the fact that some yet remain in pristine condition suggests that it was not universally read, even within a relatively small US Army. Nevertheless, the wholesale adoption of the Garand – what Patton called 'the greatest battle implement ever devised' – was an inspired move, especially at a time when the US Army had little slack and other nations had doubts about the wisdom of giving soldiers weapons so apparently profligate in terms of ammunition expenditure. Indeed, it is arguable that it was the Garand – alongside the BAR – as much as the troops themselves that gave the US infantry its unique character.

The invention of leading gun designer John Moses Browning, the BAR was more than twenty years old on the eve of the Second World War, having been introduced in the closing stages of the First. Yet whilst its reputation was not entirely spotless, it had been extremely advanced at the time of its appearance, being a weapon able to provide full automatic fire, at least in short bursts, but still light enough – at just 22lb – for one man to carry. In the event the basic concept remained good enough, and the guns serviceable enough, to be continued in use in one country or another throughout the twentieth century. Initially, it had been imagined that the BAR would be used mainly on the move, providing 'walking fire' from hip, or even shoulder, during the attack, but it was really too much hardware to make such an option very practical or accurate. As a result, it was normally fired prone from a small integral bipod – a posture well calculated to be least obtrusive and best protected in battle in any case. Latest thoughts on BAR fire and training were summed up by the official pamphlet *Basic Weapons: Marksmanship – the Automatic Rifle* of 1937.

The key attributes of the successful BAR gunner were accurate delivery, 'mechanical skill' where needed in distribution of fire over targets, and 'maintenance of fire' by quick re-aiming and reloading. In training gunners fired from various positions and distances, 'but the soldier must be taught that the prone position is the normal position, and that he must seek firing positions which will enable him to use the prone position'. When lying down behind the weapon the firer was encouraged to position himself so that his right shoulder and hip bone were in line with the barrel of the gun, and the butt well into the shoulder. Legs were well spread, and the toes could be dug in for additional bracing. Left-handed use was actively discouraged as this impeded ejection of empty cases to the side. The sitting and kneeling fire postures were essentially self explanatory, but the 1937 instructions also continued to feature an 'assault fire' position. In this the butt was held under the right armpit, clasped firmly between the body and the upper portion of the arm, the sling being over the left shoulder for support. Soldiers practised quick magazine changes, counting the rounds as they were expended and allowing the box to drop under its own weight on release of the catch. A fresh magazine from the waistbelt carrier was then 'placed in the receiver with one rapid, smooth movement'. The usual number of rounds to be fired in a burst was five, this being calculated as likely to be effective and about the maximum before the muzzle wandered far from point of aim. This allowed for four such bursts from the twenty-round magazine.

At the end of the 1930s BARs were still considered platoon assets that could be disposed as the commander required, with manuals of 1940 referring to the existence of 'rifle' and 'automatic rifle' squads within the rifle platoons. The BAR was seen as a 'reserve of automatic fire for use in the critical emergencies of combat'. By US entry to the war the BAR had become an integral asset of the squad, the automatic rifle 'team' being three men providing,

> the rifle squad leader with an easily controlled and manoeuvred weapon capable of a large volume of fire. It is used against ground targets in a manner similar to

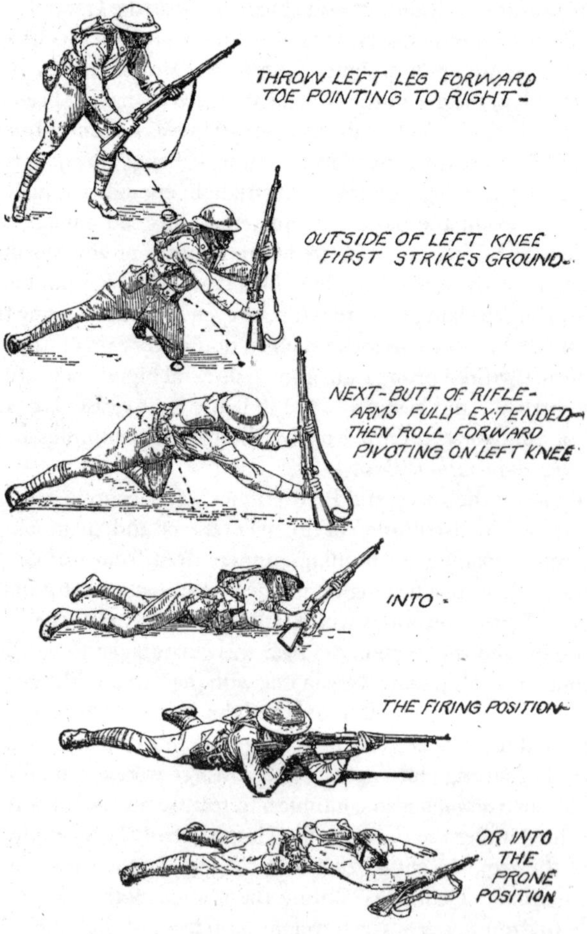

Some basic tactical movement from FM 21-45 *Protective Measures, Individuals and Small Units*, 1942. The rifleman drops to the ground from the run, breaking his fall, and quickly adopts a fire position or ducks flat to avoid fire.

> the light machine gun, and also engages air targets. Its light weight permits the automatic rifleman to maintain the rate of advance of riflemen and to fire from any position.

So it was that US practice fell into line with the basic tenets of squad operations as already practised in the German and British armies in which there was one basic type of front-line infantry squad, based around a light automatic support weapon. As of 1940 the small 8-man US squads of yesteryear were reorganised on a strength of 12, being a 3-man BAR team, 8 armed with semi-automatic rifles, including the leader and his assistant, plus the sniper with his bolt-action rifle. Remarkably, the BAR was useful enough during the course of the war that many squads took to carrying two of them, and eventually this practice was formally recognised.

Whilst the BAR had arguably taken time to prove itself and find its optimum tactical niche, it was almost immediately apparent at introduction that the M1 Garand rifle was a significant advance. Designed by Canadian-born John Cantius Garand of the Springfield armoury, the weapon seemed vaguely conventional at first glance, and at over 9lb weighed a little more than German and British manual bolt-action comparators. Nevertheless, appearances were deceptive, since the Garand was in fact the culmination of about half a dozen experimental pieces that the inventor had produced since 1919. At its heart was a gas-operated system working a piston, which, by means of a cam, opened the bolt and recocked the gun. Unlike many previous attempts at the mechanisation of military small arms, the Garand proved reliable and relatively straightforward to produce in numbers, and its drawbacks were few. Perhaps most obviously its eight-round clip could not be topped up, and when empty was ejected from the gun with an audible 'ping', but in the great scheme of things these were minor criticisms.

The firepower of the Garand gave the individual US soldier a potential advantage over opposite numbers in other nations. Perhaps unsurprisingly other US Army commentators apart from Patton were not shy about this morale-raising fact. As the Infantry Journal publication *How to Shoot the US Army Rifle*, of 1943, put it, 'your rifle is better than the enemy's'. Besides, 'the last war proved that if you hit a German in the right place with a caliber .30 rifle bullet, he falls over dead. This is also true in this war. It applies, moreover, to Japs as well as Nazis.' The 1942 *Rifle Company* manual took a somewhat more detached view:

> The M1 rifle is the principal individual weapon assigned to rifle company personnel. On account of its long range, ease of operation, and light weight it is well adapted for all types of infantry combat. These characteristics enable a rifleman or group of riflemen to deliver promptly a large volume of accurate fire upon any designated ground and air targets within range.

The new M1 cost $80 and was an innately a faster weapon than its competitors, but like all firearms required its user to know what he was doing with it. In *How to Shoot* the GI was offered a six-stage programme, dealing with aiming; positions; trigger squeeze; rapid fire; sight adjustment; and a final examination.

Practice was key, and ideally there was an element of one-to-one tuition with a 'coach' and 'pupil' working in pairs. It was not necessarily the case that every coach was a fully experienced expert, and the two could change places. This enabled correction of errors that one could not see in oneself, and at the same time it taught soldiers to teach others – 'for an army as fast growing as ours, we need men to train new men coming into camp'. There were also some wrinkles that traditional training might otherwise miss, tips such as removing oil from sights and blackening them with lamp or candle black to create a clear and matt-black 'sight picture' even in unfavourable glare, careful breath control, and the use of the sling tightly looped around the arm for steadiest aim. Posture advice also stressed steady support, with the arm directly under the weight of the rifle, rather than reliance on stressed muscles. The prone firing position was naturally preferred, but only on level ground, being significantly improved by means of a rest, such as a sandbag. The trainee was taught to sink quickly down, bending both knees, placing butt and elbows to the ground and sliding smoothly but promptly forward into position. As alternatives during combat the soldier could go prone using 'skirmisher' or 'rush' techniques. In the skirmisher's method the soldier went down initially by placing the right foot well back and bending the left knee as low as possible. The rush method integrated brief forward rushes with throwing oneself to the ground in a safe and controlled manner, advancing the left foot whilst dropping to the ground with the weapon held to the fore. In a less-tidy emergency variation, the soldier could also execute a 'cover to cover' manoeuvre, springing up from a flat position pushing from arms and right knee, dash forward, then fling himself down 'breaking his fall with butt of rifle'.

Other firing possibilities included sitting, which was good for ground sloping downward to the front; kneeling, good for upward slopes; and standing, a versatile posture, though too obvious to the enemy unless cover was involved. A squat position was recommended as being quick to adopt, and 'desirable when firing in mud, shallow water, snow, or a gas contaminated area'. One of the most important aspects of the training recommended by *How to Shoot* was rapid fire, which, to be effective required both timing and good posture. Some exercises were conducted as 'dry firing' without live ammunition, and given how quickly the M1 could be emptied in an uncontrolled manner, some of the training appears to have been geared to ensuring deliberation and aim between rounds. How not to do things was illustrated by a character called 'Joe Jerk' who 'sleeps through demonstrations' and learned his technique on Coney Island shooting galleries. Joe commits errors such as closing his eyes; failure to put himself squarely behind the rifle; poor grip, jerked trigger, and misplaced sling. The antidote to the antics of Joe Jerk was for the soldier to think of his M1 like his girl – something that 'has habits for which you must allow'.

Training literature of 1940 assumed that what riflemen actually did in battle would be defined by mission, but there were common basics. Cover was expected to be used to best advantage as matter of course – crests for example being only occupied whilst actually firing. On an order to cease the soldier resumed his 'cover position', looking to his squad leader for fresh directions. Soldiers were to learn to distinguish between good fire and good cover positions: the former gave good observation and field of fire, the latter protected him from 'hostile flat trajectory fire'. The ideal spot for a rifleman was one where a cover position was located just behind a fire position – with the two not more than three paces apart, allowing him to duck in and out of complete cover as required. 'Aimed fire' was the point of the rifleman, but this did not mean that individual enemies would always be there to be shot at. Fire could be directed at muzzle flashes, emplacements, or cover. The rifleman,

> fires his first shot on a part of the target corresponding generally to his position in the squad. He then distributes his fire by aiming at selected points a few yards to the right or left of his first shot. A slower rate of fire than standard for rapid fire practice will often be advisable because of the difficulty of selecting indistinct targets on the battlefield.

When acting as a skirmisher rushes were to be kept short, from one piece of cover to another, as directed by the squad leader. Walking was only possible under cover; creeping and crawling could be used to advantage for short moves, or through partial cover; often the soldier would have to rush as rapidly as possible, combining this with other moves as necessary. Squad rushes would be executed with the rifle locked and loaded, the leader warning the squad with 'Prepare to rush', then the command 'Follow me'. That safety locks should be kept on during movement was seen as important – as the *Soldier's Handbook*, 1941, explained, 'as you may catch your trigger in brush and kill yourself, or a comrade'.

Another semi-automatic seen in the hands of many US soldiers was the M1 Carbine. In theory this should not have seen much combat action, for at the time of introduction in 1941 it was not regarded as an infantry weapon but a defensive arm for specialists such as weapon crews, drivers, cooks, and others, who might have to protect themselves or fight in an emergency. The logic behind the specification for a semi-automatic weapon that weighed only 5lb, and used only a relatively low powered Winchester .30 'short rifle' cartridge, was that pistols proved problematic in the hands of non-experts attempting to engage anything more than a few yards away and had a poor safety record, whilst on the other hand it seemed unrealistic to expect personnel who had other tasks to perform to tote about full-sized rifles. In the event Winchester's handy little carbine, using a gas tappet mechanism by David M Williams, was designed and built in record time, and fitted the bill almost too well. It was quickly popular on account of its light weight and rapid fire, and was soon being used in many circumstances far beyond the original brief. It saw duty as squad leader's weapon, parachutist's arm, and in many other front-line combat situations. Many of its users were perfectly content, but a few complained, unfairly, that it lacked punch. Not many seemed to have realised that the request for its production had required only an effective range of 300yd. Interestingly, there was also an M2 version of the carbine produced towards the end of the war capable of full automatic fire.

According to the 1942 manual FM 23-7, *US Carbine Caliber .30 M1*, use of the weapon should have been governed by its characteristics,

> It is highly effective at close quarters and at ranges up to 300 yards. Its 15 round magazine and semi automatic action, together with its greater effective range,

> make it much superior to the pistol or revolver as a close defence weapon. Men armed with the carbine are capable of dealing effectively with parachutists landing in their immediate vicinity, and with other hostile personnel encountered at up to 300 yards. Carbineers are not organised into squads or other fire units, but deliver their fire as individuals. However a small group of such personnel may be collected for the execution of group fire in situations where this action promises the best results. Carbines may be grouped with other available weapons, especially automatic rifles.

Commonly, niceties such as target designation were unnecessary for such a close-range weapon and range estimation was 'by eye'. Nevertheless, users were encouraged to become familiar with, and hold in their minds, the appearance of objects and possible targets at 50 and 100yd distant, as this allowed pointing and shoot naturally and fairly accurately without undue delay or too many first-time misses. Carbine training involved the teaching of a variety of standard firing positions, as for example prone, kneeling, sitting, and standing. Pupils were taught rapid fire by gradually building up speed of delivery, beginning with a fairly leisurely and carefully aimed round every 5 seconds, until finally they were able to fire '25 or more accurate shots per minute'.

The opposite side of the close-range combat question was the fact that sub-machine guns were not standard issue to the ordinary US infantry rifle squads, and in contrast to the M1 carbine do not seem to have been particularly popular. The Thompson SMG had great historical reputation, was well made, and boasted massive close-range stopping power: but against this was heavy, old fashioned, expensive, and not of much use in open areas. The M3 'grease gun' introduced at the very end of 1942 was actually disliked by many, though it did what it set out to do tolerably well. A cheaply stamped weapon, it cost less than half the price of the Thompson, also used the powerful .45 round, and had a thirty-round box magazine. So it was that relatively small numbers of SMGs available to the infantry – some accounts speak of a dozen, or less, per company – were used as HQ assets. These could be distributed as and when needed for particular tasks, as for example in street fighting, or to arm patrols at night or in close country. SMGs also saw some use as junior commanders' arms.

The Browning-designed Colt model 1911A1 semi-automatic .45 pistol was the standard side arm of officers and 'second weapon' of many specialists. Adopted before the First World War, it had been trialled against a range of other possibilities including the 9mm 'Luger' Parabellum, and a Savage arm. By 1917 the US Army had in excess of 75,000 of the new pistols. The original 1911 model was slightly remodelled in the early 1920s to make it more ergonomic, thus becoming the model 1911A1. Arguably one of the best combat pistols of any nation, it had the valuable characteristics of good stopping power and reliability, combined with a seven-round detachable box magazine integral to the butt, though to shoot such a powerful weapon accurately requires some practice. Like the M1 Garand, the semi-automatic service pistol was seen as sufficiently ubiquitous to be featured in the *Soldier's Handbook* and was thus one of a relatively few pieces of equipment that pretty well every soldier had instructions on, whatever his duty or designation.

Good as it was, the Colt 1911A1 still had many of the faults inherent to most pistols. Its effective range was short, even in the hands of an expert, and it was much easier to have accidents with than long arms. So it was that the 1942 *Rifle Company* manual described it as 'an arm of emergency' intended for 'individual defense' at ranges up to 50yd. Whilst the Colt was the main combat pistol, it is often forgotten that there were others that saw at least limited use. Production of pistols was not top priority, and so it was that 'substitute standard' arms were used as supplements, though as far as possible front-line troops got the 1911A1 Colt. The additional arms were mainly .38 revolvers by Colt and Smith and Wesson, and these, as well as other second-line pistols and revolvers, were also supplied to Britain during the emergency that followed Dunkirk. Though semi-automatic weapons now predominated, it remained usual for at least one bolt-action 1903 model Springfield to remain part of squad assets. The reason for this apparent anomaly was that there were still a few things that the Garand had not been designed to do, or had not yet been adapted to perform. Chief amongst these were sniping and grenade launching.

Most destructive against close-range targets, especially those within fieldworks and pillboxes, was the grenade. US types included a Mark III 'offensive' model with a fibreboard casing and other specialist munitions, but the one that saw most use in combat was the Mark IIA1 fragmentation grenade. It looked very much like a small pineapple, and was sometimes nicknamed accordingly. The parentage of this bomb was French, being derived from a type used in the First World War. The thrower pulled the pin, and the side lever was released as the grenade left the hand, allowing the 'Bouchon' or 'mouse-trap' igniter to snap initiating the fuse. After 4½ seconds the bomb exploded into lethal fragments. Whilst theoretically antiquated and less than perfect, nothing better was devised before the end of the war, and the fragmentation grenade did most of what was asked of it. Indeed, in terms of sheer destructiveness it was found more potent than the German stick grenade, as 36th Division infantryman Michael Stubinski explained, 'I captured a German potato masher, my first, and threw it. It went off just like a concussion grenade, not like ours, which we carried on our belts. Ours . . . tears a body to pieces whereas the potato masher shook the hell out of you'.

The key infantry manual at the time of US entry to the war was FM 7-5, *Organisation and Tactics of the Infantry: The Rifle Battalion*, 1940. This was particularly significant since nothing of such a comprehensive nature had been produced since the 1920s and it superseded a whole raft of other documents. Its publication by the War Department that October post-dated both the invasion of Poland and the *Blitzkrieg* campaigns in the West, but how much it was able to take note of both latest campaigns and recent home exercises is open to some debate as at least part appears to have been prepared earlier in the year. Nevertheless, in many aspects the new bible was already influenced by European examples and interwar German tactical manuals in particular. Whilst the US had already begun a titanic struggle of rearmament and recruitment, *Rifle Battalion* accepted that material factors were only part of the problem as, 'Man is the final and decisive element in war. Combat is a moral struggle, and victory goes to the side that refuses to be discouraged. Numerical factors, armament, equipment and technical training affect morale but at the same time derive their full value from the moral qualities of the soldier'.

The infantry was charged with 'the principal mission in combat' and decisive results were usually to be obtained by 'offensive action', though numbers, materiel, and other factors would often mean that defensive missions also had to be tackled. It was assumed that infantry units could overcome 'improvised' resistance, or 'isolated hostile elements' unaided, but that 'co-ordinated continuing resistance' would be likely to require the assistance of 'powerful supporting weapons' for successful outcome. Whilst the three-battalion regiment was the 'complete tactical and administrative unit', the rifle battalion was regarded as the 'complete tactical unit'. It was capable of 'assignment to a mission requiring the application of all the usual foot Infantry means of action'. All the weapons of the rifle battalion could be 'manhandled over a distance of several hundred yards'.

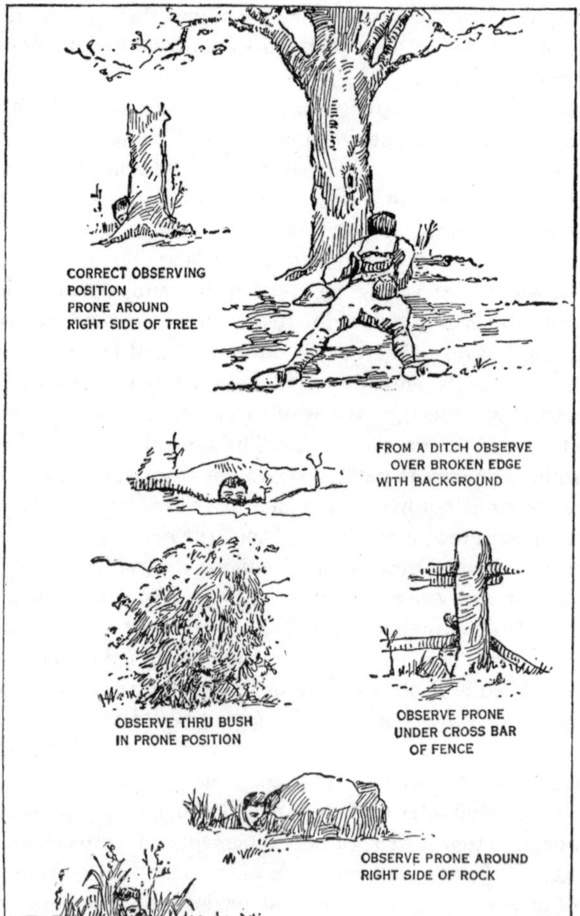

Some US fieldcraft for individual observation on the battlefield. From the *Soldier's Handbook*, 1941.

The 'approach march' was defined as commencing once a battalion came within medium artillery range, or about 10 miles, of the enemy. In daylight it was then assumed that the advancing force would have to abandon 'the route of march' and adopt other formations, such as platoon single files or 'column of twos', going forward by 'long bounds' from one objective to the next. Dispersion did not need to be great where there was cover from fire or observation, and friendly formations in front, but units could cross dangerous areas 'by infiltration', gathering together again once an open space was crossed. Within the rifle platoons commanders nominated a 'base squad' to which the tactical deployments of the others conformed. By giving personal direction to the base squad the platoon commander could thereby effectively regulate the movement of the whole. Within companies it was usual for the rifle platoons to go first, followed by the weapons platoon. Commanders had to be suspicious of

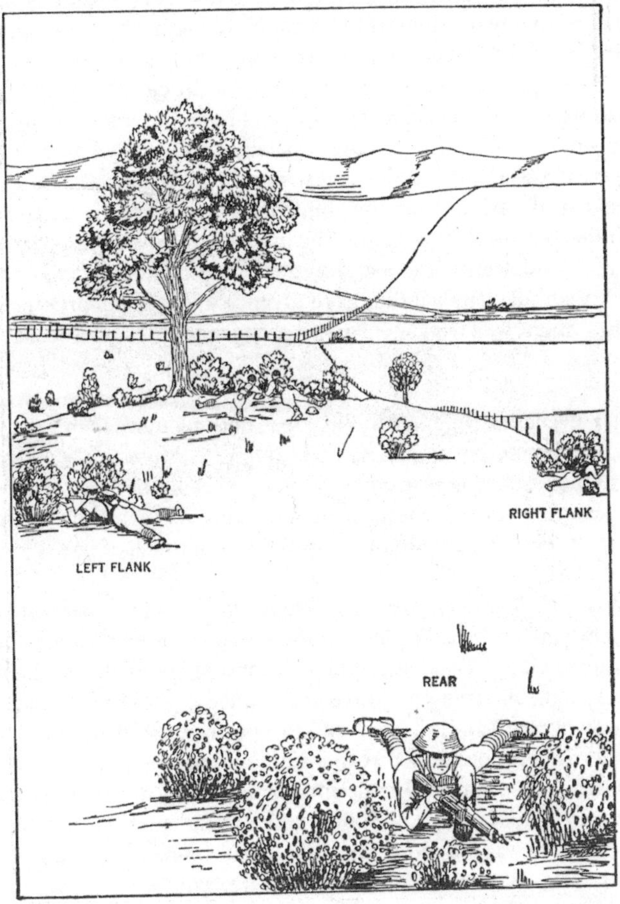

A US patrol adopts a covered position for observation: from FM 7-5 *Organisation and Tactics of Infantry: The Rifle Battalion*, 1940.

previously shelled areas or isolated features as these were likely to be pre-registered by the enemy and decide whether these should be skirted round or simply moved through as rapidly as possible. The ultimate objective of the approach march was to get the troops close to the enemy ready for action, but with minimum loss. The approach march was at an end as soon as the zone of effective small-arms fire was entered. For an attack of any scale, or had benefit of thorough preplanning, initial advances could be to designated 'assembly areas' in relatively safe spots that allowed units to reform before the assault.

When in proximity to the enemy leading rifle units progressed in extended order 'reconnoitring so as to prevent elements other than patrols being taken by surprise fire by infantry weapons'. Designated reconnaissance teams were allowed freedom of movement, and encouraged maximum use of cover – as for example in crawling carefully to breaks in a skyline rather than wandering over a crest, remaining still to observe and check that no enemy overlooked the path, climbing trees, and keeping back from doors and windows of buildings. Wide detours were fully acceptable in avoiding open spaces or too close a proximity to an enemy post. For the close security of platoons two men per squad were also designated as 'scouts'. These were more limited in that they were to move 'boldly' from cover to cover, usually within 500yd of their parent body. Often they were close enough to give visual signals, perhaps with one a little in front of the other so that the signal from the point could be relayed via his comrade back to the squad. Unlike reconnaissance teams, the main job of which was to collect information on the enemy and details of topography and equipment, platoon scouts performed their task more than adequately if they gave advance warning and prevented ambushes. In doing so they might well trigger enemy fire. As jaundiced squad scout Henri Atkins put it,

> A point man needs a willingness to die. He is nothing more than a decoy. When he is shot, the enemy position is revealed. Don't confuse this willingness with 'bravery'. A point man is just doing his job, what he has been trained to do. Usually a scout is way out ahead of the attacking forces, ready to signal back enemy contact. He has a chance of survival, but not much of one.

According to *Rifle Battalion*, weapons were the 'means of combat', and the building block of all higher infantry formations was the squad – 'the elementary combat unit' – with a rifle squad being defined as a leader, second in command, and a minimum of five riflemen, ten at full strength. Three such squads, plus an automatic rifle squad of leader, second in command, six men, and two or three automatic rifles, made up the platoon. Three rifle platoons and a weapons platoon made up the rifle company. For general purposes, 'short range' was defined as anything up to 200yd; 'close' up to 400yd; 'middle' to 600yd; 'long' to 1,500yd; and 'distant' anything greater. Ideally, the frontage of a battalion was not more than 1,000yd; a company 500yd; a platoon 200yd; and the squad 75yd. Where wider frontages were required the practice was not to increase the distance between individual troops, but to leave gaps between the elements. An uneven distribution was perfectly acceptable, and could be turned to advantage by using such gaps for the flanking fire of machine guns. The preparation of the battalion-level attack was estimated to take a minimum of 1½ hours, commencing with the commander's personal reconnaissance, followed by issuance of oral orders to a brief officer-group meeting, transmission of orders to all parts of the unit, and finally the advance.

In developing the attack it was expected that the commander would issue tasks to sub-units in terms of initial positions, directions of attack, zones of action, and objectives, but the smaller the unit the less detailed the instructions would be. A commander 'prescribes a detailed tactical plan only so far as he can reasonably estimate the hostile resistance to be expected'. However, in attacks against co-ordinated resistance fire plans for support weapons were prepared,

> When practicable, fires to dominate located resistance and neutralise areas from which hostile fire would be most dangerous are prearranged. Provision is made for engaging targets revealed during the course of the attack. Each unit seeks necessary augmentation of its own fire support by requesting that higher headquarters provide support from means under its control . . . In the absence of tanks, the fire of divisional artillery constitutes the basis of the fire plan of infantry regiments and battalions. The artillery neutralizes target areas in successive concentrations; it shells the nearer targets until the progress of the attack makes it necessary to transfer fire to a more distant zone. Fires are arranged in consultation with the commander of the supporting artillery.

It was a company commander's job to ensure that supporting fires co-ordinated with the actions of the platoons 'in place and in time', perhaps by designating successive objectives and pushing in his light machine guns close behind the platoons. He was also to look for the ideal places to launch assaults, checking where resistance might be weakening. The infantry support weapons concentrated on targets too close for the artillery to hit safely, point targets revealed during the action, and 'opportunity' targets, though heavy machine guns could also be used to reinforce artillery by long-range fire. Mortars were placed as far forward as cover and ammunition supply permitted, with the 60mm type 'within 400 yards of the front line'. In using them effectively observation was crucial. Light machine guns were used to fire through gaps in depth across the front of their own companies, or to flanks. Frontal fire was regarded as reserved for emergencies. Some weapons were held ready for rapid advance to positions for flanking fire. Others displaced forward as necessary.

The key offensive technique was 'fire and movement', and the closest possible co-ordination of the two was required so the infantry 'may close with the enemy and break his resistance'. Indeed, as was explained in a passage that was but modest rephrasing of a passage from the book *Infantry in Battle* a few years previously, 'Fire destroys or neutralizes the enemy and must be used to protect all movement in the presence of the enemy not masked by cover, darkness, fog or smoke. Through movement infantry places itself in positions which increase its destructive powers by decrease of range, by the development of convergent fires, and by flanking action'. Commonly, supporting weapons were well forward, allowing visual observation from emplacements: the infantrymen themselves were assumed to have highly destructive fire potential against 'unsheltered personnel' but against those under cover flat trajectory weapons were only of a neutralising effect. In moving sub-units were to take full advantage of broken or rolling terrain, avoiding whenever possible conspicuous or isolated features upon which the enemy might easily focus his fire. The very fact that progress against enemy concentrations was likely to be uneven could be used to advantage by taking flanks as they appeared, as for example by moving machine guns into new positions. As one terrain feature was occupied the advance to the next was organised – 'fire bases' being prepared for the next move. In close assaulting the enemy the best technique was to advance to the nearest available cover, then,

> The assault of rifle units is usually initiated by units whose close approach has been favoured by the terrain or those which have encountered weak enemy resistance. A heavy burst of fire is delivered by all available weapons, following which the troops rush the hostile position. The assault of a unit is supported by every element in position to render resistance.

On arrival troops securing a lodgement in the enemy position were to turn their automatic weapons onto the flanks of any adjacent resistance, or upon retreating enemy. As far as possible, successful attacks were pushed right through the enemy lines, and the most advanced detachments 'pushed forward without regard to the progress of units on their flanks'.

Details on tactical movement were filled in by the 1941 *Soldier's Handbook*. Some of the advice was fairly obvious, as for example in lying flat and moving extremely cautiously when there was danger of being observed, or taking advantage of hedges, walls, and folds in the ground. However, a number of patrol formations and drills were also included, dependent on mission. 'Security patrols' for example might be used as advanced guards, rear guards, or flank patrols. Advanced and rear guards were likely to be disposed on both sides of a track or road, and 'so arranged as best to let the leader control it, to make a poor target for enemy fire, and to permit all members to fire quickly to the front or either flank'. Such patrols were usually under standing orders to engage any enemy within effective fire range, and to send report of anything seen if they could not. Flank patrols could move alongside the route way at a given distance, or be concealed static protection. Extensive use of patrols was to be made in any direction where a flank might be exposed to the enemy. When in danger areas and until actually engaged, stealthy patrol movement was assumed, with for example streams being crossed one man at a time whilst others covered the ground. Reconnaissance patrols taken by surprise used a drill in which the first man to apprehend the threat called out the direction of the enemy. His comrades could then come to his aid on either side, and by doing so any small or isolated group of the enemy could be flanked. Wherever possible, patrol-squad leaders were encouraged to rush unprepared enemy individuals or small bodies. Night patrols required particular planning, and for these prearranged recognition signals were particularly vital.

Defensive infantry combat might take the form of 'sustained defence' or 'delaying actions' – these might be adopted deliberately, or be forced by the enemy. In sustained defence the usual infantry mission was to 'stop the enemy by fire in front of the battle position, to repel his assault by close combat if he reaches it, and to eject him by counter attack in case he enters it'. As defending forces were likely to be weaker than attacking ones that had been concentrated for the purpose, defenders made maximum use of screening and concealment. Protection was not to be sought at the expense of disclosing dispositions as, 'unmasked defensive positions will be promptly neutralised, if not destroyed, by superior hostile means of action'. Accordingly, the defence acted 'by surprise', varying its procedure and making every effort to keep the enemy in doubt about the main line of resistance and its principle elements. The enemy might be misled by camouflage, dummy works, screening by security detachments, and activity ahead of the main position. Whilst defenders relied heavily on fire, they were to remain 'mobile and aggressive. Weak 'holding elements' at the front took advantage of the power of modern weapons to cover large areas and were reinforced by reserves shifted to meet the attacker with maximum strength and counter attacks.

Though main lines of resistance were often selected by higher authority, battalion and company commanders were to pick 'detailed locations' for smaller units taking particular account of observation and natural obstacles. Troops were to see, but not be seen, denying the enemy ability to view approaches to the position from the rear. Good communications in the rear were desirable to allow flow of men and materials to vital points. Sometimes reverse slopes would be adopted, with just small posts and machine guns on crests. Salients and re-entrants in the defensive position allowed for flanking fire from machine guns. Defenders were not to be distributed evenly, but to take maximum advantage of terrain and depth of positions and concentrate on key locations. Defending units might usefully be divided into three: the 'security' echelon; 'combat' echelon; and reserve.

'Combat outposts' on the German model formed the main element of security detachments beyond the main 'battle position'. In larger defensive zones complete battalions could be given over to outpost duty together with artillery and anti-tank weapons. One outpost battalion might be given 2,000 to 2,500yd frontage to cover. Within the battle position itself were concentrated and co-ordinated all the resources required for 'decisive action', including a network of 'fortified supporting points' prepared for all-round defence. 'Lines' were to be avoided unless a defence was regarded as a 'delaying action' as a system based on holding successive lines was likely to result in dispersion of force. The 'holding garrisons' of points would consist of small groups usually built up around automatic weapons, positioned in depth and in 'such a manner that the fires of each cross the front or flank of adjacent or advanced elements'. Unoccupied areas were covered by fire and counter attack. Frontages, though based on the 'general' figures already given, were varied according to terrain and situation, with narrower unit frontages and greater firepower devoted to vulnerable places where the enemy had benefit of covered approaches allowing them to get closer to the defenders. Conversely, obstacles allowed fewer troops to cover greater distances, and hence wider frontages for given units. Boundaries between units were not, however, to be on critical localities, as this would tend to divided responsibilities and confusion in event of attack.

Defensive fire was crucial,

> The skeleton of the main line of resistance is constituted by machine guns and anti-tank weapons. Close defence of the position is largely based upon reciprocal flanking action of machine guns. The direction of fire of flanking defences often permits their concealment from direct observation of the enemy and their protection from frontal fire. They therefore have the advantage of being able to act with surprise effect in addition to that of protection and concealment. Frontal and flanking defences mutually supplement one another and subject the attacker to convergent fires. Gaps in the fire bands of machine guns are covered by artillery, mortars, automatic rifles and rifles. Riflemen and automatic riflemen furnish enough close protection for automatic weapons executing flanking fires and cover frontal sectors of fire. Premature fires from positions in the main line of resistance disclose the main defensive dispositions to the annihilating fire of the hostile artillery.

The best antidote to defending weapons being knocked out by enemy artillery was for them to wait until the enemy infantry got close enough that their supporting guns had to cease fire. At that point defenders could open fire on the attacking infantry, gaining surprise, and without fear that they would be hit in return.

The effectiveness of defensive fire positions could be much improved by the use of obstacles, such as wire, but they were not to be positioned in such a way as to telegraph the location of the main line of resistance. Wire could be disguised by being discontinuous, laid in vegetation, or put in stream beds. Where time allowed the protection of a position was progressively improved, not only by building up physical defences and digging trenches and bunkers, but by improving communications, stockpiling munitions, and protecting defenders against weather. Shell-proof shelters for reserves were regarded as a priority. Trenches were not, however, to be allowed to become conspicuous. Within battle position fire zones were adjusted so as to leave no gaps.

Though *Rifle Battalion*, 1940 was actually quite a good grounding for action at the time it was introduced, it was largely based on second-hand experience, and produced at a time of great change. As a 'battalion' instruction it was also not highly detailed on matters pertaining to squads. All these factors set limitations on its effective shelf life and scope. A number of other manuals and documents were, therefore, used as supplements or updates, especially where new weapons were introduced or new factors encountered. One of the most important of these was FM 21-45 *Protective Measures, Individuals and Small Units*, signed off by the Secretary of War at the end of 1941, and published in March 1942. This filled in many gaps, notably detail of concealment and cover, camouflage, digging of foxholes and trenches, awareness of booby traps, communications and information security, and protection against aircraft, chemical weapons, and tanks. It was intended to supersede the single chapter devoted to some of these aspects in the 1938 'Basic Field Manual', which was by now pretty much out of date.

Significantly, *Protective Measures* acknowledged that modern war put a higher premium than ever upon 'individual initiative' and stressed both the role of the soldier and the 'small group', on whom rested 'more and more' the course of battle. It mattered little whether the task was bringing up a truck load of ammunition, preparing a meal, or outflanking a machine gun: if all these could be accomplished intelligently and

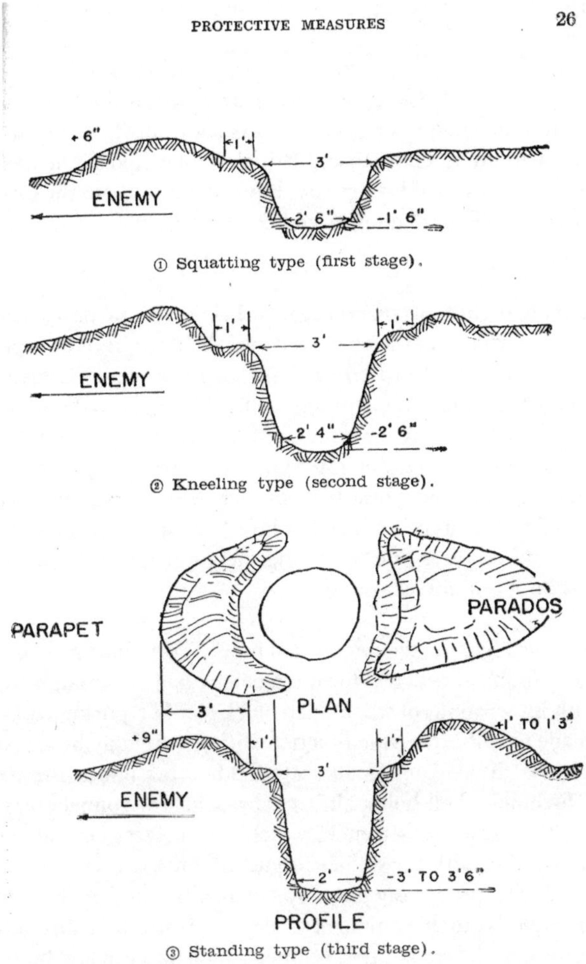

The development of the foxhole, from squatting, to kneeling, and finally standing cover for the rifleman, as described in FM 21-45 *Protective Measures, Individuals and Small Units*, 1942.

unseen by the enemy every one of them would contribute to the probability of success and the 'destruction of the enemy'. As if to emphasise how personal war could be, and the importance to the individual, *Protective Measures* and the latest soldier's handbooks now spoke to the US private soldier in person. 'You' were told how to protect yourself and handle your weapons — this was not some exercise in describing someone else in the third person, this was very much as though Uncle Sam was speaking direct to the citizen about his own responsibilities and the best way to stay alive whilst fulfilling them. Of course these manuals could be, and often were, used as teaching materials by others – and it is a fair guess that even the most conscientious and literate only dipped into them in places, but the message was clearer and more a matter of the individual knowing his job than ever before.

Interestingly, some of the material from *Protective Measures* did also appear in FM 21-100 *Soldier's Handbook* of 1941, republished in a revised edition in March 1942. The information on camouflage and concealment was significant, but in many respects repeated that already found in German and British publications. The new material on 'hasty entrenchments' was arguably of greater interest, but was not the easiest to impart to reluctant soldiery for whom digging large holes was often not thought to be part of the job description,

> In order to provide natural protection against hostile fire by hasty construction you must have a knowledge of the tools available, their use, and the types of hasty entrenchment which will afford cover. Permanent or semi permanent cover requires a long time and many men to construct, and will normally be done under the supervision of an officer. When your mission permits, you should provide or improve your cover by digging. You must know the various types of cover which you can provide and learn how best to construct them by digging them. These types have been developed by survivors of hostile attacks and tested under fire. It is hard work, and requires practice to dig them quickly and properly. Learn how before hostile action forces you to.

Many who did not learn how to dig quickly had indeed very short military careers: but some lazier GIs also found short cuts, for if the enemy had not thoughtfully ploughed up the ground with his weapons of war a small block of TNT purloined from the engineers might be made to fulfil the same function with gratifyingly little spadework.

Protective Measures divided up small-scale field works under the heads of skirmisher's trench; foxholes; shell holes; slit trenches; shallow connecting trenches and squad positions. The skirmisher's trench, which had in fact been taught during the First World War, was dug with the soldier prone, head towards the enemy. Naturally, it was best executed with proper digging implements, but under fire anything would suffice, as for example 'your bayonet, mess kit cover, sticks or any other available object'. Lying on his left, the soldier first scraped a hole for head and body, then rolled into it. Then, lying on his right, excavated to his left enlarging the hole enough to get his head, shoulders and hips well down. Earth was thrown to the front so improving cover for the head and shoulders as quickly as possible. This accomplished the soldier then extended his scrape backwards enough to get his legs under cover.

> In average soil you can get fair protection in about 10 minutes and finish the trench in less than an hour. The finished trench will give you protection against flat trajectory small arms fire but only partial protection against high explosive shell or bomb fragments. You should enlarge the forward portion into a foxhole as soon as enemy fire permits.

The foxhole was described as the 'more usual form of hasty entrenchment' and gave fair protection against bombs and shells as well as direct small-arms fire. It could be dug prone or crouching but was better made from standing when not under fire. It was dug progressively allowing squatting, kneeling, and finally standing fire positions as time allowed. With full-sized dedicated tools a standing foxhole could be completed in less than an hour, but with infantry implements in cramped conditions an hour and a half was considered more normal. In firm soil the lower portion of the hole could be enlarged to allow the occupant to curl up at the bottom, and so secure the best possible protection, even against tanks driving over. The last refinement was a sump at the bottom, 'larger than a canteen cup', to allow for bailing when thc hole got wet. Shell holes were a good starting point for battlefield cover as much of the hard work was already done, and the enemy might not be able to distinguish which were being used as infantry cover.

Where a shell hole was purposely converted to best effect it was recommended that the soldier dig '2 or 3 feet into the forward slope to get a good firing position and lateral protection from shell fragments and enfilade fire'. Similar improvements could be speedily made to roadside ditches, banks, or other ready made features. In practice and with time it was found that two-man positions were often best, as a buddy allowed one soldier to rest and act as lookout during construction, or both worked together for maximum speed and encouragement. With the double foxhole, pair of holes, or converted shell hole complete it was now possible for one man to sleep whilst the other acted as sentry. In any event, morale was better and nasty surprises fewer with a second man in the hole. As the 1944 *Infantry Anti Tank Company* manual later explained, the two-man hole gave only slightly less protection, but was used when men needed to work in pairs, or 'for psychological reasons, battlefield comradeship is desirable'. Once everyone in a unit had cover it was sometimes useful to link the individual positions using the 'shallow connecting trench'. For creeping, crawling, and occasional use a depth of about 2ft was deemed adequate, though such slender cover was not ideal to fire from or occupy for protracted periods.

The slit trenches also had uses.

> It gives excellent protection against all types of fire, air attack, and in firm soil, or when revetted in soft, provides protection against tanks passing overhead. It is excellent type of cover for the immediate protection of gun and vehicle crews and for anti tank lookouts. A slit trench is less visible to ground observation if it is dug parallel to the front and the spoil (dug out earth) scattered and concealed rather than used as a parapet. The cut sod should be saved and used for camouflage. Such a trench can be concealed by methods similar to those used in camouflage of a foxhole. A slit trench should be as narrow as possible and still admit you, and deep enough to permit you to get below the surface of the ground. A standing slit trench may be caved in by concentrated artillery fire. For this reason one dug in soft ground should be well braced and revetted. A single such trench should not be required to hold more than two individuals. When more are to be protected, dig more trenches. Slit trenches in the shape of a chevron or cross, about six feet on a side, will ensure enfilade protection against fire from tanks.

The basics of 'squad positions' were not hugely changed, but *Protective Measures* was far more detailed in its advice, perhaps more so than might be practical under many battle conditions. Ideally, the squad leader deployed each man personally with an eye to 'all-round defence'. Every soldier was also allotted primary and secondary 'sectors of fire' – primary sectors usually being those areas fronting the squad in the direction of the enemy, whilst secondary sectors covered across the flanks to the frontages of adjacent squads at maximum distances of perhaps 200 to 400yd. Supplementary positions were also prepared to allow riflemen to shift to cover the flanks and rear of the squad position.

> Fox holes for each primary and supplementary position are started as soon as possible after you deploy your squad and more fully developed as time and situation permit. Individual fox holes should be about five yards apart or they may be placed in pairs. If the position is to be held for some time, have the fox holes connected where necessary by shallow connecting trenches. If your men are to occupy the holes overnight, have them extend the fox holes on each side or deepen the connecting trenches so they can lie prone while sleeping . . . If an automatic weapon, automatic rifle, machine gun or submachine gun is available you should site it in an advanced position near the centre of your group of fox holes so that its fire can cover the entire sector of your squad and adjacent squads. Select an alternative position nearby to which it can move, if necessary, and deliver the same fire. Select a secondary position to permit its fire to cover to the rear.

From mid-1942 the US infantry manuals were comprehensively updated with the appearance of FM 7-10 *Rifle Company, Rifle Regiment* in June, and a new *Rifle Battalion* that September. Arguably, the new company manual was significant in that it appeared to suggest greater responsibility at lower levels of command, and that companies might themselves have greater combat significance than had been imagined before December 1941. For whilst the company acted in accordance with the battalion commander's plan and mission, and was likely to be assigned either to the battalion 'forward echelon' or the 'battalion reserve', many of the smaller decisions could fall to the company commander. This was especially true when the company was detached,

> When the company is acting alone, it is employed as directed by the commander who assigned the company its mission. The company commander will, of necessity, have to make more decisions on his own initiative than he will when operating with his battalion. His major decisions, as well as frequent reports of location and progress, are submitted promptly to the higher commander.

As a matter of course the company commander was responsible for administration, discipline, supply, training and control of his company: but *Rifle Company* also made it clear that he had an important tactical role. He was to anticipate and plan for prospective missions, supervise his subordinates, and decide on a course of action 'in conformity with orders from higher authority'. This required a good 'estimate of situation' before the issuing of clear orders,

> Having decided upon a detailed plan of action to carry out an assigned mission, the company commander must assign specific missions to his subordinate units. Company orders are usually issued orally to the leaders concerned or as oral or written messages. Sketches are furnished when practicable. Prior to combat, subordinates frequently can be assembled to receive the order. This facilitates orientation prior to the issuance of orders and enables the company commander to ensure that orders are understood. . . . Whenever practicable, the order is issued at a point from which terrain features of importance to subordinates can be pointed out. In attack, this often will be impracticable because of hostile observation and fires. If time is limited and leaders are separated, the company commander will issue his orders in fragmentary form. Leaders of units which are engaged with the enemy will not be called away from their units for the purpose of receiving orders.

Once combat was joined the company commander's job became complex indeed. He was expected to know where the enemy was, and was capable of doing; keep track of both front and flanks, ensuring 'all-round protection'; anticipate the needs of his platoons for supporting fire, and ensure that the sub-units supported one another; and check that his orders were carried out, whilst controlling company transportation and ammunition resupply. Nevertheless, he was still expected to find time to make 'frequent reports' to the battalion commander. Crucial to the performance of these tasks was the 'Command Group', comprising a second in command, first sergeant, communications sergeant, bugler, messengers, and orderly. The second in command, usually a first lieutenant, was expected to keep abreast,

> of the tactical situation as it affects the company, replaces the company commander should the latter become a casualty, and performs any other duty assigned him by the company commander. During combat, he is in charge of the command post until he assumes command of the company, or of a platoon. He maintains communication with the company and battalion commanders. He notifies the battalion commander of changes in location of the command post.

The first sergeant usually assisted the second in command, and in combat might take responsibility for aspects of administration and supply, though *in extremis* he was used as a platoon commander, or as a substitute taking charge of the command post in case of casualties.

The communications sergeant naturally took charge of all aspects of communications, as well as assisting in preparation of sketches. Though often unsung, the duties of the communication sergeants were crucial, and when well performed could give the US infantry an advantage over both friend and foe as US units were usually better equipped in this department. The SCR 300 ('Signal Corps Radio') was a conventional-looking 32lb backpack model, giving a range of about 5 miles and was used between company and battalion. It could be operated by one man, but also be carried by one person whilst a handset was used by another. The little SCR 536 'handy talkie' eventually issued down to platoon level was a genuine innovation. First produced in

1941, it weighed only 5lb, had an integral antenna, and a battery life of about a day in normal use. The whole set was held up to the ear and the operator depressed a switch to talk and released it whilst receiving. Though the range of the SCR 536 was less than a mile over some types of terrain, this was often adequate to bridge the gaps between company and platoons. Often at lower tactical levels voice-to-voice communications were used 'in the clear' and with no scrambling and only modest use of codes. It was reasoned, probably correctly, that in fast-moving situations swift delivery of accurate information was more important than a high level of security. In any event, when sets were first captured by the Germans in Sicily they were very impressed with them. Taking no chances, *Rifle Company*, 1942 also prescribes that as soon as a company is deployed each platoon should have a messenger report to company HQ.

In offensive situations it was expected that until the company left the route of march many decisions would be taken at higher levels, but as soon as deployment took place, or the unit was endangered, or under fire, the company commander would have responsibility. His orders, often issued in 'fragmentary' form due to pressures of time, would inform the platoons of known dispositions of both enemy and friendly troops; mission, objectives, and directions of march, including landmarks; frontage and reconnaissance requirements, and what actions to take in the event of being attacked. Where his company acted as part of a larger movement his 'base' platoon would act in conformity with that of the company designated as 'base' company within the battalion. Usually the company commander's position would be at the front, and he was encouraged to make 'personal reconnaissance', but not attempt to tell his platoon commanders what precise formations and dispositions to adopt, unless what they were already doing disagreed with overall objectives and mission. In open terrain it was perfectly acceptable for platoons to be anything up to about 300yd apart so as to make best use of any cover or vantage points, but in close terrain, and especially woods, the platoons were to close up sufficiently that they were in visual contact.

The drill on contact was that only the element under fire would engage where they were – other platoons, and any squads not engaged, attempted to continue toward the objective, taking 'every advantage of concealment and cover and assuring security of their flanks' as they did so. By this method and 'fire and movement' they worked round the enemy and thereby assisted those held up. Where attacks on specific points were pre-planned the platoon commander had several options; perhaps holding back a part as a 'manoeuvring element', or sending forward a few riflemen aided by a BAR able to creep forward under cover and engage the enemy by surprise in a manner impossible for the whole platoon.

In any event, the platoon commander followed his attacking echelon closely, so as to be able to observe and direct his men.

> When the platoon comes under effective small arms fire, further advance is usually by fire and movement. The enemy is pinned to the ground by frontal (and flanking) fire, under which other elements of the platoon manoeuvre forward, using all available cover to protect themselves against hostile fire. In turn, the original manoeuvring elements may occupy firing positions and cover the advance of the elements initially firing. The platoon leader hits the weak spot in

the enemy position by having his support attack against the point of least resistance, or by manoeuvring his support around a flank to strike the enemy with surprise fire on his flank or rear . . . When fire from other hostile positions situated to the flank or rear makes it impossible to launch a flanking attack against a particular area, an assaulting force is built up by infiltration close to the hostile resistance. This force is protected by the fire of the rest of the platoon and of supporting weapons. One or more automatic rifles may be employed to neutralize the fires of the hostile flank or rear elements.

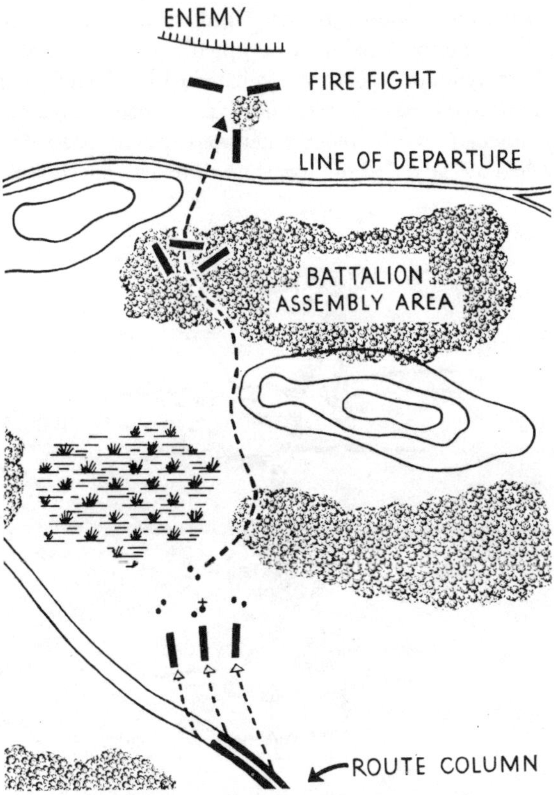

RIFLE PLATOON IN APPROACH MARCH

The above diagram is schematic and illustrates the leading platoon of a rifle company from the time it leaves the route column until the fire fight commences.

A typical sequence of events for the US rifle platoon as part of a battalion attack from the approach march. The platoon deploys from the road it has been using and advances in lose columns to the battalion assembly area. In co-ordination with the remainder of the battalion and the covering fire of artillery and other units it crosses the 'line of departure', arriving at the firefight with two of its three sections deployed in rough skirmish lines and the third in support. Taking advantage of cover, the enemy is now brought under effective fire until opportunity for close assault. From *The Rifle Platoon and Squad in Offensive Combat*, 1943.

Having achieved a final jumping off point close to the enemy, this being defined as being as close as the troops were able to get without masking their supporting fire, the assault could begin. Though this might be a 'general assault' ordered by a company or battalion commander, it was equally likely to be started 'in the heat of battle' on the initiative of a squad, or even 'a few individuals'. Any such attack warranted the immediate co-operation of every individual or unit within sight. Whilst platoon commanders would give the signal to stop supporting fire as his men crossed the last few yards, the attackers were to 'assault fire' during their final progress, bayonets fixed. At this crucial moment they would take 'full advantage of existing cover such as tanks, boulders, trees, walls and mounds, advance rapidly toward the enemy and fire as they advance at areas known or believed to be occupied'.

Gung-ho as this may sound, the battle of what one Free French commentator in Italy called the 'last hundred metres' was often illusive, a fugitive beast, rarely seen, and less often caught on camera. Not infrequently men were nerved for final assault only to find that the enemy had already fled, or were, more or less successfully, attempting to

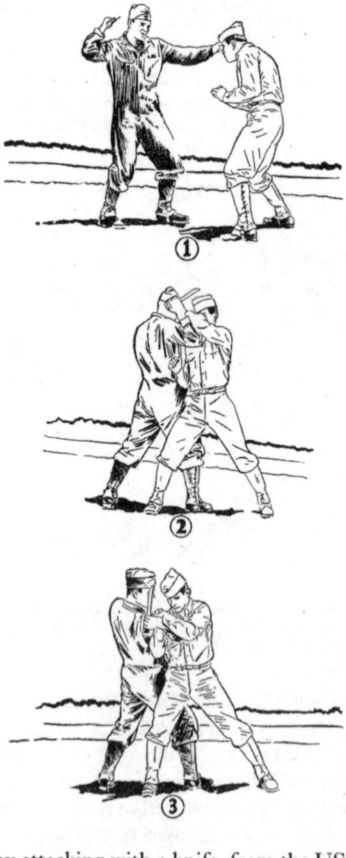

Disarming an enemy attacking with a knife, from the US manual *Bayonet*, 1943.

surrender. The empty battlefield was so for a reason, as to linger was to invite death. As a US observer, also in Italy, described,

> One never saw masses of men assaulting the enemy. What one observed, in apparently unrelated patches, was small, loose bodies of men moving down narrow defiles or over steep inclines, going methodically from position to position between long halts and the only continuous factor was the roaring and crackling of the big guns. One felt baffled at the unreality of it all. Unseen groups of men were fighting other men that they rarely saw.

What actually happened at such decisive moments in the infantry battle was analysed by Major GS Johns of US 29th Division in Normandy. First a machine gun might be knocked out. A man or two was killed or wounded, then:

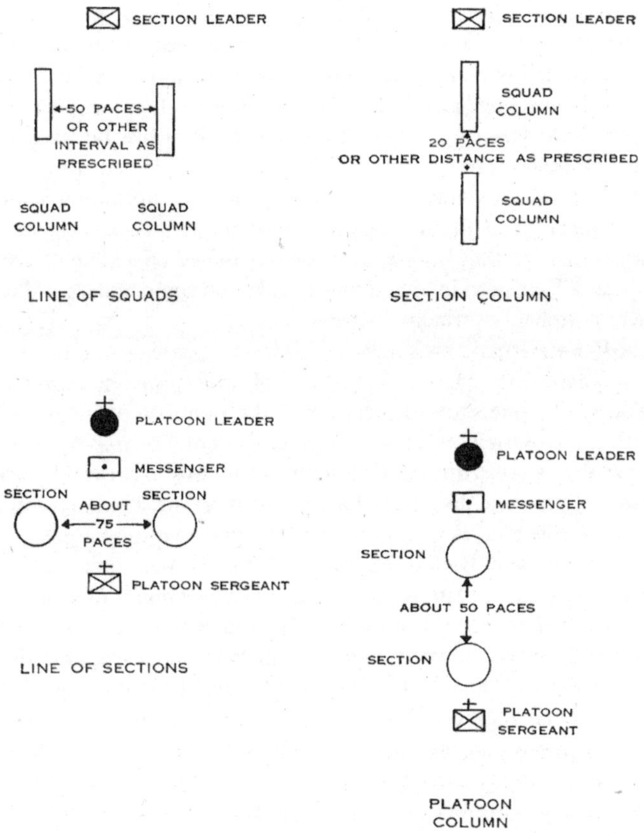

Possible arrangements of squads during the approach march from FM 7-10 *Rifle Company, Infantry Regiment*, 1944.

> Eventually the leader of the stronger force, usually the attackers, may decide that he has weakened his opponents enough to warrant a large concerted assault, preceded by a concentration of all the mortar and artillery support he can get. Or the leader of the weaker force may see that he will be overwhelmed by such an attack and pull back to another position in his rear. Thus goes the battle – a rush, a pause, some creeping, a few isolated shots here and there, some artillery fire, some mortars, some smoke, more creeping, another pause, dead silence, more firing, a great concentration of fire followed by a concerted rush. Then the whole process starts all over again.

Useful as it was, the advice of the 1942 manual was not given in isolation, nor was it regarded as the final word. In addition to two formal amendments, *Infantry School* offered a series of pictorial supplements, intended not only to keep the subject fresh and up to date but to present what might otherwise be dry and dense material in a fashion accessible to the NCO. *Training Bulletin* GT-20 of March 1943 for example expanded specifically on the subject of the approach march. By means of cartoon-style sketches, a simplified text, and tactical diagrams it showed exactly how the squad and platoon were expected to look, lined up for inspection, and in a series of tactical situations. Pictures showed how useful the informal platoon column was in moving through woods, fog, smoke or darkness, narrow spaces, and artillery fire, but also how dangerous it could prove if exposed to fire from the front. Also explained were the ideas of the 'base squad', tactical movement, and scouting. Platoon formations such as line of squads, and dispositions with one squad forward and two back – or vice versa – were similarly illustrated. As the *Training Bulletin* was issued on a scale of one per platoon it would appear to have been intended to reach platoon commanders and sergeants, and through them – probably verbally, their men.

The final US statement on small-unit infantry tactics prior to D-Day was the deservedly well renowned March 1944 edition of *Rifle Company, Infantry Regiment*. A solid 300 pages, this managed to incorporate the minutiae of several previous field manuals with some of the handy pictorial references of *Training Bulletin*. It encapsulated, so far as they were required for infantry, diagrams of the field works pioneered by the *Protective Measures* and *Field Engineering* manuals. Updated information was also given on the role and issue of individual weapons within platoons. Rifle grenade launchers were now widely distributed, ideally three per squad, plus one each to communication sergeants, platoon guides, squad and section leaders in light machine-gun squads, and even to truck drivers. Carbine launchers were also on hand, with one specifically allotted to the company bugler. Launchers were used for both the anti-tank grenade and, by means of an adaptor, the anti-personnel Mark II type. Hand grenades were described as being 'especially useful' against weapon crews or other small groups where they were located in places inaccessible to rifle fire, but inside the minimum range of high-angle rifle grenade fire.

For basic fire and movement the squad was regarded as three teams 'Able' which was the two scouts; 'Baker' comprising four men with the BAR; and the 'Charlie' five-man manoeuvre and assault team. The leader initially attached himself to the scouts. Where casualties intervened it was actually often the practice to make do with two

British troops pause during the advance on Venlo, 1944. Nearest to the camera is a Bren gunner, weapon reversed over the shoulder for comfort. The rest of the team carry the No. 4 rifle. Officially adopted in 1941, this was a slightly modified version of the old Short Magazine Lee–Enfield, or 'SMLE'. The helmets are worn with nets and garnished with hessian as recommended in *Infantry Training*.

How to Shoot the US Army Rifle, 'a graphic handbook on correct shooting' published by the *Infantry Journal* in 1943. Popularly written and well illustrated, *How to Shoot* drew on the editors of *Life* magazine and made use of 'repetitive flash' photography to show not only how to use the Garand but how to adopt prone, kneeling, and sitting positions and rush from cover to cover in infantry combat. Arguably, it was not bettered until long after the war.

British infantry take some questionable cover behind munition boxes during combat in Italy. The sergeant is a photographer, armed only with a holstered .38 Enfield revolver. The next man is throwing a No. 36 Mills grenade. Originally designed in 1915, this powerful bomb was the main British high-explosive grenade of the Second World War, and could be rifle discharged from a cup attachment as well as hand thrown. It was best used from cover, or with the user flinging himself flat to avoid fragments.

Soviet archive picture showing a German NCO of the *Grossdeutschland* division armed with the 9mm MP 38. Not enough had been produced to arm all squad leaders at the beginning of the war, but the MP 38, and its slightly simplified successor the MP 40, were soon iconic arms, and over a million were manufactured by 1945. The MP 38 was well made, compact by virtue of its folding stock, and good enough for Allied infantry to want to pick up and use them whenever they could. For maximum effectiveness they were best used in very short bursts – this gave better accuracy and fewest stoppages whilst conserving ammunition.

Nicknamed the *Ofenrohr*, or 'stove pipe', the *Panzerschreck* was a German 8.8cm anti-tank rocket launcher inspired by the US bazooka, and first used in 1943. The example seen here is the second-generation type incorporating a shield with a small window to protect the user from the exhaust of the rocket as it left the barrel. Considerably lighter than small conventional anti-tank guns, the weapon remained in use to the end of the war.

The 1942 edition of Dr W Reibert's *Der Dienst Unterricht Im Heere*. Though not an official publication of army command or war ministry, 'Reibert' was one of the most popular manuals and frequently used in training. In its 342 pages it covered not only infantry tactics but highlights of German history; remarks on duty; a summary of orders and decorations, uniforms, ranks, and badges; weapons; gas defence; maps and navigation; field works; fieldcraft and even the basics of military duty with horses. Official instructions were supplemented by many semi-official and unofficial booklets in the Britain and the USA as well as Germany.

The *Panzerfaust* as featured on the front page of the *Berliner Illustrierte Zeitung*, 29 June, 1944. Whilst Nazi propaganda made much of the potential of the 'tank fist' as the personal 'anti-tank gun' of the individual, the ability of infantry to take on even heavy armour with all sorts of rocket weapons and shaped charges did herald a new chapter in the infantry-armour balance. For the Allies, often attempting to attack through built-up areas and fixed defences during 1943 to 1945, such innovations came at entirely the wrong moment.

The German *Granatwerfer 36* in the snow, c.1939. This little 5cm mortar was a standard-issue platoon weapon for much of the war. Over ½ million rounds were expended from this type of mortar during the French campaign of 1940 alone. However, production ceased in June 1943, and many were passed on to Croatia in 1944. The mortar broke down into two loads for transport, with the three-man team also able to carry five tin boxes of bombs. Its maximum range was about 575m.

Before sunset a US patrol moves off to its jumping off position near Klein Blittersdorf, Alsace, March 1945. After dark they will advance into the Siegfried Line to probe enemy defences. The men are well armed for maximum short-range night firepower with M3 'Grease guns', grenades, and at least two Colt Model 1911 semi-automatic pistols: the leader has a .30 cal carbine. All faces are blackened and soft caps worn.

The US M2 infantry mortar. This 60mm weapon originated from a French design, and was a good example of the class. Having a range of almost 2000yd, it fired a 3lb high-explosive bomb, or specialist rounds such as the 'illuminating' M83. If there was enough ammunition the mortar could be fired at anything up to eighteen rounds per minute for short periods, with more than one bomb in the air at any given moment. The M2 continued in use in various parts of the world long after 1945.

Men of 41st US Armoured Infantry aboard an M2 half-track during Operation Cobra, France 1944. The M2 was slightly shorter than the M3 that carried the basic armoured infantry rifle squads, and this example is fitted with the old 37mm anti-tank gun as well as two machine guns. Amongst the many items stowed on the carrier are coiled barbed wire, picquets, and tools, allowing for the preparation of a defensive position.

US infantry of 'Big Red 1' Division advance down a narrow lane near Faymonville during the battle for the Ardennes. Even at this stage of the war there was still much infantry movement on foot, and weather and terrain conditions as well as fuel shortage could limit the ability of troops on both sides to transport large numbers of men in motorised vehicles. Though fairly sophisticated snow camouflage clothing had been used as early as the First World War, the dress seen here has a distinctly improvised appearance.

A German soldier explains the *Steilhandgrenate* during weapons training, c.1939. Based on a First World War design, the grenade consisted of a thin metal cylindrical head mounted on a wooden stick. Through the centre of the stick ran the fuse, ignited by a pull on a cord. Capable of being thrown about 30m, the grenade relied mainly on blast effect, though a steel fragmentation sleeve could be fitted around the head.

The German MG 08 heavy machine gun firing during an exercise, c.1939. Introduced in 1908, the hefty water-cooled, belt-fed Maxim was theoretically no longer a front-line infantry weapon. Nevertheless, shortages of more modern machine guns and almost limitless demand for fixed position weapons made sure that it was still seen on the battlefield throughout the Second World War. The performance of the MG 08 was similar to that of the slightly more modern British Vickers machine gun, introduced in 1911.

A German *Richtschütze*, or machine gun 'No. 1', advancing with the MG 34, a holstered semi-automatic, ammunition belt, and belt kit for the machine gun. Usually, the gunner's belt pouch contained an extra bolt; oil bottle; anti-aircraft sight; tools; and other spares. When moving in squad column the gunner was close to the front, usually just behind the squad leader, and followed by the 'No. 2' who carried a spare barrel and ammunition box in addition to his own weapon. This picture was taken by a *Propaganda Kompanie* photographer during the advance into France in June 1940.

Men of the King's Own Scottish Borderers doubling on the town of Ulzen, April 1945. A Bren gunner is closest to the photographer, but further down the column can be seen riflemen and a PIAT gunner. Close examination shows that several of the team are carrying full-size spades, heavier than entrenching tools, but much more suitable for swift 'digging in'.

British infantry escort a Sherman tank during 'mopping up' operations in the Cantania sector of Sicily. As the original caption to this photo observed, the 'wooded and cultivated' areas of the island offered 'excellent cover' for anti-tank weapons and machine-gun nests. Accordingly, a platoon of infantry was attached to each tank, and the platoon and company commander of the infantry were linked to the tank commander by wireless. Whilst the tank rooted out machine-gun nests, the infantry concentrated on threats to the tank. These methods were a precursor to similar ideas used by both US and British forces on the Italian mainland and after D-Day.

A British sniper amongst woodland equipped with the No. 4 Mk 1 (T) sniper rifle. Essentially similar to the standard issue bolt-action No. 4 with its ten-round magazine, the Mk 1 (T) was fitted for a telescope and had a wooden cheek rest added to the butt. Many of the conversions were executed by London gunmakers Holland and Holland. This man, like many British snipers of the late war period, wears the Denison airborne-type smock. An extra layer over the battledress was useful when keeping still for long periods, but more importantly the Denison was printed with a camouflage pattern.

US troops examine an enemy hedgerow position in Normandy, 1944. The *bocage* terrain with its small fields, hedges, and walls formed a natural defence. In some instances the Germans burrowed through obstructions to form concealed rifle and MG positions, or climbed trees to create sniping and observation posts. Here a bivouac has been created in a ditch between hedges, concealed from both air and ground observation. The user has made himself more at home with overhead weather cover, bread, bottles of wine and champagne, and books to while away the time.

A mud splattered GI fallen on a pontoon bridge. Crossings and defiles presented rich pickings for snipers, machine guns, and artillery alike, as there was often nowhere to hide and units were sometimes forced to bunch dangerously together. Situations such as this give graphic illustration of the natural combat advantages reaped by intelligent defence.

A photograph from the series *Unsere Waffen SS*, showing troops armed with the K98k bolt-action rifle and Mauser *Schnellfeuer* R713 pistol. The *Schnellfeuer* was a good illustration of the fact that not all German weapons were perfect, nor did the *SS* always get the best weaponry. First introduced commercially in 1930, and later used in small numbers by the military, the R713 system consisted of a modified version of the old C96 'broomhandle' with wooden shoulder stock and distinctive twenty-round magazine. In theory, the result was a well-made, handy, selective fire, short carbine. In reality, it was far less effective than a sub-machine gun, fired a relatively light 7.63 round, and emptied at an impractically fast 15 rounds a second on full automatic.

A British PIAT gunner on the march. Whilst tolerably effective against tanks at close range and useful as a sort of miniature infantry howitzer out to several hundred yards, the 'Projector Infantry Anti-Tank' was a clumsy beast weighing 32lb, firing 3lb bombs. So it was that whilst enemy armoured vehicles were knocked out and the PIAT did some good work against pillboxes and bunkers, especially on D-Day, it was not really in the same league as the bazooka or other new rocket weapons. This infantryman has another trick in his arsenal; for tucked between his pack and gas cape is a No. 75 'Hawkins' anti-tank grenade. Introduced in 1942, this was best thrown, or dragged, in front of moving vehicles.

Abandoned German half-tracks in front of the Senate House casemate, Paris, 1944. Though the German Army used half-track vehicles for a multitude of different purposes and as mounts for a variety of weapons, there were never enough to provide all the *Panzergrenadiere* with armoured battle transport. The result was that aggressive fully fledged armoured infantry tactics were not always possible. Both US and British forces adopted rather less high-risk methods by 'debusing' before transport came under effective fire. This was probably wise given the improvement in hand-held anti-tank weapons later in the war.

Firing the MG 34 on exercise in a 'heavy' machine-gun role. Arguably the first true 'general-purpose' machine gun, the *Maschinengewehr* 34 served the German Army well – the only genuine reason for seeking replacement with the MG 42 later in the war being that the latter was simpler to produce. For accurate long-range support fire, as is seen here, the MG 34 was mounted on the *Lafette*, or tripod with sprung cradle. The gunner fires by means of a remote trigger, so that he does not even have to touch the weapon, and could even duck his head below cover whilst continuing to shoot.

DAS ALLES SIND INFANTERIEWAFFEN
Zielfernrohr-Scharfschützen unserer Grenadiere setzen mit sicherem Schuß den Gegner außer Gefecht

A German sniper with observers from the postcard series *Das Alles Sind Infanteriewaffen*. The bolt-action Kar 98k standard infantry carbine of the German Army in the Second World War II was little more than a short version of the old G 98 infantry rifle introduced at the end of the nineteenth century. It was handy, but inferior to both the US and British arms. The example seen here is fitted with the small *Zielfernrohr*, or telescopic sight. The team have been grouped unrealistically close together, presumably to create an interesting picture, but this shows that observers might be equipped with either binoculars or small periscopes.

A Spigot mortar at work with the Kent Home Guard. Whilst it threw massively destructive bombs, its weight made it far more useful as a position weapon than as a true infantry anti-tank piece. So it was that the much smaller PIAT was developed from the original concept. Spigot mortar pits, such as the one seen here, are still occasionally encountered as the archaeological remains of British anti-invasion defences.

Feuer und Schwert!

'*Feuer und Schwert*!', 'fire and sword!'. A German 1935-type manpack flamethrower as illustrated in the *Wehrmacht* picture series. The integration of flamethrowers and other battlefield engineer assets into the infantry attack against fixed positions began as early as 1915, and was a key feature of German assault methods from 1939. Similar ideas were revived, or newly adopted, by the Allies both West and East, as the war progressed. Both British and US forces would also have success with tank- and vehicle-mounted flame weapons in support of infantry attacks against defences later in the war.

US infantry just a hundred yards from the enemy near Alsdorf, Germany, during a brief period of what was effectively trench warfare. The M1 Garand of the NCO nearest to the camera is fitted with the grenade launcher.

A *Waffen SS* junior NCO runs past a half-track recently abandoned by the US 14th Cavalry at Poteau in the Ardennes, December 1944. His weapon is the *Sturmgewehr 44*, the world's first genuine 'assault rifle', capable of both selective and full automatic fire using a 'short' cartridge. Though crudely finished, it was a highly effective weapon, the introduction of which was accompanied by a new manual for small-unit tactics. It was intended to replace both the MP 40 and K98k bolt-action rifle. Note the distinctive pouch designed to hold three thirty-round magazines.

British Home Guards using just one of the many versions of the 'Molotov cocktail': in this instance a spirit bottle of fuel, wicked with a length of film. Two men work as a team from cover close to a road, one ready to pick off the opposition with a P17 Enfield bolt-action rifle, the other throwing the incendiary. Molotovs were surprisingly widely used, from the Spanish Civil War right through to some of the street battles in Warsaw and other towns in the late years of the Second World War. Though a poor substitute for genuine infantry anti-tank arms, they were simple to produce, lucky hits were sometimes scored, and flame weapons always had morale value.

A captain and guardsman of the Grenadier Guards, armed respectively with the .38 revolver and Thompson sub-machine gun, January 1941. The revolver was handy and sturdy, but outside of confined spaces of little account on the modern battlefield: most front-line junior infantry officers carried other weapons in addition. The Thompson has the early drum magazine. The first appearance of the US .45 Thompson was a godsend as the British Army had no other SMG and it was powerful and well made. Against this it was heavy, initially available only in small numbers, and cost a ruinous $225 each. The mass production, cheap, but shoddy looking Sten gun made its appearance in 1941.

Men of 2nd Royal Norfolks during street fighting at Kervenheim, Germany, March 1945. There is no bunching and no hanging around in open spaces. As this team crosses the street at the double, only one man is fully exposed in the road.

teams, the smaller having the BAR. When one team was moving another was the 'foot on the ground', much as on the British model. Yet fire was also seen as antidote to many an adverse situation. As George S Patton put it,

> The proper way to advance, particularly for troops armed with that magnificent weapon the M-1 rifle, is to utilise marching fire and keep moving. This fire can be delivered from the shoulder, but it can be just as effective if delivered with the butt of the rifle half way between belt and the armpit. One round should be fired every two or three paces. The whistle of the bullets, the scream of the ricochet, and the dust, twigs and branches which are knocked from the ground and the trees have such an effect on the enemy that his small arms fire becomes negligible.

Raids received more detailed treatment than before. Rifle companies were most likely to be committed, day or night, in 'supported raids'. Ordered by battalion commanders who set the mission, time, and objective, these depended on both the element of surprise and the fire of supporting weapons. Details, however, were left to the company commander, who was usually given discretion regarding training, equipment, and conduct of the raid. His course of action would be informed by a preliminary reconnaissance. Important decisions included the designation of leaders and objectives for each party, and how to deploy the weapons platoon. Given that raids would not generally require heavy weapons to displace forwards, possible options included using its elements to protect flanks, assist in covering the withdrawal, reinforcing support fires, or provide men to carry captured materials or guard prisoners.

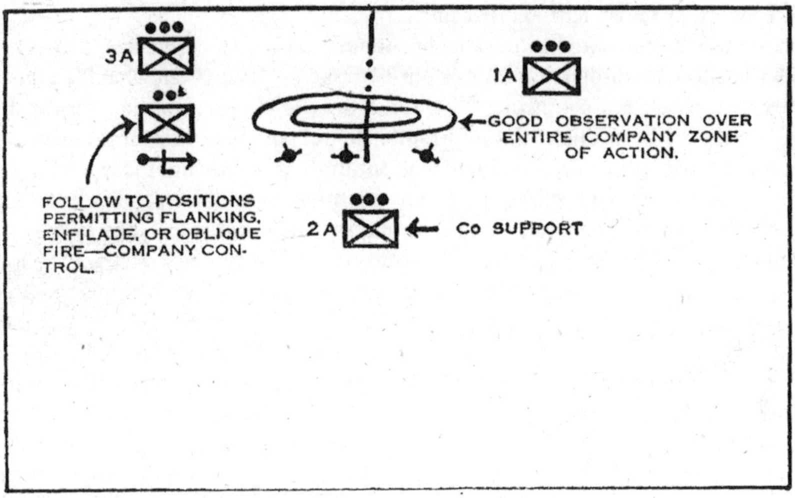

Initial dispositions of platoons for a 'strong attack', with the majority of the company forward. This could be developed into an enveloping attack if circumstances allowed. From FM 7-10 *Rifle Company, Infantry Regiment*, 1944.

Company commanders were also well advised to keep in hand a support party, including rocket launchers, to use against unexpected enemy resistance or counter attack. This was particularly necessary since positions left vacant during the day might well be occupied by enemy reserves at night. Indeed, US instructions on night deployment specifically recommended that platoons close up tighter to each other at night, as this enabled them to keep in touch and reduced the possibility for infiltration under darkness. If a raid proceeded without preparatory fire by support weapons, the company commander had to be particularly careful to plan the timing of 'protective fires' by means of which objectives could be 'boxed in'. Premature shooting roused the enemy, late firing might mean enemy units adjacent joining in the fray. Daylight raids were almost always 'supported'.

'Infiltration', already mentioned in earlier manuals, was further elaborated in *Rifle Company*, 1944. Not an easy technique to achieve successfully it was defined as, 'a method of advancing unobserved into areas which are under hostile control or observation. It requires decentralization of control; it means giving a unit, small group, or even an individual soldier a mission to accomplish, unaided. Upon the success of this mission often depends the success of larger actions.' Infiltrations might be accomplished under any condition of 'limited visibility', as for example darkness, fog, heavy rain, very rugged terrain, or undergrowth. How many troops were committed to infiltration depended on the mission: small patrols of two or three might be all that was required for information gathering, anything up to an entire company might make an attempt if the objective was to launch an attack against the rear of a hostile position. In any case, secrecy was crucial, both to success of the mission, and the extraction of any who objectives required that they be returned unseen. In many instances security was better maintained under cover of distractions or ruses such as firing, racing engines, pyrotechnics, or movement of other units.

Extremely useful were infiltrations in conjunction with a co-ordinated attack, and in such tactics the infiltrating unit might be tasked to launch an assault against the enemy rear, single out command, communication, or supply facilities. Ideally, if the main attack was by daylight the infiltrators should complete their movement under darkness at least half an hour before dawn. Infiltrating bodies and those working with them needed careful preparation, as for example an initial assembly area within friendly lines, instructions on passing through friendly outposts, gaps in fronts and information drawn from prior reconnaissance. Standard practice was to have guides leading the infiltrating body to their departure point, and where possible guides into and through the enemy position chosen from previous patrols. Scouts and patrols could usefully screen and protect movement. The main body of an infiltration team moved in column, dispersed as the unit commander saw fit, but with any heavy weapons having to be carried by hand, preferably toward the centre of the column. Speed of movement would necessarily depend on circumstances such as visibility, terrain, and enemy activity, but with infiltration secrecy was more important than haste and allowances had to be made that enemy patrols might appear and cause delays. With this in mind, radios and pyrotechnics were not to be used during an infiltration but men were to have silent weapons to hand such as trench knives, small axes, 'blackjacks', and clubs.

Small groups could also perform useful infiltrations during larger attacks or in defence,

> When the attack is slowed down or stopped, or when the attack is endangered, infiltrating elements may be able to work their way into enemy controlled terrain to cause confusion, give the impression of an attack from a different direction, disrupt communications or supply, or in other ways confuse or harass the enemy. They may move around organised localities and threaten them from the rear. These elements may consist of two or three individuals, or of entire squads.

It followed that units also had to be vigilant against the possibility of enemy infiltration, with observers covering open ground, and 'roving combat patrols' in places that could not be overlooked. Night patrols and 'listening posts' might substitute for conventional techniques after dark.

As before, the lighter weight Infantry School illustrated *Training Bulletins* supplemented the main manual. That of 30 June 1944 dealt with 'security missions', and was, in effect, a punchy aide-memoir against being taken unawares, it being 'inexcusable for a commander to be surprised by the enemy'. The *Training Bulletin* therefore included not only pictorial refreshers on outposts, advanced, flank and rear guards, and the duties of the 'point' during the advance, but handy tips on civilians and sentries. The possibility that civilians might be something other than refugees or innocents was addressed by injunctions on preventing them preceding an advanced guard and prohibiting them from passing through outposts. In the event of encountering large numbers of refugees it was expected that 'higher authority' would issue orders on 'collection and subsequent disposal'.

Given the special conditions encountered in the close *bocage* of Normandy such reminders were timely indeed. As Lawrence Nickell of 5th US Division recorded, the countryside here was cut into tiny parcels by old walls and hedges,

> They were stone walls erected hundreds of years ago as the rocky fields of Normandy were cleared for cultivation. Over the years they had become overgrown with vines, trees had grown up on them and they were often three or more feet in thickness and six feet or more high. The Germans dug deep, standing depth foxholes behind the hedgerows and punched holes in the base of the hedgerows to permit a good field of fire for the machine guns they relied on so heavily.

Multiplied hundreds of times this became a whole new system of defence requiring new methods of attack, as was made clear by a 1st Army report,

> In effect, hedgerows subdivide the terrain into small rectangular compartments which favour the defense. With careful organisation each compartment can be developed into a formidable obstacle to the advance of attacking infantry. By tying in adjacent compartments to provide mutual support a more or less

> continuous band of strongpoints may be developed across the front. Handicapped by lack of observation, difficulty in maintaining direction, and inability to use all supporting weapons to their maximum advantage the attacker is forced to adopt a form of jungle or Indian fighting in which the individual soldier plays a dominant part. The most effective attack proved to be by the combined action of infantry, artillery and tanks with some of the tanks equipped with dozer blades or large steel teeth in front to punch holes through the hedgerows. It was found necessary to assign frontages according to specific fields and hedgerows instead of by yardage and to reduce the distances and intervals between tactical formations. Normal rifle company formation was a box formation with two assault platoons in the lead followed by the support platoon and the weapons platoon.

Often the link between arms of service had to be closer still. Reports of the US 90th Infantry Division for example mention the motto 'one field, one squad, one tank'. On approaching the enclosure the tank broke through into the field first, under cover of the infantry weapons. Inside it took position to cover the foot soldiers who advanced along the field edges. After initial heavy going the 29th under Major General Gerhardt adopted, and may even have initiated, much the same tactic, going so far as to practise and demonstrate the method at the divisional training centre at Couvains. On occasion the relationship of armour and infantry was reversed so that an infantry battalion was attached to a tank battalion for local security and ground holding. For bigger attacks the new *Infantry Battalion* manual of 1944 prescribed careful thought as to whether one arm should precede the other into action, or whether in the face of a well-prepared enemy 'composite waves' of tanks and infantry, following hard on indirect artillery and direct support fire, was the most flexible option.

Though Normandy was rightly regarded with huge mistrust as a hotbed of enemy snipers, and frequently trees and hedges were riddled by BAR men on the least suspicion of enemy activity, 1944 also saw the ultimate fruition of US techniques with the publication of FM 21-75 *Scouting, Patrolling, and Sniping*. As this appeared as early as February there was certainly opportunity for it to be seen, if not exhaustively practised, by the time of Overlord. As in earlier British summaries, the link between intelligence gathering, and the arts of stealthy movement, patrols, and sniping was seen as crucial. It brought together many of the earlier summaries of fieldcraft, stressing individual concealment, the need to remain motionless, and the value of observing and shooting through, rather than over cover. 'Cover' itself was now differentiated as a matter of course from 'concealment': the former protected against hostile weapons, the latter only against observation.

Whilst various forms of diamond arrangement for patrols of 8, 9, 12 or larger numbers were outlined, US patrolling formations were now regarded as 'fluid and flexible' with individuals taking their cue from the patrol leader and having regard to their ability to see each other whilst making 'full use of cover and concealment'. Patrols could indeed change shape as they proceeded, and there was a general intention that should a patrol be fired upon the minimum number would be 'pinned down' by the enemy intervention:

> Within a designated formation, points and flank groups move in and out as required in order to observe any cover for an enemy up to 100 yards, provided the inside man of the group can maintain visual contact with the patrol leader. Individual patrol members automatically move closer together in thick cover, fog, and at night; and farther apart in open terrain, clear weather, and in daylight. In general however, the lateral movement of flank groups is limited to 100 yards from the axis of advance.

Patrols were divided broadly into reconnaissance and combat missions. As in the British model, the former were the minimum size to achieve the objective, two or three men often being sufficient unless the excursion was expected to be protracted, or spares were needed as messengers. Reconnaissance patrols were not to indulge in combat unless for self protection or out of vital need to complete a mission, but specialists such as radio operators, mine technicians, or pioneers might be included as required. Examples requiring such special skills might include reconnaissance of mine fields, checking of friendly or enemy wire, or missions requiring rapid transmission of information to other units or HQs. Combat patrols could be both offensive and defensive. They might for example be required to screen a position, maintain a presence during darkness, or protect outposts, flanks, or important features and supply routes. Offensively they could be tasked for missions such as the capturing of prisoners or materiel, infiltration, destruction, or the interception of enemy patrols. Specific patrols were also mounted for sniper clearance.

US snipers were now defined as, 'expert riflemen, well qualified in scouting, whose duty is to pick off key enemy personnel who expose themselves'. Eliminating enemy leaders and harassing the enemy by sniping softened enemy resistance and weakened morale. Snipers could be operated singly, in pairs, or small groups, and might be mobile or operate from stationary 'observer-sniper posts'.

> The mobile sniper acts alone, moves about frequently, and covers a large but not necessarily fixed area. He may be used to infiltrate enemy lines and seek out and destroy appropriate targets along enemy routes of supply and communication. It is essential that the mobile sniper hit his target with the first round fired. If the sniper is forced to fire several times, he discloses his position and also gives the enemy opportunity to escape. Therefore, although the mobile sniper must be an expert shot at all ranges he must be trained to stalk his target until he is close enough to insure that it will be eliminated with his first shot. Stationary observer-snipers: teams of two snipers may work together, operating sniping posts assigned definite sectors of fire. Each sniper is equipped with field glasses. His rifle has telescopic sights. One man acts as observer, designating the targets discovered to the firer and observing the results of fire. Using field glasses, the observer maintains a constant watch. Because this duty is tiring, it is necessary that the observer and sniper change duties every 15 to 20 minutes.

Sniper posts were chosen as good for concealment but offering excellent fields of fire. The exits from the post to the rear were to be well concealed, though covered approaches from flanks were avoided as far as possible. Actual firing points were not to be on skylines or against contrasting backgrounds, and so arranged that the muzzle of the rifle did not project obviously or dust was kicked up when a weapon fired. Snipers could not smoke in the post, and alternative posts were provided so that locations could be changed frequently. Individual snipers were usually armed with the sniper rifle, but for close country carbines might be chosen, and for missions behind enemy lines might carry other weapons such as a pistol or sub-machine gun. British sniper officer Clifford Shore considered the M1 Carbine the ideal mate to a telescoped rifle, with the second man firing the semi-automatic, as 'for handiness mobility and ease of shooting this little carbine was certainly the finest weapon I ever handled'.

'Several men' per platoon were to be trained in the sniper role, though only one or two might actually be needed at any given time. The ideal candidates were already good shots with a sense of fieldcraft, and these were further trained in camouflage, navigation, silent movement, and made 'physically agile and hardened, and able to sustain themselves for long periods of detachment from their units'. Contrary to popular belief, US snipers were not usually employed at very long ranges, nor did they constantly reset their telescopic sights to various ranges. Normally, sights were left set at 400yd and the sniper adjusted his own aim and sight picture automatically to compensate for distance, movement, and other factors. When the target was at 400yd and stationary the sniper aimed directly at the centre of mass, dropping his aim a foot for closer targets. For further objects he aimed higher, as for example at the top of an enemy's head at 500yd. At 600yd the point of aim was 52in above the point to be hit, and much more than this was deemed impractical under normal battle conditions where targets were small or fleeting.

Chapter Five

Fighting in Built-up Areas

'In street and house to house fighting, the attacker's allies are darkness, a good plan of attack, ingenuity, surprise, audacity and speed'
– Andrew G Elliot, *The Home Guard Encyclopedia*

In 1939 most armies had healthy respect for street fighting. Bitter experiences and many historical examples – from biblical times through to the suppression of the Paris Communards and the bloody end of Republican Spain – suggested that attempting to fight within built-up areas gobbled up time and troops and sapped morale. Textbook expectation was that battle within towns would be avoided wherever possible. Largely the German *Blitzkrieg* of 1939 and 1940 did exactly this with its armour tipped *Sichelschnitt* or 'scythe cut' passing through rural areas and around cities. Built-up areas were shelled and bombed with concomitant loss of civilian life, but only when the end game was reached, as at Warsaw and Calais, did German infantry entertain the ticklish job of winkling the enemy from houses and cellars. Whilst it was unusual for infantry to tackle settlements of significant size during the early phase of the war in Europe, nevertheless, theory and training existed for this eventuality. Notes from the 1939 German instruction on *Ortskampf*, or town battle, were later translated by US Military Intelligence as *German Notes on Street Fighting*, and these, together with observation of both British training in 1940–1941 and the opening campaigns in the East, laid foundations for future Allied practice.

German ideas suggested that best practice was to begin by moving rapidly to surround a town, and so cut off water and power supplies as well as routes of reinforcement. This achieved, first attacks into the settlement aimed at cutting it into pockets, denying the enemy freedom of movement, and creating zones that were small enough to be successfully assaulted. Forces advanced along parallel lines, capturing prominent buildings, this being calculated to avoid confusion and friendly fire incidents as well as taking useful observation points overlooking hostile areas. Infantry advanced close along both sides of streets, as comrades went from house, or across rooftops. Troops on one side of the street were able to cover the other, whilst men on vantage points manned machine guns. Firing into structures where there was no clear target was best aimed low. A shot at thigh or groin height disabled an unseen standing enemy and might well kill one seated or kneeling: shots at head height would be lucky to hit a standing soldier, and miss anybody in any other position. Individual buildings that fought stubbornly were treated as small fortifications, and when isolated could be attacked by specially formed 'assault detachments' of selected men under a platoon commander. Whilst general equipment was cut back to improve personal mobility, specialist weapons were deployed according to mission and situation. So it was that engineers might be included and charges, flame weapons, grenades, smoke-producing and wire-cutting equipment all used.

When fighting defensively the German method was to create a reinforced perimeter with strongpoints, but to hold back the majority of the available force in the interior, where they were less vulnerable but could be used to reinforce or for counter strokes. Buildings were loop holed, roof tiles removed in places to create sniping and observation points, and windows left open. With nothing in the way and many apertures to choose from defenders could operate from well back in rooms, and the opposition left guessing. Confined blast effects were also likely to be lessened as were the dangers of flying glass. Obvious landmark buildings were not held with large garrisons but

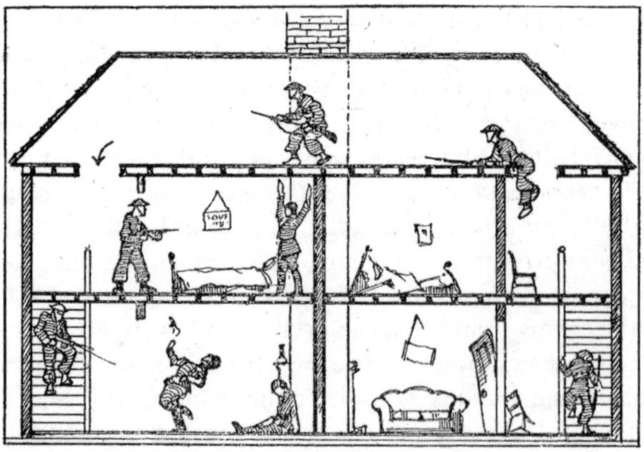

ATTACK THROUGH COCK-LOFT

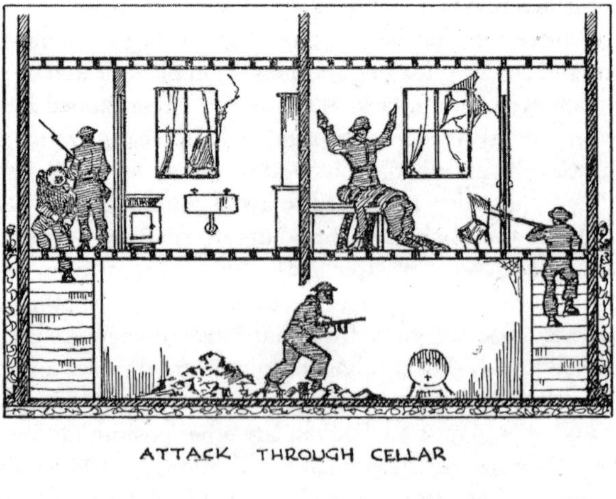

ATTACK THROUGH CELLAR

Attacking through lofts and cellars, from Colonel GA Wade's *House to House Fighting*.

defended from outside, where there were good fields of fire and opportunities for surprise and few would be hit by missiles aimed at the key structure. As opportunities arose the defence launched its own counter attacks aiming to break up the enemy forces by taking them on flanks and splitting them into pockets.

Though less developed, British techniques showed distinct parallels. Street fighting was seen essentially as a war of section commanders, to be indulged mainly as a 'mopping up' exercise after the main decision had been achieved elsewhere. Main attacks were not to be pushed into properly defended towns. However, in the event of having to advance through a village the right-hand side of the street was thought to be safest as right-handed defenders in houses would find it difficult to fire without showing themselves. Formations were adapted to circumstance, but a good option was to send two scouts ahead of a section in order to check vantage points before hazarding the main body. At the rear two men were deputed to look backwards. If there was a serious problem it might be necessary to abandon a street altogether and take to backyards and gardens. Advances were covered by an overviewing light machine gun, positioned on a roof or within an upstairs room. Where a building had to be cleared grenades and mortars came into play, and the task was undertaken systematically and men given proper instructions in advance.

In defence of built-up areas British troops were to create 'self-contained' and tank-proof strongpoints, limiting enemy freedom of movement and creating 'pivots' around which counter attacks were launched. Positions, though planned, were not allowed to become 'predictable' but force the enemy to slow and attack building by building, creating delay and disorganisation. The heart of a village defence was usually a 'keep' with good observation, and machine guns positioned both outside and within the settlement. Structures on the perimeter of the defence were not to be heavily defended, but might be booby-trapped to good effect. In individual buildings doorways were barricaded in such a way that the occupiers could still exit in an emergency, and hold cellars and roof spaces from which they could fire from 'unexpected directions'. Where time allowed, loopholes, sandbagging, and knocking additional passages between buildings were all employed. Defence works divided into those that were the province of engineers, and those that could be deputed to infantry pioneer platoons. Engineers were best for structural and technical work, such as strengthening buildings, demolitions, securing water supply, and arranging booby traps, whilst knocking glass from windows, setting up machine guns, trench digging, clearing fields of fire, and laying barbed wire could all be left to pioneer platoons. *Field Engineering*, December 1939, offered some elaborate schemes including shoring up cellars, fitting steel plates, and infilling door and window cavities with splinter-proof rubble packed between boards or corrugated iron.

The crisis of the summer of 1940 made it appear very likely that British troops, regulars and auxiliaries, would soon be fighting the enemy in their own home towns and villages. As Churchill put it in one of his most famous speeches, 'we shall defend every village, every town, every city'. One immediate result was renewed interest in experiences of veterans of the Spanish Civil War who had fought in similar circumstances: another was an outpouring of literature, some official – but much unofficial – on the conduct of street defence. In John Brophy's *Home Guard: A Handbook for the LDV*,

September 1940, the emphasis was on surprise, tank ambush, observation, reporting, and defence works. In John Langdon-Davies' *Home Guard Training Manual*, December 1940, coverage of what he called 'this most exciting form of warfare' was more systematic with village defences being considered as 'outer' and 'inner', with roadblocks so disposed as to hamper the enemy yet allow flow of defenders. Schemes were to embody well-sited anti-tank blocks and concealed posts for riflemen, grenade throwers, and flamethrowers, but again, very much like the old 'keep' idea, villages were to include a 'stronghold'. Yet, unlike medieval castles, modern strongholds were not to be so conspicuous as to invite attack. They were suitable to stop mechanised

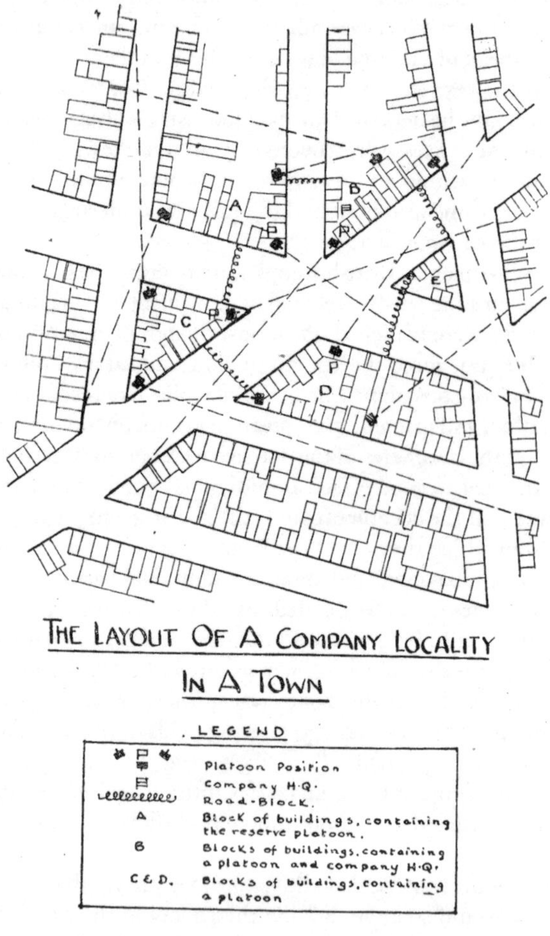

The layout of a company locality in a town from *The Organisation of Home Guard Defence*, 1943. Streets are blocked with wire and other obstacles whilst fire positions are arranged to create interlocking zones, along and across streets from different angles. The posts are so arranged that fires cross, but positions are not directly opposite each other so minimising the possibility of 'friendly fire' accidents.

attack; as sound and fireproof as possible; give both cover and fields of fire; and well camouflaged. Larger villages were to be subdivided with several independent strongholds, each capable of holding out even if neighbours fell. When street fighting became imminent defenders were not to have scruples against destruction, but be prepared to demolish houses, create bullet-proof cover, smash glass from windows, take off plaster to prevent it falling during battle, clear flammable materials and loophole walls. Whilst reminding that poison and fighting in civilian attire were against the laws of 'civilised war', defenders were encouraged to use many ruses including booby traps, dummy trenches, smoke, noise, and lights. Ingenuity was to be used where materials were scarce, as for example the simple expedients of leaving manholes and gratings open at night, and turning on gas and water mains.

One of the most interesting of the post-Dunkirk British urban warfare instructions was Captain SJ Cuthbert's *We Shall Fight Them on the Streets*. For Cuthbert the significance was strategic as well as tactical, as seaside and port towns in particular either covered, or actually were, ideal landing places. Road, rail, and canals likewise either passed through, or intersected in, built-up areas – towns being for the most part rows of houses and commercial structures, and between them various types of communications. As he put it, 'towns are the ready made answer to Blitzkrieg'. Importantly, the townscape was tall as well as broad, lending a 'third dimension' and many vantage points to combat, but at the same time built-up areas presented 'blind and disjointed conditions' so that no country was at the same time so closed, or so open. In defending commanders had to consider that attempting to protect everywhere was a recipe for holding nothing, and more often than not the solution was to balance fixed defences and mobile reserves. Which took precedence might depend on the form of assault being faced. Against parachutists fixed defences were pointless, but given sufficient resources defenders could form stop lines, and then clear areas, so in effect becoming the attacker. Against land attack there would probably be more warning, and thereby more opportunity to create 'overwhelmingly strong' defences that required only more limited mobile reserves.

As in pre-war schemes, Cuthbert saw machine weapons and particularly light machine guns as the pivots of defence even though topography might limit fields of fire. In defending individual structures consideration had to be given to all-round defence, albeit that only the most important avenues could be covered by machine guns, other angles having to be filled in by rifle fire. Though positions might be cramped, defenders had advantage of 'interior lines' and were thus able to deploy fire rapidly from one place to another: equally towns had plenty of places where men could 'lie low', allowing the enemy to pass before opening up on him from behind. In general, the average suburban house was not sufficiently large for a section, but was likely to be subject to two or more lines of approach. Rule of thumb was that a house should never be held by less than two men, who gained psychologically as well as practically from a second pair of eyes, but rarely required more than five. Light machine guns were best placed unobtrusively but in a house with dominant field of fire and strong construction. Houses on corners commonly offered three directions of fire, but conversely might be vulnerable. Such posts therefore needed strengthening, and alternatives nearby to which weapons could displace.

With enough time improvements to structures could be made virtually infinitum, with fields of fire, strength, and concealment all to be 'exaggerated in every conceivable way'. Fields of fire might be improved by choosing some basement apertures to sweep open ground at low level, or making loopholes, perhaps by removing a ventilator. Machine-gun positions could be better protected by riflemen firing at different angles from loops nearby. Strength was a question of taking away as well as adding: glass, curtains, and any breakables or flammables tended to weaken, whilst sandbags, rubble, joists, and furniture packed with earth tended to strengthen. Wire mesh over apertures made throwing grenades into a room very difficult, but canny defenders also left a small slit just large enough for them to drop bombs out. Crucial, but sometimes forgotten, were the need for a 'line of withdrawal' and alternative positions. In terraces and semi-detached houses a good ruse was to find a cupboard against the party wall, and knock the connecting hole through inside. Defenders could then pass from one side to the other very easily, but make it look as though there was no connection during a superficial search. Holes in other buildings might be concealed with any bulky object that was relatively easy to move, or apparently 'blocked' by a dummy booby trap.

When works of fire and strength were settled more detailed consideration was given to matters of concealment, removing all clues that betrayed defenders as well as installing actual camouflage. Trails of sand and rubble were removed, and net curtains were added in some places – it being often more easy to see out than in. Where works could not be well concealed or camouflaged they were duplicated. Dummy loopholes, additional barricades, covering extra windows with wire netting, removing glass from nearby houses, and other tricks all left the enemy guessing where the defenders actually were, and might serve to disperse his fire across many different locations. Equally, real positions could be created in less-obvious places outside buildings, as for example in piles of rubble, trenches, trees and bushes. These, however, required the very best of camouflage and concealment as often they gave more limited, or no, protection from fire. Barbed wire was the ideal adjunct to a street defence, placed so that it impeded the enemy where machine guns could strike them, but not so close to defended buildings that grenades could be thrown over. A street 'properly wired' under machine-gun fire was a 'death trap'. An additional refinement was to hang tins containing pebbles in the wire, so that attempts at removal or crossing at night would alarm the defence.

As to attacking methods, *We Shall Fight Them on the Streets* recognised that different objectives required different approaches, depending on whether the mission was to capture an area, or merely to penetrate or cross. In the latter event neutralisation or infiltration, stealthily executed, might be more effective and less costly than full assault. In all events, however, fighting in towns characteristically induced chaos and confusion, and usually forces would become disorganised. Losing touch with comrades, friendly fire, loss of control, and missing pockets of the enemy were constant hazards. In order to minimise such risks simple plans with limited objectives were recommended. The battle was likely to depend 'on the initiative of subordinate commanders' who were to act 'swiftly and with enterprise' in the spirit of the objective rather than hanging about aimlessly or sending back for orders at every pause. As street fighting was thoroughly unnerving with unexpected shots coming from unexpected angles, speed was 'of the essence' and any advantage being pressed before defenders had chance to react or redeploy.

Though it was probably impossible to give main bodies absolute security, advanced guards could do valuable work, finding observation points, covering crossroads with fire, and questioning inhabitants. Sentries were posted in covered tactical positions. Bricks and mortar made for poor visual horizons but to some extent this was compensated by maps, aerial photos, and oral reports from civilians and scouts. Ideal scout movement consisted of short, rapid 'bounds' by one or two men on either side of a street, dropping quickly into cover behind buttresses, alleyways, and gateposts. On 'no account' were scouts to keep their heads poked up above or round obstructions, and if possible were to be provided with a periscope. If fired on scouts were to go straight into cover and try to work to a position where they were able to give covering fire to assault parties that followed. Scouts might be shadowed by dedicated observers, sufficiently far back that they could communicate to the rear what had been seen.

Main bodies followed up, usually on one side of the road, keeping in shadow. 'Single attacks' were more likely to succeed than multiple thrusts, but these could be made across back yards as well as along thoroughfares. Indirect approaches gave better cover, but even so men might be forced to clamber over obstacles slowing them as well as momentarily exposing them to fire. 'Single attacks', though in one general direction, did not mean taking only one building at a time. In favourable circumstances a big thrust might indeed attack several streets at once – but all such efforts were to be mounted co-operatively. 'Cordons' of fire helped to keep areas clear, or prevented enemy reinforcement or movement. 'Covering fire' was crucial to the advance, and absolutely necessary to the crossing of an open space, and troops had to be aware that if the enemy saw them taking up positions, or positions were obvious, it would never be possible to fire from them. How high or how low the best covering fire positions might be depended on a number of factors. Low positions gave good 'beaten zones' with bullets skimming along just above the ground and ricocheting dangerously for distances that easily exceeded the normal visible range. However, where men advanced between those who covered them and likely locations of the enemy troops covering fire had to be high enough to shoot over the heads of their comrades. Even if no enemy was encountered, nowhere could be considered clear until 'mopping up' had been completed. To mop up properly LMGs were positioned to cover the backs of houses, and sections moved from house to house searching every structure. During the process men worked in pairs, but it was reasoned that every small space did not need to be examined since a single enemy left behind would be 'cut off from his friends and in no mood for a stout resistance'.

Though any weapons from aircraft to incendiaries could be used to attack an enemy in built-up areas, often infantry assault would be necessary; either combined with other arms or mounted independently. Wherever possible surprises were best, and movements over roof tops and through sewers might be made unexpectedly. However, there were certain techniques that proved useful in almost any event. Strongpoints were best encircled, with attackers aiming to occupy houses on either side. Entering the houses down one side of a street from the rear often saved having to go down the avenue under fire. Where to take next might often be decided by which structures were most naturally threatened by one's existing positions. Delay in the open was proved to be, 'the most suicidal occupation in war'. Usually the shortest routes and the greatest practical speed were best, but any exposed movement had to be accompanied by the 'heaviest possible covering fire to the last possible moment'.

Explosives were ideal to force houses, but failing this crowbars and heavy axes might do duty *in extremis*. Where an explosive charge was used to blow a hole only the minimum number of men would be used to set it, the main assault party being under cover nearby until the detonation. Then they rushed not only the hole torn by the explosion but other apertures, such as skylights, as the enemy were likely to be distracted and occupied. As far as infantry weapons were concerned the sub-machine gun and grenade were the best for close quarters. Pistols were also good but only if the user was well trained. The light machine gun was the ideal thing for covering fire tasks, rifles being used for the 'less important fields of fire', though mopping up with fixed bayonet had both 'moral and actual effect' at very close range. The 2in mortar lacked power for great effect, but was extremely useful to provide smoke. Anti-tank rifles were clumsy for small spaces, but might nevertheless smash through cover to hit targets otherwise safe from ordinary rounds. Where there was choice a commander should chose weapons that were capable of 'high volume of fire in proportion to weight', or those that could go over, or through, cover. Troops in street combat were to go as lightly equipped as possible, with even heavy army boots dispensed with as too noisy and lacking in grip. However, a few periscopes and one short ladder per company would pay dividends. House clearances had to be systematic to the extent that the officer or NCO in charge allotted specific tasks to individuals. If possible, the attack was top down, from an entrance in the roof. This made 'an ally of gravity' with grenades being dropped down, rather than thrown up and falling back onto their users. If forced to attack upwards bursts of fire through the ceilings were 'a prudent action'. Floors were then cleared one at a time. Halls and staircases were problematic, being natural traps, and might be mined. In some instances the use of fire escapes was useful, and where booby traps were suspected grenades or poles came in handy to clear the way.

Interestingly, many of the techniques that would later become staples of urban combat had appeared in British training and manuals by 1941. In Lionel Wigram's *Battle School* for example are to be found drills for both village and house clearance very similar to those later used in the classic *Fighting in Built Up Areas*. Villages were 'sealed off' with 'stop sections' and light machine guns firing down streets. Clearance teams, composed of a 'clearing group' and a 'covering group', worked together to take a house. The covering group took up its positions overlooking doors, windows, and other openings, whilst the clearing group undertook the actual entry. Men were deployed either side of the door, moving under cover of the sub-machine gun, then flung it open allowing a grenade to go in. Following the explosion, the clearance team rushed in, with the 'right door man' getting his back against the wall and covering the room as quickly as possible. The remainder then cleared the house floor by floor, preferably downwards from the top towards the cellar.

European developments were a wake-up call on the other side of the Atlantic, for in 1940 the US Army was ill prepared indeed for any sort of urban warfare. Arguably, the best repository of knowledge was the Marine Corps, though its training and literature was geared to the possibility that it would be used against civil unrest in the Third World as part of an expeditionary force, rather than to combat a thoroughly modern and well-trained enemy. This was disappointing to say the least since considerable advances had been made in the closing stages of the First World War, first in co-operation with British and French allies, then in the establishment of 'Hogan's Alley' type urban shooting training areas on US soil. Changing this situation would take considerable efforts, but in the months after the fall of France study of recent operations was a priority. At the forefront of improving US street fighting capability was Captain Paul W Thompson, who wrote pieces for the *Infantry Journal* stressing that co-ordination between elements of a combat team was key to success. Clearly, combat engineers would have a significant role, but as yet both the wherewithal and trained men were seriously lacking. Nevertheless, the US Engineer School instituted a series of committees in 1940–1941 and observers were sent to other countries so that such subjects received consideration, even if practical experience was still largely absent at the beginning of 1942.

If British urban techniques improved significantly in the first two years of war, those of the Germans were honed close to perfection in a much more dramatic, and costly, fashion from late 1941 to 1943. Barbarossa and other attacks to the East had begun with the familiar *Blitzkrieg* ideal that open areas were to be dashed through, preferably by armour, and communications nodes struck mainly by bombers and artillery. Stunned, undermined, and mystified enemies, communications severed, might then be surrounded if they did not retire rapidly out of the way. Where settlements had to be attacked due to the presence of a bridge or some other strategically important feature this was best done on the run, perhaps even before the enemy realised that they were in danger. If possible whole cities were encircled. Attacks were to be made from 'an unexpected direction', with the enemy distracted by bombardments and smoke elsewhere. In the event that towns had to be taken infantry did the job systematically, probably using a whole company with support weapons concentrated on a single row of houses, or even a battalion for a street should resistance prove stiff. Wherever possible, attached engineers with flamethrowers and explosives would help smooth the path. German instructions were that tanks in particular should avoid fighting in towns. If an armoured division was 'compelled' to fight in built-up areas, the job was best tackled by the armoured infantry, supported by single heavy tanks and engineer assault detachments.

However, it was not many months before this pattern began to unravel. Huge spaces and numerically superior enemies in the East made surprise and running through built-up areas progressively more difficult. As the seasons wore on, and reserves were depleted towns took on other significances. For one thing, the Nazi leadership, especially Hitler, regarded the taking of important towns as valuable in its own right. For they were both supply centres and names on maps with which to encourage the war effort and demoralise the enemy. As Russian winter approached settlements also beckoned as sources of shelter, fuel, and survival. The upshot of these pressures was that fighting in towns became ever more common in the East, and ever more bitter as the tide began to turn, and German armies were ordered to hold on to symbolic cities – often at horrendous cost.

Initially, Soviet street-fighting methods were primitive, with an emphasis on barricades and massed counter attack. By the latter part of 1942, however, the Red Army was employing much more sophisticated tactics. Though none liked to admit it, these almost certainly grew from emulation of enemy methods, combined with on the spot improvisation. In the 'academy of street fighting' that was Stalingrad, Chuikov's 62nd Army used 'Storm Groups' to wrest the city back from the Germans, block by block and building by building, combining the micro tactics of the *Rattenkrieg* – or 'rat war' – in sewers and basements with the tried and tested techniques of encirclement. Storm group actions, usually initiated at night, involved three types of ad hoc sub-unit; the assault team, reinforcement team, and reserve team. The assault elements, just six or eight strong each, comprised men armed with sub-machine guns, grenades, daggers, and entrenching tools. These crawled to within grenade-throwing range, stealthily, and under cover of darkness and supporting fire. They then lobbed their bombs, and, hard on the explosions clambered in through windows or forced doors. As battle commenced within a structure the larger reinforcement teams followed up, entering from different angles and seeking out vantage points. These reinforcements included not only riflemen but snipers, anti-tank men, and machine gunners. Their task was both to support the assault teams, and take up positions from which to dominate the area surrounding the building. By their fire they prevented enemy reinforcements coming to the aid of the garrison. The reserves were used in a number of different ways. If the fight was going badly they added their weight so the defenders were totally overwhelmed. If progress was better reserves might be deployed to the flanks against enemy counter attacks, used to form 'blocking parties', or broken down to form new assault teams. Consolidation of newly captured buildings involved digging new communication trenches, inserting reinforcements to floors, walls and cellars, establishing machine-gun positions on roofs, constructing new block houses, and placing obstacles. On occasion entrances on the friendly side were enlarged and anti-tank guns and other artillery pieces pushed inside to fire out through embrasures.

Whilst at first the Russians had gleaned more from their enemies than the other way about it cannot be doubted that the protracted urban battles of the Eastern Front, and especially Stalingrad, and later Warsaw and Budapest, lent the German infantry many painful practical lessons regarding technique. A number of these actions were followed by after battle analysis and specific advice. In the case of Warsaw in 1944, for example, it was noted that even now too much use was made of streets. In future going through walls was to be regarded as normal, especially for the movement of wounded and ammunition. Ruined buildings were to be regarded as just as dangerous as those that were still intact: patrols should be used to winkle out stragglers, rubble was to be occupied and covered by fire. Random destruction often inconvenienced friends as well as foes: for this reason buildings to be destroyed should be specifically targeted for good reasons, such as to deny the enemy means of covered approach. Captured buildings were to be consolidated as a matter of course, and any subterranean passages that could not immediately be cleared, barricaded and guarded, or blown in. Tanks were now regarded as an integral part of urban combat, but used in a productive and carefully husbanded manner. They were not bulldozers, nor were they to go in first against barricades and obstacles so as to become easy targets for anti-tank weapons. Infantry would go first, and infantry fire used to maximum effect concentrating on group targets to be neutralised and forced under cover. In particular circumstances self-contained tank and infantry groups might be used for mutual close protection. Nobody was to be allowed to stand around doing nothing in a contested town.

Though the Western Allies fought in North Africa and British troops raided Norway and France, it was arguably the invasion of Italy that brought home the realities of this particularly bloody form of combat on a large scale. Experience led to the revision of tactics, and eventual emergence of the detailed doctrine and instructions used in North West Europe after D-Day. Ortona, captured by the Canadians at the end of December 1943, came to be regarded by the Allies as a textbook example of what to expect from the enemy. As one Canadian report repeated in the US *Intelligence Bulletin* explained,

> The defensive layout was based on intimate knowledge of the town, the approaches, the streets the alleyways, and the best routes from street to street, building to building and even room to room. With this detailed knowledge, the enemy sited his weapons and carried out a determined defence, the outstanding feature of which is acknowledged by our troops to have been 'sheer guts'. The enemy had chosen a 'killing ground', and all his weapons were sited to cover this area. Where the approaches to the 'killing ground' could not be covered by fire, the Germans had demolished buildings to create debris obstacles. The enemy could, and did, cover these obstacles by fire. Groups of machine guns were always sited so that the fire of one supported the fire of another.

So it was that at a crossroads, for example, a heap of debris about 12ft high was formed – mainly by dint of collapsing the buildings on the corners – and no less than four machine guns might be placed so as to create interlocking zones of fire. Only one of these was actually behind the obstacle covering its crest and aimed more or less directly ahead down the main street. A second gun, further back, high up in a building, and slightly to one side, aimed so that it fired over the debris and covered the approaches. Guns three and four were located in the side streets of the crossroads, and shot obliquely in such a manner that their rounds created a web of fire on the German side of the obstacle, protecting the other guns, but angled in a way that did not endanger their comrades. Just to make doubly sure the debris hill was booby-trapped and mined with anti-tank *Teller* mines and anti personnel S-Mines.

Other weapons were worked into the defensive web formed by the automatic weapons. The few flamethrowers were also used in conjunction with physical obstacles, sited at ground level behind debris, covering street crossings. Anti-tank guns were cunningly camouflaged in positions enfilading vehicle approaches, their own flanks and rear being covered by machine guns and snipers creating an all-round defence. Mortars were not necessarily used with observers in the usual way, but dropped their rounds on pre-registered sectors that the Canadians were known to have already occupied.

> As the enemy were driven back, he carried out a planned demolition of buildings. In certain instances, he had prepared buildings for demolition and blew them immediately after they had been occupied by our troops. At no time did he

make a determined counter attack to retake buildings that we had occupied. However, he immediately reoccupied any building that had been recaptured by our troops and later evacuated to permit our tanks and anti tank guns to place fire on adjoining buildings. He surrendered none of his positions readily. They had to be knocked out one by one, and if our troops did not get forward to occupy them promptly after disabling the German holding force, the enemy would re-occupy them almost at once. It was a grim and bitter defence, and a very costly one for the Germans. The enemy frequently replaced personnel in positions as often as four times before our troops were able to occupy and consolidate the ground or the building.

Given their knowledge of the town defenders were able to use successive 'killing grounds' as they were pushed back. Only by 'attacking with the greatest determination' were the Canadians eventually able to overcome resistance. In the forefront of the clear-

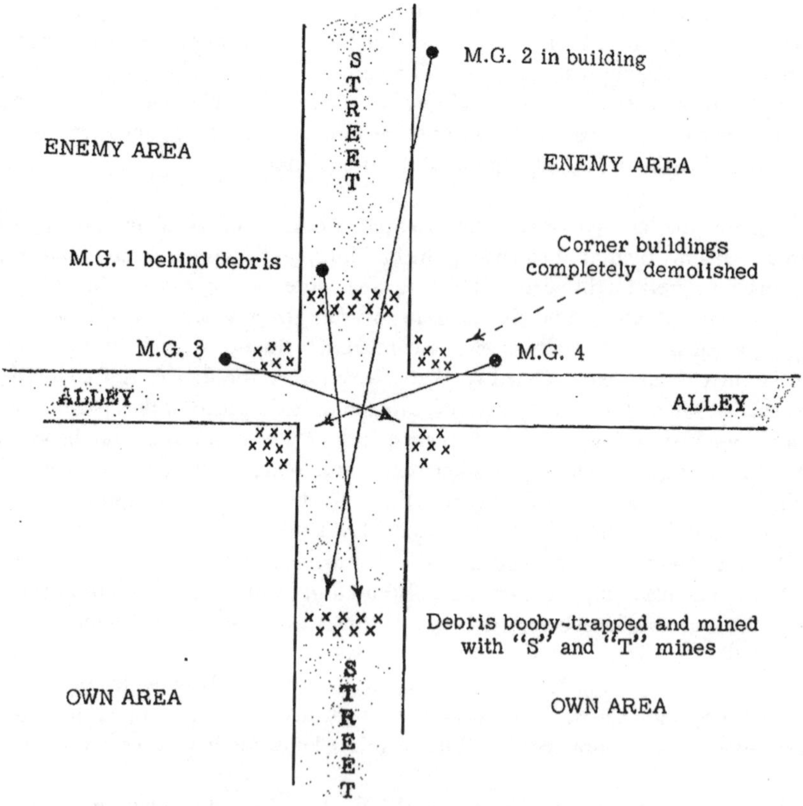

A German method for creating a crossroads 'killing zone' during fighting in built-up areas. From the US *Intelligence Bulletin*, July 1944.

ance was the Loyal Edmonton Regiment, who pressed down the main road to create a protected path for supporting armour. By Christmas Eve the unit had just three companies of sixty men apiece left in the line. On Boxing Day they reached Cathedral Square, only to discover that the enemy had planted charges, one of which buried an entire platoon on detonation. Heavy mortar fire and shaped charges to break through walls on upper floors eventually allowed further progress, but Canadian 1st Division had taken over 2,300 casualties by the time Ortona was taken.

Early the following year, at Anzio, US Fifth Army made uncomfortably close and detailed observations on enemy house-defence methods when two houses, 'reduced to rubble' by US artillery, were turned into a 'formidable strongpoint' covering a bridge on the Carano road by two platoons of German infantry. The larger of the two was set further back from the bridge, surrounded on three sides by wire and anti-personnel mines, and on capture was found to contain no less than five main machine-gun positions, plus alternatives.

> Machine gun No 1 was fired from a table in the ruins of what had once been a room; the gun's direction of fire was through a hole in the main wall and then through the archway of a cowshed. By emplacing the gun in this manner, the Germans concealed its muzzle flash from all directions except to the front, and even from that direction it was not conspicuous. The gunner was well protected from small arms fire and grenades, and was not exposed when he moved to his alternate position. From [there] the gunner was able to cover an additional area to the front and also protect the flank of the strongpoint against any attack from the road. Three Mauser rifles loaded with anti tank grenades were found leaning against the wall to the left of the doorway.
>
> Machine gun No 2 was in position inside the same room, and was sited so that it could be fired through a window facing the stream. It is interesting to note that when our forces secured the south side of the building and attempted to toss grenades through the window at machine gun No 2, the gunner ricocheted bullets of the wall in an effort to forestall the grenade fire. Machine gun No 3 was sited in a corner of an adjoining room, where the walls were still standing. This gun was so sited that its plane of fire was close to the ground; during the course of the action, the gun delivered continuous fire, ankle high, toward the stream and alternatively, to the south. The walls afforded protection from the south and west. (This gun was finally knocked out by rifle grenades.)
>
> The siting of machine gun No 4 shows how the enemy utilizes the characteristic outdoor oven as a machine gun emplacement. By siting his weapon in the part of the oven normally used for storing wood, the gunner protects himself against small arms fire from the flanks and rear, and enjoys a certain amount of protection against artillery fire. During the action, the No 4 gun delivered grazing fire ankle high. (Hand grenades and rifle grenades wounded the two man crew of this gun, and destroyed the gun itself.)
>
> The No 5 position, in the remnants of the second floor, was occupied by a German soldier armed with a machine pistol. Selecting a number of suitable points, he delivered close range fire from them during the attack, and had good

concealment. When our forces succeeded in reaching the southern wall, he delivered plunging fire over the wall. (However, grenades lobbed over the wall put an end to this.)

Concertina wire, in poor condition, was found about 50 yards from the house, on the west, south and east sides . . .

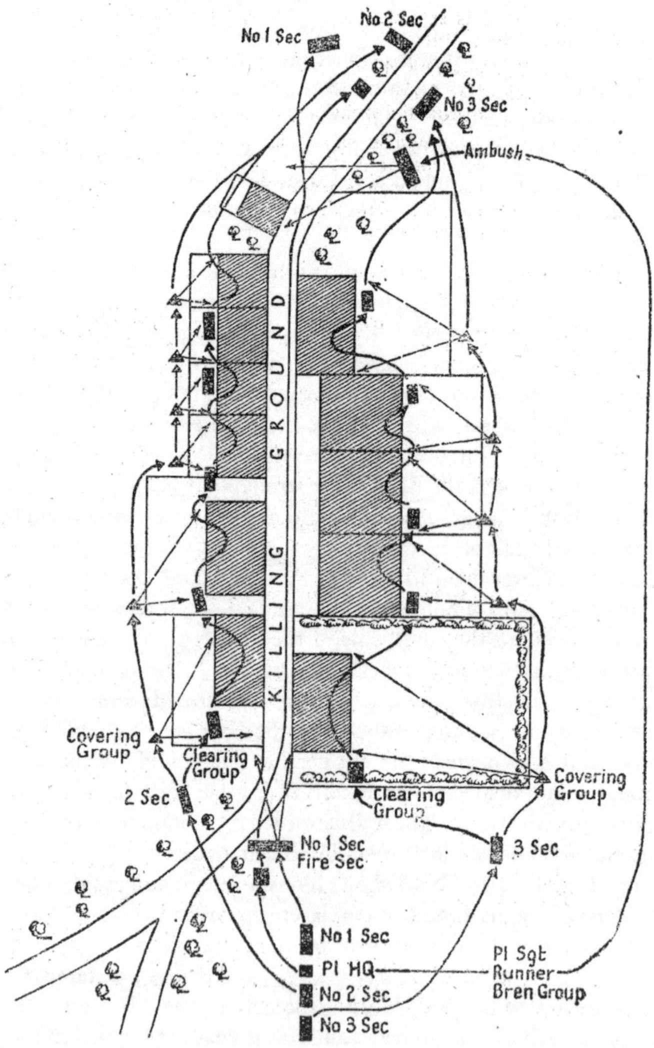

Method for clearing a small village from *Infantry Training*, 1944. The platoon breaks into covering and clearing groups, using Brens to cover open spaces and the 'killing ground' of the road. Small teams work their way along the backs of houses clearing as they go. Any enemy who escape are caught by the ambush group that has skirted around to the rear of the village.

The second house, not far from the first, was equipped as a communications centre and command post, with a small dugout between the main structure and a nearby shed. The dugout was roofed with heavy beams and contained a field telephone and pyrotechnic equipment. An MG 34, complete with tripod, was in position in the outdoor oven of the second house, so aimed that it could deliver fire down the road and give mutual support to the main strongpoint. A pit dug on the north side of the oven allowed a rifleman to protect the machine gun. About 100yd of concertina wire stretched away to another machine-gun position, so sited that any gun here gave enfilade fire onto the bridge, into the stream bed, or backwards to the rear of the whole complex. Part of the purpose of this gun was to give covering fire to yet two more machine guns within another wired enclosure surrounding most of the area around the bridge. Both of these weapons had alternate positions nearby, and that on the western bank of the stream was a heavy weapon capable of fire along the stream and supporting the second house. Happily for the attackers, both of the machine guns closest to the bridge were knocked out by artillery fire, though preparations had been made to mine the bridge itself.

Perhaps the ultimate Italian test of street, or rather rubble, tactics was Cassino in early 1944. Fought over a period of about five months by not only US and British forces but Free French, Indians, Poles, and New Zealanders, the town was but part of a bigger battlefield – but like the nearby monastery on the hill, a veritable fortress. As a US 34th Division report explained,

> The quadrangular arrangement of the houses round central courtyards, the irregular layout of the streets, and the heavy masonry of the buildings prevented our driving the enemy out into the open to destroy him, and fields of fire for our weapons were very limited. The enemy was constantly aggressive and alert, and hand grenade fights were frequent, with grenades being thrown back and forth between buildings. The enemy employed his self propelled guns audaciously, running them into the open to fire a few rounds, and then withdrawing into cover. Our tanks were hampered by narrow streets . . . but on several occasions were able to destroy enemy strongpoints in buildings with point blank fire. During the entire occupation of Cassino by our troops, the enemy held portions of the town were subjected to extremely heavy artillery concentrations, including 8 inch and 240 mm fire, but his attitude remained unchanged.

During the third battle at Cassino an already battered town was laid waste by artillery barrages dropping hundreds of tons of shells, and waves of bombers. According to one calculation, more than 4 tons of high explosive was used for every German defender. Following rain the remains of the buildings were reduced to what one commentator was moved to describe as the 'consistency of dough'. The enemy had moved Mark IV Panzer tanks into the ruins of the buildings around the Continental Hotel, and though several of these were destroyed by bombs, many pillboxes survived. So did a number of *Nebelwerfer* rocket projectors, the fire of which was later focused on a battalion of the Rajput rifles. Also too tough to be totally obliterated were some of the cellars, reinforced by a sandwich of beams, earth, and shock-absorbing air spaces. In confused fighting the attackers moved over and around German positions, sometimes not realising that they were still occupied until they were intermingled with the enemy. In one celebrated incident a platoon of New Zealanders spent 36 hours in a house upon which enemy soldiers could be heard moving around on the roof.

Private EH Groves of 25th battalion was one of the New Zealanders who joined the battle after bombardment, having been told that the attack was going to be 'a walk through'. His company began the ascent, in single file, with the men about 5yd apart, and headed for the outskirts,

> Up on the ridge we approached the town following B Company. Once we were there we slipped upwards leaving them to go on to clear the town. There was practically no fire. We got into a house on the hillside and found enemy in the lower storey looking down on the town away from us. The section leader and I killed four with a grenade and a Thompson Machine Carbine. We could not see if there were more. Found another house from which the enemy was pinning down B Company men. We got round the house and killed three with TMC. We think we left enemy there too. But it takes time to clear houses and press on. Ahead on the hillside were two dugouts or tunnels. My section leader stepped out from behind a wall to fire into those holes and was shot through the head by a sniper from below us. Our section was now down to three men and I was section leader. We tried to move round the other side of the wall and a Spandau opened up so we were held on both sides. We waited for two hours. Then our own company appeared on our right going up the stone wall on to the ridge. We had got ahead by following B Company. We sang out to them and leapfrogged across. Joined them below the Castle. They were 17 Platoon and the remainder of my 18 Platoon. We moved up to the Keep and established ourselves around the broken walls. The enemy had moved behind the Keep in the quadrangle. Two of us moved through the archway but a Spandau round the corner got the Corporal section commander. I moved back and found a hole through which to throw grenades down into the Keep.

It was during the Italian campaign that the British Army published *Fighting in Built Up Areas*: arguably its most important ever street-combat manual. First appearing in 1943, this booklet saw out the war, albeit with amendments and reprinting in April 1945. In its parentage 'FIBUA' was catholic, drawing upon, without distinction, the best to be had. In its pages are found elements of the drill approach of *Battle School* and the *Instructor's Handbook*, various things first found in Home Guard authors and *We Shall Fight Them in the Street*s, German sources, and the familiar direct method of address that would characterise *Infantry Training*, 1944. At about fifty pages it said what needed saying without prolixity, and importantly regarded urban combat not as a specialist skill, but something integral to every soldier's training. Nor was assaulting built-up areas seen as hopeless, for whilst towns were rightly regarded as suitable for defence, they could also serve as traps for their garrisons and focus for concentrated attacks of all sorts. Street fighting was bound to be expensive at close quarters – but urban areas also had dangerous open spaces. The result was high casualties and 'nerve strain' for all concerned.

> Fighting in built up areas reduces the advantages enjoyed in open warfare by the side that is superior in mobile equipment and vehicles; it involves chiefly infantry action, in the form of small, numerous, and independent battles; and its dominant feature is an abundance of cover interspersed with short, open fields of fire. Such fighting favours the defence, except possibly at night. In addition, it requires increased man power for given area. Above all, because of the enclosed nature of the fighting, success depends on the determination, cunning, and trained observation of the individual.

For *Fighting in Built Up Areas* the nature of the terrain was all important, but not static. Buildings became debris and rubble, fields of fire might open up or close in. Nevertheless, the average town offered three distinct types of landscape: on the outskirts, isolated dwellings, or groups of houses surrounded by gardens, trees, and allotments; further in more closely spaced buildings and semi-detached property; and finally blocks of houses and large buildings. Clear demarcation between town and country was, however, rare. In many instances the third dimension of height, the ability to climb quickly, smoke and dust, and the abundance of cover set conditions for 'a constant drain on manpower'.

> Because the major part of cover is rigid and set out in straight lines, movement is easily seen. This rule applies especially to individual men, if they do not remain motionless when observing or firing from behind cover. Therefore small parties must move well dispersed, from cover to cover, and always under the keen observation and ready fire support of their nearest neighbours . . . The point of origin of fire is difficult to locate on account of the noise of discharge being drowned by the crack of a bullet as it passes by or by the noise of impact of a projectile, and because of the bewildering number of points from which fire can be brought to bear in a relatively small area. It is also difficult to recognise and distinguish between the noise of strike and the noise of discharge. Consequently false rumours and information are apt to arise concerning such points as the presence of enemy snipers. What may sound like the enemy firing from adjacent rooms or buildings may mean in reality that the latter are being subjected to fire from elsewhere. Such situations occur frequently when a house is being searched, and may cause operations to be unduly slow.

In this close environment the first shot, aimed and accurate, was disproportionately valuable, and neutralisation and covering fire essential for 'the smallest operation'. Indeed, a single marksman left to his own devices might be able to prevent any small tactical operation. The only antidote was to stop the enemy's fire, and this was achieved either by getting in the first shot, or by 'getting in more shots and from more directions than the enemy can'. In terms of economy of lives the first was preferable, but the second had also to be taught by means of observation and an 'organised system'.

Fighting in Built Up Areas saw the offensive urban battle in three phases; gaining the first foot hold; 'progression'; and the reduction of 'individual centres of resistance'. The first footing was best achieved on as wide a front as practicable, so as to deceive the enemy as to where the main attacks might originate, and offer as many 'jumping off points' as possible. In gaining the first footing artillery, air support, and incendiaries were all used to maximum potential, and centres of resistance bypassed if not neutralised. Progression might well entail a frontal attack combined with envelopment. Smaller forces could operate by converging along narrow lines from the perimeter to seize vital centres, advance on a broader front to systematically 'encroach' upon one area at a time, or proceed on 'concentrated and narrow frontage' to cut off and divide part of the defences. Once isolated an area was then reduced before new attacks were launched elsewhere. 'Cordons' were used to cut off the enemy. In every attack 'rallying points' were identified in advance, and troops given specific orders on how far to go. With these firmly in mind troops would be more prepared to use infiltration to achieve their objects.

Exactly how to advance was a matter of judgement, for whilst streets were obvious invitations to ambush, they were quick ways from place to place that might allow an element of surprise against poorly organised defenders. Control of forces also tended to be better on main thoroughfares. In some instances tanks could be used down the centre of a street, its flanks protected by machine guns and 'small active groups of infantry' on either side. Covering fire was arranged at the entrance to a street, then at points along it. Infantry went from cover to cover, with individuals keeping as close to buildings as possible and ready to drop into the next position instantly. Smoke was useful, but had to be dense, as wispy smoke concealed defenders better than attackers. Going along behind houses gave good cover, though best concealment was maintained by breaking through fences rather than going over them. To get covering fire into areas behind houses mortars and anti-tank guns pulled on drag ropes were effective. When the going got really tough attackers might resort to going through the houses, wall by wall. In doing so they had to be ready to fight at point-blank range, but it might be possible to attach a field gun. Once this was established in the first of a row of houses it was used to smash holes in nearby walls which were then assaulted with grenades and flamethrowers. Men could go over rooftops unexpectedly and obtain cover behind the ridges. Tunnels and sewers also offered opportunities, particularly if an enemy was ill prepared, but troops using them had to be wary of gases and flooding as well as the ease with which the opposition could enfilade or block them.

House clearances were tackled by means of 'drills'. For the task sections divided into two: the 'clearing group' comprising the section commander, a 'bomber', lookout, and two 'entry men'; and the 'covering party' being the Bren team and remaining riflemen under the second in command. With the 'covering party' established in positions to command the approach of the clearing group, possible enemy firing positions and exits from the building, the clearance then proceeded by stages:

a) The section commander and bomber take up an intermediate position from which to direct and cover the entry men towards the point of entry.
b) Entry men approach the point of entry at best speed according to cover available. Their means of entry will depend on the type of defences, and may be either through an open door, window, or other aperture, or through a hole made by use of suitable demolition equipment. At the last moment before

entering a room it may be advisable to search it by fire (machine carbine, grenade, etc.) and follow up at top speed before any inmates have time to recover.

c) On gaining an entrance entry men get away quickly from the point of entry and stand with their backs to the wall covering the rest of the room and any doors.
d) Section commander and bomber follow up the entry men (as a result of observation or on signal from the latter).
e) All four men move out of the room in the order: section commander, bomber, first entry man, second entry man.
f) The lookout man stays at the entry, watches for signals, and acts as a guide, runner, etc., for liaison with the covering group and with platoon headquarters.
g) The remainder aim at getting to the top of the house as quickly as possible, leaving the second entry man near the entrance of the room to cover any stairs and passages. This is the ideal method, but it will not be possible if the staircase is strongly defended or heavily obstructed.
h) The covering group follow up, and if so ordered by the section commander, enter the house as soon as the entry group have successfully completed their entry. They will assist the second entry man in covering points from which the enemy may approach and, under the section second in command, will be prepared to join in searching the house or to provide fire outside the house.
i) The house is, if possible, searched downwards from the top, the first entry man opening the door of each room in turn, and providing protection against enemy approaches to the landing or head of the stairs. The section commander enters each room first at speed and turns quickly with his back to the wall. The bomber throws grenades as ordered by the section commander, and generally acts as the section commander's assistant and escort. If search from the top is not possible, it will proceed upwards floor by floor, using the ordinary methods of fire and movement, with the ground floor held as a relatively secure base for operations.
j) The section commander reports, by word of mouth or signal, that the house is clear.

Though this was normal procedure, the section commander could decide to enter the house first, followed by the bomber, his way having been prepared by them. In the event that adjoining houses were dealt with it might be possible to enter successive houses through party walls, or alternately over the roofs. The top downward search had the benefit that the enemy might be driven out into the street where they were easy meat for the covering party: searching bottom up was perfectly feasible but had the disadvantage that enemy trapped on the upper floors were likely to become desperate and fight back. In carrying out clearance men were warned not to stand in doorways, against doors, or out in the middle of rooms, as in all these cases the enemy would find them easy to locate and might shoot through the door or floor. When entire platoons were engaged in clearing streets or groups of houses one section was used as an overall covering unit and the other two assaulted the buildings to the left and right respectively using the basic drill or variations thereon. In such actions more than half of the total weapons available were devoted to covering fire, a proportion likely to overwhelm or neutralise all but the best prepared and armed garrisons.

For defence it was recommended that buildings should be occupied to suit tactical requirements: as for example in providing firm bases around which mobile elements of a garrison operated; to overlook obstacles and deny approaches; to create communications links; or give support. To do this effectively durable buildings were required, those of reinforced concrete and steel being the best choice, followed by stone. Brick was relatively weak, and wooden structures, once targeted, became 'death traps'. Adequate fields of fire and protected approaches were vital, though conversely occupied buildings should be inconspicuous and not easily observed from a dominating feature. One house in a row could answer on grounds of anonymity, but care had to be taken regarding approaches. Weapons slits at the edges of gardens were particularly valuable, being difficult to observe, even from the air, and not vulnerable in the event of house collapse. Light machine guns in such places could sweep ground very effectively, and moved to alternative posts as needed. When examining a structure with defence in mind all-round defence was important, as were possible observation posts, fields of fire, entrances and exits, communication with nearby houses, water supply, general strength, and the availability of materials. Prolonged occupations also required that thought be given to provision of dressing stations, latrines, and cookhouse.

Local protection for a building might include one or two positions outside to prevent the enemy from getting close, particularly at night when patrols were also mounted. Sentries, both outside, and on the roof, covered obstacles placed across approaches. Dummy and alternative positions, particularly those suitable for cover from bombardment and air attack were also needed. Within the structure machine weapons were best placed at ground level, riflemen and grenade throwers higher up. Weapons were used as far back from the windows and apertures as was constant with maintaining field of fire. Both doors and loopholes were kept to a minimum, too many providing opportunities to the enemy. Ideally, loopholes were cone-shaped for ease of aim from the inside, and required some form of cover and camouflage. Ground-level fire slits and cellar gratings were useful, but needed a small trench dug in front so that the enemy was prevented from rolling in grenades. Loopholes in internal walls gave the enemy a nasty surprise if he succeeded in entering a house. Additional internal protection might also be had from shoring up; sand bags and earth-filled furniture. Even mattresses provided some cover from falling debris and small fragments.

In both offensive and defensive urban combat there were certain tips useful to all individuals. In shooting at loopholes and slits single-accurate shots were encouraged, unless the object was to 'brown' the enemy through doors, walls, or ceilings, or 'snap' shots were taken on the move. The best shooting was done at the right psychological moment, sometimes held so that the enemy was entrapped or killed rather than simply repelled. Frequent changes of position kept the enemy guessing, but movement was by crawling and worming about as low as possible. To fire or observe positions were slid into slowly, avoiding eye-catching movements. Looking round a corner was best done at ground level: the enemy would not be looking for you there, and in such a posture only the top of the head was exposed, not the shoulders. Troops were to think ahead, planning what might be done in an emergency – buildings were to be 'read', perhaps from a distance using binoculars, taking note of approaches, firing points, and other significant features. Buildings were also to be imagined from the point of view of the enemy. 'Jabbering' in action was to be avoided, it could unnerve one's fellows and might conceal noises made by the enemy. A few words at the right moment, to encourage, or to deceive the enemy, were much better than constant chatter. Sturdy tables were particularly handy and could be turned on their sides for use as screens, perhaps combined with a mattress or other protection.

Though US street-combat theory made a slow start, 1942 and 1943 taught many valuable lessons, some of them being transmitted into practice by means of *Training Circulars*, *Intelligence Bulletins*, and other updates. As in the British instance, Italian examples loomed large. Nevertheless, the end of January 1944 would see the appearance of an intelligent work, comprehensive in scope, and timely in the sense that it was issued some months in advance of Overlord and the invasion of France. FM 31-50 *Attack on a Fortified Position and Combat in Towns* linked together the techniques needed for fortresses and urban areas with something of the combat-group approach advanced by the Germans at the outbreak of war. It also drew on *Fighting in Built Up Areas* to a surprising extent, repeating almost word for word, for example, its categorisations of terrain, and notes on location of enemy fire. A key realisation was that whilst attacking forces sought to 'isolate and bypass' fortified towns, defenders would hope to occupy such strategic settlements as to make this impossible, forcing the adversary to make costly attacks. At worst a well-fortified city was 'a tank-proof island'. All too clearly German forces were now usually defenders, and Allied forces attackers. Nevertheless, *Combat in Towns* was hard-boiled in its methods, reminding readers that settlements of flammable construction could be 'rendered untenable' by incendiary action. The surest, quickest, and most economical way to dislodge an enemy from a building was to burn it. Spies and 'fifth columnists' were to be sought out and 'mercilessly dealt with'.

US assaults on towns were to be conducted in two phases. The first was to 'capture an initial position within the built-up area' in order to eliminate or reduce the effectiveness of hostile fields of fire and impede enemy observation. This would also be aided by the capture of supporting fire positions outside the town. Supplies, particularly of grenades and other munitions, would be pushed as far forwards as cover and concealment permitted. In the second phase came advance, plans for which would take into account needs for:

a) Decentralisation of infantry control to subordinate units.
b) Regaining control at stated times or on designated positions. Control will be facilitated by frequent reports from subordinate units, either periodically, or on reaching predetermined objectives.
c) An organised mopping up of hostile resistance. In strongly defended areas it may be necessary for the leading element to mop up as they advance. In

lightly defended areas, it may be possible for leading elements to push forward rapidly, leaving mopping up activities to supports and reserves.

d) Steps to insure the maintenance of communication between the artillery and supported units, between adjacent units, and from front to rear.

Attacks were made on a narrow frontage, with a battalion taking on from one to four city blocks using 'a large proportion of supporting weapons' and heavy weapons, anti-tank gun, and cannon platoons attached as required. As a rule of thumb the cutting edge was not more than two companies abreast, and these were not to be given more than two blocks each. In taking on a building it was to be regarded as an objective in its own right, and the responsibility of a single commander. Interestingly, *Combat in Towns* thought that direction would usually be aided by the geometric layout of a built-up area. This might have been a fair deduction in the USA where grid patterns were more common, but in Western Europe – where cities had grown up over centuries, often from a medieval nucleus of narrow winding streets, suitable only for small carts and barrows – it was an optimistic assumption. In case of need infantry were specially equipped and organised as 'assault squads'. Reserves required careful handling as there was little room for manoeuvre, but they could be used to repel counter attacks and mop up elements not subdued by the main thrust. In ideal circumstances they might also be directed off the main route of advance to take other resistance in a flank.

> Available tanks are kept in reserve for the performance of suitable missions, including meeting hostile counter attacks. Individual tanks and tank destroyers may be used as accompanying guns to attack by fire strongly fortified buildings and to assist in reducing barricades. Tanks so used must have close infantry support. The use of long range flamethrowers installed in tanks will have the effect of neutralising enemy resistance and possibly in driving him from cover.

At ground level the burden of combat fell to platoons and squads, and in strongly defended areas platoons were normally assigned 'not more than one block'. Flamethrowers and explosives were attached at platoon level.

> The block by block attack of a rifle platoon requires alert aggressive leadership on the part of the platoon leader. After the attack has been launched, he maintains close contact with his leading squads and promptly supplies covering fire and support as needed. When he observes that smoke or additional supporting fire will facilitate the advance, particularly across parks and open areas, he calls for it promptly. When the platoon must attack on both sides of a street the platoon leader uses his platoon sergeant or platoon guide to conduct the advance on the side where least resistance is expected.

Attached machine guns were used to assist the entry of attacking squads into the first buildings to be cleared, and to cover streets and alleys. Mortars could be used in various ways, but the 60mm, being too light to smash buildings, was to be regarded as a 'weapon of opportunity', perhaps to engage snipers on roofs, or search behind barricades. The

81mm had enough punch to wreck 'lightly constructed' buildings, or to penetrate most roofs.

Though every circumstance required initiative and judgement, squads were trained to advance house to house, 'through side yards; over rooftops; by breaching walls; or through back yards, streets or alleys'. The 'zone of advance' of a squad was normally on one side of the street only, and streets themselves were normally avoided by leading squads, but when they had to be used the advance was on both sides in two or more parties, each covering the opposite side as they went forward.

> Troops engaged in house to house fighting should be lightly equipped. Steel helmets, rifles, bayonets, and hand grenades are essential items. Special equipment, such as rubber or rope soled shoes, sub machineguns, pistols, knives, toggle ropes and grappling hooks are frequently useful. An extra pair of socks pulled over the shoes, or burlap strips wrapped around the shoes, may be used

Figure 34. Loopholes in unexpected places.

A. Loophole behind vine.
B. A few tiles have been lifted on roof. In this case the same thing should be done in several places or dark patches painted on roof as dummy loopholes.
C. Loophole under shadow of porch, over the door.
D. Loophole at ground level behind bush.
E. Loophole under the eaves. Dummies should be painted all along under the gutter.
This illustrates the axiom, "If you cannot entirely conceal it, make dummies like it."

c. Use great care in the selection of firing positions. Always try to fire from unexpected places. Weapons which are to be fired from windows or large openings should be located well back in the rooms. The area in front of the weapon should be wet to avoid dust and consequent disclosure of position by muzzle blasts. Do not allow the muzzle of a weapon to project from cover. Snipers should make frequent changes of position

The defence of a house from FM 31-50 *Attack on a Fortified Position and Combat in Towns*, 1944.

> in lieu of rubber soled shoes. Each squad or detachment should have heavy tools, such as crowbars and axes, for breaking in through doors, walls and roofs.

Where the enemy had prepared defences 'assault squads' of the type formed for use against fortifications could also be used. Typically, about a dozen strong these might include a two-man demolition party with charges; a BAR team; a flamethrower; bazooka team and a few rifle and carbine men with plenty of grenades.

It was difficult to plan in advance for all eventualities, and decentralisation of command and teamwork were crucial, but often attack on buildings required 'covering' and 'searching' parties. Squads were therefore divided into two or three parts with the covering men deputed to 'protect and facilitate' the advance of the searchers. According to the most basic 'Standard Operating Procedure' (SOP) the searching party was the squad leader with four to six men, the covering party the second in command and remainder of the squad, very much as in British practice. The search parties were best kept small because too many men got in each other's way in close-quarter combat. One or two of the team forced entry to a building, the rest of the search party followed promptly, and one or two were posted inside the building to prevent surprise. Ingress could be virtually anywhere, perhaps through the roof or upper windows aided by ladders, grapples, toggle ropes, or the help of comrades; through a hole blown in a wall; or less adventurously through the ground-floor doors and windows. The place was then searched according to prearranged plan, preferably top downward:

> After clearing the rooms of an upper floor, a grenade may be thrown down before descending. One man follows quickly, covered by his partner. Sometimes it will be impossible to use the staircase. In such cases, a hole chopped through the floor will do. A grenade dropped through this hole before descending may be effective. Another method of causing confusion amongst the enemy below is to place two or three grenades on the floor, pull the pins and quickly cover them with a mattress so that the force of their explosion is directed downward. If this accomplishes nothing else, it will usually dislodge the ceiling plaster of the room below, thus filling the room with dust, confusing the enemy, and handicapping his observation.

Conversely, if teams were forced to attack a house bottom upward they fired upward systematically through floors and attempted to remove any obstructions to stairways. If a room was believed to be occupied walking in was the least desirable option: ideally, a grenade was thrown through a window, or a small hole created for the purpose. In breaching any wall precaution was taken against both enemy fire and the possibility that a grenade would come through from the other side first. When throwing grenades into doors and windows men had to be sure the aperture was not covered with wire or anything else as the result might be the bomb bouncing back, or rolling away. Failing other options, a man worked with a buddy, one throwing in a grenade, the other rushing in after the explosion. The best way to move was to crouch low and jump across the threshold to one side or the other of the entrance. It was not to be assumed that a grenade would incapacitate everyone in a room: the enemy had learned the same tricks and sometimes rigged internal barricades and refuges behind which they took shelter. For such an eventuality an entry party had to have another grenade ready to hand. Searching parties also had to look out for booby traps, and checked for the presence of holes or tunnels to other buildings.

Whatever built-up area was being taken had to be cleared systematically section by section to obviate danger of leaving 'hostile centres of resistance in the rear'. In combat individuals were encouraged to hug walls, quickly roll over walls and roofs if they had to be traversed, and select cover in advance rather than be forced into somewhere unsuitable at the first shot. Machine weapons were to seek out the better fields of fire, as for example down streets and over open areas. Wherever practicable cover was to be fired round or through, as bobbing up from behind an object broke its silhouette, attracted fire, and exposed too much of a target. In firing round corners soldiers had to be prepared to shoot right or left handed, thereby keeping as much of the body under cover as possible. In close proximity to the enemy covering fire was vital. The worst sin was bunching together, from which 'more unnecessary casualties result than from any other cause'.

Such were the theories: but French towns still presented many a surprise. Brest with its pillboxes and town cemetery covered by interlocking zones of machine-gun fire took ten days to subdue. In textbook fashion Major General Troy Middleton first surrounded the town with 50,000 men, then secured key terrain around the city whilst subjecting it to bombardment. Tanks and explosive charges were used as the infantry fought their way towards the centre. Finally, 2nd battalion of 23rd infantry came up against the cemetery, and blew in buildings either side, pushing assault teams from house to house.

In defending built-up areas FM 31-50 reasoned that many of the tactical parameters of any other terrain also had relevance. Positions required purpose, all-round defence, mutual support, and very probably the general usefulness of forcing the enemy into expensive attacks if he wished to master the town.

> The main line of resistance may be either inside or outside the built up area, but never along a clearly defined edge. The near edge of a built up area is a convenient registration point for artillery and is likely to be subjected to the most concentrated fire. In the usual situation, the main line of resistance may be advantageously located in suburban districts so as to command avenues of hostile approach and take full advantage of observation, fields of fire, and opportunities for flanking fire against attacking forces. The holding garrisons consist of a series of unit defence areas with supporting weapons attached, each occupying a separate tactical locality (one or more buildings, or blocks of buildings) permitting small unit control. The defence areas are distributed laterally and in depth in such a manner that the fires of each cross the front or flanks of adjacent elements.

Within a defended area units were usually disposed as 'security' forces, the holding garrison, and a reserve. A three-battalion regiment might for example commit two battalions to the garrison and a battalion to reserve, initially supplying the outer security detachments from the reserve. Obstacles and improvements such as pillboxes, defended

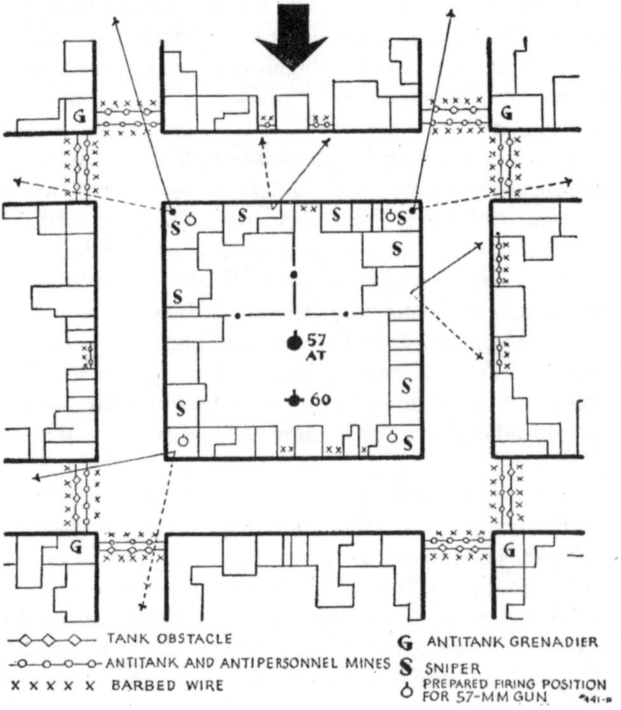

Figure 33. Defense area of rifle platoon in built-up area, with one machine-gun section, one 60-mm mortar squad, and one 57-mm antitank gun squad attached—schematic diagram. Positions of the relief on duty only are shown; the other relief is resting.

US deployment for platoon defence in a built-up area, as described in FM 31-50 *Attack on a Fortified Position and Combat in Towns*, 1944.

roadblocks, mines, barricades, and barbed wire were limited only by time and resources available. Nevertheless, they had to be created with discretion so as not to hamper friendly movement, nor give away to the enemy main positions of the defenders. In town defence a front-line battalion in the 'main line of resistance' was likely to be allotted a frontage from 4 to 8 city blocks, and a depth of from 3 to 6 blocks. Within this area two companies forward and one back, and with heavy weapons attached to the rifle companies was a basic deployment. Individual platoons constituted their own 'defence area', usually with crew-served weapons directly attached. Each squad took its own posts, with individual positions and fields of fire supervised by squad leaders. During prolonged occupation the squads were divided into reliefs allowing half the strength to rest or undertake other duties whilst maintaining vigilance and a strong defence.

Squad leaders and individuals were given practical hints on defensive preparations:

a) Every defensive measure should be taken to prevent the enemy getting above the defender and fighting his way down.
b) Principal, alternate, and supplementary loopholes for all riflemen and weapons should be prepared, reinforced and camouflaged. Loopholes may be made high so that the firer can fire from a platform, or low so that he can fire from a prone position. Low loopholes are blocked with sandbags when not in use. It is good practice to fire successive shots from different loopholes, if practicable. Dummy loopholes and heads may be used to draw enemy fire.
c) Use great care in the selection of firing positions. Always try to fire from unexpected places. Weapons which are to be fired from windows or large openings should be located well back in the rooms. The area in front of the weapon should be wet to avoid dust and consequent disclosure of position by muzzle blasts. Do not allow the muzzle of a weapon to project from cover. Snipers should make frequent changes of position.
d) Remove or sand bag windowpanes to prevent injury from flying glass. Screen or close openings, including the chimney, to exclude grenades. Place curtains over the upper portions of openings to darken the room and prevent observation by the enemy.
e) Guard against surprise, demolitions and fires. Trip or barbed wires with tin cans may give timely warning against enemy approach. The floor over basement dugouts or occupied rooms should be reinforced and fireproofed with wet earth or masonry. Keep some firefighting equipment in readiness for instant use. Remove inflammable materials.
f) Prepare one or more well camouflaged and sandbagged observation posts in the attic or upper storey. These locations may also be used for sniping or to prevent enemy infiltration over the roof.
g) Look out for booby traps, especially if the enemy has previously occupied the building.
h) Always keep one exit available. Breach the walls of interior rooms in concealed places, such as behind heavy furniture, under stairs, or other places not easily discovered by the enemy.
i) Barricade the openings. Doors required for your own use should be bullet-proofed by placing sandbags behind them, and the opening restricted to the minimum necessary for passage. The opening should be so located that the enemy cannot see into the room. In some cases it may be necessary to rehang the door to effect this safety precaution.
j) Bullet-proof parts of all upper floors, particularly the landings. This can be done with sandbags and will afford protection from enemy fire directed up through the floor.
k) Try to keep an empty room between you and the enemy if he is attempting to breach the wall of the building you are in; otherwise you may be killed by the blast. Immediately after the explosion, take position to fire through the hole keeping alert for any hand grenades thrown through the hole.
l) Drop grenades out of windows on an enemy in the street below. A slit in the

screen will permit this. Remove down spouts, or anything by which an enemy may climb the side of the building.

m) Fire through the walls or door if the enemy gains access to an adjoining room; fire through the ceiling, if he is upstairs; fire through the floor if he is downstairs. The caliber .30 bullet will penetrate most interior walls and floors. . . .

o) Prepare observation holes in the floors and walls and cover them with a sandbag.

p) If you are forced out, retreat towards the upper storey, unless you have a safe exit prepared in the cellar. It is easier to throw grenades downstairs from upper landings than to throw them upward. Prepare a means of escape from upstairs rooms.

q) Prepare a barricade in the corner nearest the door, if you are unable to escape from a room, and fight.

By the latter part of 1944 it would be no exaggeration to say that with the exception of the Ardennes offensive and some other limited counter attacking, the vast majority of German infantry were on the defensive – and many of these found their best positions in towns and the rubble left by bombing and bombardment. In village strongpoints a designated *Kampfkommandant*, or 'battle commander', pulled together disparate formations to create co-ordinated local defence schemes. In bigger towns and cities a series of concentric rings was the ideal plan, allowing defenders to fall back progressively whilst taking their toll on the attackers. Support weapons and dug-in tanks were deployed to cover defence works and individual guns placed to deny crossroads and approaches. Patrols without the defensive rings gave warning of enemy movements and mounted surprise ambushes as opportunity arose. Some of the details of street defence were repeated in the US *Handbook*. Both occupied and unoccupied buildings were booby-trapped, entrances to buildings blocked, and all windows opened so as not to disclose those from which fire is maintained. Rooms were darkened, and passages cut in walls. To avoid detection, the Germans fired from the middle of rooms and frequently changed positions. When houses collapsed, the defence was carried on from cellars, and rubble heaps of destroyed areas organised into strongpoints.

At the time of the taking of Aachen in mid-October 1944 US urban combat tactics had reached their final form, with full integration of armoured support as well as on the spot improvisations. Though not of great strategic significance, it was the first German city to be threatened, and 246th *Volksgrenadier* Division was devoted to its defence. Much of the work in clearing the town fell to the 26th Infantry, with Colonel Derrill M Daniel's 3rd Battalion ploughing, sometimes quite literally, through the maze of rubble and damaged buildings, whilst at the same time maintaining contact with Colonel Corley's effort against the northern hills. Tactical air missions delivered 160 tons of bombs, and light artillery and mortar fire swept forward block by block several streets ahead of the infantry. The corps and divisional artillery heavy artillery pounded communications farther to the rear with 10,000 shells. Yet the advance was still no easy matter,

> The fighting in Colonel Daniel's sector quickly fell into a pattern. Dividing his resources into small assault teams, he sent with each infantry platoon a tank or tank destroyer. These kept each building under fire until the riflemen moved in to assault; thereupon the armour would shift fire to the next house. Augmented by the battalion's light and heavy machine guns firing up the streets, this shelling drove the Germans into the cellars where the infantry stormed them behind a barrage of grenades. Whenever the enemy proved particularly tenacious, the riflemen used other weapons at their disposal, including demolitions and flamethrowers employed by two man teams attached to each company headquarters. The men did not wait for actual targets to appear; each building, they assumed, was a nest of resistance until proved otherwise.

To facilitate contact between units check points were set up at street intersections and the more obvious buildings, and units only proceeded beyond them after the adjacent sub-unit had been contacted. Each company maintained a specific zone of advance within which a platoon was generally allotted to one street: 'after a few bitter experiences in which Germans bypassed in cellars or storm sewers emerged in the rear of the attackers, the riflemen soon learned that speed was less important than pertinacity'. The US infantry answered by locating every manhole and blocking them one at a time. On occasion the infantry also had to rescue the tanks that had come to their support. Sergeant Alvin Wise and two privates managed to drive away a burning tank that had been hit, complete with wounded members of its crew. Close to the stone centre of Aachen tank rounds were found to be ineffective against the most solid structures so the Americans called up a 155mm self-propelled gun and used a bulldozer to clear its path to the strongpoint. The results, as Colonel Daniel remarked, were 'quite spectacular and satisfying'. Colonel Wilck, commanding the German defenders, regarded such tactics as 'barbarous', but, nevertheless – and despite orders to fight to the last, surrendered the final 3,000 troops. Aachen's cathedral, however, largely survived.

Chapter Six

Anti-tank Tactics

'Tank hunting must be regarded as a sport – big game hunting at its best'
– *Tank Hunting and Destruction*

A particularly distinctive aspect of infantry tactics in the Second World War was the invention of new weapons for use against armour, and development of tactics that gradually began to balance the playing field between the foot soldier and the tank. Tanks had been used since September 1916, and various anti-tank methods were quickly devised – notably the anti-tank grenade, the concentrated charge, anti-tank artillery, and, in 1918, the first anti-tank rifle. Yet for various reasons the advance of infantry anti-tank tactics made only limited progress in the First World War. For one thing, the overall armoured balance was very one sided: the Germans had very few tanks, and though rifle-launched anti-tank grenades were in fact made by the British, there were few opportunities to use them. Another factor was the very vulnerability of the armour of the period. For whilst later tanks like the Mark IV of 1917 were fairly resistant to armour-piercing bullets and machine guns, they remained highly susceptible to virtually any type of shell or mortar round. A very sensible option for the Germans was therefore to attempt to turn their artillery on the tank, and this they did, either without modifying existing weapons, or by mounting them on less obvious – and slightly more manageable – carriages with smaller wheels.

Infantry were left with the options of attacking tanks at close quarters with grenades, going to ground, or, in the final months of the war, attempting to pick off enemy vehicles with the limited numbers of rather heavy Mauser 13mm anti-tank rifles that had reached the front. A *Merkblatt*, or 'instructional memorandum', for tank fighting issued to German 2nd Army in January 1918 pointed out the vulnerable areas of British vehicles and what weapons should be used to attack them. Armour-piercing small-arms ammunition was to be aimed at the rear and vision ports, concentrated charges and grenades thrown onto the top decking. The light mortar, also deployed by the infantry in the latter part of the war, was regarded as the *ideales Tankbekämpfungsmittel*, or 'ideal anti-tank equipment', being capable of penetrating virtually any part of a tank, and by damaging tracks in particular bringing it to a standstill. A couple of the Mauser *T-Gewehr* rifles were recorded as captured by the Australians at Hamel in July 1918, where most of the tanks got through and 'many instances' were recorded of the vehicles overrunning and crushing German machine-gun positions.

Nevertheless, a number of new anti-tank rifles were developed between the wars, and by 1939 they were the prime anti-armour weapon in the infantry arsenal. Arguably, however, it was the experience of the Spanish Civil War that had most direct relevance to what happened in Europe after September 1939, for in Spain about 600 reasonably up-to-date tanks were deployed, including the Panzer I, as well as Soviet and Italian models. In some battles, as at Malaga in 1937, poorly trained militiamen broke and ran in the face of tanks, but in the defence of Madrid important lessons were learned. Both sides gained experience of infantry anti-tank combat, and, in the case of the multi-national force of the international brigade fighting on the side of the Republicans, quickly carried this knowledge back to other countries.

Though technically an infringement of the Treaty of Versailles, the Germans appear to have kept about a thousand *T-Gewehr* after the end of the First World War, and a self-loading rifle for close combat against tanks was suggested, but apparently not produced, by engineer W Brandt in 1925. The *Reichswehr* attempted to revive an officially financed anti-tank-rifle-development programme as early as 1929, but little progress was made for several years due to lack of resources. By the early part of the Second World War, however, the German Army fielded several types, notably *Panzerbüchse* models 38 and 39, plus some captured Polish weapons from September 1939. The *Pzb 38* relied for its power, and almost 4,000ft per second muzzle velocity, on its extraordinary round. This consisted of a 13mm cartridge, but a steel-cored bullet of only 7.92mm. The operator loaded the hefty 35lb weapon by swinging the pistol grip forward and down to open the breech, into which was slid a single round. On firing the gun recoiled, ejected the spent cartridge case, and returned to position with the block held open for the next round. The penetration of the bullet was 25mm, or about 1in at 100yd. The *Pzb 39*, which largely superseded the *Pzb 38*, was a much simpler and cheaper weapon to manufacture. For whilst its performance was very similar, the 'semi-automatic' recoiling feature was dispensed with, but a muzzle break was added so as to make the stress on the firer not appreciably greater. Something that readily distinguished the old and new models of German anti-tank rifle was the addition of two ten-round cartridge boxes on brackets either side of the mechanism. These could be reached easily by the gunner and made it unlikely that he would arrive in position entirely devoid of ammunition even if left to use the weapon solo. Interestingly, and even though the *Pzb 39* was still seen on the battlefield as late as 1942, after the opening campaigns of the war it was realised that the performance of anti-tank rifles was marginal, especially against the latest tanks. Therefore, some *Pzb 39* weapons were converted to grenade dischargers or *Granatbüchse 39*. In this the barrel of the rifle was cut down and fitted with a 3cm rifled discharger unit. The firing of a special propellant round could throw the little grenade about 500m.

According to standard instructions pertaining in 1941 the German AT rifle team was two men. The *Richtschütze* carried the gun, cleaning kit, and a pistol for personal defence, and the *Munitionschütze* was armed with a rifle and was equipped with an ammunition carrier. In action the *Munitionschütze* also observed fire, helping his colleague to correct aim. Both men carried short entrenching tools, and a total of forty additional rounds for the gun were held in pouches on their belt equipment. The anti-tank rifle team was commonly deployed as a platoon asset, but the AT rifles of a company could be grouped for a specific purpose. As the British summary *German Infantry in Action, Minor Tactics* explained,

> On the march, when attacks by AFVs may be expected, AT rifles should be located at the head and rear of the company. Protective detachments on the march should as a rule be allotted AT rifles. When deployed and in the attack the AT rifles may be allotted to individual platoons. Attacks on isolated, stationary or immobilised AFVs can be carried out with success. If the situation permits personnel of the AT section should also be employed in bringing up ammunition supplies and similar tasks.

Whilst a semi-automatic German anti-tank rifle was developed in 1940, and a very advanced looking bull-pup design was developed by the Czech firm ZB for the *Waffen SS* in 1941, it was already clear that the technology had a limited lifespan. Tank armour was swiftly increasing in thickness and effectiveness – whilst at the same time larger or higher velocity anti-tank rifles would be circumscribed by the physical ability of the crew to carry the weapon and use it on the battlefield. By the middle of the war German AT rifles were rarely seen, and totally superseded with the advent of rocket-type arms.

The British equivalent of the German AT rifles was the Boys, Mark 1, .55in. Originally codenamed 'Stanchion', its final name came from one of its designers, Captain Boys, who died during its development. So it was that Britain's first general-issue AT rifle entered service in 1937 as the Boys. At the time it was one of the best in its class, having a top-mounted five-round box magazine, bolt action, and a muzzle brake, sprung recoil mechanism, and rubber padded butt that helped absorb at least some of its backward kick. The penetration of the round against armour was much the same as German equivalents, being 23mm at 100yd, and 19mm at 500yd, with this performance dropping off to about half at an angle of 40 degrees to the target. Interestingly, it was also useful against up to 14in of brick, and 10in of sandbags. Weighing in at 36lb, it was not an easy burden for one man, but was ideally carried in the platoon truck, or between the two-man team.

The Boys was essentially intended as a platoon weapon: the usual deployment for an infantry battalion being described in the *War Equipment Table* of 1941 as 25 per battalion, divided 3 per rifle company and 13 amongst the carrier platoon, headquarters, and other sub-units. The ideal ammunition distribution was 200 rounds per weapon in the carrying vehicle, 40 rounds being held in 8 magazines and 160 in 5 round clips in bandoliers. A further 40 rounds per rifle were held as reserve. A basic AT rifle course was described in the February 1940 *Supplement* to the official manual. Some training was done on .22 rifles to save on both space and full-size rounds, and some on a 'pointing and swinging' basis with the Boys, but without live ammunition, before trainees progressed to shooting actual .55 rounds. Though the final aim of the courses was to train all troops in the firing of AT rifles, efforts began with three men per unit, preferably the best rifle shots. On the miniature ranges silhouettes of tanks were arranged to run on wires by means of winding drums, so creating 'crossing targets' at different speeds, and representing different distances. On the AT rifle range proper the weapons were shot from pits representing flanking positions against paper targets showing tanks. Troops were taught to give sufficient 'lead' toward the front of a moving vehicle to allow for speed, and in most instances to aim for crew areas, or the centre of the target, rather than attempt to stop the tank itself. Fully trained gunners were expected to be able to fire about nine rounds a minute, though probably at the cost of a battering to both eardrums and body.

The tactics for the Boys were described in passages of *Infantry Training*, 1937, and the manual *Anti-Tank Rifle* – composed the same year and reprinted with amendments in 1939. In defence use of the Boys was fairly straightforward, commanders being encouraged to integrate them within company positions for 'local protection' disposed with 'due consideration to the anti-tank plan for the defence of the sector'. Ideal positions had a 'good field of fire' up to 500yd, allowing the AT riflemen to track targets from flanks, perhaps with interlocking zones of fire. Properly concealed, AT rifle positions gave opportunity to obtain surprise, and were particularly effective if they covered a defile, natural feature, or man-made defence that tended to force enemy vehicles to follow restricted routes. Wherever possible, Boys positions were improved into pits or trenches deep enough to allow firers to sit or stand, as this gave greatest cover and possibility for traversing. Lying down was to be regarded as a posture for emergencies. When in action both members of the team played an active part with the ammunition carrier becoming both observer and protector of the firer. When protecting units on the move a number of AT rifles were deployed with the advanced guard and rear, or piquets to the side, preventing surprise by armour. How best to use the Boys in the attack was more problematic, as was explained by *Infantry Training*,

> The weight of the anti tank rifle compels careful consideration as to whether forward rifle companies should carry them into the attack. Every effort should be made to protect these companies against tank counter attack by independent means so that their own freedom of manoeuvre is not restricted . . . In any event the battalion commander must arrange for anti tank protection immediately his leading troops have captured their objective, if necessary by sending forward anti tank rifles with reserves for consolidation.

That the Boys had strict limitations was realised even by 1939, instructions recognising that it was a 'means of protection against light armoured fighting vehicles' but even then, if the crew were not hit, it might not 'seriously damage' the vehicle. By 1940 unease about its efficacy increased. According to the commercially produced Gale and Polden manual,

> After the battle of France the returning members of the BEF had many hard things to say about this weapon, the general impression being that as a weapon designed to stop modern tanks it was out of date, but – and this is a fact that cannot be avoided – it was never intended to stop modern tanks. This weapon is designed to afford a means of protection against light armoured fighting vehicle, i.e. the type of vehicle which the Home Guard is likely to have to deal with, certainly in the early stages of either an air borne or sea borne landing on our coasts. It is very important that the Home Guard realize this before doubts arise as to its capabilities.

With the evacuation from Dunkirk it became frighteningly obvious that the enemy had achieved armour superiority – partly through tactics and modernity of vehicles, but also for the simple reason that the vast majority of British tanks had had to be abandoned on the Continent. Given the nature of the emergency the advice of General Paget to the new Prime Minister was that in addition to 'irregular units' such as the Home Guard efforts should focus on the formation of 'tank-hunting platoons'. The rush to create an effective anti-tank infantry arm from almost nothing was impressively swift, even if the methods and materials were woefully inadequate, and the cost to the inexperienced tank hunters might have been horrendous had the *Panzers* actually landed in Kent and Sussex. The new bible *Tank Hunting and Destruction*, numbered as 'Military Training Pamphlet 42', was issued by the War Office on 29 August 1940 and was staunchly upbeat:

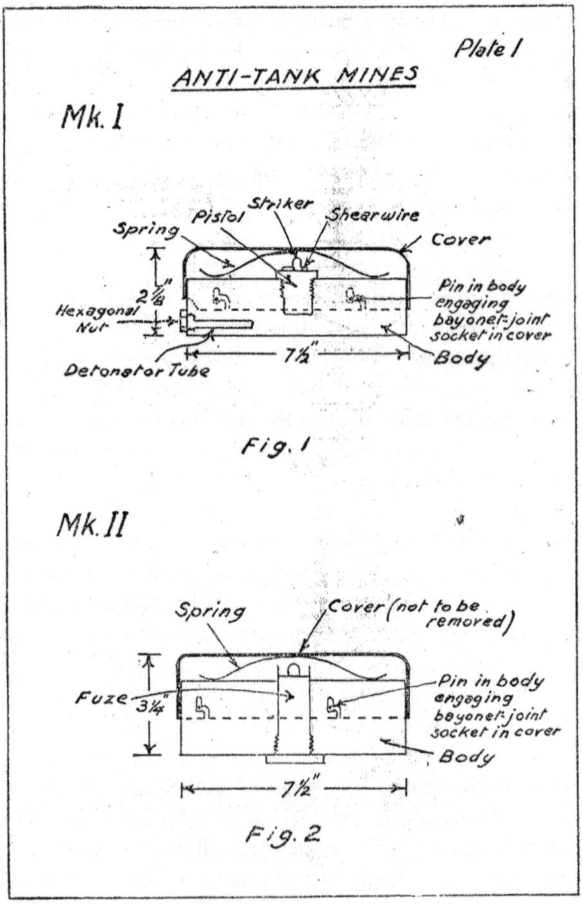

Anti-tank mines Mark I and II, from the British manual *Anti-Tank Mines*, 1939, reprinted with amendments, 1940.

> It has been proved that tanks, for all their hard skin, mobility and armament achieve their more spectacular results from their moral effect on half-hearted or ill led troops. Consequently, troops which attempt to withstand tanks by adopting a purely passive role will fail in their task, or at best only half complete it. Tank hunting must be regarded as a sport – big game hunting at its best. A thrilling, albeit a dangerous sport, which if skilfully played is about as hazardous as shooting tiger on foot, and in which the same principles of stalk and ambush are followed.

It was explicitly stated that British efforts would take note of the 'lessons of Spain and Finland', where tank hunters had operated with 'bravery, resource and determination'.

Defensive tactics were to take advantage of enemy attacking methods, with their 'bold infiltration' and 'complete disregard for open flanks', and a speed of advance that generally precluded thorough clearance or occupation of the country through which it passed in early stages. Likewise, advantage was to be had of the specific design features of tanks. These might be relatively easy to blind, given that most vision was obtained through relatively small forward-facing slits giving poor coverage of ground-level objects close to the vehicle. Infantry could fire at slits or shutters forcing them to be closed down, and ground-level fire directed slightly upwards 'under the eyebrows' could be effective. Glass and optics could be smashed or cracked even if crew were unharmed, whilst flamethrowers finding an aperture were devastating. Also sensitive to flame and incendiary bombs were louvres and air vents, whether these serviced crew or engines. Top decking and belly were often of thinner armour than fronts and turrets, anti-tank rifles and other weapons might therefore cause more damage than usual by being planted to cover banks and ditches, firing at close range as the vehicle bucked up or nosed down.

Much was also to be made of fields of fire limited in elevation and depression: so if tanks passed close to houses they were frequently incapable of engaging targets in upper windows. Similarly, most of a tank's firepower was concentrated in its turret, attacks from different angles therefore stood significant chance of success as the crew struggled to engage in a variety of directions. Tracks, fuel, and crews also presented opportunities. Tracks could be attacked in a conventional way with grenades, mines, or anti-tank rifles, or, more alarmingly, tank-hunting teams were encouraged to pop out from cover and attempt to ram crowbars and wooden spars into the running gear, preferably aiming for the space between drive sprocket and track. Interestingly, a number of other tacticians of 1940 suggested that a charge on the end of a pole ('pole charge') could accomplish much the same thing with slightly less risk to the anti-tank team, thus anticipating methods used by the Japanese later in the war. Crews could be picked off, and were especially vulnerable when they left their vehicles for food or sleep. Darkness enabled tank hunters to get much closer with less danger, and few tanks were run at night and often those that were required the hatches to be left open for maximum crew vision. Tank-hunting platoons could much improve their chances by operating on an 'area basis' knowing the ground far better than the enemy, and identifying in advance any bottle necks, ambush points.

In addition to AT rifles and small arms, *Tank Hunting and Destruction* described a variety of grenades and flame weapons for use by anti-tank teams. Prominent amongst these were the 'Molotov Cocktail', an improvised device perfected in Spain, and other types of petrol bomb. As Tom Wintringham explained in *Picture Post* on 15 June 1940,

> We made use of 'petrol bombs' roughly as follows: take a 2lb glass jam jar. Fill with petrol. Take a heavy curtain, half a blanket, or some other heavy material. Wrap this over the mouth of the jar, tie it round the neck with string, leave the ends of the material hanging free. When you want to use it have somebody standing by with a light. Put a corner of the material down in front of you, turn the bottle [or jar] over so that petrol soaks out round the mouth of the bottle and drips on to this corner of the material. Turn the bottle right way up again, hold

PLATE 3

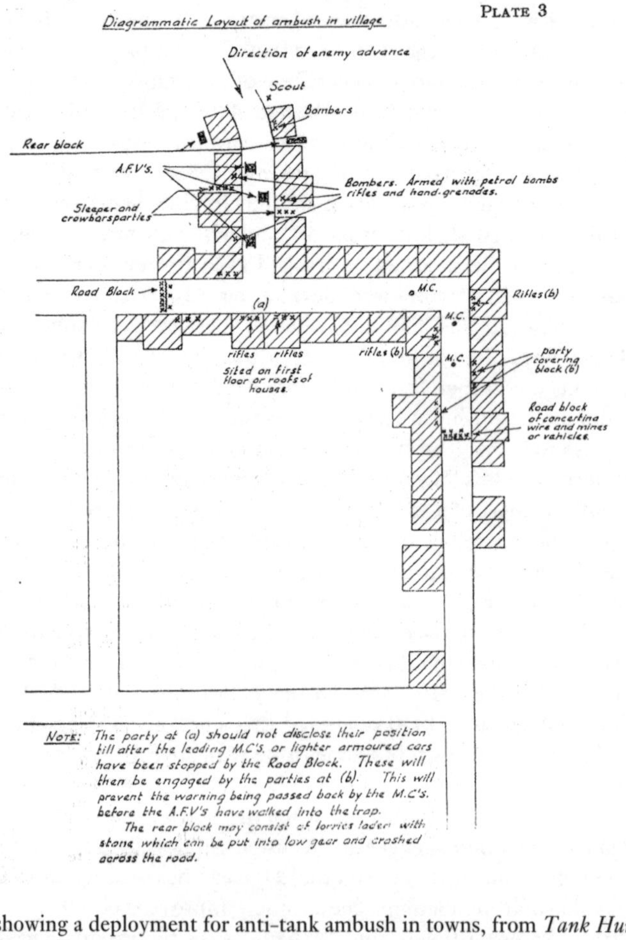

Diagram showing a deployment for anti-tank ambush in towns, from *Tank Hunting and Destruction*, 1940. The streets are blocked at locations out of sight of the approaching enemy, and whilst troops engage with small arms from upper floors a roadblock – perhaps created by a lorry – is driven out behind the enemy column. Tank hunters equipped with Molotovs, grenades, and crowbars then assault the trapped vehicles.

> it in your right hand, most of the blanket bunched beneath the bottle, with your left hand take the blanket near the corner that is wetted with petrol. Wait for your tank. When near enough, your pal lights the petrol soaked corner of the blanket. Throw the bottle and blanket as soon as this corner is flaring. (You cannot throw it far.) See that it drops in front of the tank. The blanket should catch in the tracks or in a cog-wheel, or wind itself round an axle. The bottle will smash, but the petrol should soak the blanket well enough to make a really healthy fire which will burn the rubber wheels on which the tank track runs, set fire to the carburettor or frizzle the crew. Do not play with these things. They are highly dangerous.

Tank Hunting favoured a handier bottle version, or 'Molotov', thrown directly onto the tank, adding other refinements to increase the stickiness and staying power of burning fuel. In one recipe petrol and tar were used in equal proportions, in others 'naphtha, paraffin, or diesel oil' were added, all of which helped 'the substance cling more to the surface of the tank'. Some sawdust or cotton waste in the mixture lengthened total burn time. As far as containers were concerned, a 1-pint capacity was deemed about right, but beer and champagne bottles were best avoided as they were tough and did not always break. Better were spirit or lime-juice bottles that smashed more easily, and could be encouraged to do so reliably by two or three longitudinal scratches 'with a diamond'. Ignition devices included not only flaming cloth but a length of cinema film, or alternatively, 'two lifeboat matches bound to the bottle with adhesive tape. Matches liable to be affected by damp may be covered by cellophane paper held in position with rubber bands'. The best places to throw the Molotov were high on the tank, so allowing the burning liquid to trickle downwards, preferably being sucked into louvres or vents.

> The first inclination to throw the bomb hard at the tank must be avoided: an underarm lob will often be the best method of throwing unless the bomb can be dropped from the windows of a house or some other position above the tank. After the first bomb has hit the target and ignited successive bombs can be thrown without themselves being ignited.

Of rather greater sophistication were the Albright and Wilson phosphorus grenade; 'sticky bomb'; and anti-tank percussion grenade. The 'AW' – made by Albright and Wilson of Oldbury, also known as the 'SIP' or 'Self Igniting Phosphorus' grenade, and finally as the 'No. 76' – first appeared in July 1940. Initial tests involved throwing the prototype against pieces of wood, or into a hut, and 'in every case a fierce fire was started'. This being proven, large numbers were manufactured. Described as 'an improved type of Molotov', it weighed 1.5lb and consisted of a short-necked half-pint clear glass bottle, sealed with a crown cap, containing yellow phosphorus, bezene, a strip of crude rubber and water. During storage the rubber dissolved into the liquid, making it tacky. These bombs required no special ignition, for as soon as the glass shattered the phosphorus came into contact with air resulting in dense fumes, smoke, and severe burns for any hit by the contents. An interesting ruse to allow timed ignition, or to make sure the grenade broke, was illustrated in *Home Guard Instruction* 51, of 1943. In this a length of safety fuse and a detonator were taped to the bomb. The user could light the fuse and throw the bomb reassured that it would go off whether or not it hit a hard surface, or simply light the fuse and retire. In the Home Guard the AW could also be shot from the Northover Projector. This was effectively a crude breech-loading mortar on a heavy tripod that projected bombs at modest velocity using a small charge. The range of the Northover was a modest 300yd, with fair accuracy to about 200yd. At very close ranges a 4ft square was regarded as virtually unmissable. The two-man team consisted of the operator (No. 1) aiming and firing the weapon, and a loader (No. 2) who also acted as observer. AW bombs were supplied in wire-bound wooden cases of twenty-four, but would not tolerate any careless handling. *Tank Hunting* suggested that they should actually be stored under water, or failing this in a cool place, but never inside houses. They could be transported in open lorries, but were regarded as too dangerous to be moved by rail.

The sticky bomb, 'ST' or 'No. 74' was scarcely more user friendly. Privately developed in the summer of 1940, it was a powerful charge of over 1lb of nitroglycerine in a spherical glass flask, mounted on a metal handle containing the striker mechanism. The sphere was covered with an adhesive envelope, protected prior to use inside a metal outer casing. The bomb had first to be fitted with its detonator. To throw the user pulled out the first pin and released the clip of the outer casing allowing it to fall away. Being careful not to touch the adhesive surface against anything, the second pin was now removed whilst the thrower kept a firm grip on the handle. The bomb could now be lobbed, or for a certain kill, jabbed into a vulnerable point on the enemy vehicle. In either event the bomber had 5 seconds to get under cover before detonation. *Tank Hunting* described the tactical use of the sticky bomb as follows,

> The ST grenade is most effective against baby tanks and armoured cars having plating under one inch in thickness. It is not effective against plating exceeding this thickness. Medium or heavy tanks encountered will probably be vulnerable only on the roofs, engine casing and under parts. The ST grenade should be considered a portable demolition charge which can be quickly and easily applied. One of the safest and easiest methods of application is to drop the grenade from the upstairs window of a building overlooking a road along which a tank is proceeding. Alternatively, these grenades may be used from some form of ambush within ten or fifteen yards from a road or track along which tanks are likely to pass. A position on a bank overlooking such a road has obvious advantages. The use of a smoke screen for such operations should be considered. Some form of road block may also prove most useful. For use during a night raid on tank parks the ST grenade is an ideal weapon. It can be planted by hand instead of thrown so long as the operator retreats in such a direction that he is protected from the explosion by part of the tank. If desired, the grenade can be planted in position and fired by pulling out the safety pin with a long piece of string. When this method is adopted it is essential first to close the ends of the safety pin to make sure that it will slip out easily. When applying an ST grenade by hand, it must be banged down with considerable force to ensure that the flask breaks and

Attacking the Track and Delivering a "Sticky."
(These operations are not performed simultaneously.)

Near suicidal anti-tank tactics from Derek Whipp's *Anti-Tank Weapons*, 1942. To 'smash the tank' by these 'audacious' methods members of the team lurk in cover waiting for a vehicle to slow as it negotiates a bend or obstacle. One attempts to ram a 'length of iron' between tracks, another executes a close-range 'sticky bomb' attack.

that as large an area of contact as possible is obtained. The bigger the area of contact, the more effective will be the explosion.

The hand percussion bomb, later known as the 'No. 73', appeared in *Tank Hunting* initially described only in outline as a 3lb explosive charge in a light casing, to be thrown into the tracks and wheels of tanks. When aimed well forward the vehicle would quickly run off its tracks, becoming immobilised or capable only of turning on the spot. It appears to have been introduced just after the manual appeared, and a final diagram was issued as an amendment in February 1941. To throw the No. 73 the bomber removed the safety cap, positioned the bomb vertically, and threw the grenade with a bowling action. A tape pulled the final 'safety bolt' allowing the bomb to explode on impact. Described as 'extremely powerful', it was recommended that they should only be used from cover. Though declared obsolete in October 1941, the grenade was brought back again in guise of a 'demolition charge'.

Flame did not necessarily have to come from a bomb or bottle, for *Tank Hunting* and its amendments also described the use of 'petrol ambushes', and two flamethrowers. The 'petrol ambush' was brutally simple:

> Petrol and oil poured on a road and ignited will, in suitable conditions, form an effective ambush, the intense heat and flame resulting in the destruction or immobilisation of enemy vehicles. The use of this means is restricted to defiles which the enemy is likely to use (for example to debouch from the coast or landing grounds). Consideration must be given to the effect of fires started in the vicinity. The method employed is by gravity or by trailer pump from a reservoir hidden and protected at a distance from but within view of the defile. Surprise is important and the reservoir should be camouflaged. The oil is led by 2 inch pipes to the defile, discharged from jets or sprays and ignited electronically or by some

> other simple means. The composition recommended is 25 percent petrol and 75 percent gas oil, which being of no value for the propulsion of motor vehicles is of little use to the enemy. The reservoirs may be static or mobile, preferably the latter – any tank with the necessary capacity may be used either mounted on a lorry or built into a previously prepared position. Fuel is required on a scale of 2 gallons per square foot per hour. Thus to cover an area of road 50 feet long by 20 feet wide requires 200 gallons for every six minutes of burning. To sustain a fire of great intensity a head of oil of only a few feet is necessary and a pump is not an essential.

An interesting variation on this theme, not contained in *Tank Hunting* but mentioned in other period literature, was the flame 'fougasse', developed by the British Petroleum Warfare Department. This consisted of a hollow dug into the side of a lane, or strategically positioned near to a bend around which might be a roadblock or ambush to halt a column. When a suitable target appeared a charge in the cavity was detonated and a 40-gallon drum or similar container of fuel was blown out into the enemy, simultaneously igniting. As with petrol bombs, the fuel might be mixed with gas oil, tar, or other ingredients to create a sticky mass of dripping flame, difficult to remove from men or machines. One example of the hundreds of fougasses positioned in Britain was left in situ near the village of Poynings in West Sussex after the war. Like many, it consisted of two 'batteries', totalling four barrels of fuel, one battery pointing up the road the other down. Earthenware pipes allowed charges to be lowered down behind the barrels to arm the trap that could be fired electrically using a battery or exploder and wire. Simultaneous firing of both elements would engulf both sides of the target area in flames ensuring that troops behind a tank did not survive to return fire.

The *Home Guard Training Manual* by Major John Langdon Davies detailed another simple method that required neither digging, nor even barrels, though its real practicality was dubious,

> In a village street, or at a suitable position with trees on both sides of the road it is possible to suspend blankets thoroughly soaked in paraffin in such a way that, just as the tank is about to pass them, they can be ignited and dropped so as to cover the whole tank. This blinds and suffocates the tank crew, and before the blanket has burned out masses of inflammable material can be piled up on the place. For this purpose a supply of dead bracken or branches may be kept by the side of the road, and hay forks to pitch them at the tank. As the object is to suffocate and deprive the crew of sight, this material should be flung on top of the tank and over the side slits. Where it is possible to arrange to obstruct a tank in a village street and attack it by this method, a barrel of tar, mixed with paraffin, should be kept in a first floor room, and once the blanket or other material has become well ignited, this should be poured on to the flames . . .

Whilst fuel-soaked blankets may seldom have worked, one instance of success – or even one serious attempt – was enough to endow the idea of hanging up suspicious looking things with some potency. Moreover, as Derek Whipp advised in his street-fighting volume, sheets suspended across a street screened whatever was going on further up the road. *Tank Hunting* remarked that a crew that came across blankets slung across a street would almost certainly be stopped the first time, and could never be sure whether there was a roadblock or ambush hidden somewhere nearby. Other ruses might include random excavations, or strips of canvas and dummy pillboxes that also distracted and slowed, whether or not they were associated with real threats. As Major Langdon-Davies observed,

> Anything unusual left in the village streets will have to be investigated. A soup-plate can be made to look exactly like a mine, and it will be very useful to hold up the enemy while he is under your fire by leaving a few dozen soup-plates for him to examine. Naturally there will be mines left at other places or he will soon ignore the plates. Buckets, dustbins, barrows etc. may or may not conceal danger and will waste his time.

The flamethrowers detailed by *Tank Hunting* were the Harvey and the Marsden. The Harvey was described as a 22-gallon cylinder 'mounted on wheels in the same manner as a porter's barrow', with a 25ft-long nose terminating in a nozzle. The flame could be projected up to 50yd, though as the device emptied pressure gradually dropped. It was envisaged that their primary use would be as part of roadblocks, where they would be best placed to a flank. The duration of the flame was about 10 seconds. An amendment to *Tank Hunting* in May 1941 added the recommendation that the Harvey should be aimed low, preferably from a concealed position, and perhaps sand-bagged. Troops nearby armed with rifles should be ready to deal with crews or infantry accompanying vehicles. Details of the backpack Marsden flamethrower, which weighed in at 82lb, were contained in an amendment of June 1941:

> The Marsden flamethrower consists of a gun and pack which is slung on the back of the operator and which can be handled in much the same manner as a rifle. A flexible pipe attached to the gun is connected to the pack by means of a bayonet fitting when in the alert position. The fuel from the pack is forced by nitrogen gas pressure through this flexible pipe to the control valves of the gun. The control valves are operated by a single lever which on initial pressure opens the pilot jet, this jet is ignited at will by pressing the push button beneath the trigger guard. By fully depressing the control lever a jet of flaming fuel is ejected and can be directed on the target. Maintaining a full depression on this lever allows a continuous stream of flaming oil on the target for approximately 12 seconds. Moving this lever from the pilot open position allows a number of intermittent spurts. By completely releasing the lever, operation may be suspended at any time.

Whilst immediate post-Dunkirk British anti-tank methods, particularly those of the Home Guard, may appear ludicrous, it has to be remembered that few of the most primitive were used in anger as the predicted invasion never came. Conversely, the German Army was actually forced to use many similarly desperate schemes, especially on the

Eastern Front in late 1941 and 1942. Equally early US tactics were scarcely better than their British counterparts, and it was perhaps fortunate that US infantry were not immediately brought face to face with German armour. In all three instances there was still heavy reliance on small anti-tank guns. In the German case these were mainly the 37mm *Panzerabwehr Kanon*, first field trialled in Spain and later forming a battalion within each infantry division. As *Handbook of the German Army*, 1940, explained, the 37mm 'PaK' was 'the main anti-tank weapon', capable of using a range of shells and fitted with a crew shield and low-pressure pneumatic tyres, it could be towed behind a vehicle or dragged cross country by its detachment. The British had 2pdrs that were initially part of the artillery 'Anti-tank Regiments', though a considerable number of these were left behind in the evacuation of France.

The US Army used a rather similar gun to the Germans, in the form of the 37mm M3 type introduced in October 1938. According to the *Organisation and Tactics* manual of 1940 these were usually fielded by the anti-tank platoons of the rifle battalions. Each weapon required three crew to operate the gun in action, though all members of teams were to be trained to handle the guns and replace casualties. As with the Germans, AT teams were taught to move their pieces by mechanical means as far as practicable, situation and terrain permitting, then resort to manpower. Where necessary the equipment could be broken down into loads light enough 'to permit manhandling over considerable distances' with gun, mount, ammunition, sight, and accessories carried separately. Wherever possible, platoon leaders were to assign 'sectors of fire', whilst section leaders exercised 'fire control' over a pair of guns, often in protection of a company sector. Individual gun commanders were regarded as effectively 'squad leaders', directly supervising the preparation and occupation of individual gun positions, camouflage, and the fire discipline of the crew. The pair of guns forming the section were to be positioned not only in a manner to conceal and protect them whilst giving a good field of fire, but at a distance from one another that prevented both being destroyed 'by a single projectile', yet close enough that the section commander could control them. Wherever possible, 'alternate positions' were prepared to allow flexibility and security in combat. In the attack the gun teams had to be prepared to advance with their company comrades by means of a series of forward 'displacements', though it can be imagined that even the best drilled gun team was going to arrive and prepare for action much less quickly than the average rifle squad. All three of the early light anti-tank guns, 37mm and 2pdr, were progressively outclassed by increasingly well-armoured tanks, and though newer and more powerful AT guns like the 50mm, 57mm, 75mm, and 6pdr were developed these were also larger and heavier and less likely to be able to go where the foot soldier went.

The US Army covered the subject of 'anti-mechanised protection' for the foot soldiers of the ordinary rifle squads in Basic Field Manual 21-45 *Protective Measures, Individuals and Small Units*, of March 1942. US instruction began with a basic summary of the characteristics of armour, and the need for both vigilance against its sudden appearance and training in vehicle identification. By way of example *Protective Measures* offered cutaway illustrations of the Panzer II that appear to have been lifted almost directly from British documents. Similarly inspired were lists of the vulnerable characteristics of tanks, and the possibilities for inflicting damage with small arms and grenades. US infantry also had the slight advantage that the .50 heavy machine gun had originally been designed with anti-armour work in mind, and was still capable of inflicting serious damage to scout cars and other vehicles lacking decent armour.

When it came to specific tactics the key features of anti-tank fighting were 'ingenuity' and 'aggressiveness':

> Study the terrain about you from the point of view of the crew of an armoured vehicle. Plan the action you will take in the event it uses any possible approach. Make full use of the presence of large boulders, stumps and trees. Your concealment should include all measures by which you can remain concealed whilst firing at the vehicle. In dry ground the dust raised by the blast of your weapon will be more apparent than the flash. Such ground should be wet down if possible, or covered with wet sacks, mats, or small branches, leaves or grass. Select nearby alternative positions to which you may move if the enemy discovers your first position . . . If your position is discovered, some vehicles will fire on it whilst others try to approach by covered routes from the flank and rear. Study such approaches and plan your action to counter such a move. Locate or dig cover so a tank cannot run over you. Hold your fire until it will be effective. The success of your efforts will depend upon the surprise with which they are made. All members of your squad must exercise self control to avoid premature disclosure of their positions.

Most effective was the ambush, preferably executed in a defile of other confined space-limiting options and movement of the armour.

> You should scatter your group throughout the length of the defile. Antitank mines, mounted on a plank or other means so as to be easily pulled over the ground, should be hidden and drawn under the tanks as they pass. Some mines may be laid to block the exit from the defile and others arranged to be drawn under tanks after the leading tank is stopped. When only small arms and grenades are available, self control will have to be used and your future action will depend upon what the uninjured tanks do. Watch for well aimed shots at the periscopes, the vision slits, or at the turret track. If you are close enough to make your fire effective, you will be close enough to see what the crew members are doing. If the turret guns are pointing in your direction, remain concealed. If you have fired and the turret turns towards you, shift quickly to your alternate position and let someone fire on the tank from another direction. If smoke grenades and candles are available use them to blind the crews and you can approach close to the tank. Remember the smoke will be drawn into the tank by the ventilating system, so watch for the turret to open and use your rifle, pistol or hand grenade. If several tanks are blinded by the smoke and try to move they may put themselves out of action by collision and the crews may be destroyed when they attempt to leave the crippled tanks.

Forest provided ideal terrain for tank ambush, where snipers could be deployed close enough to pick off tank commanders before they had the opportunity to close hatches.

In bad terrain wheeled vehicles might find themselves effectively restricted to roads with dire consequences for columns shot up by armour-piercing bullets. All in all this was quite like the doctrine evolved in the latter part of 1940 in Britain, and in retrospect may be seen as an indicator of dire need for a new generation of infantry anti-tank weapons on both sides of the Atlantic. Interestingly, instructions issued to US umpires for training manoeuvres in 1942 assumed that all infantry within 100yd of a tank were automatically 'neutralised', and the only weapons to be regarded as 'effective' against light or medium tanks were the 37mm and other artillery of 75mm calibre or greater.

The main points of German tactics were summarised in the manual H.Dv. 469/4 *Panzer Abwehr Alle Waffen*, or 'anti-tank defence all arms', of 1942. The ways and means of achieving successful anti-tank defence were defined as twofold, being those intended to blind the tank, and those for actually destroying the vehicle. Blinding involved some of the ruses already mentioned – everything from shelter halves to cloths and paint being used as improvised methods to obscure vision slits. Particularly extensive use was made of smoke grenades, the commonest type of which was the *Nebelhandgrenate 39*, being of very similar design to the explosive stick grenade, but identified by means of white markings. One particular special technique was recommended. First two smoke grenades were tied together with a cord or wire about 2m in length, and the tank fighter took his post under cover within the company position, so placed that he was close to the likely avenues of tank movement. On the approach of an enemy vehicle he pulled the cords of both bombs and threw them over the barrel of the enemy tank. The vehicle was now blinded, at least briefly, by billowing smoke. It was forced to stop, or risk running off the track. In another version of the same ruse there was only one smoke bomb, teamed with a suitable weight. Smaller pear-shaped glass-

A German illustration showing how enemy tanks might be blinded using smoke grenades and lengths of rope. The tank hunter hides until the enemy armour passes, then throws his device to entangle the barrel of the tank gun. Whichever direction the turret turns vision is obscured by smoke. Other teams now have opportunity to attack with projectile weapons, grenades, or incendiaries.

bodied smoke grenades, the *Blendkörper* 1H and 2H were also brought into use. Owing to their chemical composition these gave off a particularly acrid smoke and a lucky or skilful user could hope to force a tank to retire, or even make a crew bale out. Being of glass these grenades needed careful handling, and came packed like light bulbs in cardboard containers, some tubular, others hexagonal. British testers who experimented with captured munitions were sceptical as to how effective these really were.

The Army *Waffenampt* or weapons office had made experiments with various types of Molotov as early as 1940 using captured French vehicles as test pieces. Despite unimpressive results, shortages of effective anti-tank weapons on the Eastern Front soon forced their use in battle. Following Russian and British practice the German Molotov usually consisted of a mixture of petrol and oil, fused with a cloth wick, or heavy duty 'storm matches' taped to the neck of the bottle. Gun cleaning cloth was handy as wicking, being found readily to hand and of suitable scale for the job. Naturally, such weapons could only be used if close enough to hit the enemy tank, and – assuming that it was unaccompanied by enemy infantry, or that these had been discouraged by other troops – it was recommended that the throw be taken from within about 30m. Arguably more effective, yet even more suicidal in use, was the jerry can incendiary. This consisted of a fuel can, about three-quarters full, to the side of which was tied a smoke-stick grenade. To use it the tank fighter got as close as possible and simply loosened the lid, pulled the grenade cord, then heaved the can bodily onto the decking of the tank. There was just 4½ seconds for the soldier to escape before the grenade ignited, lighting the 15 litres of petrol that were now leaking over the tank. It was recommended that one of these fuel-can incendiaries should be carried ready prepared in every vehicle at the front for emergency use in the event of surprise encounter with the enemy. In a variation on the theme, German soldiers in Russia made the interesting discovery that though many openings in enemy tanks were too small for grenades, or difficult to access with a long-barrelled weapon, there were at least some that were vulnerable to the humble flare pistol. As Hans Werner Woltersdorf described,

> Then I thought of my flare pistol . . . carefully I inserted the muzzle of the flare pistol into the hole . . . Very quickly: muzzle in. They fired immediately, but I had the pistol out again already . . . They were shouting, loud commands and shrill voices of fear . . . Then there was a fearful thunderclap . . . The turret rose a few centimetres, tilted to one side, and came crashing down . . . I could not get the men from the Moscow tank brigade out of my head. What a drama must have played out in their coffin!

More powerful, but just as hazardous, were the various forms of hand-thrown, or placed, charges and grenades. An early example was the 2kg *Panzerhandgranate 41*, a hollow charge bomb that was not easy to throw any distance and had a fairly disappointing armour penetration of about 35mm, though this was enough to attack the top decking of most tanks, or lighter vehicles. A larger *Panzerwurfmine* compounded the weight issue and danger to users but offered better performance. Another ruse was to use ordinary anti-tank mines as mobile weapons, with troops lurking in ambush ready to throw a fused mine out directly in front of – or even on top of – passing armour.

In late 1942, however, much improved hollow charge devices were introduced. These accepted that the user usually had actually to place the bomb on the tank, but conversely had much-improved armour penetration. The *Hafthohlladung 3* consisted of a cone-shaped 3kg bomb, containing a 1kg hollow charge, mounted on three large magnets. The user prepared the weapon by inserting the fuse at the apex, and removing an iron keep ring from the magnets. The bomb was then placed on the tank where it stuck firm and the yellow fuse activated. The attacker then had 7½ seconds to escape back into cover before the explosion – which was particularly effective because the size of the magnets was calculated to create an ideal 'stand off' distance from the cone of explosive giving 140mm of armour penetration. An improved model increased this to 160mm. A 4½-second blue fuse was supposed to be used if the bomb was thrown: this was not very practical, but did have a point if the bomber was able to activate the weapon in an upstairs room and drop it onto vehicles passing below. Between the introduction of the *Hafthohlladung* and discontinuance of production in May 1944 well over ½ million were made. They could be converted to be placed on concrete by means of a hook and chain attachment, and so also used against fortifications.

German rifle-launched anti-tank grenades commenced with the P40 type, devised early in the war. This was a fin-stabilised model launched from a spigot, and saw service in 1941 and 1942. Despite a hollow charge head, it was not greatly effective against tanks, and was superseded by a number of slightly differing models shot from a 3cm discharger – or *Schiessbecher* – clamped to the muzzle of the rifle. An armour penetration of 40mm was claimed. These early *Gewehr-Panzergranate* were initially limited by the diameter of the discharger, but later large, or *Grosse*, types were made with a bulbous head and just the narrower rear portion slid into the rifled discharger. Accessories for the discharger kit included a sight with a bubble, not unlike that of a spirit level, allowing the user to judge the correct elevation for the range required. Though a fairly decent armour penetration of 100mm and a range of 100m was claimed for the best of the German anti-tank rifle grenades, they were nothing like as effective as the rocket and recoilless devices that began to come on stream from the middle war period. Nevertheless, German rifle grenades of various sorts were still being used late in the war. British technicians who examined them questioned whether they were really worth the amount of time, effort, and materials that went into their production.

Whilst in retrospect this opinion may have been valid, British forces also used a rifle-launched anti-tank grenade on at least a limited scale from 1940 to about 1942. This device was the 'Grenade, rifle, No. 68', a dumpy looking, flat-headed munition, weighing just under 2lb, also shot from a discharger cup. The genesis of the idea appears to have been an attempt to marry up the potential of rifle projection, the 'Munroe principle' of the shaped charge, and the already existing 2in mortar bomb. In production by May 1940, some appear to have reached France before the end of the Dunkirk campaign, and more went to the Western Desert. On a good day it could cope with 50mm of armour at about 100yd. A number of variants were made and there were attempts to use it from the Northover Projector, and even a catapult. However, like the German rifle AT bombs, it was too small to deal with the latest tank armour, and was comprehensively overtaken by later developments.

The US Army also invested in anti-tank rifle grenades in late 1941 and 1942, and indeed issued them far more widely, and for much longer, than their British Allies. The initial M9 model was launched from a spigot very much like German counterparts, but was not very efficient. It was, therefore, replaced by the M9A1 type improving upon the basic design by means of a nose cone to create the right 'stand off' distance from armour plate on detonation, and a more sensibly placed base detonating fuse. At first these rifle grenades were shot from the 1903 bolt-action Springfield rifle, but later in the war a launcher was issued for use with the M1 Garand. Though one launcher per infantry squad was usual at first, later two, or even three, were carried as the spigot was relatively light compared to its supply of bombs. What the M9A1 could achieve depended very much upon range and type of target as the *Cannon Company* manual of 1944 explained. Its 'effective' range against light and medium tanks was regarded as no more than 75yd, but it could also be used as an 'anti personnel grenade, employing high angle fire, at ranges up to 260 yards. With the use of the auxiliary grenade cartridge ranges up to 320 yards are possible'.

One of the key limiting factors of the M9A1, as with many other rifle-launched bombs, was slow speed of travel, as *Grenades, Hand and Rifle*, 1943, makes clear. To hit a target just 55yd away a grenadier armed with M1 rifle and launcher had to hold his piece at 5 degrees elevation, and the time lapse between squeezing the trigger and striking, or indeed missing, the target was a whole second. At 260yd the rifle had to be canted to 45 degrees. The M9A1 then spent a leisurely 7½ seconds in the air before impact, plenty of time for all and sundry to hear the discharge and for even strolling and deaf infantrymen to have walked a considerable distance away. When the launch weapon was a carbine with M8 launcher the problem was compounded, a grenade taking more than 6 seconds to cover 184yd at maximum elevation. Whilst field works did not move around tanks certainly did, so hitting them at anything but close range was more a matter of luck than judgement. Armour penetration appears to have varied considerably with anything from 75 to 100mm being quoted in various sources. In most circumstances it was expected that US rifle grenadiers would remain with their squads during combat forming last ditch close anti-tank defence, or high-angle nuisance fire against concealed infantry.

Arguably, it was the latter part of 1942 that saw the beginning of a real turning of the tide in favour of the infantry. For up to that point if armour was well handled, and adequately supported by its own infantry and artillery, there was very little – not potentially suicidal – that the foot soldier could do to stop it. From this time, however, were devised new weapons and tactics with sufficient potential to even up the odds and make tanks extremely wary of infantry, especially in any close country that made it probable that they would be encountered at close range. These developments were extremely significant as they also had a tendency to favour the defence, and ability to slow tank attacks of the sort that had previously characterised armoured warfare. One of the first weapons seriously to challenge the new tyranny of the tank was the US 'bazooka', more properly known as the 2.36in Rocket Launcher. A lightweight rocket firing tube had been proposed by US inventor Goddard as early as 1918, but lack of tactical niche and end of hostilities ensured that it never saw action in the First World War. However, the need for a new anti-tank arm, plus development of hollow-charge munitions in the interwar period, gave the concept a new lease of life. The fact that though the USA had developed anti-tank grenades she had never invested in anti-tank rifles, and came to the problem effectively with a blank sheet made the bazooka a highly practical proposition. Key advantages of the system were the recoilless nature of the weapon tube – open at both ends – and lightness for the relative power and range of the projectile, both properties well suited to infantry use. More problematic was the back blast from the tube, but so long as users never attempted to fire within a confined space, and loaders kept clear of the rear end, this was not dangerous.

The smoothbore bazooka that entered service in 1942 weighed just over 13lb, was electrically initiated by means of batteries in its pistol grip, and fired a 3.4lb high-explosive anti-tank rocket capable of penetrating a maximum of 80mm of armour. The projectile flew at a fairly leisurely initial velocity of 300ft per second, making crossing targets moving at speed rather difficult to hit, but the performance of the weapon was remarkable for the time it was introduced. It was claimed to be 'reasonably accurate' against moving targets at up to 300yd, with effectiveness against an 'area target' at up to 650yd. Its round was stated to be 30 per cent more effective against armour than the anti-tank rifle grenade. The bazooka was supplied in small numbers to both the British and the Soviets in the latter part of 1942, with distinctly mixed results. The only place that British troops faced German armour at that time was North Africa, and here it was reasoned that infantry would be unlikely to get close enough to tanks in open terrain to deploy a hitherto untried weapon. The Soviets, by contrast, were short of almost everything and fighting along a huge front. The bazooka was found useful immediately, but its quick deployment landed examples in enemy hands, and observations on these were soon fed into the development of German anti-tank weapons. The US Army was confident enough to deploy the M1 bazooka in combat from November, with the improved M1A1 coming on stream the following year. The M9 that reached the battlefield in 1944 was made with the barrel in two pieces, folding neatly for easy transit. As the mainstay of infantry anti-tank defence the bazooka was issued on a scale of twenty-nine per battalion, five with each infantry company, others going to headquarters and support elements. Later models of the rocket were also improved so before the end of the war armour penetrations of 120mm or so were being achieved under ideal conditions.

According to the *Rifle Company* manual of 1944,

> Rocket launchers and high explosive rockets are provided primarily for use against armoured vehicles; secondary targets are crew served weapons, embrasures, pillboxes, and grouped personnel. Rockets are also effective against buildings and masonry. However, ammunition must be conserved to ensure effective use against primary targets. For necessary assistance in loading and reloading, rocket launchers are normally operated by teams of two men each. Selected individuals will be specially trained to function as rocket teams and all members of the company will be given sufficient training to familiarize them with the use of rockets and care and cleaning of launchers. A practice rocket is provided for instruction in mechanical use, marksmanship, estimation of leads, and techniques of fire. The rocket may be fired from the prone, standing, sitting or kneeling positions; it may also be fired from the pit, fox hole and pit type emplacements.

Standard forms of rocket launcher 'pit foxhole' and 'pit' positions were later described in the 1944 *Anti Tank Company* manual. The 'pit foxhole' was,

> a circular pit, 3 feet in diameter and about 3 and a half feet deep. It is large enough for two men. It permits the assistant rocketeer to rotate as the rocketeer traverses the weapon in order that the former will never be in the rear of the weapon when it is fired. Is depth is such that the rear end of the launcher at any elevation in any direction will clear the parapet, in order that the back blast from the rocket will not be deflected into the emplacement and burn the occupants. Except in firm soil, this requirement can be met only by an emplacement which is too shallow to give protection against the crushing action of tanks; in such a case, fox holes for the rocketeer and assistant rocketeer are dug nearby.

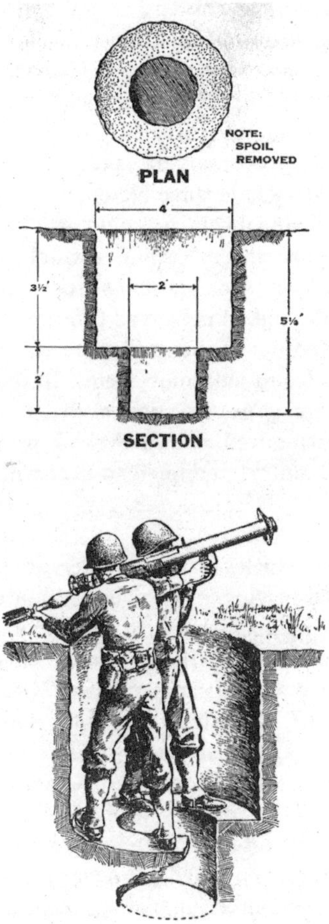

Textbook US bazooka pit from FM 7-10 *Rifle Company, Infantry Regiment*, 1944.

In case of emergency the anti-tank team could abandon the firing position of the 'pit foxhole', taking refuge in the deeper excavations. It was estimated that the basic firing position could be created in about an hour, but a total of 4½ hours were needed if the deeper refuges were added. The 'pit' rocket launcher position was simpler, but really only suitable for firm soil. In this instance a small cylindrical refuge space was dug into the bottom of the shallow firing pit. When tanks appeared to be about to overrun the position the team crouched, or perhaps more accurately crammed themselves, down into the lower area. This must have been uncomfortable to say the least but the simpler pit with refuge at the bottom could be excavated in 3 hours.

The usual mobile deployment of the two-man bazooka teams was by weapons carriers or other vehicles, dismounting as action threatened. Where time allowed the infantry company commander then placed his teams in the most advantageous positions according to mission. They could for example be used from cover to intercept incoming enemy tanks – or at the end of an advance placed near to the perimeter of the company position to block most likely 'avenues of mechanised approach'. Since enemy tank attacks were rare, especially against units not in direct contact with the enemy, it was to be expected that rocket teams might be given other duties much of the time. This being the case, early warning from 'anti-tank guards' and sentries was vital, as was pre-reconnaissance of possible firing positions. Standard warning signals might include three blasts on a klaxon, whistle or horn, or three equally spaced shots. Individual soldiers could also give a visual 'enemy tanks in sight' warning by striking 'his rifle or carbine several times between the upper sling swivel and front sight'. When such warnings were given troops on the march were expected to clear the roads, and all personnel take cover in any holes or ditches. Vehicles other than tanks moved out of the immediate vicinity 'into suitable nearby locations which provide obstacles to tank movement'. In the event of any stabilisation of the situation troops were to use any time available to dig entrenchments or weapons pits. Under actual armoured assault the AT weapons focused on tanks whilst the remainder of the infantry attempted to deal with attached infantry and vehicle crews.

> When attacked by armoured vehicles, primary targets are hostile foot troops, or exposed personnel riding on or closely following armoured vehicles. Infantry small arms fire is relatively ineffective against the armor of armored vehicles; however, under favorable conditions, the cumulative effect of armor piercing ammunition may be effective against tank sprockets, bogie wheels, and track suspension. For the most part, when hostile infantry does not afford a target, small arms fire will be directed against armored vehicle crews who seek to operate with open turrets, doors and vision slits in order to improve their field of view, In no circumstances will defending infantry be diverted from its basic mission of engaging and destroying hostile infantry. Defenders employing small arms fire against accompanying infantry, or employing anti tank rifle grenades, rockets and small arms fire against hostile armored vehicles, will continue to fire until forced to take cover to protect themselves and their weapons from the crushing action of such vehicles. They return to their firing positions as soon as the tanks have

passed, to fire on approaching foot troops or exposed personnel riding on or closely following other attacking tanks.

In terms of the bigger picture US doctrine also called for the deployment of regimental anti-tank guns within both the main line of resistance, and with combat outposts, perhaps with tank destroyer units in an immediate counter-attack reserve. Generally speaking, AT weapons were not to be distributed evenly, but intelligently, taking regard of likely avenues of advance, mines, obstacles, and general risk. Sometimes it proved possible to create channels into well-covered areas so as to create possible tank killing zones.

Though the British slowly introduced new anti-tank guns, had used anti-tank grenades, and the Home Guard and others were issued with a variety of flamethrowers and more or less improvised weapons, it was some time before the infantry arm as a whole could be re-equipped with a modern, man-portable, anti-tank piece. However, in August 1942 the new Projector Infantry Anti Tank – or 'PIAT' – was finally introduced. In developmental terms the roots of the PIAT went as far back as the early 1930s, and in 1937 Colonel Blacker of the artillery had patented a spigot discharger dubbed 'Arbelast'. Though there was no immediate requirement, Blacker reworked his idea in the dark days of 1940 to become the 29mm Spigot Mortar or 'Blacker Bombard', an unwieldy, but very powerful, anti-tank and bombardment weapon soon issued to the Home Guard. According to *Spigot Mortar*, 1942, it was possible to discharge this weapon at either low angle, to engage armour and direct targets, or at high angle, as heavy mortar. The 14lb anti-personnel bomb would fly 1000yd, but the 20lb anti-tank round was limited to 600yd, and was only tolerably accurate against vehicles up to 150yd. In emergency the rate of fire was up to fifteen rounds a minute, but was not usually more than half this. Often Spigot Mortars were dug into pits, and with 'portable' mounting weighed 342lb, severely limiting, if not entirely preventing, their use as an infantry weapon, but for transport the equipment could be broken down into five loads. For a mobile role a 15cwt truck could carry the mortar, 24 bombs, and a crew of 5 comprising a commander, aimer, loader, and 2 ammunition numbers.

The PIAT, first tested in early 1942, combined the idea of a spigot that shot forward into the tail of a 3lb bomb igniting a propelling charge with that of a hollow-charge warhead. The device was reasonably accurate against tanks at 115yd and had an armour penetration of about 75mm. It was issued on a scale of three per company, meaning that there were enough to put one with each platoon when a general anti-tank protection was needed, or several could be concentrated in ambush. PIATs could also be used against fortifications, houses, or area targets out to as much as 350yd. The user had first to cock the weapon: this was most easy to achieve by standing on the shoulder piece and lifting the PIAT to compress its enormous spring, but in action might entail wrestling with the beast on the ground so as to keep one's head well down. The bomb was then placed in the forward trough, usually by a team mate, and having taken aim using the simple sights the user pulled the large trigger. All being well the projector then recocked for its next round automatically. The PIAT was effective enough, reusable, and worked. Enemy tanks were indeed knocked out with it, and a number of soldiers decorated for its use in combat. Nevertheless, at 34lb it was heavy, not easy to manipulate, and had a shorter anti-armour range than the bazooka. It was also inferior to the new generation of German infantry anti-tank weapons.

According to the manual *Projector, Infantry, Anti-Tank*, 1943, when siting the weapon in its anti-tank role operators had five points to consider:

i. A field of fire of 100 yards or slightly more only is required.
ii. The necessity of gaining surprise and the consequent importance of a carefully concealed position.
iii. The desirability of shooting enemy AFVs from the flank or rear.
iv. The number of bombs carried will be limited; it is important, therefore, to get the enemy vehicle well within range to make certain of a 'kill'.
v. Probably the normal position for firing will be from a slit trench.

How the infantry unit should combat armour in general was the subject of sections in *Infantry Training*, 1944. Essentially, it was the job of infantry to 'make quite sure' that no enemy troops accompanying tanks were allowed to exploit the success of armour. The tanks themselves were to be dealt with mainly by anti-tank weapons, both infantry and others:

> infantry must, if needs be, lie concealed in their weapon slits. They must never allow themselves to be drawn off in pursuit. As soon as the tanks pass over, the

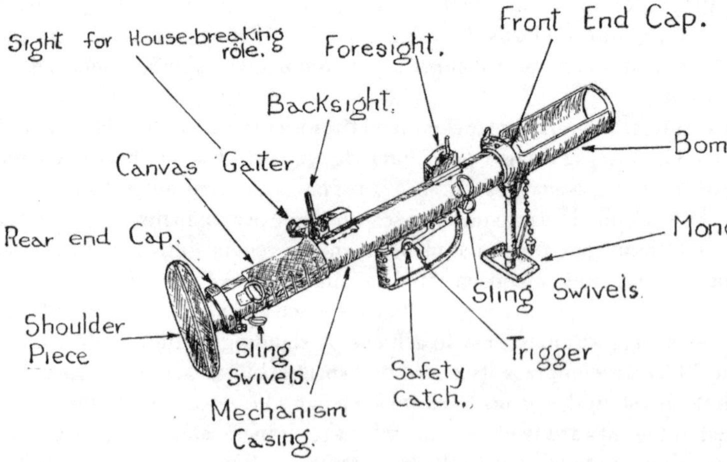

The Projector Infantry Anti-Tank – or 'PIAT' – from the provisional manual of 1943, reprinted with amendments, 1945.

> infantry task begins. They must bob up instantly and wipe out the following infantry. Tanks are likely to avoid the sort of site chosen by the defence for example woods, hedges, villages, or close country and they will then be unable to do more than by-pass the defences. They are often very chary of approaching close, for fear of anti-tank grenades, the PIAT, and other anti tank weapons. Infantry units that are in reserve or that have a mobile role may be given the task of ambushing small bodies of enemy tanks by day. Every company should therefore be prepared to carry out such roles.

In training it was decreed that every man of the platoon should be overrun by tanks whilst in a slit trench. Naturally, the troops would view this with 'considerable misgiving' in the first instance, but repeated exercises taught them that they could not be harmed if they kept down.

The key anti-tank tactic was the ambush, and in essence merely an improved version of methods devised in 1940. Much the same advice on springing an anti-tank ambush was given in the *Instructor's Handbook* of 1942, and repeated in *Infantry Training*, 1944. Ambushes were located where tanks had limited options, but not to be put in very obvious places, since 'S' bends and defiles were known danger spots that an enemy would very likely avoid. The best site, therefore, was, 'an ordinary stretch of road with a slight curve where thin cover e.g. houses, walls, banks, or a thin line of trees, make exit from the road difficult but not impossible'. The anti-tank team could practise the most probable scenarios by driving the route with carriers, seeing where vehicles slowed, or positions in the road likely to be adopted to cover each other, or see around bends and over rises. Exits from the road could be made more difficult by the use of mines.

The anti-tank team then selected three 'checking points', and a 'seal' point within which perhaps three vehicles of a tank troop could be tackled. The general rule of thumb was one ambush section to each vehicle, and the men to be placed as far as possible in perfect concealment a little back from the road, ideally in slit trenches. Tank commanders in turrets were above the level of the road, and ditches immediately adjacent likely to be shot up early in the engagement, and were, therefore, only to be used with discretion. Given smoke and confusion it was often wise to put all of the ambush team on one side of the road, so avoiding danger from friendly fire, and allowing troops to make a quick getaway after the attack. A rendezvous for the team to rally a distance away from the ambush site was designated, as was a signal for retirement. The ideal rendezvous was downwind as drifting smoke would give cover, whilst leaving any surviving enemy exposed and in doubt as to where their attackers were going. Definite orders had to be devised and issued in advance regarding enemy reconnaissance vehicles. These could be attacked, but if the point of the ambush was to hit armour they were to be ignored and allowed to pass: in this eventuality weapons had to be placed so as to deal with light vehicles that passed the ambush point but returned to assist the tanks when the ambush was sprung. Ideally, an anti-tank ambush was to last no more than 2 to 3 minutes reducing chances of loss to the attackers and increasing surprise. Ambush teams were not to be kept waiting in their positions for long periods: commanders were to place observers and sentries in positions where they could see the enemy coming a distance off and the bulk of the troops could retire to a rest place a short distance from the ambush. On warning from observers the men were sent to their positions.

The first checking point was designed to lie immediately ahead of the lead vehicle. Here the team was to conceal 'necklaces' of anti-tank mines or No. 75 grenades, tied together by cord or signal cable. As the tank approached the necklaces were to be pulled out across the road. Unless the tank stopped in time it would run over charges, disabling a track: either way it was stopped. Tanks two and three in the column now also had to slow or stop completely, deciding what to do next. Their usual drill would be to get off

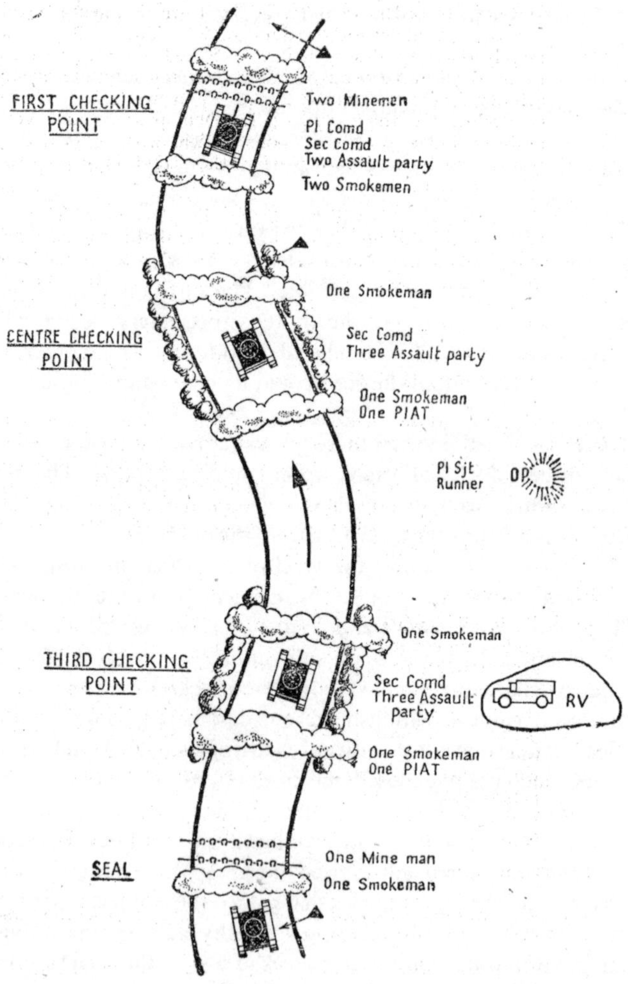

Method for tank ambush as recommended in *Infantry Training*, 1944.

the road quickly, but if checking points two and three were well placed, and 'necklaces' or bombs at the 'seal' point were pulled out behind them, this would not be easily accomplished. The actual attack was,

> all a matter of team work, and should take place under cover of smoke. Smoke grenades thrown into the air inlets of the tanks will blind the crew, cause them great discomfort and may make them sick. As soon as the some has thickened up, the assault parties go in and place their sticky bombs on to the engine covers of the tanks, if time permits on top of the turret, or on the rim where the turret meets the hull, or on the gun mountings. After penetration of the engine cover by the sticky bombs, you can, by application of fire producing agencies (such as A/W and Molotov bombs) probably set the tank alight . . . The man with the PIAT will probably have time for one shot only. The remainder of the garrison are sited to deal with any infantry who may interfere and to cover the tanks with fire to keep them closed down. The 2 inch mortar provides smoke on the up wind flank to help make the movement of the tanks off the roadside more difficult.

Another good way for infantry to attack tanks was at night when they usually laid up, often in a harbour or 'laager' of vehicles, or under cover of scrub or woods. These encampments placed vulnerable elements and supplies towards the centre, where crews might also be fed. To attack such a tank park required meticulous reconnaissance as careful commanders protected their vehicles with sentries and patrols, and one or two tanks might remain manned and ready as guards. If alarmed crews could return to their tanks, illuminating outward with their lights and very probably spray the ground with automatic fire. To deal with such precautions it was recommended that having scouted the general area the attacking platoon should approach in a night-patrol formation. Stopping short of the park at a rendezvous, two men 'expert in fieldcraft' were then sent forward to find a route to the centre of the park.

> The platoon commander's plan will vary according to circumstances, but, generally speaking, it is best to use the smallest possible force to filter through the gap discovered. This force will go right into the middle of the harbour and will begin to attack outwards. This attack will take the tanks by surprise and will avoid casualties from their machine gun fire. Tanks will be afraid to fire into the middle of the harbour lest they kill their own men. Any parts of the patrol left outside the park can add to the confusion by creating a diversion.

In such an attack tanks could be damaged, or preferably destroyed, in a variety of ways. Grenades, fire, and sabotage of vulnerable equipment was obvious, but anti-tank mines could also be placed on exit points from the laager, or modified in advance with detonator and safety fuse to create powerful time-delay bombs, preferably placed inside the enemy vehicle. Speed was essential with the attackers escaping quickly to another predetermined rendezvous well away from the area.

A significant breakthrough in German anti-tank methods was the invention of the *Panzerfaust* by Dr Heinrich Langweiler of HASAG, Leipzig, in 1942. The developmental ancestor of the finalised devices was the *Faustpatrone*, a short tube containing a gunpowder charge, held at arms length. Pulling the trigger fired the propellant and shot a large hollow-charge bomb. Three important principles were brought together: the first was the now familiar armour penetration of the hollow-charge device; the second was the fact that being open at the rear end the tube weapon was virtually without recoil; and third, the sizeable head of the bomb sat on the end of the tube with only a narrower cylindrical portion slid inside the main tube. This last meant that a large explosive charge did not have to have a commensurately big and heavy barrel.

The first of the mass-production types reaching the troops in mid-1943 was the *klein*, or *Gretschen* model *Panzerfaust*. This had a 100mm diameter warhead, a tube less than a metre in length, and an impressive armour penetration of about 140mm. Whilst it was single shot only, and limited initially to a range of about 30yd, the *Panzerfaust* offered considerable advantages. It could knock out virtually anything, was simple to use, weighed a reasonably comfortable 3.5kg, and could be mass produced and distributed very widely. This last was important since infantry units did not have to rely on the presence of a dedicated launcher or gun, but could scatter one-shot weapons around the battlefield putting them into virtually every infantry position. A larger version of the weapon soon upped the armour penetration to 150mm, and in 1944 models 60 and eventually 100 were produced increasing the range. Production climbed rapidly, peaking at 1,253,000 in December 1944, and total manufacture was over 8,000,000 units. Standard scales of issue were 36 to each rifle and pioneer company, and 12 to 18 to other small units such as artillery batteries.

Information sheets were included in every box of *Panzerfaust* weapons, and reprinted in much-abbreviated graphic form on the tubes of many. In January 1945 alone 4,000,000 leaflets for the *Panzerfaust 100* were produced, and this catchy little number commenced with an uplifting cartoon image showing a mailed fist crushing a tank: '*Panzerknacker – Heil*!', 'up the tank crusher!'. The reader was addressed colloquially as a comrade, 'The Panzerfaust is your anti tank gun. You can engage any tank up to a range of 150 metres, and the closer you let him come the better'. Probably the most valuable words in any of these documents were '*Achtung Fuerstrahl*!', or, '*Vorsicht*!', warning of the searing blast from the rear of the tube on firing. A rhyme jogged poor memories: 'Not only to the front does it go, as from the back comes the "infer-no"'. Back blast was arguably the most limiting tactical feature since, like the bazooka, the *Panzerfaust* could not be used in confined spaces without dire risk to the operator, nor could anybody put any part of their anatomy behind the tube. This aside, how it was fired was very much a question of availability of cover and comfort of the user, as the *Panzerfaust* could be shot from a variety of positions, as for example kneeling, squatting, or standing. It could be held close to the body under the arm, couched inside the elbow, or put over the shoulder.

Precise firing instructions varied slightly with time and model, but essentially the detonator was inserted into the head unit before action was joined, and prior to use any linking catches holding the head in position were disconnected. Removing the safety pin and flipping up the basic metal sights completed activation. The target and foresight were now regarded through holes in the little plate indicating various distances, and with all in alignment the trigger was pulled. Its power was impressive indeed, reports from Normandy speaking of Sherman turrets shot through with total loss of the vehicle. Wise users positioned themselves at an angle, covered frontally by the fire of other weapons, and popped up briefly, or shot through gaps in cover, to hit the flanks and rear of tanks passing by. As the bomb flew relatively slowly the shooter 'aimed off' towards the front of crossing vehicles. In the final stages of the war German youths formed anti-tank bicycle patrols with *Panzerfausts* stowed in the front forks, appearing unexpectedly on any part of a wide front. Though these were frequently exterminated before they could do damage, the very possibility that they could pop up anywhere made tank crews extremely cautious.

Just as effective, but reusable, heavier, and with greater effective range, was the *Panzerschreck*, or 'tank terror', more properly known as a *Raketenpanzerbüchse*, or 'anti-tank rocket weapon'. This looked and worked very much like a large bazooka, and not surprisingly as its development was informed by the US weapon. First introduced on the Eastern Front in 1943, this 'stove pipe' was a smoothbore, and weighed about 10kg. It cost 70 marks, and could be fired at up to five rounds per minute. The first version fired a hollow-charge 88mm projectile to an effective anti-tank range of about 150m. The initiation was electric, being derived from an impulse magneto that worked when the operator squeezed the grip. Armour penetration was a satisfying 160mm, but in early models hot waste tended to blow back over the user so gauntlets and a gas mask without filter were recommended wear for the operator. So it was that a second model was developed as well as a new projectile. In the improved version not only was a small shield fitted but the effective range also went up to as much as 180m.

As the weapon was relatively hefty and motor transport at a premium, infantry anti-tank units were issued with small trailers, the 'If.8' type cart, and limbers in which to transport rocket launchers and missiles. A single horse, or man team, could pull the equipment accommodating six launchers and thirty rounds of ammunition. Once in the battle zone the equipment was off loaded, and the loader of the two-man team carried up to five projectiles often in a wooden back frame. Such a burden was about 17kg. Over ¼ million *Raketenpanzerbüchse* were made, but interestingly cessation of production was already under consideration at the end of the war as it was reasoned that the latest models of *Panzerfaust* could do a similar job more simply especially if tubes could be reloaded , or recycled. It was therefore projected that the rocket launcher would be discontinued and facilities given over to the *Panzerfaust* with production running at about 800,000 a month.

The new German anti-tank weapons made revision of tactics possible, and instead of having to rely on small numbers of anti-tank guns, or the highly risky expedient of what amounted to hand-to-hand combat with a tank using improvised weapons, the entirety of the infantry company position could become an anti-tank zone. Whilst special attention was still given to specific terrain and avenues of approach, within a unit defensive area it was planned that anti-tank weapons would be widely distributed, ideally in a large number of posts, in depth, with trenches, weapons pits, and other cover allowing defenders mobility and concealment. Shelters were useful, both to protect and hide the troops, and to keep anti-tank weapons dry. As before, troops with machine guns and other small arms focused on accompanying infantry, or on sniping at any exposed tank commanders or open hatches. Prepared AT posts were ideally about 150m apart, so that any tank crossing the zone would be caught between triangles of posts – each of which would be able to fire on the vehicle from a range of no more than 75m as the tank passed by. Fired on both flanks and rear it was unlikely that even a group of vehicles would sustain such punishment. Surprise could be increased both by putting some weapons into combat outposts, and by the use of mobile patrols out in front of the main positions. If in danger of being overwhelmed, these could retire perhaps drawing the enemy into traps.

Chapter Seven

Schnelltruppen and Tank Co-operation

'The tanks advance by bounds from cover to cover, reconnoitering the terrain ahead and providing protective fire for the dismounted Panzergrenadiers'
– *Handbook on German Military Forces*

A highly distinctive, even unique, passage in the evolution of tactics during the Second World War was the development of special techniques for armoured and motorised infantry. Arguably Britain was world leader in this process, for as early as the 1920s it was decided that total army mechanisation should be a long-term goal. Actually to achieve something so ambitious would require overcoming not only the lobby in favour of the retention of the horse, but the financial constraints of a world in which military cutbacks were followed by depression. Nevertheless, and despite complaints of conservatism and short-sightedness, voices in favour of mechanisation gradually gained ground in the aftermath of the First World War.

Two key figures amongst these advocates were Major General 'Boney' Fuller, guru of the tank – described by one of his peers as not merely 'unconventional', but 'prolific in ideas, fluent in expression', and totally at odds with tradition and received opinion – and later Basil Liddell Hart. Fuller was lyrical, if not mystical, in his praise of tanks, at one time seeing them as replacing virtually everything else, becoming quite literally the 'fleets' of the land, made up of 'landships'. Yet, by no means all of what Fuller preached was new: there were other tank advocates, the first British tanks had been dubbed 'landships', and as long ago as 1903 HG Wells had written a story containing 'land ironclads'. In 1918, relatively swift 'Whippets' operated alongside larger numbers of slower infantry supporting tanks. The USA had embraced the tank idea first by using French machines, then taking part with Britain in the planning of the 'Liberty' tanks designed to have war-winning impact in 1919 – had the war in fact continued so long. Hart later said his conversion to the cause came in 1921, but his vision was more measured in that it included 'land marines' – or mechanised infantry – from an early stage. It also went with the flow to some degree, working as he did at various times in concert with Major Giffard Martel, Charles Broad, Colonel George Lindsay, and others. There were also some curious false starts, as for example when Martel proposed that entire units could drive into action in one-man tracked vehicles, somehow steering, shooting, communicating, and navigating entirely solo.

Though few of the pundits or visionaries would have liked the idea, eventual official acceptance of a good part of the mechanisation agenda probably did not stem from the supposed battle-winning potential of 'tankettes' or land armadas. Rather it was from a cooler realisation that the British Empire was enormous and that the nation would always be denied a large and expensive regular army, or rail transport that could be made to access every country village in India or Africa and at the same time remain invulnerable to sabotage. Another advantage appealing to those of a historical bent was that mechanising infantry and logistics might just allow campaigns to remain fluid long enough to avoid the perceived evil of trench warfare. So it was that the Mechanical Warfare Establishment was established in 1926, being re-christened as the Mechanisation Experimental Establishment (or 'MEE') in 1934. An 'Experimental Mechanised' force was started in 1927 at the instigation of the Chief Imperial General Staff, George Milne, machine-gun vehicles were tested with 2nd Battalion the King's Royal Rifle Corps in 1928, and a tank brigade set up in 1931, becoming a permanent feature a couple of years later. The tanks and infantry were not usually operated as one formation, but as two elements – and in retrospect it may be perceived that this separation did not bode well for the future. Whilst progress was slow, and mass road transport capable of bussing entire armies would not materialise for a long time, significant steps were made. The MEE tested all sorts of military vehicles and devised specifications. Governments dreamed up measures for the encouragement of the motor industry and methods to commandeer their wares in time of war. Perhaps most importantly, gun tractors and crew carriers for the artillery, and motorised platoon trucks and little carriers became standard issues for the infantry battalions. With relatively few and trivial exceptions the British Expeditionary Force of 1939 would be free of reliance on the horse, and perhaps even more significantly could usefully employ the oil found in her colonies rather than have to reap and carry mountains of horse fodder. Fuel for motor vehicles could be moved long distance by rail and ship, in concentrated form.

Having been on the receiving end of the tank from 1916 – and massed armoured attacks from 1917 onward – Germany was by no means ignorant of the advantages of engines. She was, however, at first constrained by the Treaty of Versailles that demanded the handover of 5,000 motor lorries, and later completely banned German use of tanks as well as imposing severe financial penalties. This, together with problems internally and on the Polish border and Baltic, put severe obstacles in the path of development. Even so, there were manoeuvres in the Harz mountains using requisitioned civilian lorries in 1921, and soon Germany joined together with fellow pariah state Bolshevik Russia to examine and test tanks away from German soil. Dummy tanks later stood in on home exercises. One of those really convinced that mechanisation was the thing of the future was Heinz Guderian, who was at the 'Inspectorate of Motorised Troops' from 1931. The *Kommando der Panzertruppen* was established under General Lutz in 1934, and following exercises at Munsterlager the following year the first three Panzer Divisions were formed. As distinct to the arguably more ambitious British plan to motorise the entire army and give it teeth of special brigades and divisions composed mainly of tanks – still not achieved in the run up to war, the German scheme left large portions of the infantry with nothing but the 'horse murderers', animal-drawn heavy equipment wagons. A minority of the divisions would, however, be Panzer divisions, capable of autonomous action because they contained enough supporting arms, artillery, and motorised infantry to undertake pretty well any task.

Guderian's book *Achtung Panzer*!, of 1937, showed that he had studied both French and British developments: it also gave a key vision of what motorised infantry were supposed to do,

> The truck-borne infantry are protected against the elements, and in addition to the men and their equipment the vehicles carry extra loads such as ammunition, entrenching tools and requisites, together with rations for several days . . . the main tasks of motorised supporting infantry are to follow up at speed behind tank attacks, and complete and exploit their successes without delay. They need to put down a heavy volume of fire, and require a correspondingly large complement of machine guns and ammunition. It is debatable whether the striking power of the infantry really resides in the bayonet, and more questionable still in the case of motorised troops, since the shock power of tank formations is invested in tanks and their fire power. The French have drawn the appropriate conclusion and have equipped all their infantry companies with 16 light machine guns each, as opposed to nine of their German counterparts. Combat is not a question of storming ahead with the bayonet, but of engaging the enemy with our fire power and concentrating it on the decisive point . . . What we desire is a modern and fast moving force of infantry, possessing strong fire power, and specially equipped, organised and trained in co-operation with tanks.

Guderian's work bore both tactical and personal fruit. About the time that he was writing his famous book it was decided that German motorised infantry should be given *Gepanzerter Mannschafts Transportwagen* – or armoured personnel carriers. Fully wheeled designs were rejected on grounds of insufficient cross-country performance; fully tracked designs were turned aside due to expense, complexity, and lack of production capacity. Development, therefore, focused on half-tracked vehicles, and in particular on the artillery tractors made by Hanomag, as these were the right size to carry a squad. In 1938 motorised infantry and cavalry were all designated *Schnelletruppen*, or 'fast troops', and put under Guderian's command. Four separate motorised divisions were added to the German mobile infantry arm the following year, though only a few armoured carriers were available for the Polish campaign. Success of the tanks and the conversion of existing divisions made available ten Panzer Divisions for the French campaign of 1940. Paradoxically, British tactical analysts managed to get hold of good intelligence on the new formations some time after the fall of Poland and just before the battle for France. Its translation, digestion, and printing for general circulation occurred sometime after 1 May 1940, this being the period of the latest information contained in volume 18 of *Periodical Notes on the German Army*. So it was that just as the *Schnelletruppen* were driving over France and Belgium, British officers got a belated opportunity to know what had hit them.

The key German tactical document *Provisional Instructions for the Employment and Tactics of the Motorised Infantry Regiment and Battalion* of March 1941 was translated the following year in the USA as *The German Motorised Infantry Regiment*. This document recognised that not all 'motorised' infantry could operate the latest fully 'armoured' tactics as there were not enough armoured carriers for all units. Usually, half-tracks were limited to the first battalion of each regiment, the remainder having to make do with ordinary trucks. Whilst carrier production, mainly of the Sdkfz 251 types, continued apace, this deficiency was never fully rectified. Even as late as 1944 only a minority of *Panzergrenadier* units, such as the *Grossdeutschland* corps, were fully equipped with armoured transport. Though troops in 'soft-skinned' wheeled transport might move quicker on roads, they were very much limited as to how far into the action they could remain in their vehicles, and for the most part dismounted before encountering any hostile fire.

Interestingly, German instructions of the early war period recommended a maximum speed of about 15mph for the leading carrier of a formation, with no more than 20mph for wheeled transport. Faster movement in motorised infantry action was sometimes demanded, but instructions warned unit leaders that this opened up possibility of vehicle 'strain' and increased incidence of breakdown. Much the same considerations applied to the British in general, whose explicit policy regarding motorised troops was that they should leave their vehicles before making an attack, transport being parked out of sight until needed later. Indeed, under British organisation there were not only permanent motorised battalions, but armies and corps troop-carrying companies of the Royal Army Service Corps, the job of which was to ferry any chosen infantry brigade from one point to another, but had no combat function. As of 1939 maximum British convoy speed was set at 20mph, though such a velocity demanded regular stops every 3 hours. Suitable lorries and trucks were often dubbed 'TCVs', 'Troop Carrying Vehicles'. Only in the last two years of the war were US armoured M3 half-tracks supplied to Britain.

The German 1941 instructions outlined an aggressive role for troops with armoured transport, 'The possession of armoured personnel carriers enables motorised infantry units to overcome comparatively weak opposition without dismounting. They can follow up tank attacks on the field of battle without dismounting . . . Motorised infantry is characterised by ability to alternate rapidly between fighting from carriers and fighting on foot, and also to combine these two methods of combat.

It was assumed that on firm and level ground armoured carriers would be able to move at much the same speed as on roads and tracks, with the armour giving protection against 'small arms fire, light infantry weapons and shell splinters'. Vehicles could, therefore, be 'brought up to the battle area and moved about under fire from enemy infantry'. The main purpose of the armoured infantry was close co-operation with tanks, for which they cleared a path through any difficult country, as for example in securing river crossings, villages, and woods. They also undertook the detailed work of assault on fixed positions, as well as racing ahead of the tanks to seize strategic positions, pursuing, or carrying out 'wide and sweeping envelopments'.

As of the 1941 provisional organisation the German armoured infantry regiment comprised just over 2,500 all ranks arranged in two battalions, and a gun company, plus attached engineers and signals. Altogether it deployed 153 machine guns, 36 mortars, and 16 assorted artillery pieces and anti-tank guns. The battalions contained three rifle companies, a machine-gun company and a heavy weapons company. When a whole battalion had sufficient space to deploy the normal formation was a massive arrowhead about 300m wide and 1300m deep with the three rifle companies, also in arrowheads, arranged one forward and two back. The MG company and heavy weapons took up the rear, whilst the whole was preceded by patrols to reconnoitre and seek out the route. Within each armoured carrier was a self-contained squad, essentially similar to those of the ordinary infantry, but with the important difference that each had at least two machine guns. On the march these were mounted on swinging pintles fore and aft, both capable of air and ground fire, though later models of carrier had various arrangements. The initial seating arrangement was two seats with folding backs for the driver and co-driver, and bench seats down either side at the back, lifting to reveal ammunition stowage beneath.

The 1941 instructions were fully aware that terrain and weather had crucial impacts upon tactics, and motorised infantry commanders were to take these into account in the planning of movement and operations. Snow, mud, marsh, thick woods, and steep slopes were all serious impediments: gently rolling country was best as this afforded

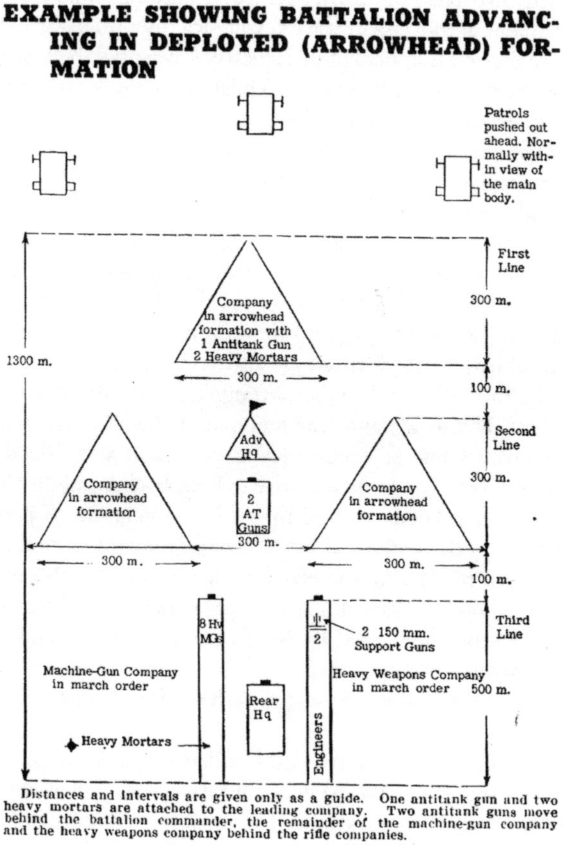

A German armoured infantry battalion deployed for offensive action, as seen in the US translation *The German Motorized Infantry Regiment*, 1942.

cover on reverse slopes, and opportunities for observation. In attacks against a demoralised enemy, river crossings, withdrawals, and advances through wooded or mountainous country small 'task-force' actions were possible, though such *Kampfgruppe*, or battle-group formations, were to be a minimum of company strength and reinforced with heavier arms, engineers, and probably tanks to suit the job to hand. Reconnaissance was to be made at the first opportunity with leaders 'determined to push forward at all costs'. Action was to be 'bold and resolute', any undue risks being mitigated by the use of adequate patrols. At the same time, commanders issuing orders were to be realistic about the time these would need to reach widely spaced sub-units.

In making their approach carriers could take advantage of their armour and cross-country mobility to attack from effective angles and concentrate fire. Moreover, the degree of splinter protection was sufficient for armoured carrier units to follow closer to barrages than dismounted infantry. Commanders were encouraged to think with 'speed and agility', view ground personally, being daring and not obsessed with their own flanks, taking their own position in the 'centre of battle'. Rapidity, concentration of force, and concealment of movement were key tactical themes likely to lend an element of surprise. Where limited numbers of carriers were available these were to be used en masse and fully utilised as fighting vehicles. Whilst using roads and tracks as far forward as possible allowed maximum speed and decreased wear and tear on both men and transport, timely deployment into broader cross-country formations was best for maximum advantage of terrain and use of weapons. Yet there was no hard and fast rule, the moment for deployment had to be left to the commander on the ground, who might choose to use speed and surprise to make an attack direct 'from the column of march'.

This was the 'attack without deployment' – made in vehicles, with dismounting only occurring when no further forward progress was possible in the carriers. Where such an attack passed over difficult ground it might be useful to halt briefly in the closest possible cover to allow 'battle formation' and concentration of the carriers to be regained before the final assault. In other circumstances a 'prepared attack' might be the preferred option. In this instance carriers halted at a distance in a safe 'assembly position' or were given a line at which they were to halt and troops dismounted to deliver the attack on foot. Even so, it was wise to keep back a mobile reserve that could be directed to wherever needed, or used for rapid exploitation. If possible, assembly positions were gained in the dark or at dusk, leaving maximum doubt in the enemy's mind about intentions. In clearing the way for the tanks it was also usual for some or all of the motorised troops to dismount and take the 'tank-proof' obstacle or objective on foot, their advance being covered by the fire of the armour and heavy weapons. When upon the enemy destruction or capture of anti-tank weapons became top priority to assist the advance of the armour. Sometimes the order of attack was reversed:

> If the ground favours an attack by tanks and if no tank obstacles have been detected inside the main line of resistance, the task of the motorised infantry units will usually be to follow the tank attack. They will remain on vehicles behind the tanks so that they can quickly exploit the success of the tanks. Narrow and deep formations will be the rule, in order to avoid as far as possible the effects of enemy artillery fire and retain a mobile reserve in the rear . . . Pockets of resistance and

defence areas which the tanks have not reduced will be dealt with as encountered. For this dismounting may be necessary. The remaining infantry will continue to follow up the tank attack in their vehicles. Contact with the tanks must never be lost.

In other circumstances the mechanised infantry was used with considerable versatility. In pursuit speed made it possible to catch up with the enemy or prevent him from taking up or improving new positions. In doing so commanders were encouraged to move forward as far as possible by road, and at night assume an all-round defensive posture. In defence mobile troops could screen broad frontages, take suitable vantage points, and redeploy quickly. Such aptitudes allowed the frontage of a motorised battalion to extend to 'twice that of an infantry battalion', typically from '1,600 to 4,000 metres and even more depending on situation and terrain'. Mobility also aided the often tricky tactic of breaking contact, where motorised troops might not only use their speed to escape, but to gain prepared defence lines further back. In disengaging it was recommended that small 'fighting patrols' and smoke be used even after the heavier weapons had departed, thus making the job of an enemy attempting to follow up all the more difficult. Engineer platoons also contributed by bridge breaking and mine laying.

Further detail on small-unit tactics was added by the manual for the *Schnelletruppen* of May 1942, reprinted with corrections in January 1943 – the year in which mechanised infantry were renamed *Panzergrenadiere*. Particularly crucial was the role of the driver who was taught to drive tactically, taking advantage of terrain to keep the carrier out of enemy fire. Rapid reversing and driving with the gas mask on and hatches shut were parts of the repertoire. Ideally, three men of each squad received full driver training, the driver, co-driver, and a reserve. Within the vehicle the team travelled in a state of 'combat readiness', weapons loaded, safety catches applied, and particular vigilance used against any enemy close by attempting to lob in grenades or Molotovs. Lookouts were detailed for all-round observation and in the event of a contact or change of orders the squad leader used a clock-face system to communicate direction – *12 Uhr* being dead ahead and *6 Uhr* to the rear.

The full-strength carrier squad was twelve, being the *Gruppenführer*, or squad leader, his deputy, or *Truppführer*, four machine gunners, four riflemen, the driver and his *Beifahrer*, or co-driver. The squad leader retained overall responsibility leading 'by personal example', maintaining contact with the platoon commander, and checking combat readiness of weapons. He might also man one of the machine guns during fighting from the vehicle. His deputy stepped in when the squad leader was absent, and also took charge of part of the squad when it was sub-divided. The driver and his assistant would usually remain with the vehicle, the driver having first responsibility for readiness, care, and camouflage of the transport, whilst the assistant manned the radio. The machine gunners usually operated as two teams of two, the first man being the firer, the second carrying ammunition and spare barrel. The four riflemen were regarded as the force of close combat and the manpower for reconnaissance and observation duties. The standard complement of light machine guns was three, two of which were intended for dismounting and one usually remaining on the vehicle. Interestingly, the MGs were each identified individually so that a member of the team had primary responsibility for its care. During motorised movement basic deployment of the MGs was one each mounted fore and aft, with the spare in the main compartment for use at will. There were two machine pistols, one to carry with the team, the other intended to stay with the vehicle. Additionally, there were five rifles and four pistols.

On the command '*Aufstizen*!' the carrier was mounted in an orderly manner via the rear door, with the squad leader assuming his normal position directly behind the driver, and his second getting in last and taking post at the rear shutting the door. If carrying gas masks, the team unfastened them from their normal low position and reattached them to the front upper body, so as to make sitting more comfortable and the mask accessible. The order for a quick tactical exit from the carrier was '*Abspringen*!'. On hearing this everybody jumped out by the nearest means, over the sides as well as through the door. The squad then took immediate cover near to the leader. The rapid remount was the '*Aufspringen*!' with everybody jumping in over sides as well as through the door. These manoeuvres were practised both at the halt, and with the carrier moving at up to 10kmph.

Combat was both from the vehicle, and dismounted. Dismounted the squad acted very much as normal infantry, but with the significant difference that the additional machine guns made fighting as two elements easier and gave greater flexibility. With the driver and his assistant still on the vehicle this also opened up possibilities of a third base of fire. On the vehicle a basic level of all-round watchfulness – particularly against air attack – was maintained at all times, but if combat was perceived to be imminent the squad leader gave the order for '*Gefechtsbereitschaft*', or 'combat readiness'. On this direction the team checked their weapons and radio readiness, and riflemen also ensured there were grenades to hand. The squad leader secured smoke grenades ready to produce screening. With hatches secured the vehicle could be driven at normal speeds through infantry fire, taking evasive action in the event of incoming artillery or mortar fire.

The squad fought from the carrier as long as enemy fire, mission, and terrain allowed:

> The main weapon of the squad fighting from the vehicle is the onboard MG. The MG in the anti aircraft mount besides being used for AA defence can be used against hostile ground targets for example adversaries in the rear and flank of the squad. As a rule it will have to fire while the carrier is moving. The riflemen participate in the fire fight at the first breakthrough of the enemy. Hand grenades with simultaneous machine gun and machine pistol fire, as well as running over enemy soldiers are the most effective means to destroy the enemy in close combat from the vehicle.

Short bursts of fire from the moving carrier were intended to force the enemy into cover and prevent return fire, but in case of sudden encounters might actually destroy targets such as moving convoys or retreating adversaries. Even so, halted fire was more effective, and when stopping the carrier positions that left the vehicle 'mostly hidden from view' were best. When halting to fire a steady machine-gun burst the vehicle was not to remain stationary for more than 15 to 25 seconds, and the squad leader observed fire, his task being made easier by tracer rounds at intervals in the ammunition belts.

Usually, the *Panzergrenadiere* fought as platoons of four vehicles, three platoons carrying rifle squads, the fourth the headquarters. In the HQ carrier with the commander travelled an NCO, two messengers, a medic, the driver, and two soldiers manning an anti-tank weapon. Other arms carried in the vehicle of the *Zugtruppführer* were six rifles and a sub-machine gun. A motorcycle messenger might also be attached to the platoon, or several pooled together within the company. What main armament the HQ vehicle had, if any, changed over time. In early type SdKfz 251/10 platoon commanders' vehicles a 37mm gun was mounted, but establishments of late 1943 show a 20mm flak gun with the commander, plus a *Panzerschrek* in each of the squad vehicles. The vehicles of the platoon might travel in closer order columns or lines but typical combat formations included the *Zugkeil* with the squad vehicles in a triangle and the platoon leader's carrier out to the front, and the loose line or *Zugbreite*. A minimum dispersion of about 50m between carriers was aimed at in action. Armoured carriers and tanks could operate fire and movement in co-operation with each other, as for example with tanks halted and firing whilst carriers advanced, or with a portion of a carrier unit halted to offer support to other carriers.

An increasingly popular form of armour and infantry co-operation in German forces was the deployment of self-propelled guns and tank destroyers with infantry. Indeed, it could be said that these required each others assistance even more than did tanks. The *Sturmgeschütz*, literally 'assault gun', was perhaps a cheaper form of tank in that it required no turret or full traverse mechanism for its gun. Nevertheless, the 'Stug' also scored in other ways because larger weapons could be mounted on a given platform, and it was possible to recycle otherwise obsolete tank chassis in very productive ways, or to continue to make a tried and trusted basic design rather than convert entire production facilities. Building guns into, rather than simply on top of, tank bodies also increased the degree of protection whilst reducing overall silhouette. Standard *Sturmgeschütz* tactics saw them deployed in the maximum strength available, with, or immediately behind, attacking infantry. They were not to give away their presence prematurely, but used 'to neutralise enemy support weapons at close ranges over open sights'. Close proximity to friendly infantry minimised their exposure to anti-tank weapons, and helped to make up for lack of a traversing turret. Similar considerations applied where small numbers of turretless 'tank-hunting' or 'tank-destroying' weapons were deployed. The fact that German forces were frequently on the defensive later in the war made them all the more profitable since they did not have to drive out exposing themselves to effective fire, but could remain and often manoeuvre within the zones occupied by defensive infantry.

By the end of 1944 the basis of tank and infantry co-operation tactics showed distinct similarities whether German, US, or British. Whether well or indifferently performed in practice, the result of six years of war was convergence of theory. According to *Handbook on German Military Forces*,

> When the enemy has well prepared positions with natural or constructed tank obstacles, the German infantry attacks before tanks and clears the way. The objective of the infantry is to penetrate into the enemy position and destroy

> enemy anti tank weapons to the limit of its strength and the firepower of its own support weapons, augmented by additional support and covering fire from the tanks and self propelled guns sited in the rear . . . When the tank obstacles in front of the enemy position already are destroyed, and no additional tank obstacles are expected in the depth of the enemy's main defensive position, the infantry breaks through simultaneously with the tank unit. . . . In most cases, the infantry follows the tanks closely, taking advantage of the firepower and paralysing effect of the tanks upon the enemy's defense. The Germans normally transport the infantry to the line of departure on tanks or troop carrying vehicles in order to protect the infantry.

Interestingly, US experiments with motorised infantry were underway as early as 1929 when a company of 34th Infantry was mounted in six-wheeler trucks as part of a 'Mechanised Force'. This did not last long, however, and rival claims were staked by the infantry and cavalry – with the former wanting 'infantry tanks' attached, the latter seeking to become the umbrella to all mobile troops. Only in 1940 was an integrated force formed with the foundation of 1st and 2nd Armoured Divisions, and in 1941 five truck-transported infantry motorised divisions were planned. In the event only one motorised division was completed, and this was never used in its intended role. Efforts, therefore, focused on the creation of more all-arms armoured divisions. Initially, armoured divisions were mainly tanks with few infantry, but observation of European experience, combined with massive infantry manpower increases, made progressive revisions possible. By March 1942 the armoured divisional establishment wedded together two armoured regiments with a three-battalion armoured infantry regiment. In 1943 'light' armoured divisions were also introduced with a better balance of three battalions of tanks with three of infantry.

The US armoured infantry platoon now numbered five squads, three rifle, one mortar and one light machine gun, each squad travelling in an M3 half-track. Capable of seating up to 13, the M3 was bigger than the M2 (that carried only 10), and was arranged with 3 seats across the front and 5 down each side. In the ordinary squad vehicle the leader usually sat front right, ready to handle the vehicle mounted .30 cal machine gun. As in the German arrangement, his assistant squad leader rode at the back next to the rear door, and more than one man was trained to drive, one of these being designated the assistant driver. The M3 armour was just adequate for protection against small arms and fragments, but would not stop much else, and there was no overhead protection on the driving compartment. Some dubbed the M3 the 'Purple Heart Box' on account of those injured in it.

Initial US theory paid relatively little heed to the notion of close integration of tanks and infantry, and early armoured establishments ensured that the latter were insufficient where they were needed. Gradually, and arguably from mid-1942, this began to change. Manuals made it very clear that the *raison d'être* of tanks, and by extension all their appendages within the armoured division, was the offensive. Within the tactical detail it was tanks that formed the cutting edge 'striking force', infantry that followed up. Yet there were exceptions. As the 1942 instructions FM 17-10 *Armored Force Field Manual: Tactics and Technique*, explained,

> In attack the combat command groups are generally disposed into four parts: a reconnaissance force (consisting of organic reconnaissance units and attacking units), a striking force (the striking echelon consisting of tanks with engineers attached), a supporting force (consisting of the support echelon, i.e. the infantry, artillery and tank destroyer units), and a reserve. Whether the striking force makes the initial attack or main attack will depend on the terrain and the extent and dispositions of the hostile anti tank defences. . . .When the striking force makes the initial attack, the support echelon follows to seize and hold objectives taken by the striking echelon. When terrain is unsuitable for tank operation or anti tank defences are strong, the support echelon, supported by medium tank units, may lead the attack to secure ground from which the striking echelon may attack. The support echelon usually leads the attack in a penetration. The support echelon may be used to make an attack initially to serve as a base of fire for the striking force in an envelopment. The attack serves to fix the enemy and attract his reserves. In this manner it assists the advance of the enveloping or striking force.

Additionally, armoured infantry had roles in both pursuit and 'encircling forces'. During an encirclement, for example, they might follow the tanks and take over and hold 'critical terrain' gained by the armour. North Africa and Italy would make it very clear that tanks without any attached infantry were at a serious disadvantage; whilst tanks, even in small numbers, lent vital fire support and morale advantages to their infantry compatriots.

Armored Force Drill, of January 1943, gave a range of formations for use by armoured infantry on the move. Whilst they could take up 'wedges' – inverted or otherwise, move in columns or stepped 'echelons', or any other form of deployment also used by tanks, the 'diamond' was described as 'the basic formation for the infantry platoon'. In the diamond,

> the platoon leader's rifle squad and the two other rifle squads form a wedge, with the platoon leader at the apex. The 60mm mortar squad and the light machine gun squad are on a line in rear of the wedge formed by the rifle squads. The company may be formed in line, column, echelon, wedge, or inverted wedge, in each formation with the platoons in diamond formation.

As may be imagined, the larger company formations described needed much open space for full deployment, so in practice, and particularly in the closed country of Normandy or Italian mountains and hills, short lines, platoon wedges, or columns of various depths and dispersions were much more commonly seen. Experience also taught that fuller integration of tanks and half-tracks was often the best option. So it was that armoured infantry platoons were paired with tank platoons, the latter giving good long-range firepower and a measure of anti-armour protection, the latter ability to counter enemy anti-tank units and infantry, or hold a terrain feature.

Though fire from the vehicle was used in emergency, and a parked half-track formed a useful base of fire – particularly if concealed and mounted with the powerful .50

calibre machine gun, US tactical theory did not regard the M3 as a 'fighting' or assault vehicle, but more as a sophisticated, and partly protected, form of cross-country transport. In any case, as the *Crew Drill* manual explained, small-arms fire was much more accurate if the vehicle stopped. Standard procedure, therefore, was that in combat the main portion of the squads alighted before meeting effective fire, leaving one, or preferably two, men with the vehicle. Those left behind could move the half-track and fire its machine gun, perhaps in support, as an anti-aircraft defence, or to protect a given locality. If not needed immediately, the M3 retired to a given rendezvous or acted as battlefield taxi for supplies and wounded. As the squad dismounted its leader gave consideration to mission and tactical requirements, for if all weapons including the main machine gun were taken off the squad had fearsome firepower but limited mobility. Conversely, if the bazooka and machine gun were left behind the team could move with great agility but little power to confront vehicles or large numbers of the enemy. As a shorthand order the word 'rockets' was recommended: on hearing this the squad debused with the bazooka using two of the riflemen as anti-tank team, but left the machine gun behind. 'No rockets' meant that riflemen went lightly equipped.

In a well co-ordinated armoured infantry attack a combined formation went to ground near the target, and whilst infantry dismounted, tanks took up covered positions from which to put the enemy under fire. Depending on the results of reconnaissance or intelligence, the action might also be supported by artillery, mortars, machine guns, and the three useful M8 self-propelled howitzers that also formed part of the armoured infantry battalion. Taking advantage of covering fire, the armoured infantry advanced in dispersed formation, using their own fire and movement as required. If all went well, the infantry took up the ground, making sure that no anti-armour weapons were still lurking before the tanks came close in: if the infantry were held up tanks might be required to neutralise machine-gun nests or other centres of resistance. Whilst tank destroyers had the main task of dealing with enemy armour, tanks would also make engaging enemy vehicles a priority. Progressively, US armoured units adopted what became known as the 'combat command' approach, bringing together units or sub-units as required for task. Though arguably less dynamic than the German *Kampfgruppe* idea, and generally enacted later, the basic notion was very similar. As the manual 17-33 *Tank Battalion*, of December 1944, explained:

> success in battle can be assured only by complete co-operation of all arms. No one arm wins battles. Success is attained when each arm, weapon and individual is employed to afford the maximum mutual support . . . tanks usually operate in close co-ordination with other arms, particularly infantry and artillery. The tank battalion may be part of a combat command; it may reinforce an infantry combat team. When operated alone, it is normally reinforced by infantry, engineers and other units.

So it was now, even when US armour was 'alone' infantry was still not far away. For defensive operations it was recommended that infantry, reinforced by other arms, should hold the 'main line of resistance', tank battalions being held as a 'local reserve' for the front-line infantry. The standard arrangement for an armoured infantry company in a defensive posture was with two platoons forward, and one back, giving support and depth to the position. Tanks could attack through infantry, though this required careful co-ordination, or support the infantry forward, and this applied to ordinary infantry as well as the armoured variety. As the new 1944 general-infantry manual FM 7-20 *Infantry Battalion*, explained,

> In infantry-tank action, there are three initial attack dispositions: infantry leading, tanks leading, and infantry-tanks together. Infantry leads initially when reconnaissance has revealed hostile anti-tank strength or when the terrain in the direction of desired use is unsuitable for tanks; in this case the tanks support the attack by fire, generally from hull defilade positions. Tanks lead initially, when suitable terrain is available, in launching an attack against a hostile position having little anti-tank strength in terms of anti-tank guns, tank destroyers, anti-tank mines and other obstacles, or when these have been neutralised; in this case, elements of the infantry battalion follow within supporting distance and aid the tanks by fire and manoeuvre.

Where neither situation applied, or was unclear, attacks were launched with both armour and infantry in the leading wave so as to promote flexibility. Such was the ideal,

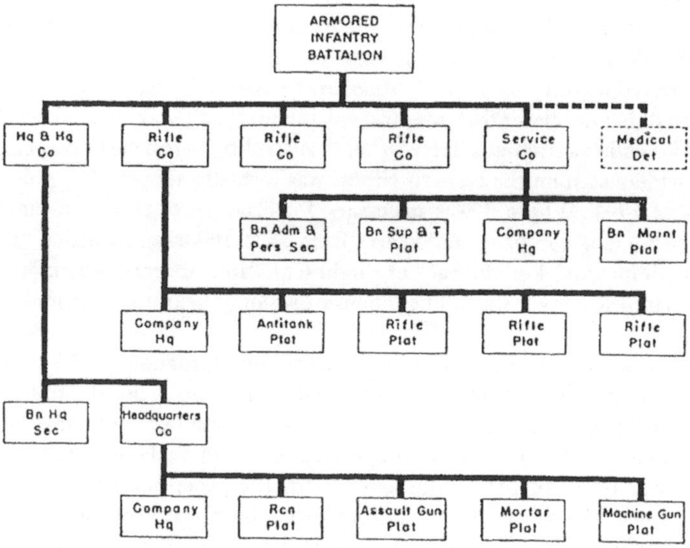

The organisation of the US armoured infantry battalion, c.1944. The three rifle companies are each divided into three platoons. Each platoon in its turn comprised three rifle squads, plus a mortar and a light machine gun squad. Platoons were thus 5 half-tracks and 49 all ranks at full strength. The battalion also included reconnaissance, assault gun, and mortars and machine guns arranged as HQ assets, as well as the 'service' company for maintenance and admin.

but as can be imagined, commanding a 'composite wave' in action was no easy task, and not always successfully accomplished.

Twelve key tasks for armoured infantry were foreseen under 1944 instructions:

a) Follow a tank attack to wipe out enemy resistance.
b) Seize and hold terrain gained by the tanks.
c) Attack to seize terrain favourable for a tank attack.
d) Form, in conjunction with artillery and tank destroyers, a base of fire for a tank attack.
e) Attack in conjunction with tanks.
f) Clear lanes through minefields in conjunction with engineers.
g) Protect tanks in bivouac, on the march, in assembly areas, and at rallying points.
h) Force a river crossing.
i) Seize a bridgehead.
j) Establish and reduce obstacles.
k) Occupy a defensive position.
l) Perform reconnaissance and counter reconnaissance.

The armoured infantry arm was described as being characteristically 'powerful, mobile and lightly armored', and in battle armoured infantry were expected to advance in vehicles until forced 'by enemy fire, or unfavourable terrain to dismount'. Generally, the 'one to one' balanced relationship of tank battalions to armoured infantry battalions held good for the remainder of the war. Post-war analysis suggested that possibly even a three armoured infantry to two tank units ratio was even better. Practical experience also suggested that the closer that infantry, any infantry, and tanks started out the more effective their collaboration was likely to be. 'Tank riding' – frowned upon early in the war – but widely seen on the Eastern Front, was formally adopted US policy by the campaigns of 1944. Where it was necessary for infantry to travel on tanks it was suggested that a tank company could carry from 75 to 100 infantry with 6 on the rear deck of a medium tank, 4 on the back of a light tank. 'In rear areas more men can ride, when rope handles are provided. The infantry dismount prior to the launching of the tank attack.'

It has been said that compared to German armoured infantry tactics those of the Americans were poorly developed and unadventurous. This is not the full story. For crucially it has to be remembered that the tactical situation pertaining in 1940 was by no means the same as that in 1944. Early in the war German methods were novel, taking opponents largely by surprise: moreover, with the exception of relatively small numbers of anti-tank artillery pieces, and somewhat ineffective anti-tank rifles, Allied infantry had little with which to counter armoured carriers effectively. German mechanised troop theory called for close integration with tanks, and also accepted casualties as a given in terms of achieving a success as part of a bigger picture. The net result was that, in both Poland and the West, German 'fast' troops scored remarkable victories in concert with armour.

Until 1940 there were no US armoured divisions, and until North Africa no practical experience of armoured combat. Thereafter, major elements of German tactics were progressively taken up, and earlier British experience studied. Later in the war, however, when the USA managed to field armoured infantry in numbers, much had changed. The basic tactics were no longer new, the enemy was already thoroughly familiar with them, and worse was already deploying hand-held anti-tank weapons down to platoon and even squad level. Usually, German forces were on the defensive, and encounters between mobile forces rarer. The result was that when an M3 confronted even a small group of German infantry there was every possibility that one of them would be equipped with a weapon capable of completely destroying the carrier with a single round. In the face of this reality fighting from the vehicle was not merely dangerous, as it had always been, but obviously suicidal. So it was, that by comparison, it was almost inevitable US techniques should appear hesitant. Conversely, it was also the case that the Germans, particularly in the West after July 1944, became progressively weaker in tanks. With fewer Allied tanks required for large armour to armour engagements this meant that tanks could be used more widely in close infantry support operations.

As we have seen, the British approach was to mechanise infantry transport as widely as possible, but following early experimental work on attacks by fully tracked, but very small, carriers, the notion of full-blown 'armoured infantry' assault in vehicles was generally abandoned. So it was that in 1939 platoon trucks were motorised, and lorry companies also existed for the transport of nominated battalions from place to place on an ad hoc basis. Within the armoured division there was provision for two motorised battalions in establishments of 1939 to 1941, and this was later raised to three in May 1942, and, by April 1943, to four battalions per armoured division. One of these was the 'motor battalion' that formed an integral part of the division's armoured brigade. The US summary TM 30-410 *Handbook on the British Army*, published in 1943 – but already slightly out of date, distinguished three types of British mobile battalion:

> *The machine gun battalion*, which is at present assigned to corps troops, is based on the caliber .303 Vickers machine gun. It consists of a headquarters, a headquarters company, and four machine gun companies of 12 guns each. Each company is composed of a headquarters and three platoons. The battalion is completely motorised and all personnel are carried in motor transport. It has a strength of 29 officers and 711 enlisted men . . . The *motor battalion* assigned to each armoured brigade, consists of a headquarters company and four motor companies. Each company consists of three motor platoons and one scout platoon (11 Bren carriers). Each motor platoon consists of three sections, each self contained, operationally and administratively, in one vehicle. This battalion, with a strength of 26 officers and 774 enlisted men, has much greater fire power than any other in the British army. . . . the *motorised battalion*, formerly assigned to the support group of the armoured division, now forms the infantry component of the infantry brigade in the armoured division. Its organisation is exactly the same as that of the rifle battalion, but it is carried in motor transport.

Additionally, divisional reconnaissance regiments were also composed of infantry riding in various forms of transport, but later these were converted into the Reconnaissance Corps. As the 1941 *Infantry Division* manual made clear, standard drill for any motorised infantry was for the transport to bring them as far forward as possible without danger, then 'debus' them to operate much as any others. Whilst not attacking in 'soft-skinned' vehicles made perfect sense, lack of suitable armoured carriers made close co-operation between infantry and all but the slowest moving tanks problematic – and was arguably a significant tactical failing – particularly in circumstances that called for swift offensive action. Moreover, early in the war there were few signs of close co-operation between ordinary infantry, operating on foot, and the tank arm. Official doctrine of 1941, as spelt out in *The Employment of Army Tanks in Co-Operation with Infantry*, was that in the attack tanks would precede the infantry, with which there would be little direct interaction. During 1942, however, individual units began to practice closer co-operation in training. This was encouraged both by the increased numbers of infantry in armoured divisions, and by the fact that a number of new tank units were created from infantry battalions – and to these working with other infantry may well have appeared far more natural.

As of October 1943 British infantry divisions in Italy disposed of no less than 3,745 motor vehicles each, including over 900 motorcycles. This gave them a degree of tactical and strategic mobility not enjoyed by the enemy, but also meant that considerable effort, logistic and otherwise, had to be expended in maintaining these fleets. By the spring of 1944 Britain had obtained enough M3 half-tracks from the USA to mount the integral battalion of armoured brigades with tracked carriers. These were again operated much on existing principles, being used essentially as a 'hardened' transport to take forward infantry and their equipment, which then alighted to fight on foot. As in the US instance it would have been highly unrealistic to expect full 'armoured infantry' tactics at this date, given that enemy infantry could now destroy carriers with considerable ease.

Issued in May 1944, the key document governing British tank and infantry collaborations was *The Co-Operation of Tanks with Infantry Divisions*. As in US doctrine, it was envisaged that attacks be made in waves of varying compositions, and in British theory the waves were built of three main parts: the 'assault', 'support', and 'reserve' echelons. Each echelon was itself likely to comprise two or more individual sub-ports. An echelon could contain tanks, or infantry, or a mixture of both, but commonly there was some infantry with every one, and tanks normally formed at least a part of the 'support' echelon. It was the job of the assault echelon to attack 'as closely as possible behind the artillery support' and disrupt and dominate the objective. The support echelon provided immediate covering fire then itself moved forward to take up ground to 'completely subdue the objective' and oppose any counter attack. The reserve was kept in hand by the commander, and deployed as necessary according to events. In these essentials British and US techniques were fairly similar, albeit the nomenclature was different. What was rather different was that under British organisation dedicated 'infantry tanks' – slow, tough, and heavy beasts like the Churchill – were allotted to infantry divisions for 'close co-operation, especially in beaching the enemy defences'. This broad concept went back all the way to the First World War, and had been reconfirmed when, at the beginning of the Second World War, a need was foreseen for well-protected armour to operate in the 'shelled area' helping the 'break in' of infantry into main defensive positions. Whilst many things had changed, and effective infantry tanks took years in development, it could be argued that in some senses things had come full circle, and the Atlantic Wall, Siegfried Line, other Axis defensive lines, and built-up areas did indeed require the attentions of heavily armoured tanks. Churchills, for example, did especially valuable service when converted for specialist roles in support of other arms; as a variety of 'funnies' on D-Day, or as 'engineer' tanks with heavy charge throwers blowing in enemy bunkers and strongpoints to allow the infantry to go forward. Conversely, the heavy infantry tanks were not of much use for rapid actions or sweeping manoeuvres.

The faster tanks, still known by the archaic descriptions 'Cruiser' and 'Light', were assumed to have specific purposes in terms of armoured exploitation by armoured divisions and in reconnaissance. Nevertheless, by this date it was acknowledged that distinctions were breaking down, for though tanks were designed for specific roles, 'there can be no hard and fast rule regarding their employment, beyond the obvious one that they must be used in the manner which most effectively carries out the intention of the higher commander. Cruiser tanks have, in recent operations, supported infantry divisions with marked success, and infantry tanks have, on at least one important occasion, carried out valuable work in a role usually allotted to cruisers.' Whilst tanks were best used offensively in numbers on narrow frontages, they could also be used successfully in smaller groups 'always accompanied by infantry'. This would be of 'moral' as well as 'material' value. They were not to be used on their own, 'for patrols or for leading the way into very close country or villages'.

How close infantry should actually get to tanks was still seen as problematic, since tank and infantry co-operation had to be close to prevent enemy infantry using hand-held anti-tank weapons, and advancing behind a tank also lent considerable protection from small-arms fire. On the other hand, armour attracted fire of all sorts and infantry very close to tanks could easily find themselves 'exposed to heavy artillery concentrations'. Several possible solutions were offered. In the best eventuality the tanks went first, 'neutralising the objective' and the infantry caught up as quickly as possible before the tanks took serious loss. However,

> A decision must be reached by the commander of the operation – usually the infantry brigadier – as to how close the infantry can move behind the assaulting tanks. Tanks normally move faster than infantry and draw enemy fire. It may, therefore, often be desirable for both to start together, with the result that the tanks draw ahead, but that the infantry will arrive on the objective while the enemy is still suffering the shock of the tank attack. In this way the infantry will obtain maximum advantage of the [artillery] fire plan which is designed for the support of the leading troops.

For a 'main attack' *Co-Operation of Tanks with Infantry Divisions* envisaged a set piece, preparation of which might take a long time, or as little as 'one to two days' or in an emergency 'hours'. Execution at night would be preferable from the point of view of the infantry, but tanks rendered their most effective assistance in daylight. In planning infantry and tank units were to co-operate closely, with as many as possible seeing the ground over which the operation was to take place in advance. For main attacks artillery was vital, and a fire plan had to be laid that 'caters for success'. The attack would ideally unfold as preparation of gaps, followed by the assault and consolidation. Assaulting infantry were not to stop to mop up any posts that remained short of the objective but to push on to it and hold it. As a British 2nd Armoured Division history explained, German troops had become very adept in their use of both the new anti-tank weapons, and snipers, sometimes holding their fire,

> until the leading troops were a mile or more beyond them. To overcome this it was necessary for the attacking troops to advance in great depth, so that when the infantry had reached their objective their rear had only recently crossed the start line. In this way the infantry and tanks were spread out all over the ground just won and in a position to help each other deal with the snipers. All round observation in each tank was vital, because the enemy were just as likely to fire from either flank, or from behind, as they were from the front.

'Main attacks' were, however, only likely to be part of the picture as many operations were 'fluid warfare'. In conducting advances in fluid warfare there was no hard and fast rule as to whether infantry or tanks should lead the way: indeed, open situations might demand tanks in smaller or greater numbers to the fore, whilst close country required infantry to lead clearing the path for armour. In the latter instance tanks would still be hard on the heels of the infantry aiming to neutralise machine-gun and mortar positions with their supporting fire. 'Tank riding' by infantry was encouraged, but only 'outside small arms and anti-tank gun range', as direct fire on tanks carrying infantry would probably result in heavy casualties, loss of morale, and difficulties for the tanks in firing back.

> When infantry are to be carried on tanks, definite organisation and practice are required. The number of sub units within the unit of both infantry and tanks is dissimilar. One tank can carry a full section of infantry with its weapons. The infantry must have a drill for mounting the tank, for dismounting, and for quick assembly. Riding on the outside of a tank, especially across rough country, requires a certain amount of practice, and, as far as possible, troops whom it is intended to carry in this manner should not have their first ride when moving up to their assembly area for action.

Whilst it may reasonably be argued that British infantry and tank co-operation, and particularly 'armoured infantry' methods, lagged sadly behind the German, and that even later in the war much depended on the availability of US-produced materiel, there were two remarkable bright spots in British performance. The first was the general level of mechanisation achieved at an early stage, the second was a belated revival of the fully tracked carrier concept that pointed the way to something of a revolution in battlefield troop mobility, still being played out decades after 1945. What had been wrong with the old Bren and Universal carriers was that essentially they were too small, and too lightly protected, to do the job of transporting a section on the battlefield. Though fine for a machine gun or a mortar, this essentially limited them to carrying support weapons and stores – useful, but no substitute for section half-tracks. A key spur came from the Canadians who pressed into action the hulls of US 105mm self-propelled 'Priests' in the breakout south of Caen in early August 1944. Soon more were being converted in Italy, as were turretless Shermans. At the end of 1944 the 'Ram Kangeroo' appeared based on a Canadian Ram tank chassis. Some British armoured cavalry units were now converted experimentally so that whilst two squadrons retained their gun tanks, the third drove infantry carriers. The whole regiment operated together so that when progress was halted by resistance the tanks took up positions to bring the enemy under fire. The carriers headed for any convenient cover and unloaded the infantry, who could now advance and attack under supporting fire disabling or capturing any anti-tank weapons. Once this was underway the troops of tanks came up, using their own fire and movement to support each other onto and through the position.

Provisional standard carrier drill was reported in *Current Reports from Overseas* of April 1945. This stressed that whilst the tanks, carriers, and their infantry passengers were to operate as a unit, the idea was not to drive the carriers into the teeth of the enemy. Individual Kangeroos drove into suitable positions and halted with one man on the Browning machine gun. The infantry spilled out as rapidly as possible from all sides of the vehicle, which remained stationary until they were clear. The stated logic to this was that if the Kangeroo moved prematurely it might detonate mines, injuring the now vulnerable troops. The troops manoeuvred or attacked on foot, carriers remaining out of the way of anti-tank weapons, but close enough to support or pick up their sections when recalled. Interestingly, these basic notes on the actions of fully tracked carriers would still form the basis of battlefield tactics more than half a century later.

Conclusion

'It is the soldier who fights that wins battles' – SLA Marshall

At heart most human activities are the interactions of people with people, or people with objects. In this infantry tactics are not the exception, but the rule. What we see in the memoirs, films, and the manuals of the Second World War was the complex result of training, motivation, experience, geography, orders – written, verbal, and transmitted, fitness, aptitude, hope, and comradeship. Often aspirations were constrained, or confirmed, by the parameters of weapons technology and supply. Tactics were buoyed or hamstrung by stategic circumstance. As in the First World War, the European conflict had finally to be resolved by determined assaults on a well-trained and prepared enemy, often with benefit of physical defences or cover in built-up areas. This meant Allied infantry doing a good deal of the hard work – and taking casualties. It did not necessarily mean that US or British tactics were, by 1945 at least, 'worse'. Few could blame a US or British commander for taking full advantage of the power of logistics, artillery, bombers, and even battleships. To do so was indeed also good tactical thinking because it saved the lives of troops, thereby husbanding the 'human resource' for those instances where there was no other choice but its deployment. As infantry officer Alistair Borthwick put it, 'We in the infantry thank the gunners for every support they gave us in every battle. Time and again we reached our objectives with negligible casualties simply because the defences had the stuffing knocked out of them before we arrived'.

Moreover, on the battlefield there were often no simple answers, and often tragic consequences. In many ways it was uncertainty that was the given, since everybody aimed at surprise, and what worked well in September 1939 might not be so effective a few months later as technology, tactics, and human organisation changed with time and circumstance. Sometimes errors were understandable, sometimes they were simply errors. Some of the participants found the whole thing unreal and incongruous. As Peter White, an officer with the King's Own Scottish Borderers, remembered,

> I felt it quite likely my hair was now grey too. Each time either of us fired we had to show our heads and shoulders for a while, and this invariably drew a hail of fire. A rotting stump of a pollarded willow tree lying just ahead of Sergeant Dickinson and myself seemed to act like a magnet to the bullets and was a Godsend to us as it was repeatedly chipped, nicked or drilled, covering my rifle with muck. The fearsome whine and twang of bullets richocheting off it

> reminded me absurdly of a wild west film. I never imagined featuring in one of those. One great joy in firing was a hot rifle to warm ones hands on!

At the root of all infantry tactics was a raft of common notions. These included the need to bring to bear superior power at specific points to force decision; 'fire and movement', or covering and supporting movement with fire; the requirement to move forces with minimum loss; organisation and division of forces into squads (or sections), platoons, companies, and battalions; separation of weapons into 'personal' and 'support' types; small-unit tactics involving light support weapons as part of squads; the recognition of the 'firefight' as a distinctive phase of combat, and the perceived need to close or mount close assaults finally to drive the opposition from his positions. The tactics of the German, British and US infantry were distinctively different, but this had relatively little to do with the convenient shorthand of 'national characteristics'. This indeed is something of a chimera – as the more it is examined, the less definable it becomes. Still less useful is the notion that men and weapons are numbers: it is barely adequate perhaps for the *Kriegspiel* as an attempt to test a theory in the abstract before real lives are risked, but something that has a horrible habit of falling apart when tested in the real world. Given changing circumstances and numerous variables, virtually every combat is different, and rarely is a mathematical calculation more than the roughest of estimates. Too often are we misled into thinking that numbers are firm and accurate science when considered in the context of human affairs.

As in the First World War, Germany had gambled on a short war in which the world would have no time to gang up against her ambitions. The 'Lightning War' was supposed to be the end, not just a beginning. Again, as in 1914, German diplomacy ultimately fell apart leaving an unbalanced war of material and populations. Whilst the *Blitzkrieg* had made victory seem likely in 1940, by the end of 1941 it was highly unlikely that Germany could ever defeat the combined production and manpower of the Soviet Union, the USA, and the British Empire – even with the input of Japan and Italy. This sounds obvious, and on the face of it, appears to have little to do with what happened on the battlefield. However, politicians and army leaders West and East could see that Germany would eventually be ground down if they could effectively deploy their natural advantages against her. High 'tail to teeth' ratios were criticised, not least by Winston Churchill, and recent calculations suggest that it took three or four times as many rear-echelon men to keep a front-line soldier of the Western Allies in combat as it did the Germans: but the other side of the coin was weight of fire, durable morale, and long-term combat sustainability. Conversely, Germany was conditioned by its history and European position and lack of world reach to seek more rapid solutions. Her army, initially very small under the provisions of the Treaty of Versailles, was formed to think of quick manoeuvre against numbers. Ultimately, the allied big picture was proved correct: it was not to be a short war, though it was a close-run thing.

This world picture and politics were to some extent reflected in the armies. Dictatorships could dictate, more or less effectively, using the full sanctions of summary execution, concentration camp, and gulag to demand the often impossible. At the same time, their rhetoric was scarcely limited by practical considerations, and only moderately curtailed by vast sacrifice of human life. In democracies it was otherwise, governments could fall without assassinations or revolutions and nations had to be encouraged as well as ordered to fight. Under such circumstances German appeals to idealism, speed, and initiative (if limited to a professional and technical sphere) are intelligible, whilst Western Allied willingness to go a little less on adventure and lightning strike, and more on the balance sheet of shells, bombs, bullets, and logistical build up have the grim but ultimately effective practicality that appeals more to the bureaucrat of war than the dynamic battlefield commander. As time progressed the US Army and the British sought to minimise their own losses – the former more by 'wall of fire' techniques, the latter by encouraging caution and a methodical approach that it has become fashionable to dismiss as too much 'leaning on the barrage'. As John English has summed it up, 'In comparision with the British, who seemed to stress keeping a tactical balance so as not to be caught unprepared by the enemy, the German army placed its emphasis on dash and deliberate acceptance of risk'. Whilst British and US infantry tactics undoubtedly made considerable ground from 1940, it, nevertheless, has to be acknowledged that much was copied from the enemy. German manuals were translated, and in certain instances sections were dropped, almost word for word, into Allied publications. By the time such paragraphs reached standard manuals they were shorn of reference to their original source. The battle-group idea was also largely lifted from the enemy, and often very effective, though in some cases German *Kampfgruppe* were actually assembled through necessity rather than positive choice – as for example when ad hoc defences were thrown together with inadequate time or resources.

Yet small-unit infantry tactics were also conditioned to a very significant extent by numbers of troops and the capabilities of men, weapons, and equipment. Each nation had squads, not only of different individuals, but of different character due to armament. The firepower of the US units was good – but fairly evenly distributed. The firepower of the Germans was better still, but concentrated with the machine gunners. The GI had the advantage of his Garand, the Germans waning numbers of men but the benefit of particularly efficient machine guns and, later in the war, good anti-tank weapons. The British sections had a light machine gun in the form of the Bren well adapted to fire and movement, and a rifle that was superior to the German but could not equal the US in volume of fire. Yet the Bren was far from ideal as a sustained fire weapon. Nevertheless, the Bren, MG 34, and BAR all made possible more potent forms of fire and movement than had previously been achievable, and their ability to operate in a self-contained manner actually caused the re-organisations of squads and platoons into a recognisably modern format from 1937 to 1940. 'Fire and movement', embryonic versions of which had existed at least as far back as the nineteenth century, developed into something of an art form and became a universal tactical mantra with the progress of war and fresh demonstrations of what could happen if one was attempted without thought to the other.

It was demonstrably the case that weaponry shaped small-unit tactics. At an early stage British trainers took advantage of the SMLE and accentuated its relatively swift fire ability, but with the adoption of the Bren quickly accepted that the remainder of the squad would act around it. The Germans shrank their squad as its machine weapon became more handy, and with generally depleted units riflemen became ever more servants of the MG. The assault rifle, which might have made a very significant impact on the infantry battle had Hitler embraced it when first recommended to him in 1942, actually turned out to be a genuinely revolutionary idea – produced too little, too late. Against roughly 9 million bolt-action rifles made for German forces during the war, only about ½ million *Sturmgewehr* were produced. These doubtless had some impact, especially on the Eastern Front, but by the time they were arriving in any numbers in the latter part of 1944 it was too late.

Other hardware also had a part to play. Aggressive German armoured infantry tactics were made possible not only by a doctrine of energetic and proactive engagement, but by early adoption of armoured half-tracks. Conversely, British tactics were not merely more cautious by choice, but formed by the availability of wheeled soft-skinned transport and the lack of an armoured half-track or carrier large enough to take a squad until much later in the war. Communications equipment similarly helped to determine just how flexible and reactive to events platoons and companies could be. Where anti-tank equipment and defences were primitive armour held the upper hand – this was realised and where such circumstances pertained armour took the lead. Where it did not the order of priorities was reversed. Unfortunately for the Allies, light anti-tank weaponry had made even greater strides than tanks by the latter part of the war – with the result that a partially trained teenager in a foxhole was a hazard that even heavy tanks were wise to hold off and destroy before advancing.

It has to be stressed that armies, tactics, and individuals alike changed very considerably over the six years of war. By the last few months of the war the US *Handbook on German Military Forces* was able to rationalise this phenomena,

> The German soldier who faces the Allies on the home fronts in 1945 is a very different type from the members of the Army of 1939 which Hitler called 'an army such as the world has never seen'. The German soldier is one of several different types depending on whether he is a veteran of 4 or 5 years, or a new recruit. The veteran of many fronts and many retreats is a prematurely aged, war weary cynic, either discouraged and disillusioned or too stupefied to have any thought of his own. Yet he is a seasoned campaigner, most likely a non-commissioned officer, and performs his duties with the highest degree of efficiency. The new recruit, except in some crack *SS* units is either too young or too old and often in poor health. He has been poorly trained for lack of time, but if too young, he makes up for this by a fanaticism bordering on madness. If too old, he is driven by fear of what his propagandists have told him will happen to the Fatherland in case of an Allied victory, and even more by fear of what he has been told will happen to him and his family if he does not carry out orders exactly as given. Thus even the old and sick perform, to a certain point, with the courage of despair. The German high command has been particularly successful in placing the various types of men where they best fit, and in selecting those to serve as cannon fodder, who are told to hold out to the last man, while every effort is made to preserve the elite units . . .

Exemptions from German military service were progressively curtailed, and theoretically 'total mobilisation' was in place from 1943. Eventually physical standards were significantly lowered and men registered for military service up to 60 years of age.

The changes in the British and US armies were scarcely less significant. The British had to change dramatically from a small professional army made up of what were effectively colonial policemen, armed much in the manner of 1918 – but possessing quite a lot of motor vehicles – to a large army of conscripts trained to thoroughly modern standards. On the way experience ran the gamut from near total defeat and desperation to victory. As a country with a relatively small population compared to either the USA or Germany and 10 per cent of conscripts earmarked for mining and industry – but a large Empire – broad conscription and very active support from, and collaboration with, Empire and Dominion forces became the order of the day. The US Army, antique and miniscule in the mid-1930s, went through even more massive expansion, more suddenly. Its troops went from no training at all, first to some good theory and no practice, and on to a size and degree of technical sophistication to match the status of military superpower.

As armies changed the progress of the individual from novice to veteran, and, all too often, to broken man, was seen fairly universally. Officers learned that there was a recognisable cycle in the service life of 'everyman'. The untrained and untried, often the young, were frequently brave beyond common sense. They had yet to see what weapons could do, nor yet to learn what sensible conduct in battle might be. Many felt they had to show they were not cowards. The first action was a test of mettle that might lead to proof or worth, or dramatic collapse. Veterans took the fewest casualties, not only because they had learned the tricks of the trade, but because usually they took the fewest risks. Often they had become veterans only by their survival skills. Proper battle experience was only to be had at the 'sharp end' but then many did not live long enough to enjoy the fruits. So it was that battle 'inoculation' and 'drills' came to be recognised as important contributions to battlefield training and efficiency.

If anything finally confirmed that men were not machines it was the phenomena of 'battle fatigue' – a slightly more humane explanation of the 'shell shock' of yesteryear. As US Army veteran Henri Atkins explained;

> This disabling condition usually strikes after a soldier has been subjected to long and severe shelling or enemy small arms fire. A soldier reaches a point of 'I can't take it any more' and slips into a state of irrational behaviour, or refusal to do anything. He just plain 'gives up'. This condition is as much a combat wound as a piece of shell piercing his body. Some never reach this point, while others reach it early. The preferred method of treatment was to pull the soldier out of the line.

Who would be struck down by mental stress, and when, was quite unpredictable, as efficient and seasoned soldiers might suddenly break down whilst others carried on – apparently indefinitely. US studies suggested that on average about 10 per cent of infantrymen would suffer battle fatigue at some point. Perhaps the most surprising thing was that 90 per cent did not.

Appendix 1

US Rifle Platoon, From the Manual *Rifle Battalion*, 1940

Command Group

Junior officer: Platoon Leader.
Platoon Sergeant: with rifle, field glasses, compass, and wire cutters.
Platoon Guide: with pistol and signal projector.
Platoon Messengers (x 2): with rifle and shovel or pick mattock.
Basic Privates (for replacements, maximum x 5): with rifles, plus axe, shovel or pick mattock.

Rifle Squads (x 3)

Squad Leader: Sergeant, with rifle, bayonet, wire cutters, field glasses, compass, and signal panel.
Second in Command: Corporal, with rifle, bayonet, axe, compass, and signal panel.
Privates and Privates First Class (x 10): with rifle and bayonet, plus 7 shovels, 3 pick mattocks, and 4 signal panels.

Automatic Rifle Squad (x 1)

Squad Leader, Second in Command, and six men: with field glasses, wire cutters, 2 (or 3) BARs, 4 rifles, 2 pistols, 2 pick mattocks, 4 shovels, and 1 axe.
Maximum Platoon Strength: 54.
Minimum Platoon Strength: 32.
Maximum Armament: 3 BARs, 48 rifles, 3 pistols, and platoon leaders arm.

Appendix 2

US Rifle Company, From the Manual *Rifle Battalion*, 1940

Company HQ

Command Group: Company Commander, First Sergeant, Communications Sergeant, Bugler, Orderly, 4 Messengers.

Administration and Supply Group: Supply Sergeant, Mess Sergeant, Cooks and assistants, Armourer Artificer, Company Clerk (Corporal).

Each member of HQ armed with rifle or pistol. NCOs of the Command Group and Bugler to have compass and field glasses, Messengers a compass, plus a total of 1 wirecutter, 4 shovels, and 1 pick mattock.

Weapons Platoon (x 1)

Command Group: Platoon Leader, Second in Command, Platoon Sergeant, Transport Corporal, Messengers (x 2), Drivers (x 2) armed with rifles or pistols, and equipped with 1 field glasses and 4 shovels.

Motor Weapons Carrier 1: 60mm mortars (x 3) with 180 rounds, 1 BAR.

Mortar Section: Sergeant, Messenger, 3 Corporals, 3 assistant gunners, 9 ammunition bearers, plus replacements (maximum x 2). All armed with rifles or pistols, and equipped with 1 wire cutters, 4 field glasses, 4 compasses, 3 axes, 2 pick mattocks, and 3 shovels.

Motor Weapons Carrier 2: Light machine guns (x 2) with 6,000 rounds, 1 BAR.

Light Machine Gun Section: Sergeant, Messenger, 2 Corporals, 2 gunners, 2 assistant gunners, 4 ammunition bearers, plus replacements (maximum x 2). All armed with rifles or pistols, plus 1 wirecutters, 3 field glasses, 3 compasses, 2 axes, 1 pick mattock, and 3 shovels.

NB Mortar and Light machine-gun sections could be broken down into squads – one weapon and its crew comprising a weapon squad. Machine-gun ammunition was packed into 250-round 'chests', a gun number 'off carrier' usually carried 1 chest plus other equipment, dedicated 'ammunition bearers' carried 2 chests (500 rounds).

Rifle Platoons (x 3)

Composition as Appendix 1.

Appendix 3

Scale of Ammunition Distribution in German Rifle Companies, From *Handbook of the German Army*, 1940

Rifle: 90 rounds (40 more in company and battalion reserve).
Machine Pistol: 192 rounds in 6 magazines.
Light Machine Gun: 3,100 rounds (divided between gun team and reserves).
Heavy Machine Gun: 5,250 rounds (divided between company limbers and reserves).
Pistol: 32 rounds.

Ammunition replacement was carried out continuously as required being delivered from transport echelons to the light infantry column, then to battalion and company reserves, and finally to the individual soldier.

Appendix 4

British Issue of Battalion Weapons, Vehicles, and Ammunition, From *Provisional War Equipment Table for an Infantry Battalion*, 1941

Strength

Battalion comprises: 4 Rifle Companies (4 x 124 personnel); Rifle Companies organised as 3 platoons of 3 sections each.
1 HQ Company (235 personnel including Corps attachments and Carrier Platoon).
1 Battalion HQ (54 personnel).
'First-line' reinforcements (157 personnel).

Arms and Ammunition

Rifles: 868 .303 SMLE Mk III* or Mk III (or Pattern 1914 Enfield).
Bayonets: 862 (to match the above).
Sniper rifles: 8 No. 3 Mk I (and bayonets).
Bren guns: 58 (with bipod, plus 58 spare barrels and 1,450 magazines).
Bren mounts: 62 (58 tripods, 4 twin AA, plus 8 x 100 round magazines).
Machine Carbines: 42 (Thompson .45, SMG).
Anti-tank Rifles: 25 (Boys .55, plus 200 magazines).
Dischargers: 24 (for rifle grenades).
Mortars 2in: 16 (with 1,152 HE bombs).
Mortars 3 in: 6 (with 936 bombs, smoke and HE).
Pistols: 53 (revolvers).
Signal Pistols: 38 (with 372 cartridges and 360 reserve).
Grenades: 732 (various types).
Ammunition .303: 42,800 rounds (bandolier packed); 70,000 rounds (reserve bandolier packed); 75,000 rounds (general reserve); and 12,000 rounds (tracer).
Ammunition .380: 636 rounds (for revolvers); and 282 rounds (reserve).
Ammunition .45: 25,200 rounds (for Thompson SMG).
Ammunition .55: 6,000 rounds (Boys AT Rifle).
Dummy cartridges: 40 various.

Vehicles

Bicycles: 31.
Cars, two-seater: 6.
Cars, four-seater: 1.
Chaplain's car: 1.
Lorries, 30cwt: 1.
Lorries, 3 ton: 13.
Trucks, 15cwt: 32.
Trucks, personnel: 2.
Trucks, water: 1.
Motorcycles (solo): 23.
Motorcycles (combination): 4.
Universal carriers (tracked): 14 (for 'carrier platoon' HQ company).
Universal carriers (tracked): 7 ('fitted for 3in mortars' HQ company).

Appendix 5

British Combat Section, From the Manual *Light Machine Gun*, 1942

Section Commander: machine carbine (SMG) with 6 magazines and 3 magazines for Bren, wire cutters, machete or knife, and whistle (total weight carried inclusive of clothing and equipment 65lb).
No. 1 Rifleman: sniper rifle, 50 rounds, bayonet, 4 Bren magazines (weight 61lb).
No. 1 Bomber: rifle, 50 rounds, bayonet, 1 Bren magazine, 2 No. 36 grenades, 2 smoke grenades (weight 61lb).
No. 2 Rifleman: rifle, 50 rounds, bayonet, 4 Bren magazines (weight 61lb).
No. 2 Bomber: rifle, 50 rounds, bayonet, 3 Bren magazine, 2 No. 36 grenades (weight 61lb).
Second in Command: rifle, 50 rounds, bayonet, 2 Bren magazine, 2 smoke grenades (weight 65lb).
No. 1 Bren: Bren gun, 4 Bren magazines, plus 50 rounds, spare parts wallet (weight 75lb).
No. 2 Bren: rifle, 50 rounds, bayonet, 4 Bren magazines in utility pouches (weight 63lb – might also carry spare Bren barrel).

NB According to *Army Training Memorandum* 38 of 1941, the eight-man 'battle' section was usual for action but the higher war establishment was one corporal and ten men. The additional men ensured that the 'basic strength of one corporal and seven men can be maintained during the absence of personnel due to sickness, leave and other causes . . . the additional men may be employed on working parties and other duties'. In the *Instructor's Handbook* of October 1942 three sections virtually identical to the one given here, plus a platoon HQ, comprised the battle platoon. The HQ consisted of the commander, platoon sergeant, a two-man AT Rifle team, a two-man mortar team, a runner, and a batman who also doubled as mortar-bomb carrier. The platoon was therefore thirty-two all ranks.

Appendix 6

German Infantry Platoon, From *The Regimental Officer's Handbook of the German Army*, 1943

Platoon (*Zug*) at full strength: 1 officer, 48 NCOs and men.

HQ	Platoon Commander, Officer.
	NCO.
	Other ranks (x 4).
Rifle sections (x 4)	NCO.
	LMG team (x 3 men).
	Riflemen (x 5).
Light mortar section	NCO.
	Mortar team (x 2 men).
Armament:	1 5cm Mortar, 4 LMG, 34 rifles, 11 pistols, 5 SMG.

NB The light mortar was out of production by 1943 and other weapons such as the *Panzerfaust* and semi-automatic rifle were being introduced down to platoon level by this time.

Appendix 7

US Armoured Rifle Platoon, Establishment of September 1943

First M3A1 Carrier (Platoon HQ and First Squad)

Platoon Commander, 2nd Lieutenant (M1 Carbine).
Platoon Sergeant (M1 Carbine).
Sergeant, Squad Leader (M1 Rifle).
Riflemen x 7 (M1 Rifles).
Sniper (M1903 sniper rifle).
Driver (SMG).
Also 1 Bazooka, and 1 .50 MG.

Second and Third M3A1 Carriers

Sergeant, Squad Leader (M1 Rifle).
Corporal, Assistant Squad Leader (M1 Rifle).
Riflemen x 9 (M1 Rifles).
Driver (SMG).
Also 1 Bazooka, and 1 .30 MG.

Mortar Squad M3A1 Carrier

Sergeant, Squad Leader (M1 Rifle).
Corporal, Assistant Squad Leader (M1 Rifle).
Mortar gunner (M2 Mortar, M1 Carbine).
Mortar assistant (M1 Carbine).
Ammunition carriers x 3 (M1 Carbines).
Driver (SMG).
Also 1 Bazooka, and 1 .30 MG.

Machine-gun Squad M3A1 Carrier

Sergeant, Squad Leader (M1 Rifle).
Corporal, Assistant Squad Leader (M1 Rifle).
Machine gunners x 2 (LMG, M1 Carbine).
Ammunition carriers x 2 (M1 Carbines).
Riflemen x 3 (M1 Rifle).
Driver (SMG).
Also 1 Bazooka, and 1 .50 MG.

Appendix 8

Organisation of a British Infantry Platoon, From the Manual *Infantry Training*, March 1944

Platoon HQ (x 1)

Platoon Commander: (arms unspecified but might include pistol and/or rifle, SMG).
Platoon Sergeant: rifle, 50 rounds, 4 grenades.
Mortar Lance Corporal: rifle, 50 rounds, 12 mortar bombs.
Mortar No. 1: mortar, Sten gun, 5 magazines, 160 rounds, 6 mortar bombs.
Mortar No. 2: rifle, 50 rounds, 12 mortar bombs.
Runner: rifle, 50 rounds, 2 grenades.
Batman/Signaller: rifle, 50 rounds, No. 38 wireless set.

Rifle Sections (x 3)

Section Commander: Sten gun, 5 magazines, 160 rounds, 2 grenades.
No. 1 Rifle: rifle, 2 Bren magazines, 156 rounds, 1 grenade.
No. 2 Rifle: rifle, 2 Bren magazines, 156 rounds, 1 grenade.
No. 3 Rifle: rifle, 2 Bren magazines, 156 rounds, 1 grenade.
No. 4 Rifle: rifle, 2 Bren magazines, 156 rounds, 1 grenade.
No. 5 Rifle: rifle, 2 Bren magazines, 156 rounds, 1 grenade.
No. 6 Rifle: rifle, 2 Bren magazines, 156 rounds, 1 grenade.
Second in Command: rifle, 4 Bren magazines, 162 rounds.
No. 1 Bren: Bren, 4 Bren magazines, 112 rounds.
No. 2 Bren: rifle, 5 Bren magazines, 190 rounds, 2 grenades.
Total platoon armament: 29 rifles, 4 Sten guns, 3 Bren guns, 2in mortar, platoon commander's weapon, 30 mortar bombs (18 smoke, 12 HE), 36 grenades, 640 rounds Sten ammunition, 4,450 rounds .303 ammunition. Some sections carried two Bren guns and PIAT anti-tank weapons were sometimes allotted to platoons rather than being reserved as company assets. A few rifles were equipped with scopes for sniping. According to *Army Training Memorandum* 47, of January 1944, the scale of issue of No. 38 Wireless sets was 8 to each rifle company, 4 per signal platoon, 13 per 3in mortar platoon, and 6 per carrier platoon. Total strength of the 1944 platoon was 37 all ranks.

Appendix 9

German Infantry Small-unit Organisations of Late 1944, From *Handbook on German Military Forces*, March 1945

Typical Rifle Company Small *Kampfgruppe* or 'Combat Team'

Company HQ:	1 officer, 1 NCO, 5 men (6 rifles, 1 LMG).
Rifle Squad 1:	1 NCO, 7 men (6 rifles, 1 pistol, 1 SMG, 1 LMG).
Rifle Squad 2:	1 NCO, 7 men (4 rifles, 2 pistols, 1 SMG, 1 LMG).
Rifle Squad 3:	2 NCOs, 8 men (7 rifles, 2 pistols, 1 SMG, 2 LMG).
Rifle Squad 4:	1 NCO, 8 men (6 rifles, 2 pistols, 1 SMG, 2 LMG).
HMG section:	2 NCOs, 6 men (2 HMG, 6 rifles, 4 pistols).
Engineer section:	2 NCOs, 28 men (24 rifles, 3 pistols, 3 SMG, 3 LMG).
Engineer AT squad:	1 NCO, 6 men (6 *Panzerfaust*, 6 rifles, 1 SMG).

Total strength 87 all ranks: the presence of attached engineers suggests the team also had access to other engineer stores.

Rifle Platoon, 1944 Type Regiment

Platoon HQ: 1 officer, 5 men, 4 rifles, 2 pistols, 1 SMG, 1 LMG; Transport: 2 horse-drawn vehicles, 2 trailers, 3 horses.

Rifle Squads (x 3): 1 NCO, 8 men, 6 rifles, 1 pistol, 2 SMG, 1 LMG.

Total strength: 1 officer, 3 NCOs, 29 men. Second and third platoons of a company were usually commanded by NCOs, in these the total would be 4 NCOs and 29 men. *SS* infantry units were of similar organisation to the 1944-type German divisions. Though the majority of rifles were still 98k and G 98 types, scoped sniper rifles and semi-automatic rifles were also used in small numbers.

Panzer Grenadier Company, 1944

Company HQ: 1 officer, 7 NCOs, 9 men.
10 rifles, 3 pistols, 4 SMG.
3 motor vehicles, 4 motorcycles.
Pz Gren Platoons (x 3): either 1 officer and 4 NCOs or 5 NCOs and 38 men.
26 rifles, 13 pistols, 4 SMG, 6 LMG.
5 motor vehicles.
MG Platoon (x 1): 1 officer, 8 NCOs, 42 men.
4 HMG, 2 81mm mortars, 27 rifles, 17 pistols, 7 SMG.
6 motor vehicles.
Total strength: 3 officers, 29 NCOs, 165 men (197 all ranks).

Volksturm Platoon (Militia or Home Guard, called out October 1944)

Platoon HQ, 5 all ranks: Platoon Leader, Squad Leader, 3 men.
3 rifles, 1 pistol, 1 SMG.
Squads (x 2 or x 3) 9 all ranks: Squad Leader, 8 men.
3 rifles, 1 pistol, 3 SMG, 1 *Panzerschreck*, 1 *Panzerfaust*.
Total strength varies from 32–41 depending on numbers of squads and weapons available.

Appendix 10

US Infantry Company, From *Tables of Organisation and Equipment*, 1944

Company HQ: 2 officers, 35 men.
Rifle Platoons (x 3): 1 officer, 41 men.
Weapons Platoon HQ: 1 officer, 6 men.
Mortar section: 17 men.
Machine-gun section: 8 men.
Total: 6 officers 193 men; Armament: 174 rifles, 9 BAR, 2 LMG, 1 .50 cal MG, 3 60mm mortars, 5 bazookas, grenades and launchers, plus pistols/carbines, 4 motor vehicles.
Rifle platoons organised as 3 squads and platoon HQ.
Platoon HQ: 1 officer, 5 men (5 rifles and officer's arm).
Squads (x 3): 12 men (11 rifles, 1 BAR, grenades and grenade launchers).
Each rifle squad: Squad Leader (NCO).
Assistant Squad Leader (NCO).
Riflemen (x 7).
BAR team (3 men, 1 BAR).
(Usually one of the rifles was a sniper rifle.)
A battalion heavy weapons company comprised 8 officers, 166 men, 8 HMG, 1 .50 cal MG, 6 81mm mortars, 6 bazookas, 132 rifles, plus pistols/carbines, 34 motor vehicles. The heavy weapons were organised into Machine Gun Platoons (x 2) a Mortar Platoon and a Company HQ.

Appendix 11

Specialist US Small-unit Infantry Organisations 1944, From FM-31-50 *Attack on a Fortified Position and Combat in Towns*, and J Balkowski's *Beyond the Beachhead*

Typical Assault Landing Craft Loading for 6 June 1944

Working from the bow ramp end toward the rear the 31-man landing craft section was accommodated in the following order:

Bow position:	Officer
	Five-man rifle team.
	Four-man barbed wire cutting team.
	Two-man BAR team.
	Two-man BAR team.
	Two-man bazooka team.
	Two-man bazooka team.
	Four-man 60mm mortar team (1 mortar).
	Two-man flamethrower team.
	Five-man demolition team (bangalore torpedoes/satchel charges).
Rear:	Medic and Assistant section leader.

Typical Twelve-man 'Assault Squad' for Attack on Fortified Positions January 1944

Leader: rifle, grenades, signal equipment.

Two-man 'demolition party': rifles, demolition charges, grenades.

Flamethrower man: flamethrower, pistol/carbine, grenades.

Rocketeer: bazooka, AT rocket, pistol/carbine, grenades.

Assistant Rocketeer: rifle, AT rocket, grenades.

Wire-cutting party: Assistant squad leader: rifle and grenade launcher, grenades, wire cutters, signal equipment.

BAR man: BAR, grenades.

Assistant BAR man: rifle and grenade launcher, grenades.

Riflemen x 3 (wire cutter): rifle and grenade launcher, wire cutters, 6 Bangalores, grenades.

NB This organisation was regarded as a 'framework' to be altered to fit the target and circumstances.

Organisation of Infantry Squad in a Defensive Position During an Alert, January 1944

The Squad is divided into two 'reliefs', one resting one watching:

First Relief:	Sergeant Squad Leader. BAR man. Rifle grenadier (assigned by leader). Riflemen (x 3).
Second Relief:	Corporal. BAR man. Rifle grenadier (assigned by leader). Riflemen (x 3).

Appendix 12

Establishment of a *Volksgrenadier* Infantry Company, From *Handbook on German Military Forces*, March 1945

Company HQ: 1 officer, 5 NCOs, 14 men; Arms: 1 pistol, 16 rifles, 3 MP; Transport, 1 horse-drawn vehicle, 1 trailer, 1 horse, 5 bicycles.
1st (SMG) Platoon: 1 officer, 3 NCOs, 29 men; Arms: 5 rifles, 2 pisols, 26 MP, 3 LMG; Transport: 2 horse-drawn vehicles, 1 trailer, 3 horses.
2nd (SMG) Platoon: 4 NCOs, 29 men; Arms: 5 rifles, 2 pistols, 26 MP, 3 LMG; Transport: 2 horse-drawn vehicles, 1 trailer, 3 horses.
3rd (Rifle) Platoon: 4 NCOs, 29 men; Arms: 20 rifles, 4 pistols, 9 MP, 3 LMG; Transport: 2 horse-drawn vehicles, 1 trailer, 3 horses.
Total strength of company: 119 personnel.
Three squads in each platoon:
The sub-machine-gun platoons comprised: 2 MP squads,1 Rifle Squad and HQ.
The rifle platoon comprised: 3 Rifle squads, and HQ.
Machine Pistol Squads comprised: 1 NCO and 8 men with 9 MP.
Rifle squads 1 NCO and 8 men with 6 rifles, 1 pistol, 2 MP, 1 LMG.
(Except Rifle squads within the MP platoons which comprised: 1 NCO, 8 men with 3 rifles, 1 pistol, 5 MP, 1 LMG. In MP platoons 2 LMG were retained as platoon HQ assets). The 'MPs' were now the new *Sturmgewehr* or 'assault rifle'.
Heavy Weapons companies *Volksgrenadier* regiments totalled 194 all ranks with 8 HMG, 6 81mm mortars, 4 75mm howitzers; Transport: 28 horse-drawn vehicles, 16 trailers, 45 horses, 5 bicycles; Additional arms: 108 rifles, 47 pistols, 39 MP, 1 LMG.
Infantry gun (13th) companies *Volksgrenadier* regiments totalled 197 all ranks with 8 120mm mortars, 4 75mm howitzers, organised in two heavy mortar platoons and a howitzer platoon; Transport: 33 horse-drawn vehicles, 1 motor vehicle, 2 trailers, 89 horses, 4 bicycles; Additional arms: 145 rifles, 21 pistols, 31 MP, 5 LMG.
Anti-tank (14th) companies of *Volksgrenadier* regiments totalled 167 all ranks with 72 *Panzerschreck*, organised in three platoons, an HQ, and reserve; Transport: 19 horse-drawn vehicles, 12 trailers, 30 horses, 2 bicycles, 1 motor vehicle, 1 motorcycle; Additional arms: 91 rifles, 63 pistols, 14 MP, 4 LMG.

Appendix 13

German Infantry in Action (Minor Tactics), 1941

German Infantry in Action (Minor Tactics) is a succinct British summary of German small-unit methods from the early period of the war. It is significant for a number of reasons, for not only does it precis in practical form the contents of a number of both official and unofficial German documents, it shows what the British had learned from enemy techniques. In their own instructional literature British and US manual writers were usually careful to avoid the impression that they were borrowing from, or inspired by, the Germans, as this would have suggested that Allied tactics lagged behind those of the enemy. In fact, there was considerable cross pollination as many details were picked up and incorporated by the Allies. Broader concepts regarding training, aggression, battle drills, and taking of the initiative also owed quite a lot to a study of the enemy. US trainers learned from both German and British methods, the US 'Combat Command', for example, being essentially a version of the '*Kampfgruppe*'. Sometimes the copying went full circle as when the Germans copied Allied anti-tank methods, some of which had their roots in the Spanish Civil War.

MGS-G32(N)
26,000

NOT TO BE PUBLISHED.

The information given in this document is not to be communicated, either directly or indirectly, to the Press or to any person not holding an official position in His Majesty's Service.

65763
G.S.—M.T. 2

GERMAN INFANTRY

IN ACTION

(MINOR TACTICS)

THIS DOCUMENT MUST NOT FALL INTO ENEMY HANDS

PREPARED BY THE
GENERAL STAFF, THE WAR OFFICE
February, 1941.
Reprinted in India.

PRINTED BY MANAGER, GOVERNMENT OF INDIA PRESS, CALCUTTA
1941

CONTENTS.

INTRODUCTION.

In this pamphlet is set out the German teaching in minor infantry tactics.

It will be seen that the general principles are very similar to those in the British manuals.

Attention is drawn to points of difference between the German and British teaching by the use of footnotes. These footnotes have been prepared by the General Staff at the War Office.

It is suggested that the reader should study carefully the German infantry organization given in Section 1. Only when this organization is thoroughly understood and appreciated is the full benefit from the study of the pamphlet to be derived.

SECTION 1.

Organization and equipment of an infantry battalion.

The organization and equipment of the infantry battalion described in this section is that of an infantry battalion of the normal German infantry division. It consists of:—

Battalion headquarters.
Signal section.
Pioneer platoon.
Three rifle companies.
One machine gun company.

Sub-units are organized and equipped as follows:—

Battalion headquarters.—Bn. comd., adjutant, assistant adjt. and three other officers, and a number of N.C.Os. and men, *e.g.*, clerks, orderlies, drum-major, transport sjt., etc.

Signal section.—Signalling officer, two telephone sub-sections, two lamp signalling terminals, four pack wireless sub-sections and one messenger dog sub-section.

Rifle company.—Coy. H.Q., consisting of the coy. comd., C.S.M., one N.C.O. i/c H.Q., three orderlies, two cyclists, one bugler, one horse-holder, one medical N.C.O. and one stretcher-bearer[1].

One anti-tank rifle section consisting of a commander and six men with three A.Tk. rifles[2].

Three platoons, each consisting of pl. H.Q. (pl. comd., pl. sjt., two orderlies, one bugler and one stretcher-bearer[1]),

---

[1] The one stretcher-bearer presumably carries the stretcher and is trained as a medical orderly.

[2] Compare this organization with the A.Tk. rifle in each platoon in the British organization. The number of A.Tk. rifles in the German and British companies are the same.

four sections each of a commander and nine men with one L.M.G., and one light mortar section consisting of a commander and two men with one 5 cm. (2 in.) mortar.

Coy., pl. and sec. comds. are armed with machine pistols[3].

Each platoon has one horsed vehicle for carrying the L.M.Gs. and mortar together with ammunition, light signals, wire, tools, cleaning material, hand grenades and camouflage equipment.

Machine gun company.—Coy. H.Q., including the coy. comd., C.S.M., and orderlies who act as signallers.

Three heavy M.G. platoons, each of two heavy M.G. sections, each with two heavy M.Gs.

One heavy mortar platoon, consisting of three sections, each with two 8·1-cm. (3·16-in.) mortars.

Pioneer platoon[4].—Formed from men detailed by the rifle companies who have been trained in pioneer duties when simple engineering tasks have to be performed.

Battle transport.—Includes field kitchens, vehicles for armourer's stores, tools, medical stores, etc. The company vehicles join the battalion battle transport when companies are in action.

Supply transport.—Consists of two-horsed vehicles and light lorries.

Baggage transport.—Consists of light lorries.

The infantry battalion may be reinforced by other units for carrying out special tasks. These units may be, for example:—

(*a*) One platoon of two light infantry guns of the regimental infantry gun company. (The latter consists of three light platoons and one heavy platoon, each of two guns.)

(*b*) One platoon of three A.Tk. guns of the regimental A.Tk. company. This platoon is fully mechanized. (The company has four platoons.)

(*c*) One N.C.O. and four to ten men of the regimental mounted infantry platoon or the whole platoon. (The platoon consists of H.Q. and three sections.)

---

[3] In the British army the section commander is armed with a sub-machine gun.

[4] Notice that the German platoon is not a permanent organization as is the British.

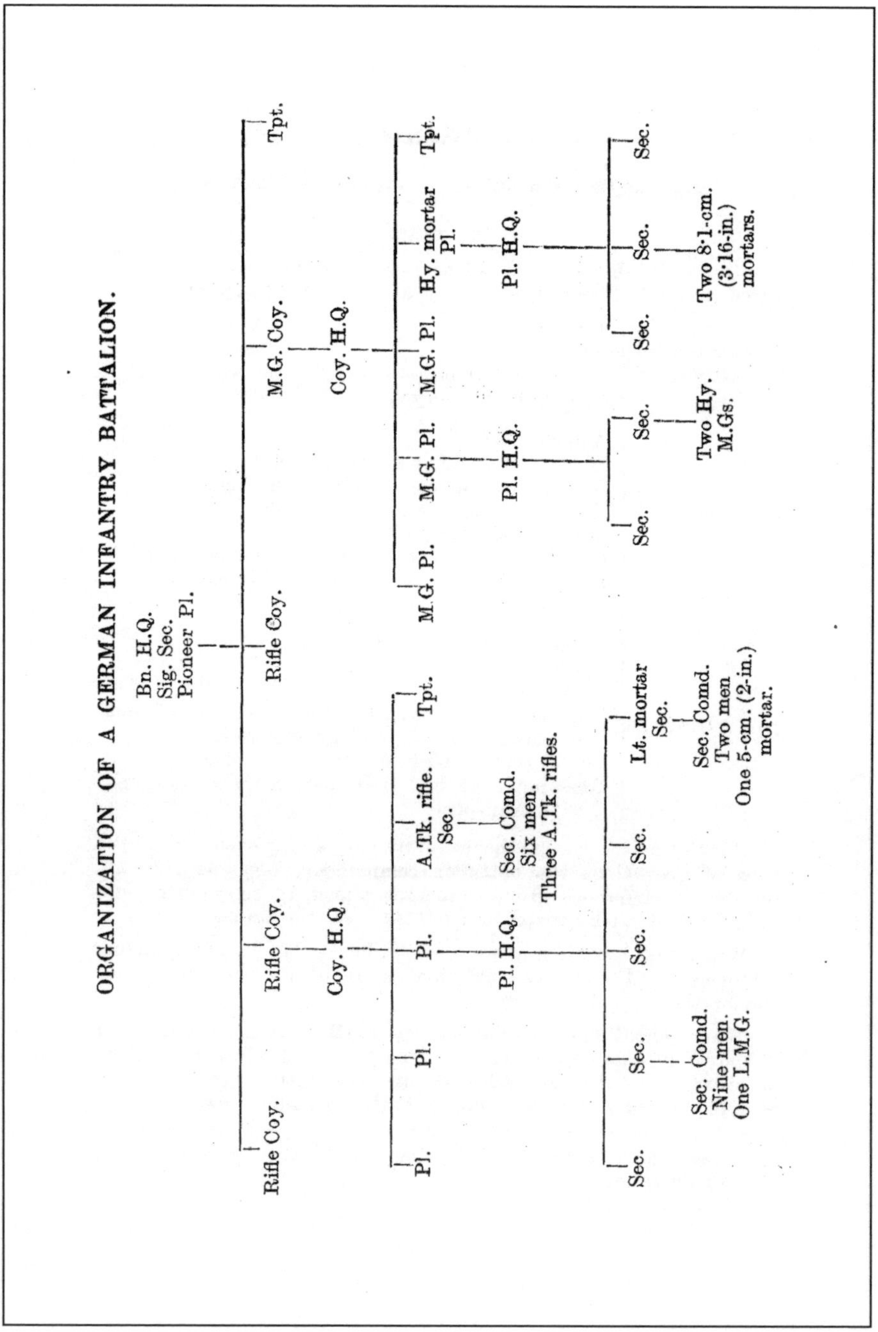
ORGANIZATION OF A GERMAN INFANTRY BATTALION.
Bn. H.Q.
Sig. Sec.
Pioneer Pl.
Rifle Coy.
Rifle Coy.
Rifle Coy.
M.G. Coy.
Tpt.
Coy. H.Q.
Pl.
Pl.
Pl.
A.Tk. rifle. Sec.
Tpt.
Pl. H.Q.
Sec. Comd. Six men. Three A.Tk. rifles.
Sec.
Sec.
Sec.
Sec.
Lt. mortar Sec.
Sec. Comd. Nine men. One L.M.G.
Sec. Comd. Two men One 5-cm. (2-in.) mortar.
Coy. H.Q.
M.G. Pl.
M.G. Pl.
M.G. Pl.
Hy. mortar Pl.
Tpt.
Pl. H.Q.
Pl. H.Q.
Sec.
Sec.
Sec.
Sec.
Sec.
Two Hy. M.Gs.
Two 8·1-cm. (3·16-in.) mortars.

SECTION 2.

Organization and duties of battalion headquarters.

(a) Organization.

In battle, battalion headquarters is organized in two or three groups. The following may be taken as an example:—

Commander's Group.	Bn. comd. Adjt. One mounted horse-holder for bn. comd. One clerk with bicycle.
No. 1 Group.	Assistant adjt. M.G. coy. comd. with horse-holder. Hy. mortar pl. comd. with horse-holder. A.Tk. pl. comd. with cross-country vehicle. Arty. liaison personnel. Comds. of other arms placed under command. Personnel of mounted infantry platoon. Motor-cyclists.
No. 2 Group.	Drum-major in charge. Clerks. Runners. Two men with scissors telescope, climbing irons, headquarters' flag and ground strips.[5] Signal section with signal stores vehicle. Remainder of bn. H.Q. less N.C.Os. and men with transport.

On the march or at the beginning of any movement in the area of operations the battalion commander, accompanied only by the commander's group, proceeds ahead to reconnoitre and gain contact with troops in front and on the flanks.

When the battalion goes into action, a battle headquarters is formed and becomes stationary to facilitate the conduct of the battle.

When choosing the position of battle headquarters, good observation is of the greatest importance. If this cannot be obtained from the site selected, an observation post must be established connected by line to battle headquarters.

---

[5] These men correspond to the intelligence section in a British battalion.

Considerations affecting the choice of a position for battle headquarters include facilities for good communications; concealment from ground and air observation; covered approaches for runners; and avoidance of places such as corners of woods, entrances to towns or villages, cross-roads, etc., which attract enemy fire.

Artillery or infantry gun observation posts should be close at hand, but several observation posts must not be bunched together in one place.

The lay-out at battle headquarters must be such that the battalion commander and his adjutant can be well served and work in quietness.

The battalion signal office, the remainder of headquarters (Nos. 1 and 2 Groups, chargers, etc.) must be sufficiently far away, at least fifty yards, so as not to disturb the work.

Figure 1 gives a suggested lay-out of a battalion headquarters.

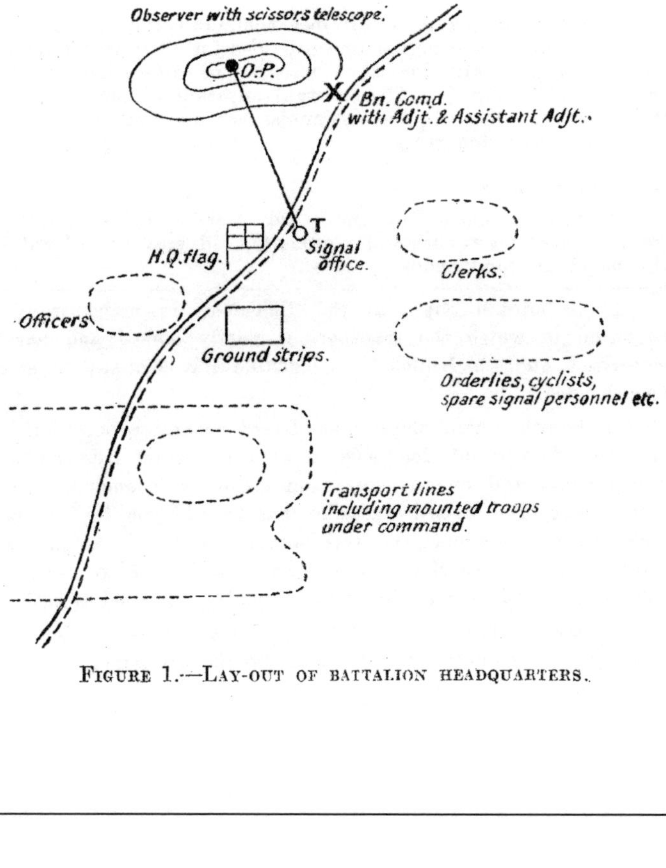

FIGURE 1.—LAY-OUT OF BATTALION HEADQUARTERS.

(*b*) *Duties.*

Battalion commander.

The battalion commander conducts the battle by means of orders and instructions and by supervising their execution[6].

Adjutant.

The adjutant prepares and issues written orders on the rare occasions when this is necessary[7]. He prepares any sketches which may be required. He transmits urgent verbal orders in person, mounted or on foot. He keeps the war diary and collects the necessary material for it.

Signalling officer.

The signalling officer establishes communications as ordered by the battalion commander and provides for their maintenance. He makes proposals for any increases or alterations in the employment of signals. The assistant adjutant frequently assists the signalling officer in the reconnaissance and establishment of a new battle headquarters.

Medical officer.

The medical officer, in some cases assisted by an assistant medical officer, establishes a regimental aid post as ordered by the battalion commander.

---

[6] It is pointed out that the difficulties in manœuvring a battalion in which the transport is partly horsed and partly motorized, and which includes a machine gun company, must be considerable.

On the other hand the commander of a German battalion has to give orders to only four subordinates, *i.e.*, three rifle company commanders and one machine gun company commander. The commander of a British battalion has in addition to four rifle company commanders, the commanders of the A.A. pl., the mortar pl., the carrier pl., and the pioneer pl. to consider. (The German pioneer pl. is not permanently embodied as such.)

[7] It seems that in the German army written orders are envisaged even more rarely than in the British army.

SECTION 3.

Equipment and duties of personnel of the rifle company.

(a) The company.

Headquarters.

The C.S.M. sends and receives messages and is responsible that the area in which the company is operating is kept under observation. He sees that visual communication is maintained with platoons and battalion headquarters.

The three orderlies, in addition to their normal duties, can be used for manning two lamp signalling terminals.

The two cyclists are used for communication within the company and to attached supporting weapons.

The bugler carries the company commander's machine pistol until the latter requires it.

A.Tk. rifle section.

A.Tk. rifles are manned by two men; one man fires the rifle, the other looks after the ammunition.

Battle transport.

A N.C.O. is in charge of the platoon vehicles and the A.Tk. rifle vehicle when these are grouped together. He is responsible for their concealment.

One man is detailed to accompany each vehicle and to supervise the issue of stores.

Supply and baggage transport.

Operates under battalion arrangements.

(b) The platoon.

Headquarters.

The platoon serjeant assists the platoon commander and usually carries the light signal pistol.

The bugler carries the platoon commander's machine pistol until the latter requires it.

Personnel of platoon and company H.Q. are trained as observers, orderlies and air sentries.

(*c*) *The section.*

The following table shows the equipment and duties of each man of the section.

	Equipment.	Duties.
Section commander.	Machine pistol with 6 magazines. Magazine filler. Field glasses. Wire cutters. Compass. Whistle. Sun glasses.[8] Pocket torch. Map case. Anti-gas respirator. Emergency ration.	Leads the section and directs the fire of the L.M.G. and rifles. Responsible for serviceability of section's arms, ammunition and stores.
No. 1	L.M.G. with magazine. Tool bag. Revolver.[9] Entrenching tool. Sun glasses.[8] Pocket torch. Anti-gas respirator. Emergency ration.	Mans and fires the L.M.G. Responsible for care and maintenance of the L.M.G.
No. 2	Barrel cover with spare barrel. 4 magazines. 1 ammunition box. Sling. Revolver.[9] Entrenching tool. Sun glasses.[8] Anti-gas respirator. Emergency ration.	Assists No. 1 to fire and clean the L.M.G. Looks after ammunition. Assists No. 1 in preparing gun for action and taking up fire position. Takes up his position to the the left of No. 1, and is always ready to assist him, *e.g.* in remedying stoppages, changing the barrel, adjusting the bipod.
No. 3	Barrel cover with spare barrel. 2 ammunition boxes. Sling. Rifle. Entrenching tool. Anti-gas respirator. Emergency ration.	Ammunition number. Lies completely under cover in rear of No. 1. Inspects magazines and ammunition.
Nos. 4—9	Rifle. 2 ammunition pouches. Entrenching tool. Anti-gas respirator. Emergency ration. In addition when ordered: Hand grenades. Smoke grenades. Explosive charges. Ammunition. Tripod.	Take part in fire fight with the rifle. The senior is the deputy section commander. He assists the latter and replaces him if necessary. Responsible for keeping touch with the platoon commander and neighbouring sections.

[8] In the German army the section commander, the No. 1 and the No. 2 are provided with sun glasses. The normal equipment in the British army does not include this.

[9] In the British army neither the No. 1 nor the No. 2 of the L.M.G. is provided with a revolver. They carry rifles when not carrying the L.M.G.

SECTION 4.

Section and platoon formations.

(*a*) *The section.*

There are two normal formations for the section when extended, *i.e.*, single file and extended line. The section should only be split up in exceptional circumstances, and if it is, must still operate as a complete unit.

Figure 2 shows a section in single file.

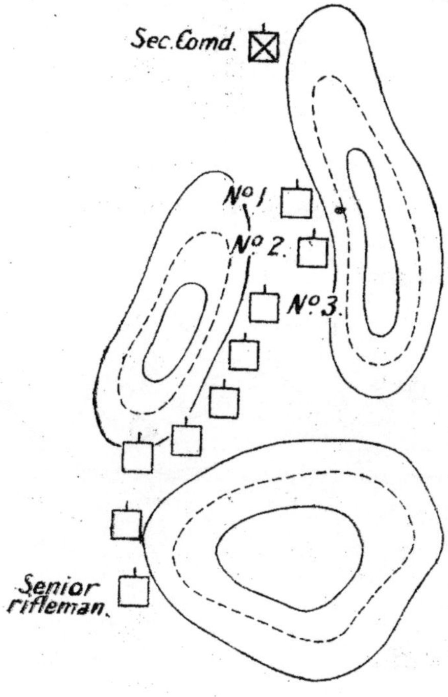

FIGURE 2.—SINGLE FILE.

This formation is used for the approach towards the enemy and in the fire fight when the L.M.G. is to be employed alone, the riflemen remaining in rear.

Figures 3 and 4 show how the section adopts extended line from single file. Unless otherwise ordered, extension will be to some five paces.

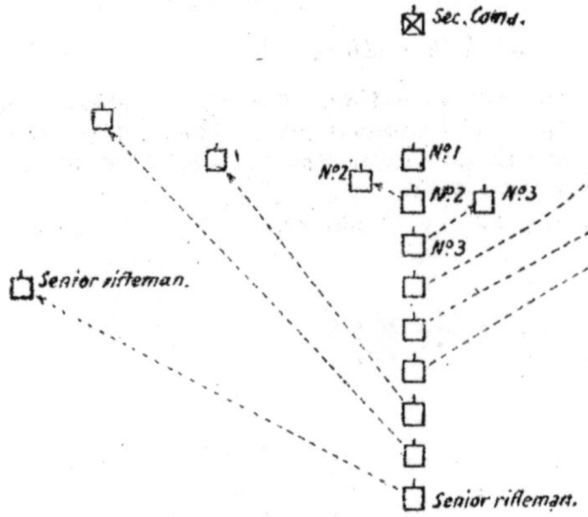

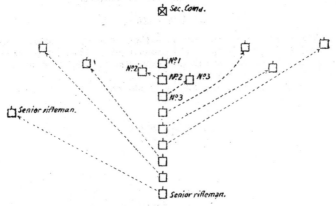

FIGURE 3.—EXTENDED LINE.

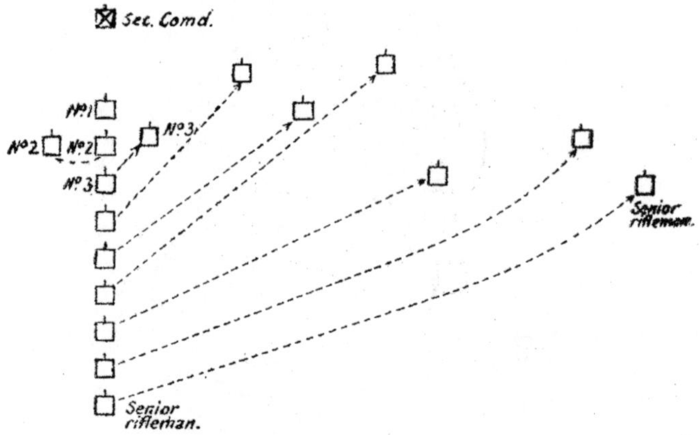

FIGURE 4.—EXTENDED LINE (TO A FLANK).

This formation is used for crossing open stretches of country and when the whole section (L.M.G. and riflemen) are required to take part in the fire fight.

(*b*) *The platoon.*

The platoon normally deploys into one of two formations, *i.e.*, arrowhead or wide arrowhead. The platoon commander can, however, order other formations, *e.g.*, sections one behind the other in file or single file or two sections forward and two in rear.

Figure 5 shows how the platoon deploys into arrowhead from column of route. The distances given serve only as a guide.

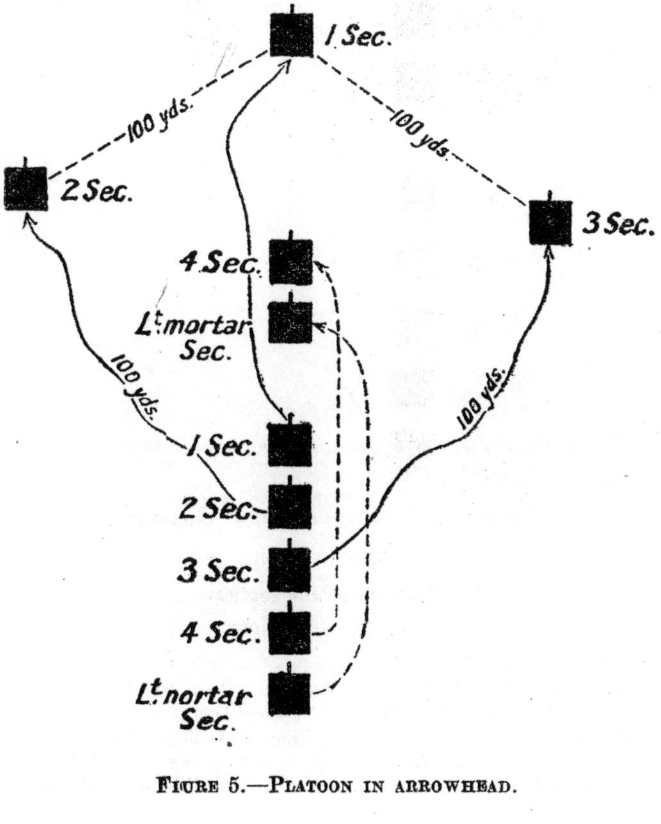

FIGURE 5.—PLATOON IN ARROWHEAD.

Figure 6 shows the platoon deploying into wide arrowhead. Again the distances given are only a guide.

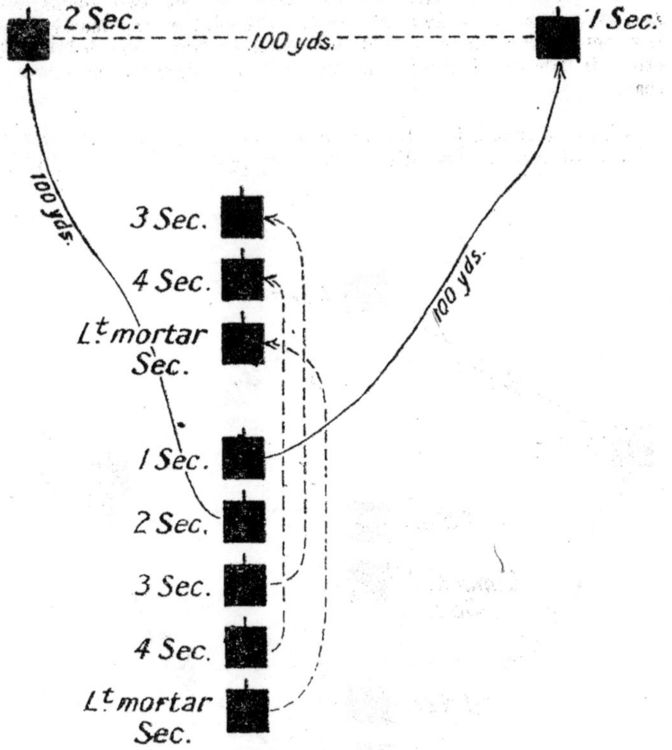

FIGURE 6.—PLATOON IN WIDE ARROWHEAD.

SECTION 5.

Tactics of the section.

(*a*) *The fire fight.*

The section is the fire unit.

When fire has to be opened, the section ommander usually opens fire with the L.M.G. only. He directs ts fire.

When good fire effect is possible and whn plenty of cover exists, the riflemen take part early in th fire fight. The majority of riflemen should be in the front lin and taking part in the fire fight at the latest when the assault is about to be made.

They usually fire independently, unless the section commander decides to concentrate the whole of their fire power on to one target.

(b) The advance.

The section works its way forward in a loose formation. Within the section the L.M.G. usually forms the spearhead of the attack. The longer the riflemen follow the L.M.G. in narrow, deep formation, the longer will machine guns in rear be able to shoot past the section.[10]

(c) The assault.

The section commander takes any opportunity that presents itself to carry out an assault and does not wait for orders to do so. He rushes the whole section forward to the assault, he himself leading the way. Before and during the assault the enemy must be engaged by all weapons at the maximum rate of fire. The No. 1 takes part in the assault, firing the L.M.G. on the move. With a cheer, the section attempts to break the enemy's resistance, using hand grenades, machine pistols, rifles, revolvers and entrenching tools. After the assault, the section must reorganize quickly.

(d) Occupation of a position.

When occupying a position the riflemen group themselves in twos and threes around the L.M.G. in such a way that they are within voice control of the section commander.

SECTION 6.

Deployment.

(*a*) *Position of commanders.*—When the company deploys, commanders go forward to reconnoitre the ground to obtain for themselves an impression of the situation. Contact must be maintained with commanders in front.

(*b*) *Maintenance of direction.*—One platoon maintains direction for the company. This will either be the leading platoon or, if two are leading, the right-hand platoon.

Sections conform to the same principles within the platoon.

(*c*) *Protection.*—The company when deployed in close country, protects itself by means of moving or standing patrols.

---

[10] This consideration affecting the formation of a section is not envisaged in British manuals.

(*d*) *Orders.*—Orders for deployment usually contain:—
i. information about the enemy;
ii. objective or purpose of deployment;
iii. formation of the company or platoon.

(*e*) *Transport.*—When the company deploys, battle transport normally follows its platoons; when the platoon deploys it follows the last section. Company headquarters normally remain with the leading platoon.

(*f*) *Formations.*—Figures 7 and 8 show the company deployed in the two normal formations, *i.e.*, arrowhead and wide arrowhead. The distances between platoons are given only as a guide.

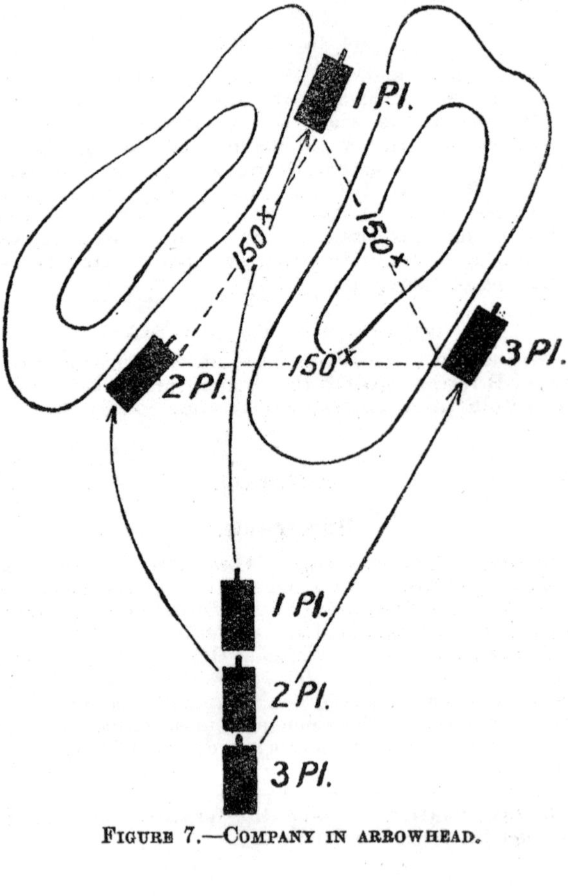

FIGURE 7.—COMPANY IN ARROWHEAD.

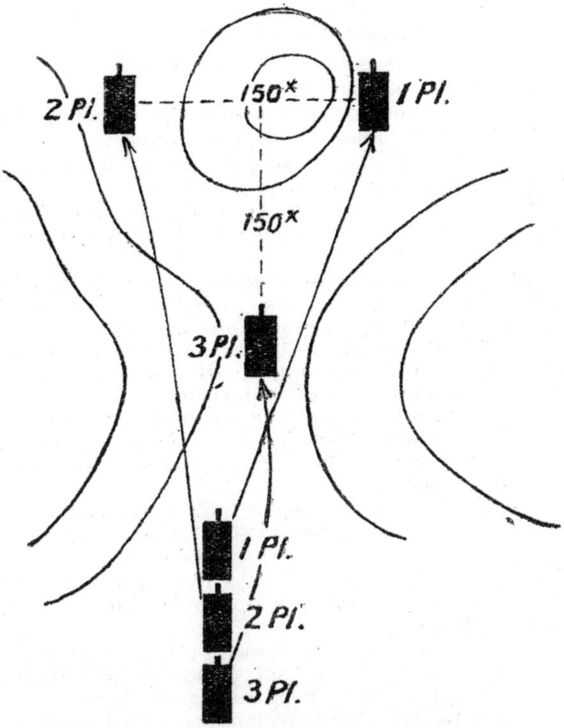

FIGURE 8.—COMPANY IN WIDE ARROWHEAD.

SECTION 7.

Battle.

(*a*) *General.*—The rifle companies are the deciding factors in the infantry battle. Close co-operation with the infantry support weapons, the artillery and on occasions tanks and aircraft, and a quick and determined exploitation of their action ensure the success of the rifle companies.

(*b*) *Duties of company and platoon commanders.*—Company and platoon commanders select their positions so that they can always exercise control and keep the area of operations in view.

It must also be possible for the company commander to maintain contact with the infantry support weapons. In cases of necessity he enters the battle at the decisive place, regardless of his own person.

The platoon commander leads his platoon in the attack, and is its mainstay in defence.

Every company and platoon commander is given a task, the choice of methods of execution being left to him.

Reconnaissance of the battle area at the beginning of an action is of the greatest importance.

(*c*) *Orders and reports.*—The type of orders must be made to suit the situation. The more pressing the situation the shorter the orders.

Company and platoon commanders, whenever possible, give out their orders verbally on the ground. Orders transmitted verbally are as a rule repeated by the recipient.[11]

Transmission of orders is facilitated if subordinate commanders and troops are kept informed of the situation. Halts and intervals in the fighting should be used for this.

Company, platoon and section commanders must render reports continuously to their superior officers about the enemy, their own positions, those of neighbouring units, the ammunition situation and casualties.

(*d*) *Recognition signals.*—To facilitate recognition by artillery and infantry support weapons of the position of foremost troops, the latter must indicate their positions by means of small coloured flags which can only be seen from the rear (grey front, orange back).[12] Light signals may also be fired for recognition of foremost troops.

Foremost troops indicate their positions to own reconnaissance aircraft by laying out ground-strips[13] (white, with red backs for use in snow) or by letting off flares.

(*e*) *Reconnaissance.*—The company commander arranges for constant close reconnaissance. Platoon commanders may have to send out patrols independently. Continuous observation of the area of operations must be ensured.

(*f*) *Ammunition supply.*—Timely replenishment of ammunition is essential.

Infantry support weapons placed under command control their own ammunition supply. The commander of the rifle company must, therefore, be informed of their expenditure in ammunition.

---

[11] In the British army, recipients of orders do not as a rule repeat them back, except in the case of runners who are transmitting orders.

[12] In the British army no flags or signals are carried to indicate the position of forward troops to supporting arms.

[13] Experiments are being made in the British army with individual strips for indicating the position of troops to the air.

SECTION 8.

Attack.

(*a*) *Duties of the company commander.*—The company commander allots deployment areas and objectives to leading platoons. The advance of the company must be co-ordinated with the fire of the infantry support weapons and the artillery. If infantry support weapons are placed under command, the company commander must allot them tasks. He always maintains a reserve. He informs platoons of his position.

(*b*) *Duties of the platoon commander.*—The platoon commander decides on the formation of his platoon and either includes in his orders the platoon deployment area and objective, or he details the sections to their tasks. He usually selects a reserve and tells the sections his position.

(*c*) *The attack.*—When the situation is uncertain, company and platoon commanders employ only weak elements forward so as to be able to push forward others later.

The attack is usually carried out in bounds, the fire of the infantry support weapons being taken into consideration. At first a limited and visible objective is given, further objectives being given as the attack progresses.[14] New objectives must, therefore, be ordered soon enough to ensure that success is quickly exploited.

Section commanders lead their sections as near as possible to the enemy without opening fire, making skilful use of the ground and areas not covered by fire and with the support of artillery and infantry support weapons. Section commanders open fire with the L.M.G. only when forced to do so by the ground and enemy fire. To open earlier is to waste time and ammunition.

Further advance is by fire and movement.

As the foremost troops of the company approach the enemy, platoon commanders must decide where to attack. Where weak points in the enemy position become apparent the attack will be pressed home.

Troops in rear should be brought forward shortly before the assault so that they can assist in the attack if required.

If the first assault is successful, even if penetration is only made on a narrow front, the attack must be pressed forward into the depth of the enemy position. At this moment the

[14] This is the same as taught in the British army. Allotting objectives which are out of sight is, however, envisaged, particularly in large scale attacks.

personal example of the platoon commander, who must concentrate on maintaining the momentum of the attack, is of great importance. Immediate pursuit at places where the enemy resistance weakens is therefore, required. Premature movement to a flank before the enemy position has been completely penetrated is wrong.[15] The flanks of attacking sections must be protected by troops in rear. It is the duty of reserves following up the attack to destroy any centres of resistance which remain.

(*d*) *Reserves.*—The company or platoon reserve reinforces the front line, usually at places where the enemy resistance has weakened. If a neighbouring unit gains ground quickly it may be advantageous to bring the reserve forward at that point. The duties of the commander of the reserve include the following:—

i. Observation of own and enemy fire.

ii. Maintenance of contact with own foremost troops and neighbouring units.

iii. Personal liaison with the company or platoon commander.

iv. Preliminary reconnaissance of possible routes by which to advance.

v. Protection of open or threatened flanks.

(*e*) *Consolidation.*—The capture of the objective must be reported immediately. Reorganization in depth must take place for the continuance of the attack or for holding the ground gained.

SECTION 9.

Assault detachments.

(*a*) *General.*—For attacks on strongly fortified positions, specially organized, trained and equipped assault detachments are employed.

These detachments consist of men selected for their courage, determination and physical fitness. The commander should be an experienced platoon commander.

Prior to the attack the detachments are carefully rehearsed in every detail, and extensive patrolling is carried out to ascertain the exact positions of fortifications, obstacles, lines of fire, etc.

[15] This teaching is the same as the British.

(*b*) *Organization and equipment.*—An assault detachment is organized in several parties, the strength depending on the task to be performed.

Personal equipment is reduced to a minimum to ensure maximum mobility. Each man carries a ground sheet (for removing casualties or captured equipment), a water bottle, one day's rations and a bayonet. The respirator is carried on the back or in a pocket of the jacket as is a revolver and ammunition.

The following table gives an example of the way in which the various parties of an assault detachment may be organized and equipped:—

Party	Strength	Equipment
Commander.	—	Machine pistol, wire cutters, light signal pistol, hand grenades, compass, field glasses, whistle.
Wire-cutting party.	3–4 men for each gap to be made.	4 rifles or revolvers, 4 entrenching tools, 12 hand grenades, 4 wire cutters, 2 claw hatchets, 8 sandbags, explosive charges.
Embrasure-destroying party.	3 men for each embrasure to be attacked.	2 revolvers, 1 rifle, 10 sandbags, 6 hand grenades, one 6-lb. charge, 2 tins of petrol, light signal pistol.
Support parties.	2-3 parties of 2–3 men each.	Hand grenades, light signal pistols, signalling flags, smoke candles or grenades. Rifles, machine pistols and L.M.Gs. according to ground and cover.
Smoke party.	2–3 men.	Rifles or revolvers, 4 hand grenades, 8 smoke candles or grenades, entrenching tool, wire cutters.

(*c*) *The attack.*—Artillery and infantry guns cover the advance of the assault detachments from the starting line with barrage fire, Machine guns, anti-tank guns, anti-aircraft guns and tanks engage the fortifications to be attacked.

The wire-cutting party clears a way through the wire under cover of smoke and supported by fire.

The embrasure-destroying party, covered by the fire of the support parties, rushes through the gaps in the wire and takes cover in the dead ground in front of the fortification.

The support parties take up positions in rear and on the flanks of the fortification.

The smoke party covers the advance of the embrasure-destroying party and support parties.

The attack on the fortification itself may be carried out in the following ways:—

i. By throwing hand grenades through the embrasure if it is open.
ii. By blowing up the embrasure if it is closed.
iii. By blowing up the gun in the embrasure.
iv. By stopping up the embrasure with sandbags if it is near the level of the ground.
v. By blowing up the entrance to the fortification.
vi. By using flame throwers.

SECTION 10.

Defence.

(*a*) *General.*—In defence the rifle company is allotted an area of the main defensive position, of which the front edge is known as the main line of resistance. The foremost defended localities are in this line. The company is so disposed in its allotted area that the ground in front of the main line of resistance is covered by fire which, as far as possible, leaves no gaps. Defended localities, disposed irregularly and in depth, render mutual support possible. This causes enemy fire to be dispersed, allows alternative positions to be occupied in the face of superior fire, and enables resistance to be continued even when the attacker has forced his way into the main defensive position.

(*b*) *Duties of the company commander.*—The company commander shows his platoon commanders on the ground the exact trace of the main line of resistance and allots them areas to defend. He orders the work to be done which frequently includes the construction of dummy works. Instructions must be given about the authority to call for defensive fire from the artillery and infantry support weapons.

The company commander ensures that boundaries between areas are completely covered by fire, especially at night and in bad visibility.

He co-ordinates the fire of the company with that of the infantry support weapons.

He always retains a reserve.

(*c*) *Duties of the platoon commander.*—The platoon commander shows his section commanders the trace of the main line of resistance and the platoon boundaries. He gives orders defining what ground is to be prepared for all round defence. The platoon commander allots tasks and localities for defence by the sections, and defines their zones of fire. He also orders what digging is to be done and what obstacles are to be constructed.

(*d*) *Reserves.*—The duties of the company or platoon reserve include the following:—

i. To thicken up the fire in front of the main line of resistance by firing through gaps.

ii. To destroy by fire enemy who have entered the position or prevent them by fire from advancing further into it.

iii. To expel enemy who have entered the position by immediate counter-attack.

iv. To protect unsupported flanks.

v. To act as protection at night and in bad visibility between and in front of defended localities.

(*e*) *Outposts.*—Sections in the outpost position commence the fire fight with their L.M.Gs. and open fire at long ranges. The duty of the riflemen is to supplement the L.M.G. fire and to protect or reconnoitre the flanks of the L.M.G.

Withdrawal from the outpost position must be carried out so that the fire of the main defensive position is not screened and the outposts themselves are not endangered.

(*f*) *The main defensive position.*—The infantry support weapons commence the infantry fire fight in defence of the main position. The closer the enemy approaches, the more the light infantry weapons take part. In this connection care must be taken that fire is not opened too early as this would give away the position of the main line of resistance and offer targets to the enemy's artillery and infantry support weapons. L.M.Gs. which open fire at long but effective ranges should do so in the first instance from alternative positions. In this way fire positions intended for the defence at close ranges will not be disclosed.

Elements of the rifle company under superior enemy fire will occupy alternative positions only on orders of the company commander, and if by so doing the defence as a whole is not endangered, and if the enemy is not thereby enabled to establish himself in the main defensive position. A preliminary condition is that the company commander has been specially authorized to give this order.

If the enemy succeeds in entering the main defensive position, every effort must be made to destroy him by fire. Elements of the company in close contact with the enemy must expel him by immediate counter-attacks, before he has established a foothold on the ground gained. When the action is broken off the main line of resistance must be in the possession of the company.

(*g*) *Defence by night.*—The necessary preparations for defence at night must be made during the day. At night, warning of the enemy's approach must be ensured by means of increased patrol activity and illumination of the ground in front of the position. Outposts may have to be reinforced.

SECTION 11.

Anti-aircraft defence.

(*a*) *General.*—The weapons of the rifle company suitable for for anti-aircraft defence are the L.M.G. up to 3,000 feet and the rifle up to 1,500 feet.

Air sentries and an alarm system ensure that weapons open fire in time.

When a company is deployed for action it does not offer a favourable target to enemy aircraft owing to its dispersion, and every effort must be made to carry out allotted tasks regardless of enemy air activity.

All commanders down to section commanders can temporarily employ men not required for ground fighting to engage air targets. They must, however, realize that in doing so they may disclose well-concealed positions.

When marching with intervals for protection against aircraft, the company is allowed twice its normal space in the column[16], and it may be necessary to have the L.M.Gs. of one platoon carried to be ready for anti-aircraft defence.

(*b*) *L.M.G. fire.*—Air targets can be effectively engaged only by employing several L.M.Gs. In the rifle company three L.M.Gs. of one platoon are usually detailed for anti-aircraft defence. They must be placed under one commander who remains with one L.M.G. which becomes the "directing gun".

The best position for the guns is some 300 yards from the troops to be protected. They should be sited with distances and intervals of some 50 or 60 yards so that the "dead zone" above each individual gun can be covered by fire.

Objects which can be quickly removed, such as branches, should be used for camouflage. The best method of camouflage is to avoid any movement until opening fire.

---

[16] The German company when deployed uses only twice its normal road space, which is considerably more concentrated than is usual in the British army where a company frequently covers up to four times its normal road space.

established a foothold on the ground gained. When the action is broken off the main line of resistance must be in the possession of the company.

(*g*) *Defence by night.*—The necessary preparations for defence at night must be made during the day. At night, warning of the enemy's approach must be ensured by means of increased patrol activity and illumination of the ground in front of the position. Outposts may have to be reinforced.

SECTION 11.

Anti-aircraft defence.

(*a*) *General.*—The weapons of the rifle company suitable for for anti-aircraft defence are the L.M.G. up to 3,000 feet and the rifle up to 1,500 feet.

Air sentries and an alarm system ensure that weapons open fire in time.

When a company is deployed for action it does not offer a favourable target to enemy aircraft owing to its dispersion, and every effort must be made to carry out allotted tasks regardless of enemy air activity.

All commanders down to section commanders can temporarily employ men not required for ground fighting to engage air targets. They must, however, realize that in doing so they may disclose well-concealed positions.

When marching with intervals for protection against aircraft, the company is allowed twice its normal space in the column[16], and it may be necessary to have the L.M.Gs. of one platoon carried to be ready for anti-aircraft defence.

(*b*) *L.M.G. fire.*—Air targets can be effectively engaged only by employing several L.M.Gs. In the rifle company three L.M.Gs. of one platoon are usually detailed for anti-aircraft defence. They must be placed under one commander who remains with one L.M.G. which becomes the "directing gun".

The best position for the guns is some 300 yards from the troops to be protected. They should be sited with distances and intervals of some 50 or 60 yards so that the "dead zone" above each individual gun can be covered by fire.

Objects which can be quickly removed, such as branches, should be used for camouflage. The best method of camouflage is to avoid any movement until opening fire.

---

[16] The German company when deployed uses only twice its normal road space, which is considerably more concentrated than is usual in the British army where a company frequently covers up to four times its normal road space.

(*b*) ***A.Tk. rifle.***—The A.Tk. rifle can be effectively used against tanks and armoured cars up to a range of 300 yards.

On the march, when attacks by A.F.Vs. may be expected, A.Tk. rifles should be located at the head and in the rear of the company. Protective detachments on the march should as a rule be allotted A.Tk. rifles.

When deployed and in the attack the A.Tk. rifles may be allotted to individual platoons or retained with the reserve platoon.

In defence the A.Tk. rifles can be employed in the company sector or allotted to individual platoons.

Attacks on isolated, stationary or immobilized enemy A.F.Vs. can be carried out with success.

If the situation permits, personnel of the A.Tk. section should also be employed in bringing up ammunition supplies and similar tasks.

Summary.

The following is a summary of the main points of interest and of difference between the German and British doctrines:—

1. The Germans place great reliance on direct observation of the battlefield. Coy. H.Qs. move well forward in the company. Bn. H.Q. has an O.P. and a scissors telescope for the use of the battalion commander or his observers.
2. The German teaching stresses concealment in the defence more than the British
3. The value of a quick local counter-attack is stressed more than in the British manuals.
4. The Germans do not mention either A.Tk. obstacles or tank proof localities in their teaching. The reason may be that they have not yet been seriously attacked by tanks.
5. In the attack, the British army does not envisage the firing of machine guns *through* attacking infantry. The Germans do.
6. The Germans regard the issue of a written order as very exceptional.

MGIPC—L—I-3-65(PD)Army—9-8-41—26,000.

Bibliography

Memoirs and General Primary Works

Anon. 'Your First Day in the Army: A *Look* Photographer Follows a Rookie and Answers Questions 16,500,000 Potential Conscripts are Wondering About', *Look* magazine, Des Moines, Iowa, 3 December 1940, 39–43

Borthwick, A. *Battalion*, Stirling, 1946

Cochrane, P. *Charlie Company: In Service with C Company 2nd Queen's Own Cameron Highlanders*, London, 1977

Forman, D. *To Reason Why*, London, 1991

Jary, S. *18 Platoon*, Bristol, 1987

Jünger, E. *Copse 125 (Das Wäldchen 125)*, trans. B Creighton, n.p., repr. 1985

Knappe, S. *Soldat*, London, 1993

Levy, Yank. *Guerilla Warfare*, London, 1941

Liddell Hart, B. *New Methods in Infantry Training*, Cambridge, 1918

Liddell Hart, B. *The Future of Infantry*, London, 1933

Liddell Hart, B. *The Way to Win Wars*, London, 1942

MacDonald, CB. *Company Commander*, Washington, 1947

Marshall, GC (et al.). *Infantry in Battle*, Washington, 1939

Marshall, SLA. *Men Against Fire*, 1947, reprinted Oklahoma, 2000

Miksche, FO. *Blitzkrieg*, London, 1941

Sava, G. *School For War*, London, 1942

Shore, C. *With Snipers to the Reich*, 1948, new edn London, 1997

Weeks, CW (ed.). *Mailing List: A Semi-Annual Publication Containing the Latest Thought on Infantry*, Infantry School, Fort Benning, 1930s

White, P. *With the Jocks: A Soldier's Struggle For Europe, 1944–1945*, Stroud, 2001

Wintringham, T. *New Ways of War*, London, 1940

Manuals and Instructions, British and Empire Subjects

Anon. *The Complete Lewis Gunner*, Aldershot, 1918, repr. 1941

Anon. *Drill in Threes and Elementary Drill*, reproduced from *MTP 18 and Manual of Elementary Drill*, Aldershot, 1942

Armstrong, NAD. *Fieldcraft, Sniping and Intelligence*, 1940, n.p., repr. 1993

Barlow, JA. *Small Arms Manual*, London, 1942

Cuthbert, SJ. *We Shall Fight Them in the Streets*, 1940, repr. Boulder, 1985

Elliot, AG. *The Home Guard Encyclopedia*, London, 1942

General Staff, India. *Close Quarter Battle: Small Arms Training vol. 1, Pamphlet 11 (India)*, Delhi, 1945

GHQ Home Forces. *The Instructor's Handbook on Fieldcraft and Battle Drill*, n.p., 1942

GHQ Home Forces. *Battlecraft and Battle Drill for the Home Guard: Part III Patrolling*, Instruction No. 51, n.p., 1943
GHQ Home Forces. *Battlecraft and Battle Drill for the Home Guard: Part IV The Organisation of Home Guard Defence, Instruction No. 51*, n.p., 1943
Humphrey, RA. *How to Teach Battlecraft*, Aldershot, 1943
Langdon-Davies, J. *The Home Guard Fieldcraft Manual*, London, 1942
Perrigard, GE. *Awrology: All Out Hand to Hand Fighting*, Montreal, 1943
Wade, GA. *House to House Fighting*, Aldershot, c.1940
Wade, GA. *The Art of Prowling*, Aldershot, c.1940
War Office (UK). *Section Leading*, London, 1928
War Office (UK). *Infantry Training*, London, 1937
War Office (UK). *Infantry Section Leading*, London, 1938
War Office (UK). *Notes on Concealment and Camouflage*, London, 1938
War Office (UK). *Anti-Tank Rifle, Small Arms Training*, Vol. I, No. 5, 1937, repr. with amendments London, 1939
War Office (UK). *Notes on the Tactical Handling of the Carrier Platoon in Attack*, MTP 13, London, 1939
War Office (UK). *Dannert Concertina Wire Obstacles*, MTP 21, London, 1939
War Office (UK). *Operations: Part II, Defence*, MTP 23, London, 1939
War Office (UK). *Individual Training Period 1939–1940*, Army Training Memorandum, No. 23, London, 1939
War Office (UK). *War*, Army Training Memorandum, No. 24, London, September 1939
War Office (UK). *War*, Army Training Memorandum, No. 26, London, November 1939
War Office (UK). *Training in Fieldcraft and Elementary Tactics*, MTP 33, London, 1940
War Office (UK). *Tank Hunting and Destruction*, MTP 42, London, 1940
War Office (UK). *Instructional Notes on the .300 Browning Automatic Rifle*, London, 1940
War Office (UK). *Notes on the Training of Snipers*, MTP 44, 1940, repr. with amendments London, 1941
War Office (UK). *Provisional War Equipment Table for an Infantry Battalion*, G 1098-708, London, 1941
War Office (UK). *The Soldier's Welfare: Notes for Officers*, London, 1941
War Office (UK). *Field Engineering (All Arms), Part IV: Booby Traps*, London, 1941
War Office (UK). *The Officer and Fighting Efficiency*, London, 1941
War Office (UK). *Operations, Part X, The Infantry Division in the Advance*, London, 1941
War Office (UK). *Operations, Part IX, The Infantry Division in the Attack*, London, 1941
War Office (UK). *Surprise The First Principle of Attack*, London, 1941
War Office (UK). *Supplement No. 2: No 73 Anti-Tank Grenade*, Small Arms Training, Vol. I, No. 13, London, 1937, rev. edn 1941

War Office (UK). *Grenade*, Small Arms Training, Vol. I, No. 13, London, 1937, repr. with amendments (1) 1941
War Office (UK). *Rifle*, Small Arms Training, Vol. I, No. 3, London, 1942
War Office (UK). *Light Machine Gun*, Small Arms Training, Vol. I, No. 4, London, 1942
War Office (UK). *Bayonet*, Small Arms Training, Vol. I, No. 12, London, 1942
War Office (UK). *Spigot Mortar*, Small Arms Training, Vol. I, No. 23, London, 1942
War Office (UK). *Operations: Part I, General Principles*, MTP 23, London, 1942
War Office (UK). *Individual Battle Practices*, Small Arms Training, Vol. I, No. 18, Supplement 1, London, 1943
War Office (UK). *Projector, Infantry, Anti-Tank*, Small Arms Training, Vol. I, No. 24, London, 1943
War Office (UK). *Operations in Snow*, MTP 62, London, 1943
War Office (UK). *Infantry Training, Part VIII, Fieldcraft, Battle Drill, Section and Platoon Tactics*, London, 1944
War Office (UK). *Shoot to Kill, Part X, Basic and Battle Physical Training*, London, 1944
War Office (UK). *The Co-operation of Tanks with Infantry Divisions*, MTP 63, London, 1944
War Office (UK). *Rafting and Bridging: Part III, Assault Crossing Equipment*, MTP 74, London, 1944
War Office (UK). *Field Engineering*, London, 1944
War Office (UK). *Machine Carbine*, Small Arms Training, Vol. I, No. 21, London, 1944
War Office (UK). *Section Leading and Fieldcraft for Cadets*, London, 1945
War Office (UK). *Grenade*, Small Arms Training, Vol. I, No. 13, London, 1942, repr. with amendments 1945
War Office (UK). *Tactical Handling of Flame-Throwers*, MTP 68, London, 1945
Whipp, D. *Anti-Tank Weapons, Know Your Weapons, No. 3*, n.p., 1942
Wigram, L. *Infantry Battle School*, 1941, repr. Cambridge, 2005

Manuals and Instructions, German Subjects

Anon. *Der Feuerkampf der Schützenkompanie*, Berlin, 1940
Bönicke, G. *Tornister Lexicon Für den Frontsoldaten*, Berlin, 1943
Center of Military History (US). *Military Improvisations During the Russian Campaign*, 104-1, repr. 1983
Dembowski. *Exerzieren und Kommandieren: Richtigkommandieren und befehlen, die Grundausbildung mit und ohne Gewehr und das Exerzieren de Gruppe*, Berlin, c.1940
Dembowski. *Der Marschkompaß und sein Gebrauch*, Berlin, c.1940
DWM. *The Parabellum Automatic Pistol*, Berlin, n.d.
Gesterding, S and Hoebel, E. *Zwanzig Offizierthemen: Ein Handbuch für den Offizierunterricht*, Berlin, 1936

Gesterding, S and Feyerabend, H. *Unteroffizierthemen: Ein Handbuch für den Unteroffizierunterricht*, Berlin, 1943
Kühlwein. *Felddienst ABC für den Schützen*, Berlin, 1934
Meusel, H. *Körperliche Grundausbildung*, Berlin, 1937
Military Intelligence (US). *German Tactical Doctrine*, Special Series, 8, Washington, 1942
Military Intelligence (US). 'German Night Fighting Tactics', *Tactical and Technical Trends*, No. 30, Washington, July 1943
Military Intelligence (US). *The German Squad in Combat*, Washington, 1944
Military Intelligence (US). *Company Officer's Handbook of the German Army*, Special Series, 22, Washington, 1944
Necker, W. *The German Army of Today*, London, 1943
Oberkommando des Heeres. *Merkblatt über Handhabung, Mitführung und Verwendung der Gewehrgranaten*, 41/23, Berlin, 1942
Oberkommando des Heeres. *Taschenbuch für den Winterkrieg*, Berlin, 1942, repr. Solingen, 1996
Oberkommando des Heeres. *Offizier Im Grossdeutschen Heer*, Berlin, 1942
Oberkommando des Heeres. *Merkblatt*, 'for the troop trials MP 43', Berlin, 1943
Oberkommando des Heeres. *Der MP Zug Der Granadier Kompanie*, Berlin, 1944
Oberkommando des Heeres. *Die Panzerfaust*, Merkblatt D560/4, Berlin, January 1945
Reibert, W. *Der Dienst Unterricht Im Heere*, Berlin, 1940 and 1942 edns
Reichsführer SS. *Dich Ruft die SS*, c.1942
Reichskriegsministerium. *Schießvorschrift für Gewehr, Karabiner, Leichtes Maschinengewehr, Pistole usw.* Berlin, 1926, repr. 1931
Reichskriegsministerium. *Schießvorschrift für das Schwere Maschinengewehr*, H.Dv. 73, Berlin, 1937
Reichskriegsministerium. *Ausbildungsvorschrift für die Infanterie, heft 2, Die Schützenkompanie*, h.Dv 130/2a, n.p., 1940
Reichskriegsministerium. *MG 34 und MG 42*, Berlin, 1943
Seeckt, H von. *Führung und Gefecht der Verbundenen Waffen*, Berlin, 1921
Siwinna, C. *Das Kommandobuch, 6, I.G.W. 36, (5cm)*, Berlin, 1939
Staemmler, M. *Deutsche Rassenplege, OKH Tornisterschrift*, 29, n.p., 1941
War ABCA (UK). *The German Army*, Army Bureau of Current Affairs, 17, n.p., 1942
War Department (US). *Handbook on German Army Identification*, Washington, 1943
War Department (US). *German Defense Systems*, Washington, 1944
War Department (US). *TM-E 30-451: Handbook on German Military Forces*, Washington, 1945
War Office (UK). *Periodical Notes on the German Army*, 18, London, 1940
War Office (UK). *Periodical Notes on the German Army*, 32, London, 1940
War Office (UK). *Periodical Notes on the German Army*, 35, London, 1941
War Office (UK). *Popular Guide to the German Army, No. 2, The Infantry Division*, London, 1941

War Office (UK). *Enemy Weapons, Part II, Italian and German Infantry Weapons*, London, 1942
War Office (UK). *The Regimental Officer's Handbook of the German Army*, London, 1943
War Office (UK). *Handbook of Enemy Ammunition, Pamphlet No. 11, German Mines, Grenades, Gun Ammunition and Mortar Ammunition*, London, 1944
War Office (UK). *Tactics of the German Army, Vol. II, Attack and Pursuit*, London, 1944
Weber. *Unterrichtsbuch für Soldaten: Ausgabe A für Schützen*, Berlin, 1938
Zimmermann, B. *Die Soldatenfibel*, Berlin, c.1935
Zimmermann, B. *Die Neue Gruppe*, Berlin, 1940

Manuals and Instructions, US Subjects

Bureau of Aeronautics. *Don't Kill Your Friends*, n.p., 1943
HQ AA Training Centre. *Resistance Exercises*, Combat Conditioning Series, No. 1, Camp Haan, 1944
Infantry Journal. *How to Shoot the US Army Rifle*, Washington, 1943
Infantry School. *The Rifle Platoon and Squad in Offensive Combat, Pictorial Supplement to FM 7-10, Part 1, Approach March*, Fort Benning, 1943
Infantry School. *The Rifle Platoon and Squad in Offensive Combat, Pictorial Supplement to FM 7-10, Part 3, Security Missions*, 1944
War Department (US). *Basic Field Manual, vol. III, Basic Weapons, Rifle Company 2A, Marksmanship – the Automatic Rifle*, Washington, 1937
War Department (US). *Infantry Field Manual FM 7-5: Organisation and Tactics of Infantry; The Rifle Battalion*, Washington, 1940
War Department (US). *Basic Field Manual FM 21-20: Physical Training*, Washington, 1941
War Department (US). *Basic Field Manual FM 21-100: Soldier's Handbook*, Washington, 1941, with amendments, 1942
War Department (US). *Field Manual FM 105-5: Umpire Manual*, Washington, 1942
War Department (US). *Field Fortifications*, Washington, 1942
War Department (US). *TB 23-7-1: Carbine*, Washington, 1942
War Department (US). *Basic Field Manual FM 21-40: Defense Against Chemical Attack*, Washington, 1942
War Department (US). *FM 17-10 Armored Force Field Manual: Tactics and Technique*, Washington, 1942
War Department (US). *TM 9-285: Shotguns, All Types*, Washington, 1942
War Department (US). *Field Manual FM 21-45: Protective Measures, Individuals and Small Units*, Washington, 1942
War Department (US). *Basic Field Manual FM 21-150: Unarmed Defense*, Washington, 1942
War Department (US). *FM 17-27: Armored Force Field Manual: 81mm Mortar Squad and Platoon*, Washington, 1942

War Department (US). *FM 7-15: Heavy Weapons Company, Rifle Regiment*, Washington, 1942
War Department (US). *Field Manual FM 23-25: Bayonet*, Washington, 1943
War Department (US). *TM 9-1985, Grenades, Hand and Rifle*, Washington, 1943
War Department (US). *FM 21-105, Basic Field Manual: The Engineer Soldier's Handbook*, Washington, 1943
War Department (US). *FM 17-5: Armored Force Field Manual: Armored Force Drill*, Washington, 1943
War Department (US). *TM 9-270: US Rifle, Cal .30 M1903A4 (Sniper's)*, Washington, 1943
War Department (US). *Basic Field Manual FM 21-22: Watermanship*, Washington, 1944
War Department (US). *TM 9-1270: US Rifles, Cal.30, M1903*, Washington, 1944
War Department (US). *FM 7-10: Infantry, Rifle Company, Rifle Regiment*, Washington, 1944
War Department (US). *FM 21-75: Infantry Scouting, Patrolling and Sniping*, Washington, 1944
War Department (US). *FM 7-20: Infantry Battalion*, Washington, 1944
War Department (US). *FM 31-50: Attack on a Fortified Position and Combat in Towns*, Washington, 1944

Secondary Works

Ambrose, SE. *Citizen Soldiers*, New York, 1997
Balkowski, J. *Beyond the Beachhead*, Mechanicsburg, 1989
Barnes, BS. *The Sign of the Double 'T': 50th Northumbrian Division, July 1943 to December 1944*, Hull, 1999
Bidwell, S and Graham, D. *Fire-Power: British Army Weapons and Theories of War*, London, 1982
Bidwell, S and Graham, D. *Tug of War: The Battle for Italy*, London, 1986
Breyette, TW and Bender, RJ. *Tank Killers*, San Jose, 2000
Bruce, R. *German Automatic Weapons of World War II*, Marlborough, 1996
Bull, SB. *World War II Infantry Tactics: Squad and Platoon*, Oxford, 2004
Bull, SB. *World War II Infantry Tactics: Company and Battalion*, Oxford, 2005
Bull, SB. *World War II Infantry Tactics: Street-Fighting*, Oxford, and Washington, 2008
Citino, RM. *The Path to Blitzkrieg: Doctrine and Training in the German Army*, Boulder, 1999
Danchev, A. *Alchemist of War: The Life of Basil Liddell Hart*, London, 1998
Delaforce, P. *The Fighting Wessex Wyverns: From Normandy to Bremerhaven with the 43rd Wessex Division*, Stroud, 1994
Delaforce, P. *Monty's Ironsides: From the Normandy Beaches to Bremen with the 3rd Division*, Stroud, 1995

Doubler, MD. *Closing with the Enemy: How GIs Fought the War in Europe, 1944–1945*, University Press of Kansas, 1994
Dupuy, TN. *Understanding War: History and Theory of Combat*, New York, 1987
Ellis, J. *The Sharp End: The Fighting Man in World War II*, Newton Abbott, 1980
English, JE. *On Infantry*, New York, 1981
Farrer-Hockley, A. *Infantry Tactics*, New Malden, 1976
French, D. *Raising Churchill's Army*, Oxford, 2000
French, D. '"You Cannot Hate the Bastard who is Trying to Kill You": Combat and Ideology in the British Army in the War Against Germany', in G Martel, *The World War II Reader*, New York, 2004
Fritz, SG. *Frontsoldaten: The German Soldier in World War II*, University of Kentucky, 1995
Gajkowski, M. *German Squad Tactics In World War II*, Pisgah, 1995
Griffith, P. *Forward Into Battle*, Chichester, 1981
Handrich, H. *Sturmgewehr!*, Ontario, 2004
Hart, P. *The Heat of Battle*, Barnsley, 1999
Hobson, CS. *US Portable Flamethrowers*, Atglen, 2010
Hogg, IV. *Infantry Weapons of World War II*, London, 1977
Hogg, IV and Weeks J. *Military Small Arms of the Twentieth Century*, London, 1977
McManus, JC. *The Deadly Brotherhood*, New York, 1998
Müller, KJ. *The Army, Politics and Society in Germany, 1933–1945*, Manchester, 1987
Nafziger, GF. *The German Order of Battle: Infantry in World War II*, Mechanicsburg, 2000
O'Neill, RJ. *The German Army and the Nazi Party*, London, 1966
Palmer, RR (et al.). *The US Army in World War II: The Procurement and Training of Ground Forces*, Washington, 1948
Pate, CW. *US Handguns of World War II*, Lincoln, 1998
Place, TH. *Military Training in the British Army, 1940–1944*, London, 2000
Purcell, H. *The Last English Revolutionary: Tom Winteringham*, Stroud, 2004
Rosciszewski, L. *Niemieckie Pancerzownice: Panzerschreck I Panzerfaust*, Warsaw, 1993
Rosinski, H. *The German Army*, London, 1966
Rottman, GL. *World War II US Armoured Infantry Tactics*, Oxford, 2009
Seaton, A. *The German Army 1933–1945*, New York, 1982
Sharp, CC. *Soviet Infantry Tactics From Squad to Rifle Company From the Combat Regulations*, West Chester, 1998
Shephard, B. *A War of Nerves: Soldiers and Psychiatrists in the Twentieth Century*, Harvard, 2003
Skennerton, I. *British Sniper*, Margate, 1983
Wette, W. *The Wehrmacht: History, Myth, Reality*, English edn, Harvard, 2006
Whitlock, F. *The Rock of Anzio. From Sicily to Dachau: A History of the US 45th Infantry Division*, Boulder, 1998
Wintringham, T. *Weapons and Tactics*, London, 1943

Index